UKRAINIAN FOREIGN
AND SECURITY POLICY

UKRAINIAN FOREIGN AND SECURITY POLICY

Theoretical and Comparative Perspectives

Edited by Jennifer D. P. Moroney,
Taras Kuzio, and Mikhail Molchanov

Westport, Connecticut
London

Library of Congress Cataloging-in-Publication Data

Ukrainian foreign and security policy: theoretical and comparative perspectives / edited by Jennifer D. P. Moroney, Taras Kuzio, and Mikhail Molchanov.
    p.   cm.
    Includes bibliographical references and index.
    ISBN 0–275–97622–X (alk. paper)
    1. Ukraine—Foreign relations—1991– 2. National security—Ukraine. 3. Nationalism—Ukraine. I. Moroney, Jennifer D. P., 1973– II. Kuzio, Taras. III. Molchanov, M. (Mykhail).
    DK508.849.U385   2002
    327.477—dc21   2001054593

British Library Cataloguing in Publication Data is available.

Library of Congress Catalog Card Number: 2001054593
ISBN: 0–275–97622–X

First published in 2002

Praeger Publishers, 88 Post Road West, Westport, CT 06881
An imprint of Greenwood Publishing Group, Inc.
www.praeger.com

Printed in the United States of America

The paper used in this book complies with the Permanent Paper Standard issued by the National Information Standards Organization (Z39.48–1984).

10   9   8   7   6   5   4   3   2   1

Contents

1

Ukraine's Foreign and Security Policy: Theoretical and Comparative Perspectives

Jennifer D. P. Moroney

Ukraine's foreign policy, particularly since 1994, has been an attempt to balance its pro-West ambitions with its historical, cultural, and other deeply rooted ties with Slavic Eurasia, particularly with Russia. For the most part, Ukrainian policy makers have leaned more toward the West, meaning the United States, European Union (EU), NATO, and other key individual Western states, as well as international financial organizations such as the World Bank and the International Monetary Fund (IMF). The main motivation for focusing on the West was to obtain the economic and political support necessary to ensure Ukraine's continued existence as an independent state.

While it cannot yet be said with any great degree of certainty that Ukraine's Western-oriented foreign policy is irreversible to the extent of Ukraine's western neighbors such as Poland and Hungary, it can be said that Ukraine's ties with the West on a political, economic, and military level are quite extensive. Moreover, these links have taken on a more objective foundation in recent years, making it ever more difficult to severely alter particularly the institutional links between Ukraine and Western states and institutions at the whim of whomever is currently wielding power. In other words, a radical reorientation of Ukraine's foreign policy toward Eurasia will simply not be supported by a majority of Ukraine's political elite, as clearly demonstrated during the Kosovo crisis, when Ukraine did not alter its overall foreign policy orientation.

However, although it is unlikely that Ukraine will, for example, halt its participation in NATO's Partnership for Peace (PfP), pull its troops out of KFOR, or refuse loans and grants from European and international institutions when the offer is made, subtle changes to Ukraine's foreign and security policy are not unlikely, and tend to reflect broader macro-level geopolitical realities, as well as the internal political dynamics of the state at any given time. Though Ukraine is often criticized for its inconsistency and unpredictability in its foreign relations, given the state's geopolitical position between a resurgent Russia led by Vladimir Putin and a West that has tended to be only half-heartedly committed to supporting Ukraine at a multitude of levels, we should hardly expect to see much less than occasional twists and turns of Ukrainian foreign policy. Yet with these twists and turns over the past decade, Ukraine has not wavered from its desire to "return to Europe." Thus, the Ukrainian government's present refocus on Russia in the new millennium should not be seen as a backslide from its rather steadfast Western foreign policy course.

It has come to the attention of scholars and policy makers alike that there are many factors that serve to influence a state's foreign and security policy orientation. One can analyze foreign policy decisions from a macro or global level, from a domestic politics perspective and the linkage between domestic and foreign policy, or even from deeper imbedded issues related to national identity. This volume considers all of these factors from a comparative perspective in an attempt to make sense of Ukraine's overall foreign policy orientation.

The following chapters analyze the interplay between domestic and foreign policy (which Rosenau labels as "linkage") and considers the impact on Ukrainian foreign and security policy when domestic and international issues converge.[1] Domestic factors tend to be broadly defined from a "bottom-up" approach, which includes the impact of economic, political, military, and identity factors on Ukraine's foreign policy orientation. However, a "top-down" approach is also considered; for example, to what extent is broader geopolitical developments in East–West relations replicated in Ukrainian domestic politics (e.g., the Kosovo conflict led to heightened tensions between Russia and the West at the macro level, which as a result was replicated on a domestic level in Ukraine when support for NATO was based on East–West internal divisions as well as political ideology).

This volume examines the orientation and trends of Ukraine's foreign and security policy from the perspective of several different and often opposing schools of international relations theory. It is, in short, an attempt to link area studies and international relations theory through a focus on Ukraine's foreign policy orientation.

It has come to the attention of the editors that there is not a single scholarly study of contemporary Ukrainian foreign and security policy that integrates area studies and international relations theory. The only volumes in this field are area studies and chronological accounts, such as Ilya Prizel, *National Identity and Foreign Policy in Russia, Poland and Ukraine* (1998), O. Hajda, editor, *Ukraine and the World* (1998), and David Albright and Semyen Appatov, editors, *Ukraine and European Security* (1999). Three others, by Taras Kuzio, *Ukrainian Security Policy* (1995), Sherman Garnett, *Keystone in the Arch* (1997), and Tor Bukkvoll, *Ukraine and European Security* (1997), are directed at the policy-making communities and are shorter monographs.

This book intends to fill a very important gap in the scholarly literature on Ukraine by using international relations theory as a tool to further Western understanding of the foreign and security policy decisions of the Ukrainian government. Previously published works on Ukrainian foreign and security policy have lacked an overall theoretical context within which the analysis is presented, and this book will indeed provide such a context. Different aspects of international relations and civil–military theory will be employed in all of the chapters to incorporate a wide array of theoretical perspectives into the analysis. Though no single international relations theory is applicable on its own, a single theoretical framework can be provided for a country in the throes of a multiple transition.

Using international relations theory, this volume analyzes the extent to which Ukraine's foreign and security policy orientation is influenced by domestic factors (something the majority of the contributors argue it is; the extent to which is the point at which they deviate). Therefore, it is argued that a comprehensive model that incorporates both structural factors and domestic issues of state building but also takes into account subjective, behavioral factors such as nationalism, national identity, ideology and political culture, nation building, party politics, and personalities of leaders is absolutely necessary. At the same time, the contributors recognize that even in established liberal democracies, domestic factors play little role in defining foreign policy. Moreover, in post-communist states such as Ukraine the weakness of civil society means that it is even more difficult for domestic factors to influence the state's foreign policy. This situation has worsened under Kuchma, where "state capture" has led to the circle of those deciding foreign policy narrowing even more.

This volume will build the discussion based around several key questions: To what extent do domestic sources influence Ukraine's foreign and security policy orientation? If they do not in Western states (as realist and neorealist theory suggest), are they likely to in Ukraine, and why or why not? Do opinion polls matter if those polled are unable to influence governmental decisions given the absence of civil society? If domestic sources do not influence Ukraine's foreign and security policy to a considerable degree, then what is stopping Ukrainian elites from fully committing themselves to the state's integration into Western structures? Perhaps it is political culture and identity that keeps them from doing so (as several contributors to this book suggest). Finally, to what degree are international relations theories applicable to countries such as Ukraine, since these theories by and large assume that nation-states are already in place and functioning effectively? If post-communist states are still being built, and national identity plays a central role in regional relations, to what extent are international relations theories applicable and thus employable in our analysis?

The book is thus divided into four parts: First, international relations theory and Ukraine's foreign policy; second, civil–military relations; third, Ukraine's foreign and security policy orientations, comparative contexts; and fourth, national identity, ideology, and Ukrainian security policy. Among the contributors are well-known scholars as well as governmental officials who have made contemporary Ukrainian studies an important focus of their professional lives. The contributors agree that a gap exists between the West's portrayal of Ukraine as a crucial component of European security and actual policy put into practice. This book investigates the issues that tend to sustain or reinforce this gap and also attempts to determine whether this trend is likely to continue in the next decade, and why.

Part I seeks to analyze Ukraine's foreign policy through several schools in international relations theory, including realism, constructivism, and globalization, within the context of broader geopolitical and psychological dynamics stemming the East–West frontier in Europe. Victor Chudowsky argues that neither realist nor ethnic determinist theories can account for Ukraine's foreign policy over the past decade, such as Ukraine's dual participation in the Commonwealth of Independent States (CIS) joint air defense system and NATO's Partnership for Peace program, or the reluctance to join the CIS Customs Union while at the same time expanding Ukraine's program of military and technical cooperation with Russia. Paul D'Anieri explains that traditional international relations theory—realism and liberalism in particular, and even the subfield of foreign policy analysis—underestimates the importance of nationalism and national identity as determining factors in international relations.

D'Anieri clearly points out the fundamental dilemma in studying international relations in the post-Soviet states, which is that scholars must leave out the politics of identity as these factors do not fit into mainstream international relations theory. Alternatively, scholars could focus solely on nationalism and identity issues, though they would run the risk of being tagged as an atheoretical "area studies" scholar. Constructivism, D'Anieri suggests, is a way to bridge the two because it shows how national identity fits into international relations theory and how consideration of it can significantly improve the theory.

Jennifer Moroney prefers to view Ukraine's foreign policy orientation from within the context of the creation of the new frontier between Europe and Eurasia. She explains that psychological and social dimensions of the frontier, reinforced by EU expansion to a selected few states in Eastern Europe, has led to a situation where exclusion from the prosperous organizations of Western Europe has led to a feeling of alienation or even resentment from the "outs" of the enlargement process. Those states not included in either the fast- or slow-track group of aspirants of both NATO and particularly the EU tend to associate this exclusion with perceptions of their own security and identity.

Part II is specifically focused on civil–military relations and Ukraine's foreign policy. James Sherr argues that the West's institutions have an important role to play in helping to bring about civilian control of the military, not just in supporting Ukraine's defense and military cooperation with NATO through PfP. Sherr points out that civil–military relations should be applied to other security institutions of the Ukrainian state that are less transparent. Only with an across-the-board institutional change aimed at bringing the military and the rest of the security forces under civilian control will Ukraine be able to move ahead with its broad program of defense reform and restructuring. Ukraine should not only look to the United States and EU member states for this model; it should follow the example of its closest neighbors in Central Europe, particularly Poland.

Yet, as Stacy Closson articulates, what this state of civil–military affairs will comprise remains to be defined, because Ukraine's primary consideration is to address economic crises as well as other serious social and political challenges. Closson argues that a consolidated national consciousness must first be formed to create new democratic and legitimate political institutions to address these challenges. The evolution of civil–military affairs is hampered by a system that has failed to address these factors. Sociologically, the Western model, for Ukrainians, is reminiscent of the Soviet system, where the Communist Party dominated the Ministry of Defense and decisions of senior officers. At the root of civil–military affairs is the notion of transparency and the role of society in government affairs. This requires an open evaluation of the "redevelopment" of the armed forces through multiple layers of society and its organizations.

Part III focuses on several other international relations schools of thought, which include the pluralist and Weberian schools, liberalism, and neorealism. Tor Bukkvoll argues that foreign policy shifts can be best explained by applying insights associated with state theory, by which he seeks to analyze Ukraine's shifting foreign policy orientation. Bukkvoll employs two main approaches: the pluralist and Weberian schools of thought. These two schools, Bukkvoll points out, coincide with the liberalist and realist schools in international relations theory, and help to explain why Ukrainian elites, particularly in the business and energy sectors, have tended to gravitate more toward Europe than Eurasia.

Joshua Spero's chapter examines two cases (Polish–German and Polish–Ukrainian relations) of cooperative behavior in Central and Eastern Europe from a neorealist perspective on alliance-building tactics such as bandwagoning. His work contributes to international relations and comparative politics by studying, in one case, the design and formulation of Polish foreign policy toward Ukraine to reveal if Warsaw–Kyiv ties showed an important conciliatory model of state behavior. Spero uses neorealist theories of bandwagoning, balancing, and aggressive alignment to examine nonthreatening and cooperative behavior among traditional adversaries. He shows that cooperative rather than competitive bandwagoning exists when weaker states align with a stronger state or coalition in order to receive a "reward," and not necessarily to improve their security situation or as a response to a direct threat. Balancing, conversely, results when a state attempts to ally with another state or coalition against a perceived threat. Jennifer Moroney and Sergei Konoplyov focus their work on the creation of new subregional organizations in Europe's gray zone of security, and analyze both internal and external hindrances to their proliferation. They argue that the establishment of GUUAM (Georgia, Ukraine, Uzbekistan, Azerbaijan, and Moldova) and other subregional organizations reflects a desire on the part of their members to bring about some kind of institutionalized security to the underorganized frontier region between Russia and Europe.

Part IV aims to bring the debate in the previous sections to fruition, focusing on the role of national identity in Ukrainian foreign policy, which all of the contributors have touched upon to a certain extent. Taras Kuzio considers the impact of Ukrainian national identity on foreign policy from the perspective of the ideological divisions that exist within the Ukrainian political elite. These two groups are the "Slavophiles," who are antireform and pro-Russia/CIS, and "Westernizers," divided further into "pragmatic nationalists" and "romantic nationalists," who are proreform. President Kuchma is a pragmatic nationalist, according to Kuzio, as he has tended to avoid antagonizing Russia (as seen through Ukraine's accession to the CIS Interparliamentary Assembly in 1999, and in the firing of pro-West Foreign Minister Borys Tarasyuk in 2000), but still has been able to pursue a clear pro-West foreign policy (for example, in the declaration issued in 1998 that stated Ukraine's foreign policy goal of acceding to the EU, and in the proliferation of closer ties with NATO since 1997).

Mikhail Molchanov, however, disagrees with Kuzio in one sense, as he argues that the construction of the Ukrainian national identity need not be based on the distancing of Ukraine from Russia and the CIS. To illustrate his point, Molchanov shows the value of the national identity connection of the Ukrainians and the Russians. Ukraine is a nation in the making that embraces many different ethnic groups and political communities whose national political visions differ, sometimes radically. Occasionally these political and ethnic cleavages overlap, but more often they crosscut each other, making attempts to rationalize the role of national identity in Ukrainian foreign policy complicated and thus incomplete.

This book is the first of its kind, linking area studies and international relations in the case of Ukraine, but it has not had the aim of creating an overarching theoretical framework. It should be clear from the wide array of plausible perspectives in this book that no one international relations theory can be used to understand Ukraine's security policy.

NOTE

1. James N. Rosenau, *The Scientific Study of Foreign Policy* (London: Pinter, 1980).

Part I

INTERNATIONAL RELATIONS THEORY AND UKRAINIAN FOREIGN POLICY

2

The Limits of Realism: Ukrainian Policy toward the CIS

Victor Chudowsky

Ten years after the collapse of the USSR, the study of foreign policies of the "newly independent states"—perhaps a rather outdated phrase— finds itself more or less firmly in the theoretical mainstream of political science and international relations theory. Alexander Motyl quickly and correctly pointed out that if Russia were to overwhelmingly dominate the Commonwealth of Independent States, then the study of Ukraine and other republics would continue as an interesting offshoot of Russian studies. However, as the republics differentiated themselves, a new type of post-Soviet studies would emerge, given common institutions and the unique political characteristics among the former republics. Yet Ukraine and other former republics have emerged as important international actors, and academics have followed by even further "mainstreaming" the study of these new nations and looking at them in the context of the main currents in political science theory.[1] As the CIS has turned out to be less cohesive then was originally expected, and as its member states have increasingly differentiated themselves in both their internal politics and foreign policies, the study of their foreign policies will be looked at less in the context of "nationalities" and more in the context of how "normal" states with (somewhat) functioning institutions and attributes of statehood relate to one another. The way we study Ukraine and the other former republics has changed, as "Sovietology" has faded into mainstream social science and the study of "nationalities" within the former USSR has changed into the study of international relations among the states of Eurasia.

This chapter seeks to explain Ukraine's policy toward the CIS in light of trends in the study of Ukrainian foreign policy and international relations. These studies might be divided into two groups. In the first group, the focus is on Ukraine's place in the emerging system of international relations. These might be viewed as realist or liberal views of how the structure of the international system, or external factors, impact upon Ukraine's foreign policy. In the second group, the focus is on how internal politics affects Ukraine's foreign policy decisions. Although they might be seen as part of the pluralist or liberal trend in international relations theory (in that they argue that internal politics and subnational actors are very important), these studies are much more focused on questions of theories of state building and national identity, and how the struggle over Ukrainian national identity has impacted upon foreign policy decisions.

Explicitly or implicitly, studies of Ukrainian foreign policy take as a given the geopolitical divide between the area of the former USSR on one side (where Russia is the dominant power), and the "West," characterized by the NATO alliance and the overlapping institutions of Europe, including, most notably, the European Union. Most are concerned with why Ukraine's foreign policy has sought to maximally differentiate Ukraine from Russia and join the West; many are also concerned with the wisdom of this effort and whether it is indeed possible. The idea of this chapter is not to place scholars in any categories or to introduce debates where none may exist, but merely to highlight what trends are taking place in the study of Ukraine's foreign policy.

REALIST APPROACHES TO UKRAINE

The nation-state is the primary unit of analysis for realists. The state is assumed to be a unitary, rational actor. Just like individuals in Hobbes's state of nature, states aim to survive in a competitive, anarchic, and hostile environment, where there is no overarching authority to dispense justice or ensure stability. Without such an authority, states must resort to their own resources or capabilities, and/or join alliances, in order to survive. Alliance systems, and the distribution of power among states, are important to realists.[2] Economic issues, domestic politics, bureaucratic politics, nationalism, ideology, and so on are of secondary importance because all states basically are rational and try to do the same thing: survive. In discussing Ukraine's security from a realist point of view then, its internal problems only matter to the extent that they interfere with its ability to make rational foreign policy decisions or interfere with capacity for self-help; that is, its ability to build a strong state and army. A greater determinant of Ukraine's foreign policy is its geopolitical position in the structure of the international system in which it is operating. Now that the Cold War has ended, this structure is in a state of flux.

In realist terms, Ukraine is definitely, to use Waltz's terms, a "secondary state"; that is, its power will never match that of Russia, Germany, or the United States. As a secondary state interested in its survival and security, it will have to ally itself with the United States and/or Germany, perhaps through NATO, or with Russia. Waltz asserts secondary states will balance against the stronger power; therefore, using this logic, Ukraine should balance the NATO alliance by joining with Russia, because U.S.–led NATO is currently the stronger.[3] However, Ukraine seems to be resisting this at all costs.

Stephen Walt disagrees with Waltz's assertion that power distribution alone determines alliances.[4] Instead, states balance against their greatest perceived threat, not against the states with the most power. Russia is Ukraine's largest perceived threat, therefore Ukraine should balance against Russia. However, there are instances where states "bandwagon"; that is, join in an alliance with their greatest perceived enemy. Small states bandwagon because they

1. may want to share in the spoils of their new ally's military victory.
2. want to appease, in the hopes that their new ally will attack other states.
3. want to ally with states with great power and offensive capabilities.
4. are within close geographical proximity to the great power state.
5. are weak.
6. are unlikely to be able to join any other alliance.

Practically all of Walt's conditions are true for Ukraine: It is close to Russia, it is weak, and full membership in another military alliance is unavailable to it. So between Walt and Waltz, both theorizing about international relations generically, we do not have agreement as to with whom Ukraine will ally itself.

The question of what sort of structure will prevail in Europe is crucial to the question of Ukrainian security. A consensus view seems to be emerging that Ukraine is important as a counterpoint to Russian power in the space of the former USSR, and would aid in the process of normalizing Russia so that it does not reemerge as an imperial power. However, Ukraine is not important enough, or is unable, to actually become a member of the NATO alliance.[5] In other words, Ukraine's role may not necessarily be of interest to the West as a member of the

Western alliance but as a check on Russian power on the other half of the divide. Europe, then, will split into NATO and the CIS, and Ukraine's role is to insure a weak CIS and "geopolitical pluralism" within the former Soviet space; thus it deserves Western support in this mission.[6] A more charitable description of Ukraine's situation is Sherman Garnett's characterization of Ukraine as a "keystone" in the development of regional cooperation between NATO and non-NATO countries; Garnett also stressed that tension in the Ukraine–Russia relationship would adversely affect Russian, Ukrainian, and Western interests.[7] Similarly, Stephen Larrabee and Tor Bukkvoll describe a delicate geopolitical balancing act Ukraine must engage in between the East and West.[8]

DOMESTIC POLITICS AND
UKRAINIAN FOREIGN POLICY

International relations theorists of the pluralist school have long argued that states do not necessarily act in optimally rational ways, and that subnational actors—interest groups, bureaucracies, domestic politics, preferences and biases of individual leaders—heavily influence foreign policy decisions. These factors are worth studying because they help to determine a state's behavior or its reaction to events external to it.[9]

In the case of Ukraine, a great deal of attention has been paid to the question of nationalism and the direction of Ukrainian foreign policy. There are a number of reasons for this. The first, obviously, is the boom in academic study in nationalism, ethnicity, and identity politics in general across numerous disciplines, from literature to sociology. The second reason is the renewed investigation into nationalism as a major factor in the breakup of the USSR; a controversy in Sovietology was whether sufficient attention was paid to national questions.[10] Third, a great deal of early research into Ukrainian domestic politics (following independence) focused on language and cultural issues.[11] These factors combined in various ways as scholars looked at how Ukraine's internal political divides affect foreign policy. The central question in this literature can be basically summed up with the phrase, "East or West?"

This literature is striking for its lack of consensus on the character and effects of Ukrainian nationalism (or lack thereof) and its influence on the foreign policy direction of the country. Some have written that Ukraine's leaders were dangerously nationalist, while others characterize their nationalism as benign, and still others discussed the weaknesses of Ukrainian nationalism.[12] Further still is the entire question of what type of nationalism the Ukrainian elite is promoting in its state-building efforts; it seems to waver between Ukrainian ethnic and "civic nationalism."[13] Indeed, the question of the nature of Ukrainian nationalism has seemed to run full circle. In the immediate years following independence, there was the fear of "suicidal nationalism" and expectations in governing circles and the popular press that Ukraine would become a new Yugoslavia. Yet ten years later, recent works have focused not only on the relatively peaceful state of ethnic relations in Ukraine, but new academic works have stressed the deep bonds between Ukrainians and Russians, not only historically but in Ukraine's current situation.

There is also the question of precisely what the majority sentiment on nationalist issues is, and how this may impact the country's future direction. The major theme in this literature is the debate between the two competing conceptions of the Ukrainian nation in domestic politics. On one side there is that conception of Ukraine as a European state, maximally differentiated from Russia and part of European institutions, including NATO. This idea, strongest in western Ukraine, also strongly supports the revival of Ukrainian language and culture. The other conception is of Ukraine as part of the Eastern Slavic family of nations, closely allied with Russia and Belarus. It views Russian culture as being an important part of Ukraine's heritage, and is based most firmly in eastern and southern Ukraine and in the political left.

Andrew Wilson and Stephen Shulman in particular have argued that in fact the latter conception of Ukraine is the more popular, and expect that in the long term the country's foreign policy will or should veer to the East, toward Russia and/or the CIS. Indeed, Wilson characterized a correction in foreign policy in the early Kuchma years as a policy of "little Russianism."[14] Shulman argues that a major problem for the Ukrainian state is lack of adherence to a unifying or majority national idea, which can be found in the idea of Ukraine as an eastern Slavic state. For the sake of nation building, Ukraine should make a strategic choice in favor of integration with Russia rather than Europe.[15] Anatol Lieven notes the deep roots of Ukrainian–Russian cultural and historical interaction and views overtly pro-NATO foreign policy decisions on the part of the Ukrainian government, and their encouragement by Western governments (the United States in particular), as destabilizing.[16]

Yet others have found the pro-European conception of Ukraine's identity to be more crucial in the formation of the nation's foreign policy. Although it not argued that the pro-European idea is carried by a majority, it has enough of an impact on elites to influence their thinking to issues related to sovereignty and relations with Russia. Taras Kuzio, for example, divides the pro-European forces into two camps, the "pragmatists" and the "romantics." The former seek integration with Europe to preserve Ukrainian sovereignty as well as for better security arrangements, capital, and so on. The latter are the afore-mentioned purveyors of the "Ukraine as part of Europe" idea. Agreement between the two forces on foreign policy issues in the Kuchma era has created the critical mass necessary for the pro-European idea to dominate thinking about integration with the West.[17] Stephen Burant focuses on the level of nationalist sentiment, arguing that Ukraine, while possessing a weaker national identity than the Baltic nations, still possesses one stronger than that of Belarus, and enough to make sovereignty a primary concern of the elites.[18] Ilya Prizel, in a less hopeful characterization, states, "It [Ukraine] will have to choose whether to resume an intimate relationship with Russia—albeit on different terms—or to attempt a 'return to Europe.'"[19] This choice is dependent on how Ukraine sorts out questions of polarized, ambivalent, and competing conceptions of national identity.

There are several problems with viewing the direction of Ukrainian foreign policy as stemming from the ethnic identification of the Ukrainian populace or its decision makers. This is not to say that ethnic identification does not matter; it is simply to say that it is difficult to quantify and to precisely conceptualize its role in the foreign policy decision-making process. How does nationalist sentiment help us to explain or predict Ukrainian foreign policy decisions?

First, there is the issue of type of nationalism, how strong this sentiment is, and whether it is a good predictor of a leader's future actions. For example, what are we to make of figures such as Leonid Kravchuk, Leonid Kuchma, and Hennadiy Udovenko? All were loyal servants of the Soviet regime and spent most of their careers interacting very comfortably and successfully with Russians. But over time, after attaining power, both became favored candidates in western Ukraine, Kravchuk's parliamentary constituency was in Ternopil, and Udovenko became a presidential candidate for one of the Rukh factions. Similarly, how does the ethnic or geographical background of a commanding figure such as Volodymyr Horbulin—a key figure in Soviet military industrial complex—inform us about the foreign policy decisions he made? For example, some scholars predicted that Kuchma would follow a foreign policy of "Little Russianism," yet Ukraine has become a lead participant in NATO's Partnership for Peace, has not opposed NATO expansion, and has developed a close military relationship with the United States.

Second, the use of nationalist sentiment in predicting foreign policy choices ignores the functioning of Ukrainian foreign policy institutions. Ukrainian foreign policy is made by a very small group of people at the pinnacle of the Ukrainian elite: basically the members of the National Security and Defense Council (NSDC). How does Ukraine's "ethnic balance" figure into their decision making? Does language matter? It is extremely difficult to say. Analytical materials prepared for the NSDC by the National Institute for Strategic Studies (NISS) indicate that analysts there recommended the *depoliticization* of language and cultural issues for two reasons: (1) to avoid giving Russia an excuse to interfere with Ukraine's internal politics, and (2) to allow leaders the ability to cooperate with Russia on certain issues without being accused of being soft on the issue of sovereignty.[20]

The focus on nationalism perhaps diverts attention away from other important domestic actors and their influence on foreign policy, such as oil interests, the military, business groups, oligarchs, and other interests; in short, the same types of policy lobbies so often studied in other nations. There is also the problem of geopolitics. Wilson, Lieven, and Shulman, in prognosticating Ukraine's future foreign policy direction, do not fully address the effects of both Russian and Western foreign policy on Ukraine. Ukraine is a secondary, status-quo state located between two power centers in Eurasia. It is a weak state, and therefore it is less likely to be an influential actor in European affairs, but rather, to a certain extent, it will be acted upon by its neighboring powers and must react accordingly. Therefore, discussions of Ukraine's future orientation must take place in the context of Ukraine's role in the security designs of both Russia and the West.

The preceding survey makes clear that simple realist or ethnic determinist explanations of Ukraine's strategic choices fall somewhat short, and that a model is necessary that takes into account both domestic politics and/or nationalism along with the explanations of power politics provided by realist theory. The problem is in explaining Ukrainian foreign policy in a manner that takes into account both domestic politics and national sentiment along with geopolitics. To date, the most successful attempt has been Paul D'Anieri's work.[21] D'Anieri argues that nationalism is an important factor in understanding Ukrainian foreign policy because of the primacy placed on sovereignty over economic well-being. D'Anieri's analysis has the advantage of embedding the examination of nationalist sentiment into realist theory. As realist theory places a great deal of importance on sovereignty, Ukrainian nationalism is a key element in the identity struggle between Russia and Ukraine. The struggle for sovereignty has been at the expense of trade ties with Russia/CIS as well as the ability to cooperate with other states to pressure Russia within the confines of the CIS. Nationalism is important in relations among states in the former USSR because new sovereignties are forming and national myths and identities may be in conflict with one another. While not a determining factor, nationalism explains the overwhelming drive for, and sensitivity about, the issue of sovereignty.

D'Anieri's arguments are based on two assumptions:

1. That nationalism and the conflict between competing Russian and Ukrainian national myths and ideas are the main reasons for Ukraine's hardline stance on sovereignty.
2. That Ukrainian positions on economic and other types of integration had a cost in terms of prosperity.

While these are fair assumptions, additional evidence must be taken into account as to why Ukraine has made the decisions it has, and there is great difficulty in fitting this evidence into any kind of parsimonious model.

First, the assumption about nationalism and sovereignty is made rather difficult when one tries to assess precisely how nationalist the Ukrainian elite actually is; other explanations have been presented, which characterize the elite as basically concerned with exploitation and hanging on to power at any cost. For example, Orest Subtelny writes,

The almost complete holdover [from before the collapse of the USSR] of personnel has its ironies. One of them is that the leadership of the Ukrainian state is in the hands of people who only a short time before vehemently opposed the idea of national independence. Self-preservation was certainly a major factor in the Ukrainian elites hasty adoption of pro-independence positions. With the Soviet system tottering, it had to embrace, or, to be more precise, co-opt the concept of a national state or go down with the crumbling empire. Less frequently mentioned but certainly crucial to this transformation was the desire of the Kyiv apparat to free itself of Moscow's overlordship. Indeed, it is quite likely that many members of the Ukrainian elite were more interested in attaining and maintaining exclusive control of Ukraine rather than achieving national independence as such. Thus, the events of 1991 might be viewed as a liberation of a regional elite as much as, or perhaps more than, the liberation of a nation from an imperial yoke.[22]

Subtelny has characterized the Ukrainian elite as being extremely exploitative and corrupt, lording over Ukraine in a rather parasitic way.[23] Indeed, the level of corruption among the Ukrainian elite is rather astounding for an elite characterized as "nationalist" or even "pragmatic." A legitimate question is whether the Ukrainian elite is concerned about sovereignty on the basis of national sentiment or simply to continue opportunities for personal enrichment while defending their turf against Russian oligarchs. While at first glance this may be seen as a somewhat cynical view, Subtelny correctly raises the issue of whether the elite is concerned more with nation building or personal enrichment. The last presidential election, as well as Ukraine's record on domestic economic reform, in particular reform of the agricultural and energy sectors, gives substance to Subtelny's suspicions. These are shared by Ukrainian political scientist and member of parliament Artur Bilous, who characterized the Ukrainian elite class as such:

They have not formalized any party ties, but instead have formalized ties with the party/state bureaucracies, and their ideological positions are quite diverse. Their ideological orientation has a concealed character, and the order of the day for them is in the direction of self-preservation in changing conditions through pliable actions and strategies. . . . Therefore the analysis of the stances and political perspectives of the state/governing elite can't necessarily be found in their value orientations, but in their concrete, practical actions.[24]

On the issue of trade and the CIS, or "sovereignty over well-being," this chapter will discuss evidence presented in Ukrainian government circles in the early years of the Kuchma administration that argued against CIS integration. These argued that entering into a customs union or taking actions to encourage trade with Russia at the possible expense of trade with other parts of the world would do long-term damage to the Ukrainian economy. There was agreement that Russia was an important trade partner, but the issues were on the terms of trade and its long-term consequences. These concerns were not necessarily related to sovereignty.

To follow is a diverse compendium of plausible explanations as to why Ukraine has chosen to avoid full integration into the CIS, as well as why it has cooperated quite readily in other areas—the degree of practical cooperation between Ukraine and the CIS has been somewhat overlooked. The purpose is to fill in the explanatory blanks, which are left over or have gone missing due to the focus on nationalism and realist-style geopolitics. Many of the arguments supporting the position that Ukraine should not join the CIS are quite rational, others perhaps frivolous, and still others are firmly rooted in domestic politics. The purpose is not to come up with a new theory about combining international and domestic factors in Russian–Ukrainian relations, but simply to enrich the current literature with "stray" factors that are nonetheless important. The sources are all Ukrainian, and are from the crucial years 1994 to 1996, when the new Kuchma administration was exploring options in the area of foreign policy before settling on its present course.

UKRAINIAN TRADE STRATEGY:
BACKWARD OR FORWARD?

In the area of trade relations with Russia and the CIS, many Ukrainian scholars and advisors quite rationally and coolly calculated the costs and benefits of entering into various types of trade agreements with the CIS, as well as Eastern and Western Europe. They found what many Western scholars and commentators have also found: that the former USSR was a zone of economic collapse, dislocation, and disintegration. At the same time, the West was integrating and was seen as a valuable potential market as well as a source of capital. From the Ukrainian point of view in the mid-1990s, it was difficult to argue that increased ties with the disintegrating zone was a rational trade policy choice.

The importance of trade as a possible means of escaping the legacies of the Soviet era was not lost on decision makers. A National Institute of Strategic Studies report frankly stated,

The entry of Ukraine into the world economic system and its participation in the international division of labor is an unavoidable condition of its transition to a democratic country with a market economy. The young country received as its inheritance threadbare manufacturing capital, exhausted and poor deposits of fossil fuels, a bulky and ineffective structure of industry, and a degraded creative potential and work ethic of its cadres. Processes of depression in the Ukrainian economy have a negative impact on the state of foreign trade. The past few years have seen a change in the participants, mechanism, investment dynamics, geographical and product structure in the area of Ukrainian foreign trade. This was conditioned by the following causes: deep economic and political crises in the USSR and Ukraine, the collapse of the USSR, the realization of socio-economic transitions in Ukraine and other nations with centralized planned economies, which were the principal trading partners of the former USSR, and the significant worsening of conditions of international trade, which happened, not in the last place, as the result of domestic changes.[25]

This from a report titled *Ukrainian Foreign Trade: Current State and Prognosis*, was not an official working document but a study prepared for use by the NSDC; it gave an indication of a strain of thinking about trade in the Ukrainian government.

After a regional breakdown of potential and existing trade partners, the authors stated flatly that Russia was Ukraine's most important trade partner and vice versa, and then brainstormed ways to both develop that relationship and widen the circle of trading partners. The main findings were as follows:

1. Investment: The authors noted that "despite the predictions of optimists," foreign capital had not rushed to Ukraine. The authors nonetheless recommended that seeking investment and foreign credits should be a "priority."
2. Barter Trade: The report stated that barter trade was a sign of the overall ill health of the Ukrainian economy, "the imperfection of the tax system, instability of the monetary system, the undeveloped banking system, the un-competitiveness of our production, the inadequate tempo of liberalization of foreign economic activities and processes of privatization."[26]

Barter trade, which took place primarily with CIS countries, was causing "highly liquid" products such as sugar and metals to leave the country at far below market prices. In addition, barter trade was difficult to regulate, deprived the country of hard currency, did little to help the state budget, and provided numerous opportunities for abuses and corruption.

The section of the report on trade with CIS countries flatly stated that the hoped-for revival of trade ties among former republics was not going to happen. CIS states were saving hard currency for overseas purchases, and were reorienting their trade to the outside world just as Ukraine was, at the expense of trade with other CIS states. In addition, "there cannot even be talk about the return to the old system of mutual ties"; instead the CIS should be studied as a place where new, "rational" types of trade should be developed on an enterprise-to-enterprise basis.

The study concluded that

1. Ukraine suffered a large trade deficit in inter-CIS trade, and too much of it was conducted in barter.
2. In contrast to the previous Soviet mechanism of integration, "integration among CIS states in current conditions should be integration between enterprises, on the basis of expedience and mutual interest."
3. Decision makers should take into account that a current decision to integrate with the CIS by whatever means could have long-lasting and drastic consequences.

Today's economic ties with the nations of the CIS look like a means of dealing with current social problems of Ukraine, but in the future they will define or determine the expansion of the spectrum of scientific–technical and economic contacts, the change in type of goods and geographic divisions of trade relations, the increase in independence and effectiveness of the national economy, the increase in well-being of the Ukrainian nation, and the interests and possibilities of not only the market of the CIS but the world market as a whole.[27]

The subtext of this passage, particularly when taken with the report as a whole, seems to be that economic integration with the CIS would lock Ukraine into an unhealthy pattern of trade relations and limit the country's future economic potential.

The report was more positive about trade with Europe, both Western and Central: It was not only profitable, but would help bring Ukraine into the democratic and market-oriented (often called "civilized") family of nations. The conclusion of the nontechnical section of the report was titled "Transition of the National Economy of Ukraine to a Market Economy of the Open Type," and the authors stated that there was no alternative to this "historical plan." However, noting that Ukraine was in a poor and uncompetitive position with respect to most developed countries, it could not simply become a completely open and free market overnight. Therefore, this process of transition, or "opening," should be done "step by step" and "selectively" and should be based on a preplanned industrial policy that combines measures of liberalization as well as protectionism. Import policy should be structured in such a way that valued industries are not destroyed; export policy should be structured such that higher-value-added items find markets abroad. Most important, both export markets and sources of imports must be diversified as widely as possible, not only for economic reasons, but for geopolitical reasons as well. A diversified group of trade partners may hasten potential political and strategic partnerships, and would solidify ties with bordering states.

The recommendations of the final "Transition" chapter of the report were to

1. increase cooperation with the EU.
2. recognize that Ukraine is not able to compete with the West in the area of more sophisticated manufacturing and services; however, a sound industrial policy and economic reforms would do much to dispel the image of the country as merely being a source of raw materials.
3. pursue the creation of a Black Sea free-trade zone that would lower trade barriers between Ukraine, Russia, Turkey, and others.
4. increase ties with developing nations in Africa and Latin America, which could be markets for the low-cost products of heavy industry Ukraine provides at a low price.
5. recognize that the zone of principal interest for Ukraine remains the CIS, and most of all Russia. The CIS was the source of Ukrainian energy and raw-materials needs, an important market for exports, and there were tight technological and cooperative ties. In addition, the report urges forming new bilateral ties with CIS countries aside from Russia, in particular Turkmenistan.

The report was fairly indicative of the thinking of the government on international trade as Ukraine pursued closer trade ties with Europe and cooperation with European multilateral organizations. What is most interesting is the way Ukraine's two main markets—Europe and the CIS—are portrayed in this report and other statements by the government on economic issues. The CIS is portrayed as an important market for Ukraine, but not a terribly lucrative or attractive one, as if ties are pursued only grudgingly; a concern is also that integration will come at the price of sovereignty. Europe, on the other hand, is portrayed as a market where opportunities abound, meeting Ukraine's potential and aiding in its path to democracy and a market economy;

this despite the realization that the obstacles to such integration are substantial.

FORWARD OR BACKWARD:
THE UKRAINIAN VIEWS OF TRADE PARTNERS

In the early Kuchma era, Ukrainian trade analysts tried to objectively view the economic situation in Europe and the former USSR and were obviously attracted by European growth and integration. Despite the constant reminders that the CIS and Russia were Ukraine's most important trade partners, there was a difference in the way Ukrainian policy makers and opinion makers viewed the former USSR and the West. In Ukrainian trade policy, at the official level, "forward" meant Europe and "backward" meant the CIS, which was associated with Russia, the USSR, infringement on sovereignty, and the general lack of realization of the country's potential.

This forward–backward dichotomy was evident in several articles appearing in *Polityka i Chas,* the Ukrainian Foreign Ministry's official journal. One article, written by a senior member of the Ukrainian National Academy of Science, was actually titled "A Step Forward or a Step Back: On Questions of Ukraine's Interests in All-European Integrational Processes."[28] The author stated, "From the point of view of the standard of economic development and the standard of living of the population, integration with Europe would be for us a step forward, and reintegration with Russia a step backward."[29]

At the semiofficial level there has been a rather vigorous debate as to which "bloc" should be Ukraine's primary economic partner: the CIS/Russia, or Europe and the West.[30] However, the "pro-Westerners" vastly outnumbered the "Eurasianists."[31] Typical were articles that "spun" economic relations with Russia, such as "With Our Strategic Partner" (meaning Russia), by O. S. Samodurov, the head of the Administration for Bilateral Relations with Russia at the Ministry of Foreign Economic Ties and Trade.[32] The author reminded readers that Russia was still Ukraine's largest trading partner, and that Ukraine should not be "afraid" of doing business with Russia. He recited positive aspects of this, such as the fact that trade was growing; Ukrainian exports were more highly value-added (such as processed foods and machinery) than imports from Russia, mostly energy, and the like. However, the article quickly took a darker turn as the Russian side was blamed for continued use of export tariffs that penalize Russian exporters of goods to Ukraine, and the failure of Russia to implement free-trade agreements.

Valeryi Heyets, an economist at the Ukrainian National Academy of Science, attacked the forward–backward issue through the prism of what is best for Ukraine's not insignificant but uncompetitive high-tech sector.[33] This included space-related industries, aircraft, high-tech defense enterprises that must be converted, and computer programming talent. The author believed that these industries should be developed to the point where they reach world standards, and that high technology would serve as the key to Ukraine's entry into the world market. Integration in the world economy would

1. realize the potential of Ukrainian science and high technology.
2. save the industrial and technological basis of the Ukrainian economy.
3. renew and widen perspectives for the use of present industrial organizations and preserve jobs.
4. increase beneficial ties with other countries.
5. aid in the import of high technology.
6. open up new sources of investment income.

At the end of the article the author asks whether the CIS would be an appropriate vehicle for the development of Ukrainian high-tech industry, as there is the possibility of the formation of "financial–industrial groups" in which Russian capital would assist in the redevelopment of Ukrainian high-tech industry. However, there were factors standing in the way of CIS integration; namely,

1. the increasing differences among CIS states in terms of socioeconomic development.
2. the worsening economic situation, which negatively affected member states willingness to enter into economic alliances.

Oleh Mirus, the head of the Administration on Europe of the Ministry of Foreign Trade and Economic Ties, applied the forward–backward dichotomy to CEFTA (the Central European Free Trade Agreement between the Czech Republic, Slovakia, Hungary, Poland, and Slovenia) and the CIS, and recommended a push for greater trade ties with CEFTA.[34]

Victor Andryichyk, manager of state regulation of foreign trade at the Ukrainian Academy of Foreign Trade stated that the primary reason for Ukraine's rather poor overall trade performance was its own unreformed economy.[35] Trade with the CIS, however, aggravated the situation because so many of Ukraine's suppliers as well as consumers in the CIS are monopolistic, and therefore prices for both exports and imports are not in accordance with world prices, thus harming Ukraine's competitiveness. The author recommended maximum diversification of trade partners, particularly those with market economies, as this would serve to nudge along Ukraine's internal reforms.

A similar approach was used by Anton Filipenko, of Kyiv State University, in the English-language version of *Polityka i Chas*.[36] Filipenko argues against full integration in the CIS because

1. it is an attempt to reintegrate an economic entity (the USSR) originally created on the basis of military and ideological factors, and not rational economics.
2. Ukraine will integrate itself with countries that are failing economically.
3. the "supranational" CIS bodies that have been formed bear an uncomfortable resemblance to Soviet-era planning institutions.
4. any attempt at integration should start with free trade, which Russia has refused to do.
5. because of her size, Russia would dominate the CIS.
6. the CIS, through a customs union and other measures, limits member states interaction with the outside world. Ukraine's first and foremost concern was with its own national interests, and some CIS efforts met these interests, such as the maintenance of a CIS-wide network of scientific research establishments. However, a number of specific features of the CIS, such as the ruble zone, in which accounts between CIS states were settled in rubles in accounts at the Russian Central Bank, merely subsidized the Russian economy and were not in Ukraine's interests.

Again, the "backward" theme is repeated: "A forced renewal of former economic ties will only recreate a poor approximation of what existed previously and drag the Ukrainian economy into the stagnant and crisis-ridden CIS economy for a long time to come. This would simply preserve the general technological and economic backwardness, low productivity, low labor quality and the extremely high levels of energy inefficiency."[37]

UKRAINE AND THE CIS:
THE MINISTRY OF FOREIGN AFFAIRS

What became of the more than 600 CIS documents signed by Ukraine from 1992 to 1996? In practice, the CIS has been of some use to Ukraine on a few narrow issues. According to the CIS desk officer at the Foreign Ministry, the following represented the greatest hopes and failures of the CIS:[38]

1. Budget problems prevented Ukraine from following through on agreements signed at CIS meetings: Ukraine's economic downturn and the nonfunctioning nature of many of its internal governing institutions made it impossible for the country to fund CIS initiatives it had signed. To the government and the *Verkhovna Rada*, funding to follow through on CIS agreements was a low priority, so nothing of great consequence happened.

2. Pensions: CIS pension agreements have been one of its few success sto-
   ries. If a Soviet citizen lived in one republic prior to 1991 and moved to another one to become a citizen, his new country provided him or her with a
   pension. The member states in general have adhered to this principle.

3. Double taxation: None of the agreements were working, because the relevant committees set up by the CIS to work on this issue never met.

4. Baikonur and Space Programs: Space cooperation programs were done
   strictly on a bilateral basis, outside of the context of the CIS, with Russia
   and Kazakhstan, where the Baikonur launch area is located.

5. Chernobyl: Cooperation in this area was limited to the exchange of information, primarily between Belarus and Ukraine, where the effects were
   most drastic.

6. Science: The CIS created a "Scientific–Technological Council" which met
   regularly and exchanged information on problems in energy, engineering, and space programs. This was another success story, and was tied in
   with the fact that space-related manufacturing systems of member states
   were intertwined and dependent on one another.

7. CIS Bank: The bank existed on paper but was not functioning due to a
   lack of funding by member states.

8. Railway freight: A CIS body successfully divided railroad stock and kept
   track of the location of cars.

So, Ukraine in fact has cooperated quite extensively with the CIS in
areas useful to it: people's pensions, meetings of scientists associated
with the military–industrial complex, and keeping track of railroad
freight cars. The desk officer then gave explanations as to why Ukraine
did or did not sign more controversial agreements:

1. "Associate membership": CIS documents did not specify what such membership status was, but Ukraine's understanding of the term was that it
   would only cooperate in areas of the CIS of interest to it; it need not attend
   every meeting or help fund every multilateral CIS institution or effort.

2. Ukraine was against forming permanent multilateral CIS institutions or
   "organs," preferring normal diplomacy, bilateral talks, and ad-hoc solutions. The fear was that permanent institutions would rapidly be controlled by Russia.

3. Customs Union: Ukraine was against a CIS-wide customs union because
   it was seen as a means for Russia, the largest industrial producer in the
   CIS, to protect its market and the continued production of inferior goods.
   For example, Russia was the leading producer of cars in the CIS; it wanted
   high tariffs on foreign cars throughout the CIS in order to protect its market there. This, however, was bad for Ukrainian consumers, who may
   have preferred other foreign automobiles.

A fuller explanation of the refusal to join the customs union was offered by Serhiy Osyka, a close colleague of Kuchma and a former minister for external economic relations. In the government newspaper *Uriadoviy Kuryer,* Osyka explained that there were differing Russian and Ukrainian interests in so far as tariff rates were concerned. Agriculture was a major sector of the Ukrainian economy; therefore, Ukraine wanted higher tariffs to protect its industry, whereas Russia did not. On the other hand, Ukraine, an energy importer, would support lower tariffs on energy than Russia. Osyka mentioned forty customs categories in which Ukrainian and Russian interests were in conflict. He stated, "It is not expedient for us to join those unions on such terms, because this would ruin the Ukrainian economy."[39]

4. Air defense: This was a controversial move attacked by the Ukrainian right, because Ukraine's air defense system is united with that of Russia. Counselor Vorontsov explained that Ukraine signed onto the CIS air defense system because (1) the system was already in place, being a holdover from the USSR, and (2) Ukraine cannot afford an air defense system of its own. The counselor stated that Ukraine would build its own once it could afford to do so.

The counselor added that the ministry is under constant pressure from Russia to join as a full member, but stated that this was mostly the product of inertia: Russia was used to thinking of itself as the "center" of the Soviet–post-Soviet space. The first main point of disagreement was the necessity of forming institutions to initiate "integration." The Ukrainian approach was to press for free trade relations and allow enterprises and people to integrate on their own, not at the direction of CIS ministries. The second point of disagreement was Ukraine's nonparticipation in CIS security structures, such as peacekeeping forces and joint border patrols. Ukraine, the counselor stated, simply had no interest in patrolling the borders of other CIS states, particularly in Central Asia, where border wars continue to rage.

In addition, documents were presented at various CIS conferences that were either reminiscent of the Soviet era or signaled the fact that Russia saw the CIS as a unified entity of somewhat less than sovereign states; for example, dual citizenship, a common CIS-wide identity card, and numerous documents on a "single information space" or a "single technical–scientific space." After the collapse of the CIS Unified Military Force in 1993 and the approaching anniversary of World War II, the CIS delegates spent a great deal of time issuing statements and decrees regarding the celebration of the fiftieth anniversary of World War II and the commemoration of Soviet era military heroes such as Marshall Zhukov. Plans were also laid to erect monuments, award medals, and conduct "propaganda" events to commemorate the anniversary of the CIS.[40]

The proposed CIS customs union presented the biggest problem to Ukrainian policy makers, due to the fear that entry into such a union would limit future options in trade policy. The amount of barter trade was also seen as harmful. The second largest problem was the developing nature of CIS "coordinating" institutions; here the fear was definitely over sovereignty, in that Russians would come to dominate such institutions and Moscow would reestablish itself as a center. More broadly, the CIS was viewed as a zone of collapse, particularly when compared to the West.

DOMESTIC POLITICS AND THE CIS

Much can also be learned about the Ukrainian position on the CIS by understanding the dynamics of the interaction between the parliament (particularly the 1994–1998 parliament) and President Kuchma. The issue of the CIS failed to appear on the policy agenda as set by the president and parliament.

For the March 1994 parliamentary elections, a database was compiled that included all campaign flyers for winners of parliamentary seats in 1994. They were coded on the question of position on the CIS: no position, against, in favor of economic membership only, and full participation and/or restore USSR or a single state.[41] A majority favored the last two positions, while almost 40 percent were hostile or did not mention the CIS:

No opinion–not mentioned	108	26%
Against CIS membership	53	13%
Pro-economic membership	137	33.7%
Full union–restore USSR	108	26.6%

It was, of course, the parliamentary left that most supported full entry into the CIS:

	No Opinion	Against	Economic	Full Union
LEFT (171 seats)				
Communists	1.1	—	4.4	94.4
Socialists	7.6	—	—	92.9
Agrarians	34	—	62.3	3.8
CENTRISTS (134)				
Center	62.9	—	37.1	—
Unity	29.4	—	67.6	2.9
Interregional	12.9	—	83.9	3.2
Independent	68	—	32	—

RIGHT (94)				
Reforms	41.7	19.4	38.9	—
Rukh	18.5	77.7	3.8	—
Statehood	29	64.5	6.5	—

President Kuchma was also quite interested in greater cooperation on economic issues with the CIS. However, the nature of the political battle that took place between Kuchma and the parliament prevented the CIS from coming to the top of the policy agenda. As two of Kuchma's political consultants, Vladimir Malinkovich and Mykhailo Pohrebins'ky, explained to me, Kuchma's first priority upon taking office was economic reform, second was concentration of power in the office of the president, and closer relations with Russia were in third place, or perhaps lower.[42]

Malinkovich attributed Kuchma's abandonment of CIS issues to a number of factors, but primarily Kuchma's own shift to the right. First, Malinkovich wanted Kuchma to start a non-communist left party in parliament that would work toward "political union" with Russia. Kuchma, however, refused, because he also wanted to work out a constitutional agreement concentrating power in the office of the president and did not feel he needed a party in parliament to do so; in fact, he felt many centrists and leftists in parliament would be opposed to a strong presidential system. This led Kuchma to rely more and more on right-wing forces for support. Second, Vladimir Grinev, perhaps Ukraine's best-known Eurasianist and a friend of Kuchma's, tried to convince the president to adopt a foreign policy friendlier to Russia, but failed because Grinev's constituency, the Inter-Regional Group–Union of Industrialists and Entrepreneurs, won few seats in parliament and was something of a spent force politically. This was complicated by Kuchma's fight with leftists in parliament over reform, the very constituency that helped him into office. In this heated political battle, Kuchma was loath to adopt any programs or policies dear to the left, fearing loss of support on the right. This caused Kuchma to drop cooperation with the CIS as a policy goal.

Both consultants also explained that Kuchma was reluctant to follow through on promises for closer relations with Russia out of personal considerations or out of vanity. When dealing with Yeltsin, Kuchma often complained that the Russian president "would wag his finger at him as if he were only a provincial party boss" rather than president of a large country, or that Ukrainians were once again being treated as "little brothers." When Kuchma visited the West, particularly the United States, on the other hand, he would receive honor guards and twenty-one-gun salutes. Both consultants were extremely complimentary on the way, for example, Kuchma was given such grand treatment when he visited the United States.

Other powerful forces in society were also against a close political union with Russia, according to Malinkovich. Much of the upper strata of Ukrainian society was enthralled with the West and uninterested in the familiar territory of the former USSR. High-level bureaucrats in the Cabinet of Ministers and the Presidential Administration profited from Western business deals by industrial cronies. High-level figures in the government collected sizable honoraria and consulting fees from various Western institutions. Opinion makers, such as journalists and intellectuals, being from the provincial Soviet-era city of Kyiv and largely barred from traveling, now reveled in numerous contacts and travel opportunities, and treated the West far more favorably in their writing. Businessmen also did not want to endanger their freedom to deal freely with both Russia and the West. This was even confirmed by former Foreign Minister Udovenko, who complained at a press briefing that his diplomats did not want to serve in the CIS, preferring the United States and Europe.[43]

Pohrebinsky suggested that in Ukraine's polarized political climate, figures who spoke out for a close alliance with Russia, even on the basis of full sovereignty, were derided as less than patriotic, unrealistic, or, at worst, traitors. Pohrebins'ky added, however, that there was no powerful interest group that supported a close alliance. The Communists siphoned off the pro-Russian vote. In addition, the major Ukrainian patronage networks, or "clans," often based in industry, did have an informal voice in foreign policy. In particular, the new business elite and clans based in Donetsk and Dnipropetrovs'k were interested in three things from Kyiv:

1. protectionist measures for the internal Ukrainian market.
2. continued exclusion of Russian capital from the Ukrainian privatization process.
3. access to Western or hard-currency markets for their goods.

In other words, they wanted protectionism while looking for lucrative deals in the West. This group of new businessmen were closely intertwined with and depended on favors from the government, and there was no strong pro-Russian sentiment among them.

UKRAINE AND CIS POLICY: RATIONAL OR NATIONAL?

Ukraine's policy of selectively participating in CIS initiatives while remaining strongly opposed to coordinating institutions based in Minsk or Moscow began under President Kravchuk around 1992–1993, and has more or less continued unchanged until today.[44] It has, in fact, been a remarkably steady policy.

The determinants of this policy cannot simply be attributed to geopolitics or Ukraine's national identity; instead, they are multifaceted and complex. The formation of this policy took place during a time of great upheaval: the collapse of the USSR and the subsequent economic collapse of the CIS, and the phenomenon of a new Ukrainian elite taking power. Add to this mix the pressures of Russian, European, and American foreign policy toward Ukraine on issues of sovereignty, nuclear weapons, Chernobyl, the Black Sea Fleet, and so on. Also, the policy was formed at a time when much of the Ukrainian elite was fascinated and excited by increased ties with the West, and the top elite was resentful of Russian pressure.

Realist theory, with its emphasis on balancing against threats, cannot account for the nuance of certain aspects of Ukraine's policy toward the CIS. It cannot explain how Ukraine can simultaneously participate in the CIS air defense system but not a Customs Union, while at the same time holding NATO military exercises on its territory and demanding attention from the European Union. Realist theory only outlines the broad parameters of policy: Ukraine must balance, bandwagon, or somehow remain neutral. But the record of Ukraine's cooperation with both Russia and the West cannot easily be placed in one of these categories.

Similarly, a focus on national identity or nationalism as an important determinant of Ukraine's foreign policy also ignores other determinants, from the personalities of leaders, to the functioning of Ukrainian institutions, to analyses of issues by Ukrainians themselves. For example, do Ukrainian experts explain by nationalist sentiment or by assessments of trade figures the fact that Ukraine has not joined the CIS customs union? Virtually every top economist or trade-related professional near the ruling elite recommended against it on the basis of the problems of barter trade, tariffs, and the possibility of closing the Ukrainian economy off from the West. While it may be true that such studies were biased (I believe that at the very least the NISS study was not) and perhaps flawed in hindsight, it is difficult to factor in how nationalist sentiment figured into the work of economists. There were quite rational reasons why Ukrainian economists wanted to avoid a customs union and the like, not the least of which was that the CIS economies were in a tailspin.

This chapter might be seen as an argument for theoretical flexibility, as different determinants of foreign policy may be accounted for by the following factors, in rank order in terms of importance:

1. Balance of power: Realist theory best highlights the security and alliance dilemmas Ukraine faces, and takes into account the important factor of how Ukraine is acted upon by Russia and the West. It alerts us to the fact that Ukraine's foreign policy will be conducted as a reaction to the poli-

cies of these power centers. On the side of Russia, crucial issues will be the extent to which Russia treats Ukraine as sovereign, the presence of troops in Crimea, and the attractiveness of Russia as a security and trade partner. On the side of the West (i.e., the United States, NATO, and the EU), a crucial question is the extent to which the West will signal its willingness to absorb and/or accommodate Ukraine and the degree to which Ukraine benefits from various types of military, political, and economic cooperation with the West, or whether it will be ignored. In a broad sense, how these issues play out will have the greatest impact on Ukrainian foreign policy.

2. Domestic politics, meaning, in the liberal–pluralist sense, the actions of interest groups and lobbies (which are murky to outsiders) and opinion makers, and the action and interaction of institutions, in particular the parliament, the National Security and Defense Council, the Ministry of Foreign Affairs, and the president. This chapter presented evidence that Ukrainian domestic politics in 1994–1996 were hostile to the CIS, and perhaps aided in the evolution of Kuchma's views of Russia and the CIS.

3. The preferences of individual elites: As we have seen, Kuchma's own preferences evolved over time, and perhaps were influenced by his interaction with Yeltsin. In addition, there is no question that figures such as Horbulin and Udovenko left an important stamp on the institutions they headed, and on the attitudes of many within those institutions. Also important are policy recommendations of those charged with the rational assessment of foreign policy options, such as think tanks.

CONCLUSION

This "levels of analysis" approach, while perhaps not very parsimonious, calls attention to various factors that result in Ukraine's highly nuanced yet fairly consistent approach to the CIS. It is also the usual set of factors we investigate when examining the foreign policies of states outside of the CIS. It is difficult to factor in nationalism, as there are different types and varying levels of nationalism in Ukraine and disagreement about precisely how nationalism affects policy. In addition, as the initial stages of nation building fade into memory, the states of the CIS may well become more "normal," and the relations among them become hopefully more "normalized." Nationalist sentiment may well play less of a role in policy formation in favor of rational calculations over power, security, trade, and prosperity.

NOTES

1. This process began fairly early; Motyl announced the "end of Sovietology" in 1992. See Alexander Motyl, ed., *The Post-Soviet Nations: Perspectives on the Demise of the USSR* (New York: Columbia University Press, 1992). Frederick J. Fleron and Erik P. Hoffman also argued for imbuing Sovietology with more

theorizing from mainstream social science in F. J. Fleron and E. P. Hoffman, eds., *Post-Communist Studies and Political Science: Methodology and Empirical Theory in Sovietology* (Boulder, Colo.: Westview Press, 1993).

2. The modern classic of the field is Kenneth Waltz, *Theory of International Politics* (New York: McGraw-Hill, 1979). See also Michael E. Brown, Sean M. Lynn-Jones, and Steven Miller, eds., *Perils of Anarchy: Contemporary Realism and International Security* (Cambridge: MIT Press, 1995).

3. Waltz, *Theory*, 126–127.

4. Stephen M. Walt, *The Origins of Alliances* (Ithaca: Cornell University Press, 1987), 5.

5. See James Brusstar, "Russian Vital Interests and Western Security," *Orbis* 38, no. 4 (1994): 607–619; Charles L. Glaser, "Why NATO Is Still Best: Future Security Arrangements for Europe," *International Security* 18, no. 1 (1993): 13. John Mearsheimer, "Back to the Future: Instability in Europe after the Cold War," in *Perils of Anarchy: Contemporary Realism and International Security*, ed. Michael E. Brown, Sean M. Lynn-Jones, and Steven Miller (Cambridge: MIT Press, 1995), 78–130. Also John Mearsheimer, "The Case for a Ukrainian Nuclear Deterrent," *Foreign Affairs* 72, no. 3 (1993): 51–66, and Zbigniew Brzezinski, "A Plan for Europe," *Foreign Affairs* 74, no. 1 (1995): 26–42.

6. Taras Kuzio, "Promoting Geopolitical Pluralism in the CIS: GUUAM and Western Foreign Policy," *Problems of Post-Communism* 47, no. 3 (2000): 25–35, and "Geopolitical Pluralism in the CIS: The Emergence of GUUAM," *European Security* 9, no. 2 (2000): 81–114.

7. Sherman Garnett, *Keystone in the Arch: Ukraine in the Emerging Security Environment of Central and Eastern Europe* (Washington, D.C.: Carnegie Endowment, 1997).

8. Stephen F. Larrabee, "Ukraine's Balancing Act," *Survival* 38, no. 2 (1996): 143–165, and Tor Bukkvoll, "Ukraine and NATO: The Politics of Soft Cooperation," *Security Dialogue* 28, no. 3 (1997): 363–374.

9. See Robert Jervis, *Perception and Misperception in International Politics* (Princeton, N.J.: Princeton University Press, 1976), and Richard Rosecrance and Arthur A. Stein, eds., *Domestic Bases of Grand Strategy* (Ithaca, N.Y.: Cornell University Press, 1993).

10. A. Motyl, *The Post-Soviet Nations: Perspectives on the Demise of the USSR* (New York: Columbia University Press, 1992); Roman Szporluk, *Russia, Ukraine and the Breakup of the Soviet Union* (Stanford, Calif.: Hoover Institution Press, 2000).

11. Dominique Arel, "Voting Behaviour in the Ukrainian Parliament—The Language Factor," in *Parliaments in Transition: The New Legislative Politics in the Former USSR and Eastern Europe*, ed. Thomas F. Remington (Boulder, Colo.: Westview Press, 1994), 125–158, and "Language Politics in Independent Ukraine: Towards One or Two State Languages?" *Nationalities Papers* 23, no. 3 (1995): 597–622; and Dominique Arel and Andrew Wilson, "The Ukrainian Parliamentary Elections," *RFE/RL Research Report* 3, no. 26 (1994): 6–17.

12. Eugene B. Rumer, "Eurasia Letter: Will Ukraine Return to Russia?" *Foreign Policy* 96 (1994): 129–144; Charles Furtado, "Nationalism and Foreign Policy in Ukraine," *Political Science Quarterly* 109, no. 1 (1994): 81–104; Charles Furtado and Michael Hechter, "Nationalist Politics: Estonia and the Ukraine," in *Think-*

ing Theoretically about Soviet Nationalities, ed. A. Motyl (New York: Columbia University Press, 1992), 169–204; David Marples, *Ukraine under Perestroika: Ecology, Economics and the Worker's Revolt* (New York: St. Martin's Press, 1991).

13. Paul J. D'Anieri, Robert S. Kravchuk, and T. Kuzio, *Politics and Society in Ukraine* (Boulder, Colo.: Westview Press, 1999), and T. Kuzio, "Nationalism in Ukraine: Towards a New Framework," *Politics* 20, no. 2 (2000): 77–86.

14. Andrew Wilson, *Ukranian Nationalism in the 1990s: A Minority Faith* (Cambridge: Cambridge University Press, 1997).

15. Stephen Shulman, "Asymmetrical International Integration and Ukrainian National Disunity," *Political Geography* 18, no. 8 (1999): 913–939.

16. Anatol Lieven, *Ukraine and Russia: A Fraternal Rivalry* (Washington, D.C.: U.S. Institute of Peace, 1999).

17. T. Kuzio, "Ukraine and NATO: The Evolving Strategic Partnership," *Journal of Strategic Studies* 21, no. 2 (1998): 1–30.

18. Stephen R. Burant, "Foreign Policy and National Identity: A Comparison of Ukraine and Belarus," *Europe–Asia Studies* 47, no. 7 (1995): 1125–1144.

19. Ilya Prizel, *National Identity and Foreign Policy: Nationalism and Leadership in Poland, Russia, and Ukraine* (Cambridge: Cambridge University Press, 1999), 10.

20. O. L. Valevskyi and M. Honchar, *Struktura Heopolitychnyh Interesiv Ukrainy* (Kyiv: National Institute of Strategic Studies, 1995).

21. Paul J. D'Anieri, "Nationalism and International Politics: Identity and Sovereignty in the Russian–Ukrainian Conflict," *Nationalism and Ethnic Politics* 3, no. 2 (1997): 1–28, and *Economic Interdependence in Ukrainian–Russian Relations* (Albany: State University of New York Press, 1999).

22. Orest Subtelny, "Imperial Disintegration and Nation-State Formation: The Case of Ukraine," in *The Successor States to the USSR*, ed. John Blaney (Washington, D.C.: Congressional Quarterly, 1995), 184–195.

23. Orest Subtelny, "The New Ukrainian Elite" (paper presented at the Association for the Study of Nationalities Conference, New York, April 2000).

24. Artur Bilous, *Politichni Obiednannia Ukrainy* (Kyiv: Ukraina, 1993).

25. O. S. Vlasiuk and I. L. Yampols'ka, *Zovnishna Torhivlia Ukrainy: Suchasnyi Stan ta Prohnos* (Kyiv: National Institute of Strategic Studies, 1996).

26. Ibid., 12. I also examined Ukrainian trade statistics to check the extent of barter trade. In 1994 Ukraine gained three times more hard currency from exports to the "outside" world than to the CIS. Its exports to the CIS were mostly paid for with barter. On the import side, almost the reverse is true: Ukraine must pay for most of its imports from the CIS in hard currency. This can be seen as a hard-currency drain on the economy: In 1994, only 16 percent of Ukrainian exports to the CIS were paid for in hard currency; however, Ukraine had to use hard currency to pay for 45 percent of its imports from the CIS. See *Zovnishnia Torhivlia Tovaramy ta Posluhamy u 1995 Rotsi* (Kyiv: Ministry of Statistics, 1996).

27. Vlasiuk and Yampols'ka, *Zovnishna*, 15.

28. Pavlo Rudakov, "Krok Vpered Chy Krok Nazad? Do Pytannia pro Natsional'ni Interesy Ukrainy u Zahal'noevropeis'kyh Integratsyinyx Protsesah," *Polityka i Chas*, November 1996, 53–57.

29. Ibid., 55.

30. By semiofficial I mean the viewpoints of mainstream academics, such as those in the Ukrainian Academy of Sciences, who are published in "official" journals, such as *Polityka i Chas*.

31. For the pro-CIS view, see Anatoliy Kredysov, "Strybok. Ale Kudy?" *Polityka i Chas*, January 1996, 42–46.

32. O. S. Samodurov, "Z Nashym Stratehichnym Partnerom," *Polityka i Chas*, February 1996, 41–42.

33. Valeryi Heyets, *The Day*, Kyiv, Ukraine, 19 February 2001.

34. Oleh Mirus, "Ne Metodom Vyrishenia, A Shliakhom Dosiahnenia," *Polityka i Chas*, May 1995, 43–48.

35. Viktor Andryichuk, "Metodom Sprob i Pomylok: Chy Stane Zovhishnia Torhivlia 'Lokomotyvom' Rozvytku Ukrainy?" *Polityka i Chas*, September 1996, 31–36.

36. Anton Filipenko, "Economic Union of the CIS: Pros and Cons," *Politics and Times*, October–December 1995, 58–65.

37. Ibid., 64.

38. Interview with Serhiy Vorontsov, counselor, Department of the CIS, Ukrainian Ministry of Foreign Affairs, Kyiv, 7 August 1996.

39. "Minister Explains Refusal to Join CIS Customs Union," FBIS-SOV-96-019, 30 January 1996.

40. Documents on various types of cooperation and coordination presented at CIS meetings and in most cases signed by Ukrainian delegations reached the level of minutiae: veterinary cooperation, discounted travel for war veterans, military sports teams, the rescue of soldiers MIA in Afghanistan, a fire at the Kamaz truck factory in Russia, predicting earthquakes, and a "happy birthday" celebration for the Artek children's camp. In addition, CIS delegates must have been cinema buffs, as they signed no less than four documents celebrating 100 years of cinema and cooperation in the field of cinema. See *Informatsoinoi Viestnyk S.N.G.*, vols. 1–4 (Minsk: Commonwealth of Independent States, 1992–1996).

41. A fuller analysis can be found in Victor Chudowsky, "The Ukrainian Party System," in *State and Nation-Building in East Central Europe*, ed. John McGeil (New York: Institute on East Central Europe, 1996), 305–321.

42. Various interviews with Malinkovich and Prohrebins'ky, Kyiv, summer 1996. Malinkovich was Kuchma's speechwriter, Prohrebins'ky a pollster and analyst.

43. Ukrainian Foreign Ministry press briefing, Kyiv, 10 July 1996.

44. Conversation with Boris Andreysuk, Chair, Parliamentary Committee on National Security and Defense, Washington, D.C., 21 September 2000.

3

Constructivist Theory and Ukrainian Foreign Policy

Paul J. D'Anieri

Putting Ukrainian foreign policy into global context is a difficult task, because Ukrainian foreign policy is conditioned by factors that seem to be ignored in the broader study of international relations and foreign policy around the world. The problem centers on national identity. To most observers of Ukrainian politics and foreign policy, the contestation of Ukrainian national identity plays a large role in Ukraine's foreign relations. This is most clear concerning relations with Russia, but extends to all of Ukraine's foreign policy problems. Conventional international relations theory, however, has almost nothing to say about nationalism or national identity as factors in international relations. K. J. Holsti asserts, "No major approach to international relations theory has emphasized the prominence of nationalist behavior as an important characteristic of the contemporary international system."[1] Even the subfield of "foreign policy analysis," which focuses on explaining and comparing various states' foreign policies, provides little insight into the effects of national identity on foreign policy.[2]

Those interested in international relations among the post-Soviet states face a dilemma: They can use conventional international relations theories, speaking the "language" that makes their analyses intelligible to the broader international relations field, but to do so they must leave aside national identity politics, which are crucial in the whole region but do not fit into the schemes provided by mainstream theory.[3] Or they can write about nationalism and national identity, and withstand accusations of being atheoretical and marginalization as an "area studies" researcher.

Fortunately, a new body of theory generally referred to as "constructivism," which is gaining increasing acceptance among international relations scholars, makes it possible to bring questions of national identity into play without withdrawing from the broader discourse of international relations. While not focused on issues of national identity, constructivist theory at least offers an opening and a set of concepts and vocabulary that can be used to analyze Ukrainian (and other post-Soviet) foreign policy in a way that is meaningful to scholars having little direct knowledge or concern about this particular case. There are two reasons why building such a bridge is worthwhile. First, by considering Ukraine within the broader context of international relations theory, we are likely to learn things about Ukraine that we otherwise might not see. Second, by showing how national identity fits into international relations theory and how consideration of it improves that theory, we can improve the theory.

The absence of a role for nationalism in international relations theory is indeed striking. Historically, much has been made of the role of nationalism in international affairs. The role of Napoleon in using nationalism to fuel his conquests has been widely written about. At the time of World War I, nationalism was seen as having a powerful and negative effect on international affairs, and Woodrow Wilson, himself a political scientist and international relations scholar, saw solving the problems of national self-determination as crucial to building a safe world. Nationalism may have played an even larger role in World War II, where the three major aggressors, Germany, Japan, and Italy, all were explicitly motivated by nationalist agendas. If the Cold War seemed to push nationalism off the agenda in Europe, this was certainly not true in the international relations of the rest of the world, as the United States found in Vietnam and the Soviet Union found in Afghanistan.

To explain satisfactorily why something so obviously important has remained untouched by contemporary international relations theory would require a lengthy history of the discipline, but a few key points help clarify what the nature of the task is today for those who would write of nationalism in international politics without abandoning attempts at theoretical relevance.[4] During the Cold War there was a sense that nationalism had become less important. The U.S.–Soviet conflict was about power or ideology or both, depending on whom one read.

The United States and the Soviet Union both professed to be nonnationalist (or "internationalist"). In Western Europe, the end of the Franco–German conflict and the progress of the European Communities seemed to show that nationalism was passé.

That international relations theory did not substantially deal with nationalism cannot be viewed simply as an indictment of the discipline. Postwar international relations theory was trying to cope with the failure of interwar international relations theory (which had focused on nationalism). Theorists such as Hans Morgenthau and E. H. Carr, learning from the interwar experience, asserted that, ultimately, intentions mattered less than power. All the good intentions had not been able to stop Hitler, but Allied power had.[5] Morgenthau went further, writing that because power was the ultimate currency in international politics, it was the ultimate aim in international politics. The resulting realist approach to international politics focused therefore on power relations and played down questions of intentionality and the role of ideas, including ideology and nationalism. This perspective also minimized the importance of ideological conflict in the U.S.–Soviet conflict. This approach fit well with the positivism and behaviorism that came to dominate political science, especially in the United States. Critiques of realism did emerge, but focused on other issues: Liberal critiques focused on realism's emphasis on conflict of interest, while pluralist critiques focused on the notion of the state as a unified rational actor.[6] They did not, however, question the underlying materialist notion of politics, and like realism viewed actors as motivated by material gain, whether defined in military or economic terms. When critiques of the "rational" actor approach in international politics finally emerged, the focus was almost exclusively at the level of individual psychology, not at societywide factors such as national identity.[7]

Just as the erasure of nationalism from international relations theory stemmed from a mix of real-world events and intellectual trends, its return to the agenda is necessitated by recent events in the world and made possible by recent developments in international relations theory. This chapter aims to show how constructivist theory can be used to understand Ukrainian foreign policy. It begins with a brief overview of constructivist theory and its place in international relations theory. The discussion then highlights how this theory is relevant to the forces driving Ukrainian foreign policy problems. The chapter then turns to empirical issues, showing in concrete terms how constructivism can be applied to the issues that define Ukrainian foreign policy. Finally, the conclusion of the chapter will discuss the implications of this analysis for Ukraine and for international relations theory.

WHAT IS CONSTRUCTIVISM?

Social constructivist approaches to international relations challenge the notion that material incentives created by international anarchy and the balance of power determine the behavior of states.[8] Rationalist accounts assume the identities and interests of the actors, and then try to infer behavior. Social construction theory does not assume the identities and interests of the actors. Rather, it sees them as contingent and therefore requiring explanation. From the constructivist perspective, identities and interests are not "given" and need to be explained prior to an examination of behavior. Rather than assuming that a particular social structure is fixed, constructivist theory sees social structures as contingent and potentially changeable.

In one of the most influential articles on constructivism, Alexander Wendt argues that anarchy does not necessarily lead to conflict.[9] In this he is questioning both realist and liberal schools of international relations thought, which in different ways trace their lineage to Hobbes. Realists follow Hobbes most closely, arguing that without a central authority, states' concern for survival will lead them into conflict. Liberals agree with the Hobbesian view of international anarchy, but follow Locke in arguing that the very unpleasantness of the Hobbesian state of nature provides states, just as it provides individuals, the incentive to mitigate anarchy through the formation of some kind of civil society. Realists and liberals disagree fundamentally on the possibility of overcoming anarchy, but they agree that unmitigated anarchy has clearly predictable effects on the actors involved.

The constructivist departure is to question three things about this analysis. First, Wendt questions whether we can in fact infer that anarchy leads inevitably to "self-help" and hence to conflict. He asks why, for example, the United States regards a single North Korean nuclear weapon as more threatening than the entire British nuclear arsenal. The obvious answer is that Britain is a friend and North Korea is an enemy. According to materialist theories, however, there are no friends or enemies, only interests that emanate from material capabilities. Thus, neither realist nor liberal theories can really account for something as obvious and as ubiquitous as the notion that some groups of countries have defined an identity of interest within anarchy, while others have defined their interests in conflictual terms. Constructivist approaches seek to answer these questions by asking about how states define their identities. The U.S.–British "special relationship," for example, has something to do with common history, ancestry, and language that have led to some degree of shared understanding and hence a sense of identity between the two societies and their governments. The questions that constructivist theories ask and the way they answer them become very useful in understanding why Ukraine and Russia, which have much in common, do not get along very well.

Second, in addition to questioning the identities that actors create between them, constructivism opens up to questioning the identities of the actors themselves. Many "substate" international relations analyses have pointed out that various actors besides "states" are important in international affairs, but constructivist approaches make a deeper point. Rather than viewing a state's identity as fixed, constructivist approaches view state identity as contingent in two ways, both of which relate to sovereignty. State sovereignty is contingent first of all in that it is granted by the international "system" to some claimants and not to others. There are no firm rules for state recognition, so that even if in the short term the existence of sovereign states seems fixed, it is in fact contingent. Moreover, what it means to be sovereign is also contingent rather than fixed. The institution of state sovereignty is in flux across both time and space. In both these ways it is not enough to say that a state is a state. Instead, constructivists ask about how states are defined and what qualities statehood carries in different circumstances. For Ukraine and many of its neighbors, these are not theoretical questions, but in fact are very practical.

Third, in the constructivist approach, the structure and its agents mutually constitute one another through continuous interaction. Instead of taking the structure as given and investigating its effects on actors or vice versa, constructivist approaches study how interaction between structures and agents lead to the redefinition of both. Actors are constrained by structure, but they do have choices, and over time the choices they make can redefine the structure or reinforce it. Mutual constitution of actors and the international situation is especially important in considering nationalism. Just as it is possible for nationalism to affect international politics, it is possible for international politics to affect the level and content of nationalism in individual states, altering the context of future interaction. In other words, the "causal arrow" between nationalism and international politics points in both directions. Not only is Ukrainian foreign policy affected by national identity, but what happens in the international arena can influence notions of Ukraine's national identity.[10] Indeed, leaders' anticipation of the domestic effects on national identity may be an important motivation for certain foreign policies.

In a constructivist approach, constraints on state behavior are viewed as constructed historically through practice, not just simply by current material factors of power. Thus, historical interaction also becomes a question. How have national identities developed historically, and with what content has history imbued them? This approach takes us beyond the simple assumption that nationalism leads to war, and provides us with a more nuanced look at its effects on international politics. We also must ask whether current practice is reinforcing or undermining the conceptions that have previously developed. Together, these questions address the main insight of social construction theory, that agents and structure mutually define each other. The legacy of interaction constrains what agents can do, but the behavior of those agents can redefine the structure over time.

Social construction approaches are useful in analyzing Ukraine (and the other Soviet successors) because they allow us to focus on the identity issues that are so salient in politics throughout the region. Indeed, scholars such as Benedict Anderson brought constructivist theory to the study of nationalism long before international relations theorists began using it.[11] So we now have an approach to international politics that is quite at ease with the issues raised by ethnicity and nationalism.

CONSTRUCTIVISM AND
UKRAINIAN FOREIGN POLICY

Constructivism is a useful approach to examining Ukrainian foreign policy because Ukraine faces many of the issues that constructivist approaches focus on. The notion of contingent state identity seems like a purely theoretical concept in connection to the United States or France, but it is a matter of practical politics in Ukraine. Ukraine's existence as an independent state is contingent: Ukraine was not independent prior to 1991; it has been independent since then, but that independence continues to be questioned. Similarly, the meaning of state sovereignty has been contingent in Ukraine in a way that is less obvious in other countries. In July 1990 Ukraine declared "sovereignty" while remaining within the Soviet Union, exhibiting a notion of sovereignty that today seems untenable. Since 1991 many of the issues that most affect Ukraine, including relations with the Commonwealth of Independent States, the status of Ukrainian neutrality, and the status of Sevastopol center on this crucial question: What does it mean to be sovereign? It is unfortunate that these issues, which lie at the center of Ukraine's foreign policy agenda, are seen as unproblematic and ignored by conventional international relations theory.

More broadly, because constructivism asks about the identity of the actors, it addresses precisely the problem that drives much of Ukrainian politics and foreign policy. It might seem silly to ask "What is France?" but debates over "What is Ukraine?" and "What is Russia?" are at the center of politics in this region today. Both Russia and Ukraine are suffering severe identity crises in the post-Soviet era, and these identity problems play an important role in international relations in the region. Constructivist approaches allow us to examine that role.

Ukraine's identity crisis involves answering the question of what it means to be Ukrainian. One view holds that Ukrainians are those who define themselves as such. Another holds that one must speak Ukrainian to be completely Ukrainian. The Ukrainian state has adopted the view that all citizens of Ukraine are Ukrainian. Even if that issue is resolved, the substance of "Ukrainian-ness" remains unclear. Is Ukraine part of the "West," with all the values and allegiances of other Western countries? Is it part of the "East" with a set of values and allegiances centered on Moscow? Can it be both of those things at the same time? Can it be neither? All these are important questions for Ukrainian society and foreign policy.

The problem is magnified by Russia's equally deep identity crisis. Is "Russia" defined by the historical borders of the Russian empire, which included much of Ukraine, or by the borders of the 1991 Soviet Union, which included all of Ukraine, or by the area inhabited by people who define themselves as Russian, which includes a small part of Ukraine, or by the area inhabited by people who speak Russian, which includes a larger part of Ukraine? Is there a notion of Russian national identity and history compatible with the idea that the history of Kievan Rus and of Ukraine is that of a distinct people and a distinct country? Is Russia's status as a "great power" essential to Russian identity, and if so, does that require some degree of suzerainty over Ukraine? While the answers to these questions may never become clear, the asking of the questions and the process of debating them is as important as the answers. Because these key identity issues are contested, they play a central role in Ukrainian domestic politics and foreign policy today.

The key point we derive from a constructivist examination of Ukrainian foreign policy is that many of Ukraine's actions in the international arena are intended not to attain some material benefit, such as an improvement in the distribution of power or in Ukraine's trade position, but to attain some symbolic benefit that helps advance a particular notion of Ukrainian identity. Indeed, in several key cases Ukrainian leaders sacrificed material gains for identity gains (the most important case being the decision to surrender nuclear weapons, which is discussed later). At the same time, events beyond Ukraine's borders have important effects on Ukraine's "domestic" debate over national identity.

This view of politics sees things that cannot be viewed through a realist or liberal lens, but it is not completely divorced from the material issues on which the analysis typically focuses. What happens in Ukraine's symbolic debates will have influence on material issues as well, including which politicians will get to rule Ukraine, how the United States and Russia will manage their rivalry, and what levels of tariffs international businesses pay in their trade with Ukraine. For these reasons, politicians strive to influence identity debates in ways that will serve their interests. Identity politics and foreign policy influence each other both intentionally and unintentionally.

In the discussion that follows, we see two key phenomena in action. Ukraine's domestic identity debates influence and constrain foreign policy choices, and Ukraine's international position influences its domestic identity debates. In some cases these two effects create a mutually reinforcing cycle, while in others they offset each other. In all cases, politicians are deeply involved in trying to shape the formation of Ukrainian identity.

ISSUES

This section presents a series of issues in which the relationship between identity and foreign policy arises for Ukraine. This series of examples serves both to illustrate how constructivist theory can be applied to this case and to provide some evidence for the utility of this approach. Hopefully it will also contribute some insight into Ukrainian foreign policy. It is not meant, however, as a formal "test" of constructivist theory or of any particular hypothesis. Across these issues, we see a common theme: Uncertainty about Ukrainian sovereignty and identity becomes a major subject of foreign policy. In some cases the West seems uncertain about the validity of Ukrainian sovereignty, and Ukrainian policy has to assert that sovereignty before working on other goals. In other cases, Russia's uncertainty about its own identity causes it to question Ukraine's identity as well. In still other cases, Ukraine's own internal ethnic, regional, and linguistic divisions create identity issues that constrain as well as motivate foreign policy.

The Ukrainian–Russian Conflict

It would be an exaggeration to say that the ongoing tension between Ukraine and Russia is only about identity politics. It is about power politics as well, and about economic gain (especially in the area of energy trade). But when we look closely at relations between the two states, we realize that even if power politics provides the means by which relations are conducted, many of the goals in Russian–Ukrainian relations are driven by identity concerns. Moreover, the two countries' domestic identity problems interact with one another in a way that tends to exacerbate relations between the two states.

Both Ukraine and Russia emerged in 1991 in historically new forms. Ukraine had been an independent state only briefly in history, and never in its post-1991 configuration. Russia's 1991 boundaries were equally new. For both countries, border and identity uncertainties went beyond the question of Ukraine and Russia, but for both that question has been central. For Russia, post-1991 identity issues boil down to four questions.[12] First, what is "Russia," if territory and populations considered to be integral parts of Russia now lie in other countries? Second, what are Russia's historical roots, if key events in "Russian" history are appropriated by newly independent states as "their" history? Third, can Russia exist without being a "great power" that dominates the countries around it? Fourth, can Russia be part of the West, and does it even want to be?

The first and second questions lead some to ask whether Russia can be "Russia" in its present territorial formation. The third question raises the question of limiting the sovereignty of the other newly independent post-Soviet states. The fourth also links foreign policy closely to identity questions. Much has been written about these issues, and there is wide acknowledgment that they are identity related. Thus, Russian foreign policy has been characterized as Gaullist, in the sense that it seeks to attain or regain a self-image of global importance that is no longer supported by its material capabilities. Russian analysts agree that Russian foreign policy is an extension of identity politics, as Sergei Stankevich shows when he states, "The practice of our foreign policy . . . will help Russia become Russia."[13]

The result is that Russia's agenda concerning Ukraine is entirely different than it would be if the issues involved were strictly those of economics or security. Economically, Russia has little reason to continue to subsidize oil and gas shipments to Ukraine, but it frequently does so in order to maintain the notion that relations between the two states are not simply relations between any two states. Russia's effort to maintain control of the Black Sea Fleet is pointless in military terms, because the fleet itself is so badly deteriorated that it does not provide for Russian security. But maintaining the fleet on Ukrainian territory achieves an important symbolic goal for Russia: maintaining the notion that Russia still extends to the Crimea, and that Ukraine is not completely distinct and separate. It is precisely for this reason that Ukraine has been so recalcitrant on the issue.

Similarly, Ukraine's identity is uncertain, and many, though not all, of the issues concern Russia. The divisions within Ukraine today, with their historical, linguistic, and ethnic bases, leave the society and its elites struggling to agree on what Ukraine is and what it means to be Ukrainian. The sheer volume of literature on this topic, both in Ukraine and in the West, attests to the problematic nature of Ukrainian national identity. At one end of the spectrum are those who see Ukraine and Ukrainians as subsets of Russia and the Russians. At the opposite end are those who see opposition to everything Russian as the sine qua non of Ukrainian identity. There are also all shades of gray in between these two extremes.

The position adopted by the leaders of Ukraine is that Ukraine is a distinct country from Russia and is Russia's sovereign equal. That view is one with both international and domestic repercussions, which is why the two levels cannot be viewed in isolation. To say that Ukraine is Russia's sovereign equal says something to Ukrainian citizens about who they are, as well as saying something to Russian citizens about who they are. In addition, and perhaps most important, it says something to the international community in general, and to Russian leaders in particular, about how they should view Ukraine and how Ukraine expects to be treated. All these issues are controversial, and they arose in 1991 because, contrary to the notion that sovereignty is a clear-cut category, Ukraine's independence and sovereignty were questioned in Ukraine, in Russia, and in the world community from the very moment they emerged.

That the properties of sovereignty are not fixed was demonstrated by the variety of arrangements contemplated for Ukraine in 1990–1991. Ukraine's 1990 Declaration of Sovereignty implied a status that had many of the trappings of sovereignty (in the sense of autonomy from Moscow), but clearly did not include the notion of sovereign status on the international stage. Following the August 1991 coup, a variety of arrangements were mooted, especially in Russia, which seemed to grant Ukraine both "internal" and "international" sovereignty while still retaining some overarching role for Moscow that would distinguish this arrangement from the classical Westphalian notion of sovereignty. The European Union, which has been leading the process of blurring and redefining traditional notions of sovereignty, was seen as a model for the post-Soviet states. Until Ukraine's December 1991 referendum, international recognition of Ukraine's sovereignty was still in question. Even after Ukraine was established as a sovereign state in the conventional sense, many saw this status as temporary rather than fixed and as incomplete. In all these ways, Ukrainian sovereignty has been a variable to be hotly contested, rather than a fixed quality that must be taken as a given.

Much of Ukraine's foreign policy for the first five years was spent relentlessly asserting its sovereign rights. It may seem ironic that Ukraine was asserting its sovereignty at the same time that the countries of Western Europe were giving ever more sovereignty away to the EU, but because the EU states' sovereignty was unquestioned, they had to guard it less jealously. Ukraine could not even think about surrendering its sovereignty until it had fully acquired it.

Thus, issues that should have been straightforward became intractable, and many of these issues involved Russia. Two examples serve to illustrate. First, following the collapse of the Soviet Union there was uncertainty over how to divide up the international liabilities and assets of the Soviet Union. One solution, which was simple, was that Russia would get both. Ukraine contested this in part because of a belief that the assets (including embassies and bank accounts abroad) exceeded liabilities. Had that been the only issue, some compromise could probably have been reached. But Ukraine has also insisted that to give Russia all the assets and liabilities of the Soviet Union would be to acknowledge some special status for Russia in the region, and would downplay the equality of Ukraine. Thus Ukraine has insisted that assets and liabilities be divided up, which, especially in terms of property, is nearly impossible. The issue has dragged on for nearly a decade, complicating both states' attempts to borrow on international capital markets. But with a series of statements from Russian and world leaders implying that Ukraine was somehow unequal in international legal terms, Ukrainian leaders found it necessary to assert Ukraine's legal equality.

A similar story took place in terms of nuclear weapons. From the realist perspective, it is extremely bizarre for one state to not only surrender its nuclear weapons but to surrender them to the country that most threatens its security. Indeed some of the most prominent realist scholars made the case for Ukraine to keep its nuclear weapons.[14] Only the politics of identity and recognition explain the Ukrainian decisions first to disarm, then to retain the weapons, and then finally to disarm.

The initial decision to pledge disarmament was strongly rooted in two aspects of Ukraine's identity, and was regarded later by many as naïve. First, Ukraine's experience as the main victim of the Chernobyl disaster produced strong antinuclear sentiment in the country. Second, Ukraine envisioned itself as a neutral (on which more later), and therefore as not needing a nuclear arsenal. Thus, when declaring sovereignty in July 1990 and independence in August 1991, Ukrainian leaders emphasized their intentions to become a nonnuclear and neutral state.

However, as Russia and the United States began treating Ukraine as a second-class country, Ukraine again saw the need to assert its equality. The first large step in this direction was the Ukrainian assertion that, if it were to be bound by the START I treaty, it would have to become a party to that treaty. Legally, Ukraine's position made perfect sense. Russia's decision to take on the Soviet obligation under that treaty and others could in no way bind a separate state. The same logic that gave Russia the Soviet U.N. Security Council seat seemed to exclude Ukraine from the "Soviet" legacy in international law. But Ukraine's position angered and frightened American and Russian diplomats, who saw Ukraine as backtracking on her commitment to nuclear disarmament. Their efforts to assert that Ukraine had no right to keep nuclear weapons simply inflamed Ukrainian sensitivities further. Had they instead responded with the clear and unambiguous acknowledgments of Ukrainian sovereignty that Ukraine sought, the issue likely could have been resolved quickly.

Instead, they did the opposite, with the United States in particular using various threats to induce Ukraine to give up the weapons, while Ukraine insisted that it could only give up the weapons when its right to keep them was acknowledged. The issue was partly resolved in May 1992, when Ukraine was added as an additional signatory to the START I treaty, satisfying the United States by gaining Ukraine's acquiescence on disarmament while satisfying Ukraine by acknowledging Ukraine's international status. Russia was less pleased by adding Ukraine as a signatory. The issue was not fully resolved until the Trilateral Agreement of January 1994 between Russia, Ukraine, and the United States. Much emphasis has been given to the financial aid promised to Ukraine to sign that agreement, but the much more significant aspect was that in the agreement Russia committed itself to Ukraine's territorial integrity, a degree of recognition it had previously refused.

The Dynamics of National Identity in Ukrainian–Russian Relations

The discussion so far has emphasized how issues of recognition—purely symbolic—have driven relations between Ukrainian and Russian leaders. The same phenomenon takes place in a more complex way between the two societies. In particular, it is important to understand how groups on the extremes in both Russia and Ukraine have been able to exacerbate the perceived tension between them. The majority of Russians and Ukrainians have no particular hostility toward the other country; it is precisely the close historical, cultural, and often familial connections that make the identity issues so vexing. But debates within the two societies evolve in contact with one another. Ironically, nationalist extremists on the two sides, who presumably are enemies, support each other's causes by providing ammunition for them. In a strange way, these two extremes in two different societies are mutually reinforcing and keep on the defensive those who might have adopted a more moderate position.

It would be much more difficult for Ukrainian nationalists to raise concerns over Russia's intentions if not for a steady stream of Russians making claims about Russian control over Sevastopol or even all of the Crimea. Even while Boris Yeltsin repeatedly said that Ukraine's borders were fixed, Moscow mayor Yuri Luzhkov's support for Russian control of the entire city of Sevastopol allowed Ukrainian nationalists to raise the alarm, and to convince more moderate Ukrainians that they really did have something to fear from Russia. Similarly, support given by Ukrainian nationalists to separatists in Chechnya gave credence to those in Russia who view Ukrainian independence as a blow to Russian statehood.

Choosing between East and West

Even before the declaration of Ukraine's independence in 1991, Ukrainian elites and citizens had debated the proper "vector" for Ukrainian foreign policy. The debates are familiar to anyone who follows Ukrainian affairs, but cannot be comprehended through standard international relations models. Both realist and liberal models, for different reasons, would lead us to expect an unequivocally Western emphasis to Ukrainian foreign policy. Realism would predict an attempt to ally with Western countries against Ukraine's primary security threat, Russia. Liberalism would predict an effort to join pan-European free-trade institutions that are rooted in the West, primarily the European Union. And to some extent we see those emphases, especially in the rhetoric of Kuchma's government.

At the same time, both rhetorically and in fact, Ukrainian leaders have been completely unwilling to let go of Russia, and a substantial minority of Ukrainian elites (based on the left of the political spectrum and generally in East Ukraine), continue to advocate a decidedly pro-Russian emphasis in Ukrainian foreign policy. Exemplified in calls for full Ukrainian membership in the CIS, for joining the Russian–Belarusian Union, and against NATO expansion, this perspective is an integral part of Ukraine's foreign policy debate, not merely an outlying extreme. Ukraine's ambivalence was demonstrated most clearly during the NATO bombing of Yugoslavia in 1999, when opposition to NATO action was high, even in normally pro-NATO western Ukraine.

Why? Because in addition to calculating material costs and benefits of various geopolitical arrangements, Ukrainian society also assesses the "geocultural" impacts of various arrangements. Perhaps the most significant aspect and irony of Ukraine's tortured relationship with Russia is that while on one hand Ukraine's identity depends on establishing a clear distinction from Russia, that identity remains closely tied to Russia. This is certainly true for a large number of Ukrainian citizens who are of Russian descent, are married to someone of Russian descent, or have relatives who live in Russia. Put simply, many Ukrainians do not consider Russia an enemy. And despite creation of a national historiography emphasizing Ukraine's distinct origins, the two societies share a great deal of history, including the crucial experience of having fought together against Germany in World War II. This intertwining of the two countries' histories makes it difficult for some to think of them as completely distinct ethnically, culturally, or historically. Obviously, Ukrainians differ widely on these issues, so it is dangerous to generalize, but the important point is that even as Ukrainians see the need to be distinct from Russia, to completely deny Ukraine's links to Russia would seem to many Ukrainians to be self-abnegating.

To the extent that this is true, Ukraine cannot simply turn its back on Russia, for whatever security or economic reasons, without fundamentally recasting the notion of Ukrainian identity. Clearly some would like to do just that, to build a notion of Ukrainian identity that emphasizes (western) Ukraine's historical links to Warsaw and Vienna and rejects those to Moscow as artificially imposed. These individuals see foreign policy as one way to do that, and they have been the advocates of an exclusively pro-Western and anti-Russian foreign policy. To those for whom Ukraine is essentially an East Slavic country, Europe is somewhat alien and Russia is much more familiar. They advocate, at a minimum, a more balanced, "multivector" foreign policy and, at a maximum, a policy that prioritizes Moscow and accepts that Ukraine is much closer to Russia than to the West.

Therefore, discussions of Ukrainian policy toward the whole range of Western institutions have been extensions of battles over Ukraine's own perception of its identity. Interaction with the European Union, the IMF, and NATO, among others, implies that Ukraine is similar to the leading states of those organizations, a notion that is exhilarating to some Ukrainians and threatening to others. This explains why Ukrainian elites spend such an inordinate amount of time debating whether Ukraine should aim to join the EU and NATO. If it were just a question of the material issues involved, the debate could be ended, or at least postponed, because everyone knows that neither the EU nor NATO is going to admit Ukraine for at least a decade if ever. The debate is carried on, and it matters for Ukrainians, because it is not only the result that matters. Even if Ukraine is never admitted to NATO but establishes NATO membership as a goal, then something fundamentally new has been said about Ukrainian national identity. If Ukraine abandons this goal, it will be an equally important statement on both foreign policy and national identity of the country.

The Western powers have at times recognized this, but only incompletely, and occasionally with bizarre consequences. The United States and the Western European countries seem to understand that for them to act to include Ukraine in their activities helps the pro-Western camp in Ukraine establish their case. Ukraine's identity will not only be established by what Ukrainians think, but by what the international community thinks. This was most clear during the uncertain period following the August 1991 coup d'etat, when it was unclear whether most states would recognize Ukraine's declaration of independence. Even now, however, when the West treats Ukraine as one of the club, conceptions in Ukraine are bound to be affected.

This has led to some care on the part of the Western states in nurturing Ukraine's European self-conception. Most notable in this regard has been NATO's policy. In establishing a NATO–Ukraine Charter in July 1997, NATO was sending out a signal that Ukraine is a "special" partner of the alliance, on an equal basis (at least symbolically) with Russia and not subordinate to Russia. At the same time, the desire to include Ukraine in the "West" (along with obvious geopolitical motives) has led Western governments to look away from, and in some instances even to deny, the increasingly authoritarian nature of Ukraine's government and the near absence of genuine reform. Confronted with clear evidence that Ukrainian authorities are behaving in a decidedly "un-European" way (both in the political and economic spheres), Western institutions, including NATO, the EU, and the Council of Europe, have prevaricated rather than stating clearly that Ukraine cannot be "part of Europe" if its government carries on this way. This policy has two seemingly contradictory results: It reaffirms Western commitment to Ukraine's membership in the "West" while also increasing the Ukrainian government's latitude to pursue corrupt statism in the economic sphere and creeping authoritarianism in the political sphere.

To summarize, Ukraine's national identity is unfixed and deeply contested, and its foreign policy is one of the main arenas in which that contest is being played out. As a result, Ukraine's policies toward the world, as well as the world's policies toward Ukraine, are influenced by, and will have influence on, the Ukrainian government's efforts to forge a coherent national identity. To some extent the process is being driven by calculated decisions by self-interested political and economic actors. To some extent it is being driven by societal forces that are under no one's control. The outcome is certainly beyond the control of any single actor. Indeed, the "neither East nor West" or "both East and West" policies that Ukraine has pursued since 1991 are symptomatic of the division in the society and among political elites, and of the inherently mixed nature of Ukrainian society.

CONSTRUCTIVISM VERSUS REALISM: WHAT IS GAINED?

Since most examinations of Ukrainian foreign policy implicitly or explicitly adopt a realist perspective, it is worth considering the possible challenge: What does this approach tell us that realism does not (and what does it not tell us that realism does)? Most analyses begin with a geopolitical perspective, perhaps due to the West's ongoing worries about Russia. Whether as a "keystone in the arch," as a piece on "the grand chessboard," or as "linchpin," Ukraine occupies a key geographical position in eastern Europe.[15] Most significant, it is believed, Russia cannot expand westward if Ukraine remains strong and independent. This simple observation can explain a lot, including why Russia seeks to establish its suzerainty over Ukraine and why the West hopes to prevent this from happening.

The difficulty in establishing the relative roles of identity and power factors in determining Ukrainian foreign policy lies in part in the fact that in some cases they push policy in the same direction. In other words, the same policy patterns seem to validate both power politics and constructivist approaches. Currently, both internal identity politics and external geopolitics motivate Ukraine toward the same policy: work to establish close ties with Europe, distinguish Ukraine from Russia, but do not make any fundamental break with Russia. In that sense policies over the last ten years have been overdetermined. This is a problem for research design that can only be resolved by the passage of more time and the accumulation of more data on Ukrainian foreign policy.

We can ask, however, what sorts of policies or events might make it easier to sort out the national identity interests from the power-politics influences in Ukrainian politics. The one event so far where the two approaches most clearly predicted opposite outcomes, nuclear weapons, seemed to support the importance of national identity factors. If, for some reason, NATO were to make more substantial overtures to Ukraine, we would see greater tension. Balance-of-power politics would dictate as close an alliance with NATO as possible, to protect against Ukraine's primary threat, Russia. Identity politics, however, dictates a much more balanced policy that would exclude neither the eastern nor western strands of Ukrainian national identity.

There are many things, some general and some specific, that a materialist approach cannot explain. Most fundamental is the question of whether Ukraine will ally with the West against Russia or with Russia against the West. The realist view is that because Russia is a greater threat to Ukraine than the West, Ukraine will seek to ally with the West against Russia. While that may be correct, it presumes that Ukraine sees itself not as part of Russia and not as part of the West, but as an atomistic actor willing to choose sides based solely on geopolitical grounds. We can only assume that Ukraine will ally against Russia once it is already decided that Russia is an enemy, and for identity reasons that conclusion is one that most Ukrainians cannot accept. It is this presumption that the constructivist theory allows us to examine and study. What we see, as a result, is that Ukraine does indeed see Russia as a threat, but that it also cannot simply turn Russia into an adversary, because the implications for Ukraine's national identity debate are unacceptable to powerful forces within Ukraine. In other words, factors highlighted by constructivism both provide the starting point for a realist analysis and highlight constraints on realist behavior by states.

Ukraine's decision to give Russia its nuclear weapons provides the best example on which to argue that constructivism explains something that realism simply cannot. From the constructivist perspective, it makes perfect sense that, once the identity goal was achieved (recognition of Ukraine's territorial integrity) the material issue could be conceded. A realist perspective would see the opposite: There is no such thing as a symbolic gain because such promises as "recognition" can easily be violated by a stronger country, but possession of nuclear weapons deters any genuine violation.

It is more profitable, however, to view the constructivist approach not as a competing theory, but as one that opens up and examines questions that realism, liberalism, and other materialist theories do not. If we imagine a future in which Ukraine's sovereignty is as unquestioned as that of the United States and Ukraine's national identity is not a matter of debate within the country, we can imagine that Ukrainian foreign policy will turn to the sorts of issues—military security and economic gain—on which most theories premise their explanations (though some might deny even this). Certainly, at a time when identity and sovereignty remain contested, theories that allow examination of these phenomena are needed as much as those focusing on power and wealth.

CONCLUSION

For scholars of Ukraine and Ukrainian foreign policy, there is little new in the description of Ukraine's identity crisis and its influence on foreign policy. Even for those whose research focuses on Russia, the connection between national identity and foreign policy seems non-controversial. This analysis becomes problematic only when brought into the discipline of international relations. Then we find that talking about national identity makes Ukraine unique, and makes the analysis appear as a case study of a single unique country with no relevance beyond Ukraine.

The promise of constructivist theory for the study of international politics is that it allows us to analyze countries such as Ukraine not as unique cases with no parallels in the world but as cases that can fruitfully be compared and contrasted with others. Because there is now an increasing body of literature from a constructivist perspective, we can think about how Ukraine's experience fits with broader findings developed looking at other cases. By asking how these findings apply to Ukraine (and how they do not) we are bound to learn more about Ukraine than we can simply by focusing on events in Ukraine. Moreover, such a project can help make Ukrainian foreign policy more relevant to the broader international relations community.

The way in which Ukrainian and Russian identity crises influence relations between the two states, for example, can demonstrate an important point in constructivist theory: Not only do shared meanings and shared identities contribute to cooperation, but unsettled identities or disputes over identities can cause conflict. Similarly, while constructivist theorists have hypothesized about the contingency of sovereignty and identity, Ukraine and many of its neighbors provide concrete empirical cases of those phenomena, and hence are worth investigating for their theoretical as well as their empirical importance.

NOTES

1. K. J. Holsti, "Change in the International System: Interdependence, Integration, and Fragmentation," in *Change in the International System*, ed. Ole R. Holsti, Randolph M. Siverson, and Alexander L. George (Boulder, Colo.: Westview Press, 1980).

2. Laura Neack, Jeanne A. K. Hey, and Patrick J. Haney, eds., *Foreign Policy Analysis: Continuity and Change in Its Second Generation* (Englewood Cliffs, N.J.: Prentice Hall, 1995).

3. As is discussed further later, national identity is also a key issue in Russia's foreign policy as well as that of other states in the region. Its importance in Ukraine, therefore, is symptomatic rather than unique.

4. Martin Hollis and Steve Smith, *Explaining and Understandnng International Relations* (New York: Oxford University Press, 1991).

5. Hans J. Morgenthau, Politics among Nations, 5th ed. (New York: Knopf, 1978); E. H. Carr, *The Thirty Years' Crisis* (New York: Harper and Row, 1964 [reprint of 1939 edition]).

6. The liberal international relations literature is enormous, but two seminar works in this vein are Stephen Krasner, "Structural Causes and Regime Consequences: Regimes as Intervening Variables," *International Organization* 36 (1982): 2; Robert Keohane and Joseph Nye, "Realism and Complex Interdependence," in *Power and Interdependence*, ed. Robert Keohane and Joseph Nye (Boston, 1977). The pluralist literature is equally large, and is most famously represented by Graham Allison, *Essence of Decision: Conceptual Models and the Cuban Missile Crisis* (Boston: Little, Brown, 1970).

7. See Robert Jervis, *Perception and Misperception in International Politics* (Princeton, N.J.: Princeton University Press, 1978).

8. Constructivism is a diverse school of thought, and various constructivists disagree on certain fundamentals. This discussion of constructivism seeks to present a general overview that is compatible with the various strands of

constructivist theory. Prominent examples in a growing literature are Alexander Wendt, "The Structure–Agent Problem in International Politics," *International Organization* 41, no. 3 (1987): 335–370; Martha Finnemore, *National Interests in International Society* (Ithaca, N.Y.: Cornell University Press, 1996); Peter Katzenstein, ed., *The Culture of National Security* (New York: Columbia University Press, 1996); and Alexander Wendt, *Social Theory of International Politics* (New York: Cambridge University Press, 1999).

9. Alexander Wendt, "Anarchy Is What States Make of It: The Social Construction of Power Politics," *International Organization* 46, no. 2 (1992): 391–426.

10. See A. Wilson, *Ukrainian Nationalism in the 1990s: A Minority Faith* (Cambridge: Cambridge University Press, 1997), 202.

11. Benedict Anderson, *Imagined Communities: Reflections on the Origin and Spread of Nationalism* (London: Verso, 1982). See also Eric Hobsbawm and Terence Ranger, eds., *The Invention of Tradition* (Cambridge: Cambridge University Press, 1983).

12. For a good overview of identity issues in Russian foreign policy, see Leon Aron and Kenneth Jensen, eds., *The Emergence of Russian Foreign Policy* (Washington, D.C.: U.S. Institute of Peace, 1994).

13. Quoted in James Richter, "Russian Foreign Policy and the Politics of National Identity," in *New Perspectives on Russian Foreign Policy*, ed. Celeste Wallander (Boulder, Colo.: Westview, 1996).

14. Kenneth Waltz, "The Emerging Structure of International Politics," *International Security* 18, no. 2 (1993): 44–79; John Mearsheimer, "Back to the Future: Instability in Europe after the Cold War," in *Perils of Anarchy: Contemporary Realism and International Security*, ed Michael E. Brown, Sean M. Lynn-Jones, and Steven Miller (Cambridge: MIT Press, 1995), 78–130.

15. Sherman W. Garnett, *Keystone in the Arch: Ukraine in the Emerging Security Environment of Central and Eastern Europe* (Washington, D.C.: Carnegie Endowment, 1997); John Edwin Mroz and Oleksander Pavliuk, "Ukraine: Europe's Linchpin," *Foreign Affairs* 75, no. 3 (1996); Zbigniew Brzezinski, *The Grand Chessboard: American Primacy and Its Geostrategic Imperatives* (New York: Basic Books, 1997).

4

Ukraine's Foreign Policy on Europe's Periphery: Globalization, Transnationalism, and the Frontier

Jennifer D. P. Moroney

In September 1999 at a Summit of Black Sea states in Yalta, Ukrainian President Leonid Kuchma expressed his concern regarding the enlargement of Western institutions, particularly the European Union, to Central and Eastern Europe. Kuchma specifically asked European nations not to construct a new "Paper Curtain" of travel restrictions across the continent in place of the Cold War "Iron Curtain," as this new barrier would certainly distance wealthy European nations from the less developed ones after decades of Cold War. Kuchma stated, "We [Ukrainians] are convinced that visa and other restrictions should not become an insurmountable obstacle for free movement of law-abiding citizens of states aspiring for European integration. . . . There is a real threat that the Iron Curtain may be replaced by a much more humane but no less dangerous . . . Paper Curtain."[1]

Kuchma also asked EU states to reconsider their stance on the issue of visa restrictions for travel between Ukraine and future EU member states, particularly Poland. According to Ukrainian leader, the possible expansion of the EU visa requirements means not only barriers in personal contacts, but also in political, economic, and humanitarian links that exist in the region.

Kuchma furthermore stated that Ukraine is less concerned about NATO enlargement than it is about the EU's expansion, because "the EU works exclusively for its own benefit."[2] With these concerns in mind, since at least 1995–1996 there has been a shift in Ukrainian foreign policy toward seeking closer ties to the EU. Ukraine views relations with the EU as one of its foreign policy priorities and its goal is to approach the EU in political and institutional terms and to move toward acquiring associate membership status and, in the future, full membership. Former Ukrainian Foreign Minister Borys Tarasyuk has referred to accession to the EU as Ukraine's "strategic goal."[3] This is logical considering that Ukraine's aspiration for EU membership is not provocative to Moscow, particularly in comparison with Ukraine–NATO relations.[4] Therefore, there exists no external barrier, at least from the East, to Ukraine's eventual full membership in the EU.

However, there are plenty of other barriers to the development of EU–Ukraine relations. This chapter will investigate the extent to which Ukraine has been successful in developing its relations with the West's key institutions and in the region. I argue that President Kuchma's fears regarding the creation of a new "paper" frontier between Ukraine and the EU are justified because of several factors, including the closed-system structure and protective nature of the EU, the rather amorphous and ambivalent response of EU officials to Ukraine, and the fact that Ukraine itself has not taken the appropriate course to the EU with regard to domestic reforms.

From a theoretical perspective this chapter focuses on the issue of the emergence of new frontiers in Europe. Some key questions I contemplate are what effects the frontier has on policy in the case of an entity in which the nation-state is still being built. On what levels and issues do Western institutions, particularly the EU and NATO, seek to engage the Ukrainian government, and why is this important? Do the United States and the EU hold similar views of Ukraine's important place in European security? The main argument concerning the frontier is that whereas the processes of globalization, transnationalism, and interdependence have tended to reduce the significance of national and other barriers throughout the world, the opposite appears to be occurring in Europe. In this respect, Ukraine's relations with NATO and the EU are discussed in the context of a reemerging political, military, economic, and cultural frontier between the post-Soviet states and the West. It will be argued that Ukraine's ties to NATO and key Western states such as the United States are more developed on many levels in comparison to the EU, which indicates that for Ukraine the EU is the more profound frontier of European security and prosperity. The EU tends to focus on question of identity, which has the effect of reinforcing the frontier. It is argued that this approach has the potential to lead to the further alienation of Ukraine from its European neighbors.

This chapter considers Ukraine's relations with key Western institutions, first from a theoretical perspective and second from a detailed analysis of the empirical evidence that supports the argument that a new East–West frontier in Europe is emerging. This approach is unique in the sense that previous studies of European security and Ukraine have tended to focus specifically on the empirical concepts, thus tending to overlook the psychological and social dynamics created by the existence of a new division or frontier in Europe.

THE THEORETICAL SIGNIFICANCE OF FRONTIERS

According to some scholars, we are living in a world where state borders are increasingly obsolete. This view holds that international borders are becoming so permeable that they no longer fulfill their historic role as barriers to the movement of persons, goods, and ideas. This withering away of the strength and importance of international borders and frontiers is linked to the predicated demise of the nation-state as the primary unit of authority in international relations. Further, the supposed passing of the nation-state is linked to the weakening of political, social, and cultural structures and institutions on the nation-state level. As a result, the role of individuals in these structures is called into question, particularly in terms of their identities and loyalties. Working alongside the reduction of influence of traditional power apparatuses is the rise of the new politics of identity (in contrast to the old politics of the bounded nation-state), in which the definition of citizenship, traditionally referring to nation-state identities, now incorporates a new political significance—gender, ethnicity, race, and occupation, among other characteristics—which struggle for control of the scholarly political imaginations of the contemporary world. These processes are thought to be intensifying, shifting the ground under which nation-states once stood, changing the framework of national and international politics, and creating new categories of transnationalism, while increasing the significance of images about the relevance of "other" world cultures in our everyday lives.[5]

Globalization seems to imply that all frontiers will eventually be effaced. However, this chapter postulates that the processes of globalization, transnationalism, and the shrinking of borders and frontiers are only one way of looking at international politics in the postmodern world. A political emphasis on self, gender, ethnicity, profession, class, and nation underestimates the role that the state continues to play in the everyday lives of its citizens and the citizens of other states. Postmodern analyses often fail to query the degree to which the state maintains its historically dominant role as an arbiter of control, violence, order, and organization for those whose identities are being transformed by world forces.[6] Such analyses are also shortsighted with regard to accounting for the sustained impact that borders, boundaries, and frontiers have on policy.

Political scientists have seldom analyzed the general role of frontiers in contemporary international relations. Malcolm Anderson explains that this is partly because boundary effects on the behavior and values of the populations enclosed by them are difficult to assess, let alone measure.[7] Attempts to measure them seem shallow and usually produce obvious results that derive directly from the assumptions upon which they are based. Perhaps more important, there are differences of viewpoints about frontiers in the historical and political science literature. Some historians and political scientists tend to regard the characteristics and functions of frontiers as dependent on the internal organization of societies and the way in which political power is exercised in the core regions of the state. Debates between realist, pluralist, interdependence, and Marxist theorists arise out of differing views regarding the nature of states. Frontiers are thus thought of as entities whose role and function is dependent on the characteristics of the state. However, for others, including political geographers, the characteristics of the frontier are important in assessing the way a society develops and on the political options available to it.[8]

I tend to agree with the viewpoint of the political geographers and thus suggest that border issues are back on the political agenda of Europe. Many internal borders have been upgraded or in some cases downgraded into external political frontiers, while other state borders in Europe have diminished in political, military, and/or economic significance as a selected few countries have been invited to join key Western institutions. For those left outside of the enlargement process, geopolitical instability has been connected to people's perceptions of security and identity and, in this regard, political borders and frontiers in Central and Eastern Europe are still problematic and warrant further study and analysis. As House notes, "There is an urgent need both for empirical and comparative studies of a dynamic nature for frontier situations, whether those involve confrontational or cooperative relationships, and for a more coherent set of theoretical frames within which to study such situations."[9]

The old concept of frontier has returned at a time when NATO enlargement and EU expansion are seen as the necessary next steps in the geopolitical reorganization of the continent, placing the fate of those countries that have not been invited to join the "clubs" in jeopardy. From the Baltic to the Black Sea, a kind of *Mitteleuropa*, or an in-between Europe, is reviving, whose fate will be decided outside the region in Brussels, Washington, Moscow, Berlin, and perhaps London and Paris.

BRZEZINSKI VERSUS HUNTINGTON: TWO SCHOOLS OF THOUGHT ON UKRAINE

Zbigniew Brzezinski and Samuel Huntington, two prominent analysts of international relations and European security, have advanced rather different schools of thought regarding Ukraine's role and place in Europe. It is interesting to compare and contrast these views and the rationale that prompted each to arrive at their respective conclusions. Brzezinski is a great supporter of the West's strategic engagement with Ukraine as an independent state. He has argued that "it cannot be stressed strongly enough that without Ukraine, Russia ceases to be an empire, but with Ukraine suborned and then subordinated, Russia automatically becomes an empire."[10] This mode of thinking falls in line with that of Sherman Garnett's "keystone in the arch" thesis.[11] Moreover, Brzezinski argues that the stability along NATO's new front line, which now lies on Poland's eastern border, depends largely on the consolidation of Ukraine's nation and statehood, success in economic reforms, and its ability to balance closer cooperation with NATO and the EU and economic and political relations with Russia.

A different line of thinking on Ukraine has since been advanced by Samuel Huntington. Speaking in Kyiv on October 18, 1999, Huntington stressed that global politics is being configured along cultural and civilizational lines and, thus, for the first time in history, global politics is truly multicivilizational.[12] The relationship between "the West and the rest" will be the most important factor in global security because the West will continue to impose its values on other structures. Indeed, Huntington argues that the "clash of civilizations" is alive and well, and the global power structure resembles a "uni-multipolar system" having four levels, with (1) the United States as the only superpower, (2) Russia and China as major regional powers, (3) the United Kingdom and France as secondary regional powers, and (4) secondary regional states such as Ukraine, Japan, Australia, Egypt, Saudi Arabia, Argentina, Pakistan, and India. This uni-multipolar system has encouraged conflicts between Europe and the United States, as exemplified by Europe's increasing resentment of its dependence on the United States, in the introduction of the euro as a rival to the dollar, and by the EU's acquisition of a military capability (which is becoming increasingly likely).

The implications for Ukraine are even more daunting. According to Huntington, the Iron Curtain has been replaced by a new line, which is Western Christianity versus Muslim and Orthodox traditions. He points to Kosovo as a classic example of the clash of civilizations, and argues that a new security order based on civilizations is taking place in Europe, where Russia will assume responsibility for stability among the Orthodox countries, and states that are "culturally part of the West" will eventually be integrated into European and trans-Atlantic institutions. Thus, Huntington does not include Ukraine in the latter category, and labels Ukraine as non-Western, culturally divided, and situated on the "break" between the Christian and Orthodox worlds. Ukraine cannot join NATO or the EU because it straddles the "great power divide" of civilizations, being therefore unable to play that central role in the stability and security of Central Eurasia that is so often ascribed to it.

After more than two generations of ideologically driven East–West conflict, it is not surprising that Western elites have often embraced images of an ethnically and culturally divided Ukraine, speculating that this situation would eventually lead to a spill-over of instability in the region. Although such simplistic images of Ukraine have diminished since 1994, Western states and institutions, particularly the EU, continue to view Ukraine as non-European, tied by culture and identity to Eurasia, and perhaps closest to the Slavs in the east than to Europe. Such an approach is problematic at a time when Ukraine's government is working to implement economic and administrative reforms with the goal of aligning itself closer to Europe and its institutions.

Overall, the United States and NATO seem to back the Brzezinski argument, while the EU backs the Huntington one. The United States and NATO, more so than the EU, recognize the importance of viewing Ukraine separate from Russia and strategically central to European security. As such, they have encouraged Ukrainian elites to continue to strengthen the pro-West vector of the state's foreign policy.

DEFINING AND REDEFINING THE FRONTIER

This section examines the extent to which a new frontier is being created along geopolitical and geoeconomic lines in Central and Eastern Europe between those states that have been included as members or prospective members in European and trans-Atlantic institutions and those that have not. During the Cold War, the East–West frontier was clearly defined as NATO countries on the one side and Warsaw Pact countries on the other. At the dawn of the new millennium, the new features and defining characteristics of "Europe" and "European security" are in the process of transition. The countries of Central and Eastern Europe desire to be members of the "civilized" and democratic world, which includes specifically Western economic, political, and security institutions. However, it is clear that not all of Eastern

Europe will be invited to join until long term. This is due to difficult economic circumstances, to military forces that are not up to Western standards, and also to the external political environment, particularly with regard to the heightening of tensions between the United States and Russia.

The historical definition of the term "frontier" had strong military connotations, or more specifically, a frontier was the zone in which two forces stood opposed. In more contemporary usage, the term has referred to the precise line where (political) jurisdictions meet, usually demarcated and controlled by customs, police, and military personnel. A frontier can also signify a region, as in the description of Alsace as the frontier region between Germany and France. For this analysis I am inclined to view the contemporary frontier as a region (not simply a specific line of demarcation), where jurisdictions, civilizations, and spheres of influence converge, and where domestic and international issues intertwine and thus become more or less indistinguishable.

John Prescott explains that subsidiary organizations can be created within political frontiers.[13] These organizations include marches or border territories organized on a semipermanent military system to defend a frontier, buffer states, and spheres of interest and influence. Buffer states have been constructed in frontiers when two strong neighbors have desired to reduce the likelihood of conflict between them. An example could be Britain's strategy in the Indian subcontinent, which involved the maintenance of a system of small, weak states between British India and Russia, France, and China. Some European colonial powers have employed neutral zones to serve the same function as buffer states. For example, in 1887 Britain and Germany separated their interests in Togoland and the Gold Coast by a neutral zone that was located north of the convergence of the Dakka and Volta rivers. More recently, Central and Eastern Europe served as a buffer zone between the West and the USSR during the Cold War. The concepts of spheres of interest and spheres of influence were developed during the nineteenth century when European powers were establishing actual and potential claims to parts of Asia and Africa. In more recent times this terminology was used by the United States and the USSR when referring to interests in Western and Eastern Europe, and by the United States in reference to its interests in South America. Both concepts are a means of excluding a portion of territory from the political intervention of another state. A sphere of interest is seen as a less significant claim than a sphere of influence; the former becomes the latter when there is a threat of rivalry from another state.

Benedict Anderson argues that all political authorities and jurisdictions have physical limits, which is a characteristic so obvious that it hardly warrants further comment. But where the limits are located and the purposes they serve influences the lives of all the people separated by frontiers. Frontiers may take the form of a terrestrial borderline delimiting one state, like a landed estate, separating it from the territory that does not belong to that state. Such a border can have different appearances and features. It may have the character of an insurmountable obstacle to everyone who wishes to enter or leave the state, which could take the form of a geographical feature such as a desert, body of water, or high mountains. It can also be created by artificial means, such as walls, barbed-wire fences, watchtowers, land mines, or shooting devices and manpower, as was the case before 1990 of landlocked Czechoslovakia in relation to Western Europe.[14] At the other extreme, once visible frontiers can fade into abstract lines that do not stand out in terms of landscape or culture, as in the borders between France, Belgium, The Netherlands, Germany, and Luxembourg.

Contemporary frontiers can be analyzed and in normative political theory criticized in the same way as other political institutions and processes. Because frontiers are no longer clear-cut lines where one jurisdiction or political authority ends and another begins, they are subject to interpretation and contestation; because frontiers establish limits to authority and define both its agents and its subjects, they are central to understanding political life. Examining the justifications of frontiers often raises crucial, even dramatic questions concerning citizenship, national identity, political loyalty, exclusion, inclusion, and the ends of the state.[15]

Frontiers between states are both institutions and processes. As institutions they are established by political decisions and regulated by legal texts. The frontier is thus a basic political institution, as no rule-bound political, economic, or social life in complex societies could be organized without them. The 1978 Vienna Convention on State Succession embodies this earlier characteristic of frontiers in public international law. When a state collapses, the agreements concerning its frontiers remain in force. Frontiers are thus regarded as prior to the reconstitution of a state and are recognized to be a prerequisite for that reconstitution. Frontiers also define, in a legal sense, the identity of individuals, as the conditions for claim to nationality and exercise of rights of citizenship are delimited by it.[16]

But the same questions that philosophers have asked about all institutions may be asked about frontiers: Are they needed? What purposes do they serve? How can they be justified? The answers will vary according to historical circumstances, as different kinds of frontiers existed before the modern nation-state.

Frontiers are part of political processes with four defining dimensions.[17] First, frontiers are instruments of state policy because governments attempt to change, to their own advantage, the location and the function of frontiers. Although there is no simple relationship between frontiers and inequalities of wealth and power, government policy on frontiers is intended to both protect and promote the interests of populations or groups protected by the frontier. Second, the policies and practices of governments are constrained by the degree of de facto control that they have over the state frontier. The inability of governments in the modern world to control much of the traffic of persons, goods, and information across their frontiers is changing the nature of states, and by extension, of the frontiers themselves.

The third dimension of frontiers depicts them as markers of identity, usually national identity, although political identities may be larger or smaller then the nation-state. Thus, frontiers in this sense are part of political beliefs and myths about the unity of the people and myths about the natural unity of the territory. These "imagined communities," to use Anderson's terminology, are now a universal phenomenon and have deep historic and cultural roots, and are linked to what he sees as the most powerful form of ideological bonding in the modern world, nationalism.[18] Myths of such unity can be created or transformed rapidly during wars, revolutions, or political upheavals.

Fourth, the frontier is a term of discourse. Meaning is given to both frontiers in general and to particular frontiers, and these meanings change over time. "Frontier" is a term used in law, diplomacy, and politics and its meaning varies according to context. In scholarly works in the fields of anthropology, economics, political science, history, geography, law, and sociology, its meaning changes according to the theoretical approach used.[19] For people who live in a frontier region or those whose daily lives are affected by the rules that govern the frontier, the dominant images of the frontier may be that of a barrier or junction.[20] On the other hand, Western Europeans, for example, might look upon the same emerging frontier in Central and Eastern Europe as a safeguard from political, economic, and social instability.

Moreover, frontiers have a psychological component. As some psychologists argue, each individual has a concept of bounded personal space, and intrusion into that space without invitation or consent will provoke an emotional response of anxiety or even hostility. Governments show sensitivity to unregulated intrusions across frontiers and to threats, real or imagined, across state borders.[21] The more closed the frontier, the stronger has been its impact as a practical and symbolic threshold, and the stronger rulers' belief that strict control of the frontier was essential to the maintenance of their power and influence. Examples include the Cold War Iron Curtain, the imposed frontier between Israel and its Arab neighbors, the partition line separating Greek and Turkish Cyprus, and the partition between North and South Korea.

With regard to the justification of frontiers, the question that has yet to be addressed is what human purposes frontiers serve. Evaluations of frontiers vary, ranging from viewing them as essential and precious protection, to accepting them as a fact of life, to considering them as a tiresome and arbitrary constraint, to outright hostility toward their existence. Liberal pacifists have condemned frontiers as instruments for turning into enemies those who would prefer to live in harmony and for helping to maintain historic hostilities when the causes for them have disappeared. Another view in the Western liberal tradition is that clearly defined frontiers are essential for ordered constitutional politics, the preservation of citizenship rights, and the maintenance of community. Liberals and Marxists may agree that boundaries are made and manipulated in order to ensure a certain power distribution, but Marxists, holding to the primacy of class struggle over any other form of conflict, contend that frontiers are transitory instruments for upholding particular forms of class domination. Without frontiers, most liberals and conservatives would agree that politics would be inconceivable and that international relations in its current sense would disappear.[22] The "concept of the political," according to Schmitt's argument, is unintelligible without the notion of "friend and foe" and thus of the boundaries between them.[23]

The Western liberal view has dominated constitutional thinking in nearly all of the highly industrialized states of the world and has also permeated international organizations and international law. Liberalism is a universal doctrine, which attributes equal rights and justice to all human beings. But vagueness and ambiguity characterize the liberal position on frontiers. Liberalism simply assumes the existence of the territorial state, standing above civil society and assuming the responsibility for regulating it. In the absence of a world government, the territorial state protects liberal values from internal and external enemies. Liberal universalism is antipluralist in a sense that liberals argue that individuals should not be bounded by parochial group values and will be better off if integrated into a uniform liberal order. Naturally, the existence of strong group identities and loyalties conflicts with the liberal individualist viewpoint.[24]

FRONTIERLAND VERSUS BORDERLAND

It is important to make the distinction between the terms "frontier" and "border" in order to be clear as to what sort of entity is being analyzed here. The term "border" has a double meaning. On the one hand, borders may be seen as ends or barriers, on the other as passages, filters, or gateways between systems contiguous to each other. The term can be applied to a zone, usually a narrow one, or it can be a line of demarcation. In addition, "boundary" is normally used to refer to the line of delimitation or demarcation and is, therefore, the narrowest of the three terms. "Borderland" refers to the transition zone within which the boundary lies.[25] English is not unusual for having more than one term; French has four—*frontiere, front* (exclusively military), *limite,* and *marche* (as in English)—with only *frontiere* normally denoting an international frontier. Spanish has three—*frontera, marca,* and *limite*—and German, alone among the major European languages, has only one term in common usage, *Grenze.*[26] Throughout this chapter, "frontier" is the term used to refer to international boundaries in a wider regional sense, although it is common for Western authors to use the terms "frontier," "border," and "boundary" interchangeably.

Some fundamental questions should be asked at this stage. First, when is a border not a frontier and when is a frontier not a border? Simply put, a border is not a frontier if there is a clear and definite line of political, economic, or cultural division between states, nations, organizations, and cultures. A frontier is not a border when, for instance, organizations or cultures overlap and there is no clear line of division. Thus, the term "frontier" is a much more comprehensive one than is border, and as such is more difficult to pinpoint and analyze. Another important question to ask is if states rigidly apply their laws at the boundary or border, or if states combine or moderate policies to minimize the adverse effects of the border region or frontier on the inhabitants? Ukraine has attempted to deal with the frontier situation in two ways: first, by advocating a multivector foreign policy that is pragmatically pro-West by simultaneously concentrating on improving relations with the West and Russia, and second, by seeking to expand and diversify its ties with regional and subregional organizations that are not dominated by Russia (BSECO, GUUAM, and CEFTA, for example).[27] Finally, how does the presence of a frontier influence the development of policies of adjacent states and institutions? Using inductive reasoning, this question will be dealt with here using Ukraine as a case study. I will focus specifically on the development of Ukraine's relations with the EU and NATO in the following sections and will argue that even in the aftermath of Kosovo, which no doubt was an important test for Ukraine's pro-West foreign policy, the state's relations with NATO are far more advanced than with the EU. This situation is attributable to three factors: first, to the closed-system structure and protective nature of the EU; second, to the ambivalent response of EU officials to Ukraine, and third, to Ukraine's failure to develop a clear plan of integration into Europe beyond general ideas that have not had the affect of bringing about economic and institutional reforms. With regard to Ukraine, NATO is more concerned with geopolitics, and the EU with geoeconomics.

UKRAINE, WESTERN INSTITUTIONS, AND THE FRONTIER

As discussed at the beginning of this chapter, the conceptualization of the term "frontier" has undergone significant changes in recent years. This chapter argues that a frontier should no longer be thought of simply in terms of a security zone held in place by two opposing forces. Contemporary analyses tend to view frontiers as regions where civilizations, jurisdictions, and spheres of influence converge. Contemporary frontiers also take account of economic and social issues. Moreover, this chapter highlights the psychological effects of the frontier, as demonstrated by the confidence in international and regional relations exhibited among those states that have been invited or are frontrunners to join NATO and the EU and those that are not.

NATO more so than the EU has been a source of confidence building for Ukraine. NATO engages Ukraine on a military level through the numerous Partnership for Peace exercises and other events and bilaterally through "in the spirit of" PfP exercises on the military front. Bilateral summits are also held at the heads of state and foreign and defense minister levels through the NATO–Ukraine Joint Commission (NUC). The NUC aims to discuss and offer practical support for Ukrainian programs in the technical and scientific spheres, as well as other programs covered under the Charter on a Distinctive Partnership between NATO and Ukraine. These activities are discussed in detail in the following section. The goal is to demonstrate that NATO is attempting to reduce the negative effects brought by the emergence of a new East–West frontier, whereas the EU, by way of its deeply integrated and closed structure and its hesitant attitude toward Ukraine, tends to reinforce the existing frontier dynamics.

Ukraine and the European Union: A Problematic Relationship

It is appropriate at the outset of this section to discuss briefly the overall structure of the EU to provide a general basis for understanding this deeply integrated regional organization, and also to differentiate it from NATO, which is largely a military and defense-oriented organization.

Founded in 1957 by the Treaty of Rome, the European Economic Community (EEC) (later called the European Community [EC], and in 1993 changing its name under a new three-pillar structure to the European Union), was based on the principles of free movement of persons, services, goods, and capital. Over the years, the EU has become considerably more integrated, causing the now fifteen member states to relinquish part of their sovereignty in various sectors to the central authorities and institutions: the European Commission (the executive), the Council of Ministers and the European Parliament (the legislature), the European Court of Justice (judicial), and the Court of Auditors.

Economically, the European Union has developed from a customs union, to a common market, and now to full economic and monetary union (EMU), including a common currency, with most of the fifteen member states meeting the qualifications for joining the EMU (with the United Kingdom, Denmark, and Sweden choosing to abstain for the time being, and Greece not meeting the criteria). EC law supercedes national law and member states have had to harmonize their national legislation to comply with EC laws.[28] In foreign policy the EU operates under the Common Foreign and Security Policy (CFSP), and although member states still retain a measure of control over their foreign policies, EU member states have attempted to speak with one voice with regard to relations with third countries and international organizations. In addition, the EU has been developing its own defense identity (EDI), including defensive and military capabilities independent of the United States. The EU has, furthermore, developed an extensive social policy, dealing with issues such as working conditions, equality, public health, safety, and security. Thus, the EU today is a deeply integrated regional organization along economic, legal, political, and social lines.

With regard to free movement, the EU has established an internal common policy on visa requirements for foreign nationals traveling within the EU's territory. This policy, the Schengen Agreement, has potentially serious implications for Ukraine and other former Soviet Union (FSU) states, which presently enjoy visa-free travel to neighboring countries such as Poland and Hungary, both of which have been named front-runners for EU membership. Indeed, the Czech Republic has introduced visa requirements for Ukraine, and in February 2000 Slovakia, having entered into integration talks with the EU, expressed willingness to follow suit.[29] But according to EU officials, Schengen must be upheld when Ukraine's neighbors join the EU so as to protect and preserve the EU's policy regarding internal movement of third-country nationals.[30]

The Partnership and Cooperation Agreement

EU–Ukraine relations have a legal basis in the Partnership and Cooperation Agreement (PCA) signed in June 1994. This was the first PCA to be signed with a country of the former USSR, although now there are agreements with ten other former Soviet countries.[31] The PCA with Ukraine experienced a lengthy ratification procedure and did not enter into force until March 1998.[32] The PCA was intended to establish a strong political relationship that would constitute a new link in the developing network of Ukraine's connection with the EU and with the West in general. The activities under the PCA offer an opportunity for Ukraine and the EU to begin to harmonize their political and economic agendas. On the political side, the PCA provides for regular dialogue at various levels, up to and including the presidential level. On the economic side, the PCA marks an important step in helping to bring Ukraine in line with the legal framework of the single European market and the World Trade Organization (WTO). The PCA's provisions govern goods, services, labor, and capital, and introduce legally binding requirements that carry considerable implications for the domestic legislation of Ukraine and the other partner countries.

The PCAs concluded between the EU and its partners were intended to facilitate the development of a free-trade area between them. The EU has concluded further Association Agreements, also called the Europe Agreements, with countries in Central and Eastern Europe that have applied for membership. In their preambles these agreements recognize the fact that the ultimate objective of each of these countries is to become a full member of the EU, and that the Association Agreements will help them to achieve this objective. Much of the text of the Europe Agreements is synonymous with the PCAs, and it is with respect to trade matters that they differ, as the former are preferential agreements geared toward the establishment of free-trade areas for goods and services.[33]

The PCA can be seen as a kind of road map for assisting in the introduction of economic policies and trade-related policies in the fields of goods, services, labor, current payments, and capital movement, while moving in the direction of a market-based economy. Although the document is in many ways evolutionary, it is clear that the implementation of the PCA is a prior condition for the development of further trade relations between the parties. The PCA is a demanding legal instrument that is far-reaching into the realm of domestic policies and regulations, which for Ukraine represents a challenge in terms of adapting its legislative framework to conform to EU standards.

Other Programs of Assistance

In addition to the PCA, the EU and its member states have provided direct financial assistance to Ukraine (ECU [European Currency Unit, later called euro] 3.9 billion between 1991 and 1998), half of which was committed by the EU and half on a bilateral basis. The TACIS technical assistance program provides grants to finance know-how to help Ukraine in its transition to a market economy. Priority areas include institutional reform and development, support for economic reforms and private-sector development, and energy reforms. Moreover, the EU has committed long-term loans to Ukraine of up to ECU 285 million and also contributes substantially (30%) to the IMF and World Bank loans to Ukraine. Finally, the EU maintains that nuclear safety is a priority, particularly the closure of the Chernobyl nuclear plant, which occurred in December 2000.

Ukraine's European-Oriented Foreign Policy

Ukraine's Ministry of Foreign Affairs declared in April 1998 that an immediate foreign policy goal was to gain associate member status of the EU. In June 1998 the National Strategy for Ukraine's Integration into the EU was adopted, which fixed full membership in the EU as Ukraine's long-term strategic goal. At the same time, the EU–Ukraine Cooperation Council (which was established under the PCA) met for the first time in Brussels and adopted the Joint PCA Work Program, consisting of seventeen priorities for cooperation. The EU reaffirmed at the Vienna conference later that month that it attaches "fundamental importance" to its partnership links with Ukraine and thus decided to develop the EU Common Strategy on Ukraine (see later). The Ministry of Foreign Affairs had hoped that this document would be perhaps similar to the NATO–Ukraine Charter, providing a long-term perspective on closer relations between the EU and Ukraine, including the possibility of future membership. In the meantime, though, the Ministry of Foreign Affairs continues to pursue associate membership for Ukraine. Yet after numerous attempts during 1998 and 1999, Ukraine still was not granted this status, even though most of the rest of the Central and Eastern European states had already become EU associate members.

Despite some progress in the political sphere, on the whole relations between the EU and Ukraine have advanced rather slowly, particularly when compared to Ukrainian relations with NATO, and are faced with a number of practical problems as well as other serious challenges of a more general nature. First, there are several trade disputes that both curtail further growth bilaterally and lead to mutual accusations of wrongdoing. For example, the EU has accused Ukraine of not meeting WTO entry requirements, specifically of excessive certification procedures, discriminatory excise duties, unexpected increases in tariff rates, and other protectionist measures. Ukraine, in turn, has criticized the EU for imposing restrictions and limited quotas on Ukrainian textiles and applying antidumping measures against Ukrainian chemicals and steel, thus practically closing the EU market to Ukrainian products. Second, EU financial assistance has been far from meeting the country's needs or expectations (compare 823 million Euros of TACIS money to Ukraine with 2,024 million Euros allotted to Poland from 1990 to 1999 under the PHARE program).[34]

The development of Ukraine's relations with the EU is more difficult than with NATO because of several other factors. First, many EU members are still not willing to view Ukraine as an independent entity separate to Russia, and are not willing to develop closer ties with Ukraine than with Russia despite the fact that Russia has not declared EU membership as its official goal while Ukraine has. Indeed, as Taras Kuzio argues, it is not even clear if the EU sees CIS countries such as Ukraine as part of "Europe," because of their history and geographical size.[35] Ukraine, in this case, is the equivalent of Turkey in the eyes of the EU. Consequently, it is difficult for them to see Ukraine as a future member of the EU if Russia is not invited to join. Second, Ukraine's efforts at economic and political reform have not been consistent and thus Ukraine has not been viewed as a potential member of the EU.[36] Third, Ukraine's integration with the EU would require extensive economic, legal, and social obligations, none of which would be necessary with NATO. On the other hand, Ukraine's cooperation and integration with the EU is not controversial either domestically or externally (from Russia's perspective) in comparison with NATO, for obvious military and political reasons. Thus, in many ways it is difficult to see why the Ukrainian executive since independence has not placed nearly as much emphasis on trying to improve the state's standing with the EU as it has with NATO.

Overall, mutual misunderstanding, disappointment, and even frustration on both sides have marked EU–Ukraine relations. Each still has limited knowledge of the other and it is clear that the EU and Ukraine view the future of their relationship quite differently. While Ukraine has declared its intention to become an EU associate member and its ambition to become a full member, the EU has not included Ukraine in either the "fast-track" or "slow-track" group of future members. The perception in Ukraine is that the EU applies double standards to Ukraine, as the economies of some of the slow-track group were not as strong as Ukraine's (such as those in southern Europe, like Albania and Macedonia, for example). This has led to the belief that the door to the EU is closed for Ukraine, whatever its performance might be, and that for the EU, "Europe" ends where the former Soviet Union (with the exception of the Baltic states) begins. In addition, Ukraine's neighbors to the west, some soon to become members of the EU, will have to introduce stricter border regulations and visa requirements for their eastern neighbors. Most problematic in this respect is the effect this will have on Polish–Ukrainian relations, which have become the most promising and dynamic in the region. For the millions of Ukrainians visiting Poland each year, Polish economic achievements are the best indication of the need for continued reform in Ukraine. Imposing new restrictions on travel between Ukraine and Poland will more than likely have a negative psychological effect on Ukrainians and Ukraine's reform-minded, European-oriented political forces, and will effectively reinforce the presence of the East–West frontier.

From PCA to Common Strategy: EU and Ukrainian Initiatives

Some optimism should also be expressed with the EU's Common Strategy on Ukraine, which was adopted in December 1999 at the Helsinki Council of Ministers Summit and modeled on the structure and main thrust of the EU's Common Strategy on Russia (as adopted in June 1999 at the EU Summit in Cologne). The document declared that the EU acknowledges Ukraine's European aspirations and welcomes Ukraine's pro-European choice, but most important, the EU declared that the door for Ukraine was not closed. The Common Strategy's objectives are to

1. support democracy and the economic transition process.
2. ensure security and meet common challenges on the European continent.
3. support strengthened cooperation between the EU and Ukraine within the context of EU expansion.

The document was intended to give a new impetus to the development of EU–Ukraine ties by calling for, among other things, the establishment of regular dialogue between EU institutions and Ukraine and between Ukraine and the Troika, the setting up of a European news network on Ukrainian television (Euronews), training courses in criminality and environmental issues, and the possibility of free trade in the future once Ukraine has implemented all PCA requirements. However, this Common Strategy was viewed by Ukrainian officials as somewhat disappointing, as no provision was made for the state's eventual full membership in the EU. The EU maintains that it is not in a position to endorse Ukraine's objective of EU membership as its own because neither Ukraine nor the EU itself is ready for such a step.

Economic problems have contributed greatly to the EU's growing sense of ambivalence with Ukraine. In 1998 and 1999 the EU was increasingly disappointed with the slow pace of reforms, the inconsistency of Ukraine's economic policy, and the state's inability to comply with the PCA requirements. Although the EU continues to recognize the political importance of working with Ukraine to ensure its transition to democracy and a market economy, the EU's policy actions do not reflect this recognition, which has led to a contradiction between political declarations and the development of an official, positive Ukraine policy. While the Ukrainian government continues to look to the EU for positive signals, the EU claims it is not prepared to send such a signal at this time due to Ukraine's failure to effectively implement the PCA provisions effectively. Moreover, most EU officials, consciously or subconsciously, continue to link Ukraine with Russia. It had become evident by the late 1990s that the EU still lacked a clear vision on Ukraine.[37] Thus, it may be concluded from this discussion that the most significant obstacles to EU–Ukraine relations are not only economic and political but also psychological. The EU continues to view Ukraine as outside Europe and in Eurasia. This is exemplified by the EU's continued focus on identity issues with regard to Ukraine.

The EU's Common Strategy was rather disappointing in that it did not amount to much more than a collection of political declarations laced with statements of positive intentions. As one member of the European Commission explained, the Common Strategy will not revolutionize EU–Ukraine relations. No one is ready to talk membership. Such an option cannot be given to Ukraine at this time. The EU tends to react to external events, from COMECON, to the demise of the USSR, to the Bosnia and Kosovo Wars, and even to the earthquake in Turkey in 1999. The sad irony is that it may take a catastrophic event in Ukraine, such as a social uprising or a natural disaster, to capture the EU's attention.[38]

On a more positive note, on July 12, 1999, Kuchma signed a decree approving a program to integrate Ukraine into the EU. The draft program provides for three stages of integration covering the years 2000 to 2007. At the first stage Ukraine aims to accede to the World Trade Organization, at the second stage Ukraine will sign an agreement with the EU on setting up a free-trade area and join the EU as an associate member, and at the final stage talks are to be held on joining the EU as a full member.[39] Clearly, the goals are in place for Ukraine's integration into the EU, but what about a plan to achieve those goals? By what means? The PCA is not even mentioned in these stages and this is a problem. The EU bases the deepening of its relations with Ukraine on Ukraine's ability to follow through with its political and economic commitments, particularly the implementation of PCA provisions.

But Ukraine may have reason to believe that associate membership is a medium-term possibility. In May 2000, after a meeting of the EU–Ukraine Cooperation Council in Portugal, Jaime Gama, the Portuguese foreign affairs minister, stated that in time the PCA may be transformed to associate membership. This is the first time a clear link has been made between the implementation of the PCA and associate membership.[40] Ukrainian Prime Minister Viktor Yushchenko dubbed the session "the beginning of the implementation of Ukraine's Europe Program," which is aimed at full membership in the EU.[41] Further, Yushchenko argued that Ukraine's European integration is a matter of time rather than choice and that the pace of this process largely depends on international financial institutions" confidence in Ukraine.[42]

In July 2000 the EU and Ukraine held their third summit, though no new policy orientations were produced. The committee meetings were dominated by trade-related issues in which the EU reportedly received little satisfaction from their complaints about Ukraine's trade restrictions that are inconsistent with PCA provisions. Both sides, however, called for greater access to each other's markets, but ultimately agreed to conduct a feasibility study on the creation of an EU–Ukraine free-trade zone. EU authorities emphasized the need for Ukraine to work harder toward WTO accession.

Former Ukrainian Foreign Minister Tarasyuk has suggested that the primary goals of Ukraine's rapprochement with the EU are the development of trade–economic relations, access to the European market, and the procurement of modern technologies.[43] In the political sphere, EU–Ukraine relations have developed rather well; however, Ukraine's economic difficulties have curtailed progress in economic cooperation. Ukraine continues to be viewed as a state with a non-market-oriented economy. The number of EU antidumping cases against Ukraine has significantly increased in recent years, thus limiting the export of Ukrainian commodities and especially industrial products.

However, on a more positive note, the Ukrainian government has responded to the EU's call to begin the process of adapting its legislation to the laws of the EU. The spheres of legislation upon which Ukraine's closer economic relations with the EU depend are entrepreneurship, protection of competition and intellectual ownership rights, customs regulations, transport, communications, certification, and standards. Ukraine intends to adapt its legislation in three stages. In the first stage, attention will be given to bringing the legal system in line with the requirements of the declaration approved by the EU in 1993. The second stage will include the revision of Ukrainian laws in line with the PCA in preparation for the creation of a free-trade zone between the EU and Ukraine, as well as obtaining associate member status in the EU. The level of ties set forth in the final stage, which is largely undetermined at present, will depend on whether Ukraine has achieved associate member status.[44]

There is certainly reason to believe that Ukraine will continue to seek closer ties with the EU because there is a clear consensus among Ukrainian politicians to strengthen the state's ties with the EU. This was exemplified in the last presidential election in October 1999. Even the leftist candidates did not appear to be against Ukraine's membership in the EU. For example, Oleksandr Moroz, head of the Socialist Party, stated that there would be no major changes in Ukraine's foreign policy orientation toward the EU (or NATO) if he was elected president.[45] Communist leader Petro Symonenko also proclaimed that he would pursue a proactive policy supporting Ukraine's membership in all global and European associations if this improves the prestige of the state and strengthens Ukraine's economic potential.[46] Progressive Socialist leader Natalya Vitrenko did not necessarily advocate EU membership for Ukraine, although she did state that she intended to build relations with the international community based on principles of peace and respect for human rights.[47] Although former *Verkhovna Rada* chairman Oleksandr Tkachenko tended to favor economic ties with Russia and Belarus and was vague on the topic of Ukraine's membership in the EU, he did not speak outwardly against it. Naturally, the center and right candidates, such as Kuchma, Yevhen Marchuk, Hennadii Udovenko, and Yurii Kostenko, unequivocally supported the development of Ukraine's partnership with the EU.

Moreover, as stated previously, EU membership for Ukraine is not provocative or controversial in Russia. Therefore, theoretically Ukraine has no external (or internal) barrier that would impede the development of its multidimensional relations with the EU. Given this scenario, how can the slow pace of Ukraine's integration into Europe from 1991 to the present be explained? This slow pace can be attributed to an amorphous and hesitant EU policy vis-à-vis Ukraine, which stems first from Ukraine's acute economic crises and failure to comply with the PCA requirements. Second, it comes from the unwillingness of EU officials to distinguish Ukraine from Russia, fearing that an independent policy for Ukraine might aggravate Moscow, thus staggering the development of EU–Russia ties.

NATO, on the other hand, has more or less managed to develop its relations with Ukraine separate from Russia, even though NATO tends to view its relations with Ukraine through the lenses of its relations with Russia and relations with Russia through the lenses of its partnership with Ukraine. This cannot be avoided, because of historical, geopolitical, and psychological reasons. The NATO–Russia Founding Act was signed in May 1997 and the NATO–Ukraine Charter was unveiled only two months later, demonstrating the high value that NATO has placed on developing ties with Ukraine.

DEALING WITH THE FRONTIER: UKRAINE'S REGIONAL RELATIONS

In addition to seeking to deepen its ties to Western institutions and key states, Ukraine has also attempted to deal its geopolitical position in the frontier by diversifying and intensifying its relations in the region. From the outset of its independence Ukrainian leaders have pursued the international recognition of the state's geopolitical identity as a Central European as opposed to a Eurasian–CIS state. Placing emphasis on its relations with Poland, Hungary, the Czech Republic, Slovakia, and Romania, Ukraine has been eager to be portrayed as a Central Eastern European nation within the larger European continent. Having achieved this recognition, Ukraine's independence, sovereignty, and territorial integrity would be more solidified, thus creating some distance from Russia as well as a diversification of its international relations. Further, Ukraine's Central European neighbors were seen as the "ticket to the West" and Kyiv counted on their support in its efforts to establish links with Western states and institutions. Therefore, it should come as no surprise that Ukraine has placed great importance on maintaining friendly relations with its closest geographical neighbors in Central and Eastern Europe, specifically Poland (Chapter 8).[48]

Regional cooperation has been viewed as a way to enhance stability, to facilitate solutions to common problems encountered in the process of state and nation building in some and in the transition to democracy and market economies in others, to strengthen the position of Central and Eastern Europe states vis-à-vis Russia, and to promote integration into Western institutions.[49] With these goals in mind, several regional organizations were formed, including the Visegrad group, the Central European Free Trade Area (CEFTA), and the Central European Initiative (CEI).[50] Ukraine views its involvement with these organizations as a means to promote its Central European identity and to participate in a forum where states could discuss their problems and concerns, thus enhancing their ability to develop collective measures to deal with these problems. However, regional cooperation failed to become a priority among Central and Eastern Europe states, and during 1993–1994 many governments gradually shifted their emphasis to bilateral contacts with each other and with the West. It is important to note that this change was a reaction to NATO and the EU's shift from a "regional" to an "individualist" approach to Central and Eastern Europe. Thus, the more economically and politically developed states in Central and Eastern Europe tended to view regional cooperation as a potential impediment to accession to Western institutions.

Ukraine, however, remained active in regional activities. Having declared itself a nonnuclear and nonaligned state, Ukraine signed several bilateral agreements on limited military cooperation with its neighbors, and the first of these was with Poland in February 1993. This agreement promoted military exchange programs and the sharing of military training facilities in each other's territories. In May 1993 a similar agreement was concluded between Ukraine and Hungary. However, Ukraine's efforts to intensify cooperation with the Visegrad group and CEFTA was hindered due to President Kravchuk's proposal to create a Central and Eastern Europe "zone of stability and security," which would include Ukraine, Belarus, Poland, the Baltic states, Moldova, the Czech Republic, Slovakia, Romania, and Austria—all Central and Eastern Europe states except Russia (thus effectively shifting the frontier to Ukraine's eastern border). The proposal, presented in 1993, did not generate a positive response from other Central and Eastern European leaders.[51] The main concern was that the development of regional security organizations would hinder their accession to NATO and the EU. Central and Eastern European leaders were also by and large against the creation of a security grouping between NATO and Russia that would potentially transform the region into a permanent "gray zone" of security and prosperity. Also, Central and Eastern European leaders sought to avoid both alienating Russia and being drawn into a potential Ukrainian–Russian dispute. The proposal was also unattractive to the West, as NATO's plans for enlargement were quickly gaining momentum. As a result of all these factors, President Kravchuk dropped the idea.

During 1993–1994 some Central and Eastern European states also became increasingly concerned about Ukraine's internal instability, stance on nuclear weapons, and the effects that an unstable Russia–Ukraine relationship would have on the region.[52] After two years of independence, Ukraine found itself in virtual isolation. The West failed to formulate a clear policy on Ukraine beyond nuclear weapons and instead tended to view Ukraine as a rogue state or as a barrier to nuclear disarmament and nonproliferation in Europe. Furthermore, Ukraine's delay in implementing economic reforms increased its political and social instability and thus widened the gap between itself and other Central and Eastern European countries. As a result, Ukraine's neighbors began to perceive it as a threat to their own security.[53]

Upon Kuchma's election in 1994 relations between Ukraine and its Central and Eastern European neighbors did not initially improve because the new president's primary focus was on normalizing relations with Russia and not on developing ties in the region. Kuchma was also fixated on securing financial support from the West so that he could implement his economic reform program. At the same time, Poland, Hungary, and the Czech Republic were encouraged by the notion of the inevitable expansion of NATO.[54] Energized by the prospects of expeditious integration, the likely candidates preferred to intensify relations with NATO and sought not to burden themselves with an unpredictable and unstable East, including Ukraine. Although publicly Central and Eastern European leaders recognized the importance of an independent and stable Ukraine, they took little notice of Ukraine's role in European security. As noted by a senior official in the Ukrainian Ministry of Foreign Affairs, "it was NATO's speedy enlargement plans which disrupted the very idea of regional cooperation."[55]

But during the spring of 1995 relations between Ukraine and neighboring countries began to improve. The change was reflected in Ukraine's new domestic and foreign policies as well as the shift in the West's policy toward Ukraine. Kuchma's initiation of economic reforms combined with Ukraine's accession to the Nuclear Non-Proliferation Treaty prompted a positive response from Western states and institutions. Further, and very important, Ukraine had altered its official policy on NATO enlargement from favoring "an evolutionary process" to outright support so long as new dividing lines and frontiers in Europe were not created. Ukraine's support for NATO enlargement naturally facilitated the improvement of its relations with Poland, Hungary, and the Czech Republic, and Poland in particular has been outspokenly supportive of Ukraine importance in European security. Poland successfully lobbied for Ukraine's membership in the Council of Europe in the fall of 1995 and has also supported Ukraine's accession to CEFTA.[56] With the support of the other Visegrad members, Ukraine was granted membership in the CEI.[57] Ukraine has also pledged its strategic goal to integrate into European and trans-Atlantic structures with priority given to full membership in the EU, but at the same time Ukrainian officials realize that this is a distant goal. Kyiv has, therefore, adopted a foreign policy approach that calls for integration into Western institutions by way of using its regional ties in Central and Eastern Europe as a stepping-stone.[58]

President Kravchuk's proposal for a "zone of stability and security" in Central and Eastern Europe as well as the energy transportation routes were not Ukraine's only attempt at creating regional security and economic organizations that would move the frontier eastward, thereby excluding Russia and preventing Ukraine's large neighbor from having a dominant role. In this regard, Ukraine has also been actively engaging its eastern neighbors in such organizations as the Black Sea Economic Cooperation Organization (BSECO) and GUUAM (see Chapter 9), where Ukraine is the leading member of GUUAM and a prominent member of BSECO. Members of the anti-Moscow group within the CIS, the GUUAM alliance, view the CIS as a vehicle to promote a "civilized divorce" of the former USSR and also as a means to support their pro-West foreign and security policy. GUUAM members support several ideological positions: combating separatism, searching for alternative energy routes, integrating into the world community, and establishing closer ties with NATO and the EU. Members have stated that an important goal of GUUAM is to focus on economic issues in order to "facilitate and speed up the fulfillment of aspirations of strategic choice integration into the European Union through regional structures."

One of the main ideas behind GUUAM was to lessen the effects of the possible creation of new dividing lines or frontiers in Europe. Former Foreign Minister Tarasyuk argued that as NATO and the EU were expanding eastward, Ukraine and the other GUUAM members should seek to prevent themselves from being defined outside Europe and thereby within Rusia's sphere of influence in Eurasia.[59]

The creation of the GUUAM subregional organization is an indication of the direction in which the CIS is moving. Although the CIS has other subgroups, including the Russian–Belarussian "union," the quadripartite Customs Union (Russia, Belarus, Kazakhstan, Kyrgyzstan), and the Central Asian Union, GUUAM represents those states that have sought to maintain Russia at a distance and have also opposed CIS supranational structures. GUUAM is also important because in a broad sense it reflects those states' concern about being excluded from Western security and economic organizations and left in an unstable frontier zone. There has been talk of the forming of a Ukrainian–Azeri–Georgian peacekeeping battalion in the GUUAM framework (though this idea has been dropped due mostly to financial constraints).

Ukraine's participation in GUUAM also draws several conclusions about its foreign policy. First, Ukraine's leading role in GUUAM is a reflection of its desire to boost its international prestige and to assume a more active role in regional issues that directly affect its security and national interests. Second, GUUAM enables Ukraine to band together with countries in the region that share in its desire to cooperate closely with Western states and institutions. Third, GUUAM provides the forum for discussing and concluding agreements in the energy sector, which, if implemented, will lessen Ukraine's dependence on Russia while simultaneously moving away from Russia.

In addition to GUUAM, former Ukrainian Defense Minister Kuzmuk has sought to heighten activity in the military in the field of creating joint military structures on the southwest salient by forging a range of multinational subunits. However, the joint actions of Ukraine and Russia deserve a much less serious attitude than other battalions created on a bilateral (e.g., with Poland) or multilateral basis, despite Russia's appeals for Ukraine's participation in the united CIS defense system. Further, the quadrilateral TISZA engineering and sapper battalion—consisting of subunits from Ukraine, Romania, Slovakia, and Hungary—is another example of Ukraine's initiatives in the region that do not include Russia. TISZA's main task is to counter negative consequences of national calamities such as floods and other emergency situations. Kuzmuk, however, continued to emphasize that these multilateral forces are neither a bloc nor a union.[60] It should become clear in the near future whether the Ukrainian military are capable of shaping developments in the region or whether the role of the state's efforts in the battalion-making activities was somewhat overestimated.

Ukraine's successful participation in these regional organizations and the diversification of its activities in the region has helped it to promote its foreign and security policy objectives by lessening the state's dependence on Russian energy supplies, gaining experience in dealing with emergency situations, and ultimately increasing its ties with those of similar pro-West ideological views that would subsequently strengthen the state's international standing. Participation in regional organizations is also reflective of the participants' desire for political normalcy in the region by attempting to bring some order to the rather underorganized frontier. The West, however, have been apprehensive in supporting the development and enhancement of subregional organizations in the former USSR, reflecting their desire not to endorse any regional alliances that might alienate or provoke Russia. Therefore, in the absence of clear and positive signals from the West, it is possible that the momentum for the development of new regional organizations and the deepening of cooperation in existing ones will be thwarted.

For Ukraine and the other "outsiders" of NATO enlargement and EU expansion processes the presence of an East–West political, economic, security, and cultural frontier in Europe is clear. Moreover, those states that have been excluded, even if only temporarily, from key Western institutions are likely to equate geopolitical instability with perceptions of their own security and identity. It is therefore crucial that those states that have not been included either in the first or second waves of enlargement, such as Ukraine, be encouraged to band together with others in a similar geopolitical position that share their pro-Western ideology.

The notion of spheres of influence is alive and well in Europe, otherwise the West would have been more supportive of subregional organizations and not fixated solely on Russia's reaction. This only proves that there are larger geopolitical forces at work that tend to dictate the degree to which regional organizations are able to develop, function, and sustain. Regional cooperation should thus be viewed as an attempt to "organize" the frontier between Russia and Western Europe and to create some kind of institutionalized security arrangement. The process of globalization has served to bring these states in closer proximity to each other, but the frontier, reinforced by instability to the east and negative economic circumstances, is preventing these states from rejoining "Europe."

GLOBALIZATION AND THE
CHANGING NATURE OF FRONTIERS

As discussed at the beginning of this chapter, the conceptualization of the term "frontier" has changed to include more than military factors. It can be argued on the one hand that the process of globalization cultivates conditions of increased state interdependence and fosters the shrinking of international borders and frontiers in many areas of the world. Moreover, globalization seems to imply that all frontiers will eventually be eliminated as the potential forces of interdependence, transnationalism, universalism, and the notion of a world society are realized. On the other hand, as states and societies move closer to one another, external barriers, particularly trade and immigration barriers, are often created in order to protect the interests of those choosing to take their integration to a higher level. Therefore, as frontiers become more defined, we must take a closer look at the frontier itself and at the ensuing implications for adjacent institutions, states, and societies.

According to James Rosenau, we are so accustomed to thinking of domestic and international politics as separate playing fields that is it difficult to conceptualize any structures and processes that may be superseding them as a new field of play.[61] The frontier is in some respects an underorganized domain consisting of fragile sources of legitimacy, while in other respects clearly defined structures of authority can be discerned. Put differently, Rosenau explains that the frontier sometimes takes the form of a market, sometimes appears as a civil society, sometimes resembles a legislative chamber, often is a crowded town square, occasionally is a battlefield, increasingly is obstructed by an information highway, and usually looks like a several-ring circus in which all of these activities are unfolding simultaneously. Given this diversity, it is not so much a single frontier but rather a cluster of diverse frontiers in which background becomes foreground, time becomes disjointed, nonlinear patterns predominate, organizations bifurcate, societies implode, regions unify, markets overlap, and issues of identity, territoriality, and the interface between long-established patterns and emergent orientations dominate the political agenda.

Rosenau's response is to treat the frontier as becoming an ever more rugged and widening field of action where world affairs unfold, and as an arena in which domestic and foreign issues intermesh, converge, and become indistinguishable within a seamless web. The new conditions, which have widened the frontier, cannot be explained by a single source. The informational revolution and other technological advances are major stimulants, but so also is the breakdown of trust, the shrinking of distances brought about by the processes of globalization, the proliferation of new organizations and the fragmentation of old ones, the integration of the regions, the surge of democratic practices, the cessation of intense hatreds, and the revival of historic animosities, all of which serve to provoke further reactions that add to the complexity.[62] This is the new politics of the frontier. The Kosovo conflict all too clearly demonstrated this fact. The political, economic, social, and military developments in Central, Eastern, and Southern Europe will continue to attract scholarly attention well into the new millennium, particularly those states that have, if only temporarily, been excluded from membership in European and trans-Atlantic institutions. In short, the presence and endurance of frontiers points to a new way of thinking about how global politics and security unfolds. Where earlier epochs had their central tendencies and orderly patterns, the present epoch derives its order from contrary trends and episodic patterns. According to Rosenau, leaders are now beginning to understand, emotionally and intellectually, that unexpected events are commonplace, anomalies are normal occurrences, minor incidents can all too easily mushroom into major outcomes, fundamental processes trigger opposing forces even as they expand their scope, and what was once transitional may now be enduring.[63]

Globalization carries with it the ability to increase the proximity of what was previously a distant dispute or problem. In other words, globalization, interdependence, and the shrinking of borders closes the distance between states and regions, often propelling previously uninvolved entities into a conflict. Realizing the reality of the situation, it is logical to assume that zones of stability and security should be cautiously expanded, but in some cases it is desirable to retain a certain distance from high-conflict zones by maintaining the frontier as a buffer region.

Overall, globalization seems to be having the opposite effect on the Central and Eastern Europe frontier. As the distance between entities in Central and Eastern Europe closes, the likelihood for conflict between the actors has tended to increase, thereby increasing their political, economic, and cultural distance from Western Europe, and thereby reducing their chances for accession to Western institutions in the short to medium term. Moreover, since our conception of the term "frontier" has broadened not only along geographic lines (e.g., from a demarcated line to a widened region), but also has expanded to include economic, social, and psychological factors, it is therefore possible to assume that the frontier in Central and Eastern Europe is not softening; in fact, it appears to be hardening. The increase in interdependence has encouraged the fifteen member states of the European Union that it is in their best interests to relinquish sovereignty (or "pool" their sovereignty) to an ever-increasing extent to become more competitive in a global economy and ultimately to increase the prosperity and wealth of its citizens. But ironically, the same forces of globalization that have pushed the EU member states together have helped to drive an economic, political, social, and psychological wedge between the EU and Central, Eastern, and Southern Europe, in the process creating, as President Kuchma describes, a new post–Cold War "paper curtain."

CONCLUSION

One question that arises from the previous discussion is if the frontier will continue to widen and the inherent contradictions on which its worldview rests continue to persist, or if new institutions and boundaries will eventually emerge and settle into place as the basis of another epochal transformation wherein the politics of the frontier becomes the politics of normalcy.[64] I tend to agree with Rosenau that the latter scenario is more likely. As the frontier widens, it will manifest the creation of unaccustomed political institutions and arrangements. This can be exemplified by the most prevalent organizations, such as NATO, the EU, the OSCE, the WEU, and the Council of Europe. Further, we should not discount the proliferation of regional and subregional organizations such as CEFTA, CEI, GUUAM, BSECO, and smaller bilateral and multilateral forces (such as UkrPolBat and TISZA) in the frontier, in which their overarching goal is to establish some level of institutionalized security or "political normalcy." These organizations provide a forum that helps these states to gain experience in international relations and to collaborate more closely with other states in the region that share pro-West–Europe ideologies.

It should be clear from this chapter that for Ukraine the most profound frontiers are based on economic criteria. Ukraine has responded by prioritizing membership in the WTO and the creation of an EU–Ukraine free-trade area as key goals. The main problem, however, is that the Ukrainian government has been preoccupied with the idea of instant integration into Western institutions without really considering exactly how to get there. In other words, the goal of integration into Europe is clearly obvious but the means to get there have not been carefully thought out and planned.

This chapter has sought to demonstrate how the processes of globalization, transnationalism, and interdependence have contributed to the emergence of a new East–West frontier in Europe. It has also argued that the EU contributes more to the maintenance of the frontier than does NATO, as the latter has been much more willing to build a multifaceted and dynamic partnership with Ukraine.

It has also been argued that whereas globalization and interdependence have tended to soften frontiers and borders in many regions of the world by closing the distance between states and increasing the likelihood for collision and collusion between them, globalization has to a considerable degree had the opposite effect with regard to the East–West division in Europe. The pending expansion of the EU in particular to selected states in Central and Eastern Europe has served to create a new division in Europe for those left outside the process and has indirectly resulted in the reinforcement of a gray zone of European security and prosperity. We can already see this happening, for example, in the introduction of visa requirements for Ukrainian citizens by the Czech Republic, Hungary, Slovakia, and in the not too distant future, Poland. Western institutions, including NATO, and key Western states such as the United States, the United Kingdom, and Germany and, to a lesser extent, France, Canada, and The Netherlands, have attempted to allay the fears of those states presently left outside the enlargement process by working with them in multilateral and bilateral forums, and by increasing cooperation in the military, political, scientific, and technical spheres. However, the EU has yet to develop clear objectives with regard to cooperation with Ukraine, and as a result, Ukraine has not developed a clear plan for integration into the EU. There is only an idea among Ukrainian policy makers as to what European integration actually entails. As a result, neither side is satisfied with the relationship as it currently stands.

The emergence of a new East–West frontier has led Ukraine to make bold strategic and foreign policy choices, such as its desire to integrate into the European Union. But the real question here is, can the Ukrainian elite actually make this pro-Western choice given its domestic situation, which includes an underdeveloped nation-state, pending institutional and economic reforms, and a society in which some identify more closely with Europe and some with Eurasia? If national identity plays a central role in relations with its neighbors, can Ukraine's European choice be seen as believable, credible, and ultimately sustainable over time?

A new security environment in Europe will more than likely create some new political and cultural frontiers perhaps, as some analysts contend, along similar lines as those suggested by Huntington's "clash of civilizations." If one follows the EU's approach, which tends to focus on the identity question, those countries that are ethnically Slav and religiously Orthodox would be the "natural" allies of Russia, whereas those countries that are religiously Roman Catholic or Protestant and linked to the Holy Roman and Habsburg Empires would align with the West. In any case, for the time being, Central and Eastern Europe is bound to remain, in Eberhard Bort's words, a "difficult frontier" at the very least.[65] It will be the terrain of political quicksands on which the Europe to come will have to be built. Frontier politics have returned at a time when the enlargement of NATO and the expansion of the EU are seen, rightly or wrongly, as the necessary next step in the geopolitical reorganization of the continent. But for those states that have been excluded, perhaps in some cases only temporarily, governments and society alike are tending to equate geopolitical instability with perceptions of security and identity. Therefore, in this regard, political borders and frontiers in Central and Eastern Europe are still problematic and warrant further study and analysis.

NOTES

A shorter version of this chapter was first published as "Ukraine's Ties to the West," *Problems of Post-Communism* 48, no. 2 (2001).

1. "Kuchma Speaks against Economic Isolation of Ukraine," Kiev UT-1 Television Network, 10 September 1999.

2. "Ukraine Worried More about EU Than NATO Expansion," *Kiev UNIAN,* 30 August 2000.

3. "Foreign Minister on Cooperation with EU" (Interview with Borys Tarasyuk), *Kiev Uryadovyy Kuryer,* 22 July 1999.

4. See Jennifer D. P. Moroney, "Frontier Dynamics and Ukraine's Ties to the West." See *Problems of Post Communism*, March–April 2001, for a more detailed discussion on Ukraine–NATO relations.

5. Thomas M. Wilson and Hastings Donnan, eds., *Border Identities: Nation and State at International Frontiers* (Cambridge: Cambridge University Press, 1998), 1.

6. Ibid., 2.

7. Malcolm Anderson, "European Frontiers at the End of the Twentieth Century," in *The Frontiers of Europe*, ed. Malcolm Anderson and Eberhard Bort (London: Pinter, 1998), 3.

8. Ibid., 3–4.

9. As cited in John R. V. Prescott, *Political Frontiers and Boundaries* (London: Allen and Unwin, 1987), 159.

10. Zbigniew Brzezinski, "The Premature Partnership," *Foreign Affairs* 72, no. 2 (1994): 80.

11. See Sherman W. Garnett, *Keystone in the Arch: Ukraine in the Emerging Security Environment of Central and Eastern Europe* (Washington, D.C.: Carnegie Endowment, 1997).

12. Samuel Huntington, remarks at the National Institute for Strategic Studies, Kyiv, Ukraine, 18 October 1999.

13. Prescott, *Political Frontiers and Boundaries*, 48.

14. Peter-Christian Muller-Graff, "Whose Responsibility Are Frontiers?" in Anderson and Bort, 11–12.

15. See Malcolm Anderson, *Frontiers: Territory and State Formation in the Modern World* (Cambridge: Polity Press, 1996), 1, and Anderson, "European Frontiers," 4–6.

16. Anderson, *Frontiers*.

17. Anderson and Bort, *The Frontiers of Europe*, 5.

18. Benedict Anderson, *Imagined Communities: Reflections on the Origin and Spread of Nationalism* (New York: Verso, 1991).

19. Anderson, *Frontiers*, 2.

20. R. Strassoldo, *From Barrier to Junction: Towards a Sociological Theory of Borders* (Gorizia: ISIG, 1970).

21. Anderson, *Frontiers*, 3.

22. Ibid., 8.

23. Carl Schmitt, *The Concept of the Political* (New Brunswick, N.J.: Rutgers University Press, 1976).

24. Anderson, *Frontiers*, 8–9.

25. Prescott, *Political Frontiers and Boundaries*, 14.

26. Anderson, *Frontiers*, 10.

27. See T. Kuzio, "Geopolitical Pluralism in the CIS: The Emergence of GUUAM," *European Security* 9, no. 2 (2000): 81–114, and "Promoting Geopolitical Pluralism in the CIS: GUUAM and Western Policy," *Problems of Post-Communism* 47, no. 3 (2000): 25–35.

28. Legal and economic aspects of European integration remain under the European Community pillar. Therefore, it is appropriate to refer to EC law and not EU law.

29. "Dzurinda (Slovak Prime Minister) Supports Visas for Ukraine, Russia, Belarus," *Bratislava Rozhlasova Stanica Slovensko Network*, 17 February 2000.

30. Fraser Cameron, Foreign Policy Advisor, European Commission DG1-A, interview, Brussels, Belgium, 15 March 1999.

31. Russia and Moldova (which have taken effect), and Armenia, Azerbaijan, Georgia, Kazakhstan, Kryghyzstan, Uzbekistan, Turkmenistan, and Belarus (which have not yet taken effect).

32. As the PCA covers matters of community, national, and joint competence, it must be ratified not only by the three European Communities (the European Community, the European Coal and Steel Community, and the European Atomic Energy Community), but also by all of the member states.

33. See Official Journal of the European Communities, Council and Commission Decision of 26 January 1998, 98/149, "On the Conclusion of the Partnership and Cooperation Agreement between the European Communities and Their Member-States, on the One Part, and Ukraine, of the Other Part," vol. 49, 19 February 1998.

34. See O. Pavliuk, *The European Union and Ukraine: The Need for a New Vision* (New York: East–West Institute, 1999).

35. Ukraine is not officially a member of the CIS, having never signed the CIS Charter. Yet Ukraine participates in CIS meetings, and is a member of the CIS Interparliamentary Assembly (the legislature of the CIS).

36. T. Kuzio, "Ukraine: Strategic Options and Obstacles" (paper presented at the conference, "Ukraine: Continuing Challenges of Transition," sponsored by the Bureau of Intelligence and Research, U.S. Department of State, and the National Intelligence Council, Washington, D.C., 30 June 1999).

37. Pavliuk, *European Union and Ukraine*.

38. Klaus Schneider, Deputy Head of Unit for Relations with Ukraine, Moldova, and Belarus, European Commission DG 1A, interview, Brussels, Belgium, 12 October 1999.

39. "Ukraine on the Verge of EU Integration," *Moscow Interfax*, 27 July 2000.

40. "Ukraine: EU Ready to Discuss Associate Membership," *Kiev Dinau*, 23 May 2000.

41. "Ukraine–EU Council Session Sees Relations Developing Well," *Moscow Itar-Tass*, 23 May 2000.

42. "PM: Ukraine's Entry into the EU a Matter of Time," *Kiev Ukrainian Television UT-3*, 22 May 2000.

43. "Foreign Minister on Cooperation with EU."

44. "Government Approves Concept of Adapting to EU Laws," *Kiev Intelnews*, 19 August 1999.

45. "Moroz Issues Election Manifesto," *Kiev Holos Ukrayiny*, 8 September 1999.

46. "Presidential Candidate Symonenko Manifesto," *Kiev Holos Ukrayiny*, 1 September 1999.

47. "Vitrenko's Campaign Platform Outlined," *Kiev Holos Ukrayiny*, 19 August 1999.

48. O. Pavliuk, "Ukraine and Regional Cooperation in Central and Eastern Europe," *Security Dialogue* 28, no. 3 (1997): 348.

49. Ibid., 349.

50. Ukraine is a member of CEI but not of the Visegrad group or of CEFTA.

51. This proposal came after the Kravchuk–Yeltsin summit in January 1993 in Moscow, at which the Russian president announced that his country would be ready to guarantee the security and integrity of Ukraine and defend her against nuclear attack. Kravchuk naturally was alarmed and dead against Yeltsin's proposed security guarantees for Ukraine.

52. Ukraine's neighbors were particularly concerned about Ukraine's refusal to sign START I and the Nuclear Non-Proliferation Treaty.

53. Pavliuk, "Ukraine and Regional Cooperation in Central and Eastern Europe," 352.

54. The Visegrad group was further encouraged by the December 1994 decision of NATO foreign ministers to undertake a study in 1995 on enlargement. NATO has published this study on enlargement (December 1995).

55. See Pavliuk, "Ukraine and Regional Cooperation in Central and Eastern Europe," 352, on his interviews with unnamed officials in the Ukrainian Ministry of Foreign Affairs conducted between October and December 1995.

56. Although it remains to be seen how important groupings such as CEFTA are in light of the likely upcoming EU expansion. Its members are sure to leave the organization upon their accession to the EU.

57. Ukraine is particularly interested in the CEI in terms of the development of European transit corridors.

58. See section on returning to Europe vis-à-vis regional cooperation.

59. *Financial Times*, 11 September 1999.

60. "Ukraine's Joint Battalions, Strategy Seen," *Kyiv Zerkalo Nedeli*, 22 January 2000.

61. James N. Rosenau, *Along the Domestic–Foreign Frontier: Exploring Global Governance in a Turbulent World* (Cambridge: Cambridge University Press, 1997), 6–7.

62. Ibid., 4–7.

63. Ibid., 7.

64. Ibid., 8.

65. Eberhard Bort, "Mitteleuropa: The Difficult Frontier," in Anderson and Bort, 101.

PART II

CIVIL–MILITARY
RELATIONS THEORY
AND UKRAINE

5

Security, Democracy, and "Civil Democratic Control" of Armed Forces in Ukraine

James Sherr

The notion that "civilian control over the military is a pre-requisite for the normal functioning of a civilized state" has become one of the orthodoxies of our time.[1] Since the collapse of the USSR, this orthodoxy has been given formal expression in numerous state and interstate documents, including NATO's 1994 Partnership for Peace Framework Document. It has also assumed a contractual form in the Charter on a Distinctive Partnership between Ukraine and NATO (1997) and a quasi-legal form in the OSCE Code of Conduct Regarding Military–Political Aspects of Security (1994). Reiterated, echoed, and amplified as the orthodoxy is, the fact is that it calls for more reflection than it has received. Where Ukraine and other countries of the former USSR are concerned, reflection is required for a number of reasons.

The first reason is that, until recently, "civilian control" has been a Western orthodoxy reflecting three classic Western preoccupations: keeping the military out of politics, keeping the military out of power, and subordinating military values to civilian ones. Given the number of overtly militaristic regimes in the world—and politically ambitious military establishments—these are sound preoccupations. But they are largely out of place in the former Soviet Union. In its prime, the Soviet system was militarized, but it was not militaristic. The Soviet military system was as rigorously Clausewitzian as, until recently, a Jesuit education was rigorously Christian. For all its deficiencies, this system inculcated a high degree of professionalism, anchored in the conviction that armed forces had to be the tool of policy, rather than the master. In this respect fortunately—if in several other respects sadly—the system of officer education has not changed in Ukraine. Today most Ukrainian military officers believe that their conditions of service are degrading and that the country is experiencing conditions of almost unprecedented trial, but the number of those who believe that Ukraine's Army can assume control over the situation in Ukraine and establish order in society remains a remarkably small 10 percent. When the selection is widened to include servicemen without an officer's education, the number rises by a noteworthy 80 percent to a still reassuringly small total of 18 percent.[2] If keeping the army out of politics is the purpose of civilian control, then many will conclude that civilian control is effective and adequate. This is exactly what a large number of Ukrainians have concluded, to the detriment of defense reform in the country.[3]

The second reason is that, as a Western concept, "civilian democratic control" is discussed in Western terms and largely in the English language. Fatefully, Russians long ago incorporated "control"— literally, the French equivalent, contrôle—into their own language as kontrol', and Ukrainians have done the same. Unhappily, the Russian and Ukrainian concepts are closer to the French and even more strict. Kontrol' is the activity of "monitoring" or "checking." At most, it corresponds to "oversight." But it does not correspond to "direction" (upravlinnia) or "supervision" (nadzor). In the Ukrainian as in the Soviet military system, nearly all would concede that, if civilians make military policy, then they need to exercise kontrol' (oversight) over the military. But should civilians control it? Should they tell military professionals how to implement policy, let alone how to conduct military operations? Should they work in Ministries of Defense, cheek by jowl with serving officers, on similar issues and on an equal or even more than equal basis? The narrow notion of kontrol'—perpetuated by poor communication as much as by post-Soviet conservatism—is another reason why many in Ukraine have concluded that civilian control is effective and adequate.

A third reason to reflect on the notion of civilian control is that in post-Communist countries it is especially important to know who the civilians are. As Francoise Thom noted at the start of the Mikhail Gorbachev era, the Communist system by its very essence made war on civil society. By comparison with Poland, Hungary, and the Czech lands, civil society in Russia and much of Ukraine was weak before this war even started. In what is now the former Soviet Union, it was waged on a unique scale, with a unique intensity and for an exceptionally long period of time. However democratic today's Ukrainian state might be in form, however European it might be in aspiration, this war has had far deeper and more lasting effects there than in those Central European countries that are now rejoining the mainstream of European civilization.

The main effect of this civic deficit is that the "collapse of communism" did not produce a real devolution of power. In Ukraine, the fundamental divisions in the country are not between left and right as they are in genuinely participatory democracies (although these divisions demonstrably exist); the core issue remains the divide between us and them, between society and state. To this day, most ordinary people in Ukraine do not start with the Enlightenment assumption that "man is the architect of his fortunes." Toward the public and political order, they are more likely to start with an attitude of resignation. They no more expect to exercise control over the state than they expect to control the weather, and they expect "them," the *vlada* ("powers") to act according to their own rules and purely in their own interests. In turn, the "powers" themselves in substantial part comprise the descendants or associates of people who had power before, not to say the products of elite institutions and the mentalities they instilled. In these conditions it is not surprising—indeed, it is almost inevitable— that "democracy" is limited to elections and that elections are managed and manipulated. If civilians elected by these norms have authority over armed forces, police, and security services, that does not mean there is "democratic control"; nor does it guarantee that these formidable institutions will be used in the interests of the country. The struggle to strengthen civil democratic control is therefore inseparable from the struggle to strengthen civil society.

The fourth reason is the need to implement civilian democratic control by means of institutions that are new, relatively untried, and of still uncertain legitimacy. The "death of the Soviet Union" might not have destroyed old elites or old mentalities, but it did demolish institutions, including the Soviet armed forces and its distinctive mechanisms of political supervision. As a newly independent and not simply post-Communist state, Ukraine faces the challenge of building statehood—not only a national security system—from scratch. At the same time, Ukraine inherits the "ruins and debris" of Soviet institutions, including military formations and infrastructure, security establishments, and defense enterprises. The military establishment might have no "lust for power," but even in the pre–Vladimir Putin era this was not so demonstrably true of other entities with a role to play in the country's security. Even where armed forces subordinated to the Ministry of Defense are concerned, the absence of political ambition is simply a negative. It begs the question as to whether there is adequate authority in the military sphere, especially in those military–technical domains that military professionals consider "the military's business."

The fifth reason for reflection is that it is easy to forget what armed forces are for. Armies must be effectively and democratically controlled; nevertheless, armed forces do not exist to promote democracy, but to defend national security. For this they must be effective, and a military establishment controlled without understanding, knowledge, and judgment will prove to be as a much of a threat to national security as a military establishment that answers only to itself. This point, which sadly is not obvious to every specialist in civil–military relations, is crucial for Ukraine and other newly independent states that face chronic security problems not only because of their geopolitical position, but because of their social and institutional weaknesses. In these countries particularly, it is essential that schemes of civilian democratic control enhance military effectiveness. If they do not, both democracy and security will suffer.

UKRAINE'S SOVIET LEGACY

The former Warsaw Pact countries of Central Europe lacked the attributes of sovereignty but possessed the infrastructure of it. Ukraine was in a different position, because it had to construct the apparatus of statehood from scratch. Nowhere was the challenge more acute than in the sphere of national security and defense.

In 1991 Ukraine did not inherit an army. What it inherited was a force grouping, without a Defense Ministry, without a general staff, and without central organs of command and control. Moreover, this grouping, its formidable inventory of equipment, and its highly trained officer corps were designed for one purpose: to wage combined arms, coalition, offensive (and nuclear) warfare against NATO on an external front and under somebody else's direction. In 1991 these formations were not equipped, deployed, or trained to provide national defense. Indeed, they lacked the means to conduct integrated military operations of any kind. As they stood, they were bone and muscle without heart or brain. Since 1991, therefore, Ukraine has not merely faced the task of "reforming" an army, but creating one. The country's unilateral nuclear disarmament (completed by June 1996) injected realism but also urgency into this enterprise.

Ukraine's challenges are multiplied by the fact that the country did inherit a relatively centralized Ministry of Internal Affairs and state security apparatus, each of them with their own substantial security forces.[4] These and other military forces have grown substantially since independence. Today, even when the *militsia* (ordinary police) are excluded, the number of armed personnel serving in what the constitution terms "other military formations" is almost as great as the number of personnel serving in armed forces subordinated to the Ministry of Defense. The risk posed by this state of affairs is not insubordination but uncoordinated action, the diminution of transparency (which multiplies opportunities for foreign penetration), and loss of control over events. In a country devoid of adequate budgetary resources for defense, swollen security establishments and duplication are also a recipe for corruption and impoverishment.

The peculiar character of civilian control in the Soviet system has not helped those seeking to overcome these problems. In the USSR, civilian control of defense was at one and the same time pervasive and narrowly focused. Commanders of the Soviet armed forces were accustomed to stand to attention before a closed circle of powerful civilians in the Party's Politburo. Through the Chief Political Directorate of the Communist Party Central Committee and the "special departments" of the KGB, these civilians had mechanisms at their disposal that not only ensured the "reliability" of the armed forces, but their total obedience. Paradoxically, the very effectiveness of these mechanisms persuaded the Party leadership to entrust the armed forces with a dominant influence in military–technical decisions and accept its monopoly of military–technical expertise.[5] Being largely unnecessary, civilian expertise was largely absent. What expertise existed was focused in narrowly confined areas where specialist knowledge was required. This system, assiduously compartmentalized by its controllers, not only restricted the vision of its participants, it habituated these participants to regard information as power and openness as a threat to survival.

The swift collapse of Communist Party authority in late 1991 created a paradoxical situation. Freed of the Party's supervisory mechanisms, armed forces in the Russian Federation did not become more open, they became more opaque. In Ukraine, the risk of such opacity was at least as great as it was in Russia, because what supervisory mechanisms and expertise existed was concentrated in Moscow. Nevertheless, in the most urgent and essential respects, Ukraine's new political authorities succeeded in bringing the newly established Ukrainian Armed Forces (December 1991) under political control, and some 11,000 unreliable officers—those who refused to take an oath to the Ukrainian state—were dismissed from service by the summer of 1992.[6] Yet in routine, administrative terms, military officers who had custody over manpower, facilities, and resources sought to control what they could control and shut out "amateurs" who "knew nothing about defense." In the emphatic and almost universal view of the military establishment, these amateurs included Ukraine's first (and only) civilian minister of defense, Valeriy Shmarov, who was replaced by the current minister, Lieutenant General (now Colonel General) Oleksandr Kuzmuk, in July 1996.

THE BOTTLE HALF FULL

In one key respect the foundations for building an integrated defense and security system in Ukraine are far from poor, indeed rather better than they are in neighboring countries, which were members of the former Warsaw Pact. By comparison with most of these countries, Ukraine possesses a key attribute: defense mindedness. One readily forgets that the Warsaw Pact was not a mechanism for creating strong armies in Central Europe, but weak ones, incapable of resisting the activity of the Soviet armed forces on their national territories and across it. Even the most senior commanders of Warsaw Pact armies were deprived of an operational (combined arms) education and command experience. Warsaw Pact countries possessed Ministries of Defense and general staffs, but in crisis, emergency, and conflict these entities had no authority. In their conduct of military operations (e.g., the crushing of the "Prague spring") military commanders took orders directly from command organs established by the general staff of the Soviet armed forces. In peacetime, they were trained, equipped, and deployed according to Soviet (and largely Soviet general staff) directives.

In contrast, Ukraine did not possess even the pretence of a national army in 1991, yet because Ukrainian officers formed a large proportion of senior command personnel in the Soviet armed forces, Ukraine's current military establishment has a collective memory and some experience in planning the operations of armies and fronts, as well as a rich military–scientific background in the "art of war." In content much of this background fails to speak to Ukraine's current security challenges, but in form it has encouraged an integrated approach and a desire to engage with first principles.

A further inducement to defense mindedness arises from the fact that Ukraine is a nonaligned country, proximate to areas of tension and adjacent to a far greater country, the Russian Federation, whose commitment to its long-term independence is questionable. This position has been a salutary discipline. It has stimulated deep if not always clear thinking about the ends and means of security policy, and it has fostered habits of self-reliance on the part of much of the political and military establishment. In contrast, the expectation and eventual achievement of NATO membership have not helped to foster defense mindedness on the part of the Visegrad three. For a great proportion of the political establishments of these countries, NATO has been seen as the solution to security problems rather than a framework for resolving them. In Central Europe, this attitude has retarded defense reform and still retards it.

In 1996, nonalignment, vulnerability, and defense mindedness combined to produce an official statement of first principles, the National Security Concept of Ukraine, which is a document of exemplary coherence and realism. As a state document, ratified by the *Verkhovna Rada* in January 1997, the Concept is legally binding. It dwells upon three dangers: that Ukraine's economic, civic, and institutional weaknesses could become vulnerabilities; that these vulnerabilities could be exploited by actors, internal or external, with harmful political ends; and that in view of these dangers, crises and "emergency situations"—ecological, industrial, or financial—could escalate in magnitude and in geographical scale into conflict.[7] By identifying the "strengthening of civil society" as the most important of nine national security priorities, the Concept's authors expressed their conviction that transparency was dangerously low and that both state and society were dangerously weak. In several other respects, the Concept is noteworthy:

- It articulates a conceptually rich catalogue of "main potential threats" (political, economic, social, military, ecological, scientific, and technological informational) based on the premise that "situations threatening our national security are in most cases *precisely regional*" and that security is likely to be threatened by the *"combination* of factors" in specific regions.[8]

- It calls for a coordinated, cost-effective division of labor between law enforcement, security, and military bodies subordinated to the Ministry of Defense. It is understood that the latter's function is to localize an area of tension swiftly and prevent the "combination of factors" escalating or being exploited by external actors.[9]

- It demands what is urgent not only in Ukraine, but throughout East Central Europe: an understanding of the nonmilitary dimensions of security by national armed forces and, on the part of civil agencies (health, safety, emergency services), an understanding of the defense aspects of their responsibilities.

A better expression of the need to integrate national security with civilian democratic control could hardly be found, but in this sphere as in other domains the contrast between thinking and action in Ukraine can be deeply dispiriting. This is not to say that there has not been substantial progress in rationalizing the military system, increasing political authority over that system, and opening it up to democratic scrutiny. In all of these respects, there has been a steady and positive trend.

Yet even success must be set against a less than favorable context. The defense and security system of Ukraine is heavily weighted toward presidential authority, even more so than the political system as a whole, and the equation between presidential control and civilian control—not to say civilian democratic control—is unquestioned in much of the defense and security establishment. In the wake of what became known as a "Kuchmagate" scandal, the dubiousness of this equation has become apparent.[10] Nevertheless, in this sphere, like in others in Ukraine, the principle of the lesser evil must always arbitrate judgment. For all its evident defects, codified and institutionalized presidential authority is preferable to the authority of "shadow structures" (who still dominate the civil economy), military "clans" (a serious problem in the armed forces until 1996), and the rule of "spontaneous processes." These processes include the plunder of military infrastructure, the suborning of military inspectors by military commanders, unregulated arms sales, and de facto privatizations of state enterprises, not to mention military gangsterism and the de facto privatization of military units. All these post-Communist "negative phenomena," readily observable in the armed forces of the Russian Federation, are below significant levels in Ukraine and are steadily diminishing. Moreover, unless a Ukrainian president wishes to violate the constitution, his authority is far from absolute. In three areas at least, there are grounds for encouragement.

The Legal and Regulatory Base

Unless the institutions and rules comprising the defense and security system are codified, clear, and stable democratic control risks producing chaos and authoritarianism risks degenerating into arbitrary power. Even if these ills can be avoided, in societies undergoing rapid transition it is almost certain that vacuums in law and authority will be filled by intrigue and trials of strength. In Ukraine and other countries, there will be no institutional stability without clear and authoritative answers to the questions, "Who commands?" "Who serves?" "Who allocates money?" "Who spends it?" "Who is accountable for what?" and "Who is answerable to whom?"

To be sure, we need to know what the laws are before we can welcome or condemn the stability they create. Adolf Hitler justifiably claimed that he had instituted a "legal revolution" in Germany. Long before Russian President Putin entered the scene, leaders of the CPSU and KGB venerated "dictatorship of the law." Where law is concerned, independent Ukraine has departed from these illiberal and totalitarian precedents. In Ukraine, the enemy of democracy has not been the country's laws, but the weakness of the legal order and the ability of the powerful to defy it. But where the armed forces are concerned (though not so clearly the security services), the legal framework has been progressively strengthened, and for the better. Between 1991 and

2000, the *Verkhovna Rada* adopted 125 laws connected with the military and security system. Particularly in recent years, the NSDC and *Rada* have given obsessive attention to providing a detailed, normative framework for those who operate in this system. These laws, which have become more specific, realistic, and internally consistent over the years, generally fall into four categories:

1. Laws promulgating security policy. As in the former USSR, the development of security policy is deemed to require a hierarchical approach. Key "blocks" in the modern Ukrainian hierarchy are Constitution of Ukraine (1996), National Security Concept (1997), Military Doctrine (1993, with probable replacement 2001), State Program on Armed Forces Reform and Development 2001–2005 (2000, superseding that of 1996), state programs for other force ministries, State Program for Weapons and Military Equipment Development (2000), and programs for individual armed services, branches, and sectors.

2. Laws governing the roles, competencies, and functioning of armed forces and security bodies: "On the Armed Forces of Ukraine," "On the Border Troops of Ukraine," "On the Internal Troops of the Ministry of Internal Affairs of Ukraine," "On the Security Service of Ukraine," and so on.

3. Laws governing the manning and supply of the services.

4. Laws governing the finance and control (oversight) of military activity.

Well before Kuchmagate in November 2000, the kindest thing a cynic would say was that defense and security bodies operated fully in accordance with legal norms except when they were overridden by "higher" considerations. Yet until norms of conduct and a body of laws exist, it is impossible to speak of departures from norms and illegal acts. The growing coherence and density of the legal framework in Ukraine's defense sphere—a world apart from the incoherence that still prevails in spheres such as finance, export licensing, and taxation—limit arbitrary actions and strengthen the risk that such actions will be exposed and censured. They are a precondition for lawful, accountable conduct, even if they do not guarantee it.

Institutionalization

Like effective laws, effective institutions are not ends in themselves. A defining feature of totalitarian systems (as opposed to simple despotisms) is that they institutionalize (and often depersonalize) the power of small groups of people. On balance in Ukraine—a country in which a balance must always be struck—the core defense institutions have tended to moderate presidential authority, modifying it into executive authority.

Moreover, a core institution with limited but not insubstantial powers, the *Verkhovna Rada*, is independent of the executive and often in opposition to it. Not only does the *Rada* possess a measure of final authority (e.g., the right to sack ministers, even if the right is circumscribed in practice); it has measurable and very inconvenient authority in several respects (e.g., over the establishment of foreign military bases and facilities in Ukraine and the deployment of Ukrainian forces abroad). Proof that these are real powers is demonstrated by the fact that only after a pro-presidential majority emerged in March 2000 was it possible to secure ratification of three long-pending items of legislation central to Ukraine's cooperation with NATO: the Status of Forces Agreement, the Open Skies Agreement, and authorization of KFOR deployment for the Ukrainian element of the Ukrainian–Polish battalion in Kosovo.

But it is in the budgetary sphere where the *Rada's* authority has grown most substantially and constructively. It is also in this sphere where the challenges of establishing civil democratic control can be seen most vividly. Until recently, the prerogatives granted to the *Rada* under the constitution to approve the defense budget did not provide a constructive check on executive power. In the absence of a transparent and disaggregated budget and sufficient corporate expertise, the *Rada's* Commission on National Security and Defense had little to scrutinize, little basis for questioning the costs and assessments presented to them, and little choice but to "take it or leave it." More than once they refused to take it, with the consequence that the armed forces suffered from ill-judged cuts. Today's realities, whilst far from encouraging, are vastly preferable to those, which existed only a few years ago. The commission's basis of knowledge has grown (assisted by growing collaboration with NGO's) and its prerogatives strengthened by the work of the *Rada's* Accounting Chamber. In addition, the chamber as well as commission members now have considerably greater possibilities to participate in state budget formation, alongside the relevant executive bodies (presidential administration, NSDC, General Military Inspectorate, and the State Audit Chamber of the Cabinet of Ministers). Not least important, the armed forces have become more open and less reluctant to share information. At the same time, they are becoming more aware of the costs of their own manpower, assets, and operations. As a result, the budget itself is presented in a more detailed form and in a format that is beginning to resemble Western practice. In view of these improvements, one congenitally skeptical set of experts has concluded that "budget formation is gradually improving and becoming transparent for the legislative branch and for the public."[11]

State institutions, too, have become more mature with the passage of time. Again, qualifications must be entered. The National Security and Defense Council—the body that according to the constitution "co-ordinates and controls [*kontroliruet*] the activity of executive bodies in the sphere of national security and defense"—is supported by a largely civilian, eighty-strong professional staff of high quality and integrity. But the NSDC illustrates the classic ambiguity present in Ukrainian institutions. Does it "monitor" (*kontroliruet*) these bodies, or does it have authority over them? In practice, the answer has not depended upon the constitutional powers of the NSDC—which the authors of the constitution perhaps made deliberately ambiguous by the use of the word *kontrol'*—but the power of NSDC's secretary and his rela-tionship with the president (who as chairman of the NSDC not only appoints the secretary but his deputies).[12] Under Secretary Volodymyr Horbulin (1996–1999) the NSDC tended to be a strong body, sufficiently strong to ensure that the armed services did not wield authority over the military members of its staff (some of whom felt confident enough to criticize the military leadership in open-source publications). Fol-lowing the appointment of one of the president's key rivals, Yevhen Marchuk, to Horbulin's post in November 1999, the relationship with the presidential administration became more competitive. Even be-fore Marchuk's appointment, Kuchma chose deputy secretaries based as much on their ability to monitor the secretary as the defense and security bodies. In October 2000, Kuchma resubordinated the National Institute of Strategic Studies—a key research arm of the NSDC with a highly respected international profile—to the presidential adminis-tration. The changing fortunes of the quasi-analogous U.S. National Security Council are a reminder that there are limits to institutional stability even in mature democracies.[13] But in an immature democ-racy, does the personalization of decisions about institutional preroga-tives strengthen stability, let alone civilian democratic control?

In principle, questions are also raised by the prerogatives of a sec-ond core institution, the General Military Inspectorate (GMI) under the president of Ukraine. A network of information-analysis depart-ments now exists in the armed forces as well as in other non-MOD subordinated security formations. On the basis of their work and the work of subordinate inspectorates specific to each of these establish-ments the GMI has powerful tools to ensure that defense and security bodies operate in accordance with executive directives. The GMI is a potent institution. It provides political authorities with an effective means of supervising military structures as well as making their ac-tivity more transparent. But the GMI is also the tool of the president. An indicator of progress toward civilian democratic control would be greater transparency within the GMI, a broader definition of Ukraine's "political authorities," and wider publication, in classified and un-classified form, of the GMI's work and findings. It could be some time before the presidential administration concludes that such transparency would be in the interest of Ukraine.

Overcoming the Tyranny of Theory

The Soviet military educational system was rigidly Clausewitzian. On the one hand, it instilled the notion that armed forces were a "tool of policy" and that only political leaders could decide whether war was an appropriate means for achieving state objectives. On the other hand, it instilled the notion that if used at all, the military tool would be used to implement state policy by means of war. The responsibility of the military establishment was to be up to the task. Far from being "unthinkable," this task was an ever-present possibility. To Soviet officers it was axiomatic that, even if war was not "fatalistically inevitable," the potential of war was inherent in the international system. To the products of this system—including the majority of Ukraine's most senior officers—the notion that the state should, even for a specified period, be without armed forces designed for general war is not only profoundly misconceived, but immoral. Fortunately, both the National Security Concepts and the State Program 2001–2005, with its emphasis on complex emergencies and "neutralizing" conflict, demonstrate that this legacy is slowly being overcome. Today, it is widely accepted that "Ukraine is unlikely to face serious threats of military aggression within the next 5–7 years."

Yet the rigidly Clausewitzian framework has imposed a further constraint on thought and action. The framework was oppressively theoretical, and theory (military science) intruded into every aspect of defense policy. As Clausewitzians, members of Ukraine's military establishment draw a strict distinction between the political leadership's responsibility to reform the entire system (military reform) and the military's duty to work out the forces and capabilities needed (armed forces reform). This has encouraged the armed forces to plan for all contingencies and wait for political will to emerge, rather than identify clear and achievable priorities today. Here, too, the State Program and the discussion surrounding it not only suggest that the military establishment is beginning to address questions of means and ends; they are beginning to recognize that it is their responsibility to do so and not somebody else's.

Independent Civilian Expertise

The emergence and development of NGOs with expertise in defense and security matters has been one of the most promising developments in Ukraine since 1991. There are now almost fifty nongovernmental research centers in Ukraine. Although only about a dozen of these are regularly active in the defense sphere, those are often of high quality and are steadily gaining in influence. Among these are the Ukrainian Center for Economic and Political Studies (whose president, Anatoliy Grytsenko, was director of analysis at the NSDC until 1999), the Ukrainian Center for International Security Studies, the Center for Peace, Conversion, and Foreign Policy, the Ukrainian Center of Independent Political Research, and the Atlantic Council of Ukraine (whose president, Major General (Ret'd.) Vadym Grechaninov, was military adviser to President Kuchma between 1994 and 1996). Moreover, the National Institute of Strategic Studies (which before its resubordination to the presidential administration in autumn 2000 was a component of NSDC) contains about sixty analysts, many of whom now write with fresh and independent perspectives. In addition, a number of media outlets also cover defense issues, some quite critically and in at least one case (the prestigious Russian- and Ukrainian-language weekly *Zerkalo Nedeli*) with commendable seriousness. Equally promising is the extent to which the armed forces have overcome their former inhibition about collaboration with NGOs.

An impressive feature of the seminar and conference scene in Ukraine is that even when attendance is restricted to small numbers and very senior official participants, representatives of the more prominent NGOs now tend to be invited as a matter of course. Although this still cannot be said of the news media, here too, shyness and hostility are disappearing. Western activity and presence by means of NATO and bilateral training programs and the funding of NGOs has reached significant levels. A number of foreign specialists now regularly collaborate with official structures as well as NGOs on defense reform and other issues relevant to Ukraine's national security. This activity has played an instrumental role in breaking down barriers in Ukraine.

In two other key areas, there has been demonstrable if still questionable progress.

1. Arms Sales. During the first three years of independence, "spontaneous processes" were the norm in this still closed and opaque area, and the persistent rumors that these processes cost the state $20 to $30 billion appear to have foundation. The sphere is now formally under the control of several state bodies, with particular influence exercised by the state company Ukrspetseksport, the State Export Control Service, and the Commission for Export Control Policy and Military–Technical Cooperation with Foreign Countries. Effectively it is under control of the State Security Service (SBU; *Sluzhba Bezpeky Ukrainy*), and Colonel General Volodymyr Radchenko, head of the Commission for Export Control Policy, was head of the SBU until 1998. Presidential and SBU control do not guarantee com-

plete correspondence between declaratory policy and state action, but it can at least be said that the activity in this sphere has become state activity and that it reflects the intentions of these authorities.

2. Defense Industry. The decision of President Kuchma to establish a State Commission for Ukraine's Defense–Industrial Complex (VPK) in July 2000 under former NSDC Secretary Horbulin could well help to consolidate and rationalize this once excessively integrated and now disembodied sector of Soviet power. Already the MOD Central Economic Department under Major General Valeriy Muntiyan has played a constructive role in providing a comprehensive audit of VPK assets and facilities. Despite nine years of post-Soviet turmoil, it is still questionable whether the key players in this sector understand market mechanisms and the "art of the possible." More questionable still is whether the closed nature of this sector is conducive to promoting such an understanding.

THE BOTTLE HALF EMPTY

The secular problems identified at the start of this chapter penetrate all spheres and elude solution. The political philosopher John Gray has defined civil society as the domain of voluntary associations, market exchanges and private institutions within and through which individuals having urgent conceptions and diverse and often competitive purposes may coexist in peace. The communist system's war on civil society was well fought. For all its failings, the system was remarkably effective in ensuring that few people possessed the knowledge, competence, and self-confidence to manage public affairs, or even their own. Without a strong civil society, there will not be a civic state: a domain of state institutions governed by a coherent and transparent body of rules and subordinate to codified, limited authority, in which the ethos of professionalism and "rightful conduct" is sufficiently developed to penalize corrupt practices, expose "subjective agendas," and resist unlawful pressure. In Ukraine the state may be overbearing, but it is also weak because the ethos of rightful conduct, the instinct of self-regulation, and the powers of resistance are deficient.[14] In the defense and security sphere, the weakness of state and society has two major consequences.

Absence of Transparency

Transparency exists when we know what decisions are taken, where they are taken, by whom they are taken, and why they are taken. Where the constitutional order has foes and the state has enemies, transparency is not always a virtue and secrecy may be essential to collective survival. In mature democracies, enormous efforts are taken to ensure that secrecy is confined to these urgent and unusual domains, that

security services answer to institutions that are themselves accountable, and that the employees of these services are a full part of the
community of people and values they are sworn to protect. The laws
do not classify as "secrets" that which is merely embarrassing to state
officials or that which reflects poorly upon their competence, and as
long as their secrets are not compromised, the law does not shield
security services from public scrutiny any more than it shields other
institutions. In these respects, democracy has yet to arrive in Ukraine.
In fact, the level of inhibition about conducting public and expert discussion is palpably greater than it was in the post-independence period. Within recent years, NGO research on the armed forces and
defense sector has become bolder, better, and more respected by the
armed services themselves. One would be hard put to find any critical
analysis, let alone an equivalent standard of analysis of the MVD, SBU,
or State Tax Administration. If the lack of transparency in these bodies
makes their lives easier, does it really help them? How many of their
accomplices are willing accomplices, and how many can they trust?
When scandals and horrors emerge (e.g., the murder in May 2000 of
the well-known composer Ihor Bilozir by assailants tied to the MVD
and SBU), will the public give these services the benefit of the doubt?[15]

Transparency is also injured by the hermetic quality of Ukraine's
defense and security bodies. So is operational effectiveness. Proceeding from the 1997 National Security Concept, the State Program of
Armed Forces Development and Reform calls for Ukraine's three Operational Commands—strategic joint commands in all but name—to
become the operational lynchpin of the defense system by 2005. Over
the next five years, they must be transformed into structures capable
of mobilizing, commanding, and supporting military forces in the tasks
of responding to peacetime emergency, as well as preventing, containing, and "neutralizing" armed conflict. This requires the capability to
command multicomponent forces, including formations not subordinated to the MOD in peacetime. But this raises fundamental questions. The State Program was drawn up by the Ministry of Defense
and is binding upon MOD armed forces. Until a state of emergency
arises, the MOD has no prerogatives over other force structures. Under the oversight of NSDC Secretary Marchuk, reform and development programs have been drawn up by other armed formations. But
has the NSDC used its authority to integrate these various programs,
and has it been given such authority in the first place? As Anatoliy
Grytsenko has noted,

Unfortunately, amendments to the Law of Ukraine, "On the Defense of
Ukraine" of October 5, 2000 replaced the term "Ukraine's Military organization" with "Ukraine's armed forces and other military formations." . . . This

(seemingly purely terminological) amendment is rather important. It poses a danger of state authorities' treatment of every power structure in Ukraine (and, correspondingly, the issues of their development, reforming and funding) in isolation from the other. Therefore, the probability of revising the present non-optimal division of functions (and, correspondingly, the manpower and resources) between the power structures that form the Military organization of Ukraine decreases. None of the previous such attempts has been a success, as corporate benefits always overshadowed state interests.[16]

Until state interests overshadow "corporate benefits," will Ukraine be able to mount multicomponent operations or will it merely succeed in appointing commanders of multicomponent forces? If these operations are to be integrated and effective, will there not have to be compatible programs of military development, compatible concepts of operations, common elements of training, and the establishment of joint committees and other linking structures between MOD armed forces and other security bodies? Will there not also have to be a far greater degree of trust than exists today?

Even in the least opaque bodies of state power, the armed services subordinated to the Ministry of Defense, the hierarchical approach that prevails in Ukraine limits the flow of information and stifles initiative. In the U.K. Ministry of Defense and at NATO headquarters there is a well-developed committee system straddling different administrative blocks. Such committees make most defense policy: interdepartmental (and civil–military) in composition, with access to all data bearing on their area of functional competence. But in the absence of such a system, blocks become compartments, and areas of relevance to the whole can be hidden from almost everyone. The General Military Inspectorate of the president was established to counter this tendency, but as an example of the top-down approach, it is also part of the problem. In Ukrainian institutions, vertical coordination has been developed to excess. There is a dearth of horizontal integration, and management from below is almost unknown.

Civilian Expertise

There is an unbreakable connection between the quality of civilian control and the quality of civilians. Where civilians are relatively ignorant about defense or, as in much of Central Europe, contemptuous of the military profession, the armed forces will naturally resist being controlled by them.[17] Given their history and corporate upbringing, it is not surprising that Ukrainian military officers find presidential control congenial and accountability to the NSDC and other state bodies normal. After eight years of living in an independent country with a limited degree of democracy, it is also not surprising that they accept parliamentary oversight and increasingly open discussion with NGOs and other public bodies. Yet they still draw the line at having a civilian minister of defense. Are they wrong to do so? Valeriy Shmarov's tenure as minister (1994 to 1996) was injurious to all parties. If it did not definitively prove that "civilians know nothing about defense," it proved that inexpert civilians will not establish good working relationships with the armed forces. Yet the presumed shortcomings of such civilians are only part of the problem. On what basis will inexpert civilians be appointed? In the view of Oleksandr Parfionov,

> The present Ukrainian practice of high-level nominations shows that they are usually the result of apparatus intrigues that are absolutely non-transparent for the public. The nominee's affiliation with a certain influential political grouping plays an important role. This practice gives reason for concern that a civilian Defense Minister appointed by the president will remain beyond the scope of control of other institutions of state power. In particular, he or she may slip beyond the control of the legislative branch, which may lead to excessive concentration of power in the President's hands.[18]

As Parfionov goes on to conclude, "the key precondition is the creation of a civil service." Yet Ukraine does not possess a professional civil service, a corps of administrators whose political neutrality is unquestioned and who are competent and expert enough to execute government policy. Instead, it has officials (many of them too politicized and many of those more interested in their careers than their work) and large numbers of *sluzhbovtsii* (functionaries): individuals whose principal ethos is deference to bosses and "work to rule." Do the armed forces resent civilian control, or do they resent being controlled by those who are less professional than they are? Whatever the answer to this question, the armed forces are probably correct that the time has not yet arrived for a civilian minister of defense in Ukraine.

Incongruence between State Policy and State Practice

Unless there is a fundamental congruence between the goals of the state and those of its core institutions and instruments, the state will have little chance of achieving its declared goals. There is, for example, a fundamental incongruence between a national security policy based on nonalignment, integration with Europe, and close partnership with NATO and the situation that O. Mykolaeva wrote about in 1996, where, "sitting in classes, Ukrainian officers are rehearsing a situation in which a coalition of western and southern states comprising 50 divisions attacks Ukraine."[19] The measure of progress in Ukraine's armed forces since 1996 is that this incongruence is recognized and it is gradually disappearing.

But the same cannot be said with confidence about the SBU and elements of the Ministry of Internal Affairs (MVS). The behavior of these bodies has led many to ask themselves what state, what political order, what community, and what system of values they are defending. Is the ethos of secrecy (and the related ethos of security) primarily to blame? Reflection suggests three other factors.

As noted, at the Union Republican level, these bodies survived the Soviet collapse relatively intact. The custodians of independent Ukraine therefore faced a stark choice: either to dismiss the greater proportion of these establishments and construct security establishments from scratch—a course pursued only in the Baltic states and post-Communist Czechoslovakia—or to do what all other successor states had done and eliminate the overtly disloyal and proceed to "reform" the structures inherited. Ukraine made the conservative, understandable but fateful choice. It took what was available. Unlike Estonia, Ukraine could not rely upon a vigilant civil society to mount guard over "their" state while a committed corps of citizens was first identified and then laboriously turned into professionals. Unlike Czechoslovakia, Ukraine faced security threats. It still faces them. The reasons that make it difficult to reform armed forces during a war—though unless they are reformed by war they are often defeated—make it difficult to reform security services under threat. Now that the dish is cooked, the country has to eat it: security services dominated by the former KGB and MVS that have preserved much of the mental inheritance of these services and some of the methods, too.

The second factor is the "objective logic" of the methods themselves in contemporary Ukrainian conditions. Unlike the FBI, MI5, British Special Branch, and other Western analogues, the internal services of the KGB (and much of the MVD) were instruments of administrative control over society. Today their successors remain networks of influence, not only in state structures but also in partnership with regional authorities and with much of the "semiprivate" sector.[20] Thanks to this influence—their ability to advance careers or obstruct them, grant licenses or deny them, provide tax privileges or tax inspections—these services not only moderate heterodoxy, they provide themselves with collaborators. One can certainly exaggerate this influence or minimize the ability of groups and individuals to resist it, and one will frequently be told that one has done both. Far less frequently will one be told such practices will be rewarded with dismissal and imprisonment. The position of Western security services could not be in greater contrast to this. These services have no "presence," let alone influence in society. Unlike SBU employees (who are paid 40 percent more than their military equivalents), they have very moderate salaries and only a moderate social status. The overwhelming majority of citizens—those who are neither subversives nor candidates for jobs requiring a security clearance—will live out most of their lives without ever needing to come into contact with them. Aside from that part of their information that comes from criminal informants, the rest comes from voluntary cooperation. But if Ukraine's special services could not exert influence over its informants, what degree of cooperation could it expect? Until civil society is strong and self-confident in Ukraine, until ordinary people see the state as "their" state, the answer is likely to be none. The conclusion is inescapable. The character of a country's security services is inseparable from the character of a country's society. The methods of the SBU and MVS reflect the weakness of civil society in Ukraine. But they also prolong its weakness. It remains to be seen whether the Gongadze affair produces a more assertive civil society or a more submissive one.

CONCLUSION

Civil democratic control of armed forces is a diminishing problem in Ukraine. Part of the reason for this is that in this sphere the Soviet legacy has not been entirely harmful to Ukraine. It has produced professional armed forces with remarkably little lust for power. Another part of the reason is that the country's leadership has not relied on the armed forces to keep themselves in power and, as a result, have not sought to politicize the military establishment. A third reason is the growing stature and competence of NGOs, the steady growth of civilian expertise, and, correspondingly, the military establishment's greater openness to criticism and discussion. Not least important is the fact, only briefly touched upon in this chapter, that international cooperation and experience, primarily through NATO's Partnership for Peace, has now exposed 16,000 fast-track servicemen to "Euro–Atlantic standards" of civil–military relations, not to say defense management, planning, and "operations other than war."

However, civil democratic control of the police and security system remains a considerable problem in Ukraine. In some spheres the problems are worsening rather than improving. Is it entirely coincidental that the MVS and SBU, largely ignored by PfP initiatives and bilateral programs "in the spirit of PfP," are not only among the least democratically minded but also among the least pro-Western institutions in the country? Yet leaving aside the problems of these services and the symbiotic relationship between security and democracy and state and society in Ukraine, an even greater problem remains. In the absence of trust between structures and echelons of power, significant levels of transparency, horizontal (interdepartmental) integration within the armed services, and working-level cooperation between institutions, can we speak of a defense and security system in Ukraine or merely of "armed forces and other formations"?

It could be harmful and not only unfortunate if current scandals and outrages overshadowed Ukraine's accomplishments in armed forces development and reform, not to say the ground gained by civilians—and independent civilian experts—in that process. Nevertheless, these outrages are a reminder that democratization is not inevitable in Ukraine and that the gains achieved can be eroded, or even reversed.

NOTES

1. Major General Vadym Grechaninov, "Truly Democratic Civilian Control over the Military Barely Emerges in Ukraine," *National Security and Defense* 11 (2000): 68.

2. The youngest officers (those with up to five years service) and the oldest (those with over twenty-five years service) scored highest in the most recent "lust for power" poll (16.3% and 14.3%, respectively). The breakdown for other years was five to fifteen years service, 9.9 percent; sixteen to twenty years service, 13 percent; twenty-one to twenty-five years service, 7.1 percent. Ibid., 23. According to another recent poll, only 7.1 percent of the Ukrainian population support "military rule." A. Bychenko and I. Zhdanov, "Poll on 'Nation, Power, Referendum,'" *National Security and Defense* 2 (2000): 9.

3. As cases in point, see Volodymyr Loginov, *National Security and Defense* 2 (2000): 63.

4. Unlike the MVS and KGB, the Soviet Ministry of Defense and Soviet general staff had no branches in the Union republics. With one exception, the organization of the Soviet armed forces was functional and operational, not territorial. In peacetime, they were organized into five arms of service under commanders in chief, who acted as administrative rather than operational heads of their services. In wartime, command and control was exercised by the general staff through "combined arms" commanders in individual Theatres of Military Activity (TVD) on external fronts. The one territorial component of defense organization, the USSR's fifteen military districts, grouped together entities responsible for conscription, training, and mobilization. But these districts were not territorially coterminous with Union republics, and they did not possess the capabilities and command structures required to plan or conduct coordinated military operations. What Ukraine inherited in 1991 were limbs without brain or body: three military districts and the forces that happened to be stationed in them.

5. This, of course, was not true under Jozef Stalin. Moreover, the Khrushchev era was characterized by numerous—and in the eyes of the military, capricious and damaging—interventions into military–technical policy. This "amateurism" and these inconsistencies and "hare-brained schemes" were a major reason that Khrushchev was ousted in October 1964. His successors placed a high premium on continuity, professionalism, and "stability of cadres," not only in the military sphere, but in others where Khrushchev had upset established bureaucratic interests.

6. The right to establish national armed forces was proclaimed in the *Verkhovna Rada's* Declaration of State Sovereignty on July 16, 1990, more than a year before Ukraine declared independence on August 24, 1991. The official

establishment of the armed forces of Ukraine did not precede but followed the establishment of a parliamentary Standing Commission for Questions of Security and Defense (February 26, 1991) and a Ministry of Defense (September 3, 1991). On October 22, 1991, units and formations of the Soviet armed forces on Ukrainian soil were nationalized. Nevertheless, concerns about the reliability of the armed forces were deemed substantial enough to justify the establishment of an altogether new military formation, the National Guard, on October 23, 1991, the day after units of the Soviet armed forces on Ukrainian territory were nationalized.

7. Albania provides perhaps the most virulent and extreme illustration of this paradigm, and also illustrates the role that political manipulation can play in such apparently "accidental" conflicts.

8. As paraphrased then by the director of the NSDC staff, O. Spirin, and V. Palamarchuk. The wording of the actual document is cautiously toned down (*Uryadoviy Kurier*, 1 March 1997).

9. In the words of Rear Admiral Yuriy Shalyt, Deputy Commander of NATO exercise Sea Breeze 1997, "In local conflicts or national disasters, which can also provoke conflicts, it is precisely military units with the right training that can and should set up a zone which would make it possible to direct or influence the processes occurring outside it, promote the consolidation of stability and order in the country or region and create the necessary conditions for the work of units from the Ukrainian emergency Situations Ministry" (*UNIAN*, 28 August 1997, cited in *BBC Summary of World Broadcasts: Former Soviet Union*, 30 August 1997).

10. In November–December 2000, Leonid Kuchma was publicly accused of overseeing a system of political intimidation and terror against independent journalists and opposition leaders in Ukraine. Several hundred hours of audio tapes, presented as secret recordings of presidential conversations with senior officials of the government, were submitted to the parliament as proof, causing an acute political crisis and mass demonstrations under anti-Kuchma slogans.

11. "Ukraine's Gains in Forming the System of Civilian Control over the Military," *National Security and Defense* 11 (2000): 19.

12. According to the constitution, apart from the president, the members of the NSDC comprise the prime minister, minister of defense, head of the SBU, minister of internal affairs, and minister of foreign affairs. The president may also appoint additional members, which include, the head of the presidential administration, chief of general staff, minister for emergencies, head of the State Committee for Protection of the State Border, minister of finance, minister of justice, minister of environmental protection and natural resources, president of the National Academy of Sciences, as well as the secretary of the NSDC, Yevhen Marchuk.

13. The strength of the U.S. NSC relative to other key departments, notably State and Defense is decided by the president, although it can also reflect competition between the personalities who head these departments. However, this writer knows of no examples where a U.S. president appointed a rival as his national security advisor and then used the appointment to undermine him. Both Yeltsin and Kuchma have done precisely this in appointing secretaries of the Russian Federation Security Council and the NSDC, respectively.

14. For a fuller discussion of the "civic state," see James Sherr, *Ukraine's New Time of Troubles* (Camberley, Sandhurst: Conflict Studies Research Center, 1998), 11–15.

15. Voronov, his assailant, was then a military officer, son of the then deputy chief of the Lviv department of the Ministry of Internal Affairs, who resigned immediately after the episode. According to several sources (e.g., the newspaper *Za Vilnu Ukrainu*, 3–10 July 2000), Voronov's companion was an officer in military counterintelligence, a branch of the armed forces subordinated not to the Ministry of Defense, but the Security Service of Ukraine.

16. Anatoliy Grytsenko, *National Security and Defense* 11 (2000): 3.

17. For a fuller discussion of these attitudes in Central Europe, see James Sherr, *NATO's New Members: A Model for Ukraine? The Example of Hungary* (Sandhurst: Conflict Studies Research Center, 2000).

18. Cited in Oleksandr Parfionov, *National Security abd Defense* 11 (2000): 8. Parfionov is executive director of the Ukrainian Center of International Security Studies.

19. O. Mykolayeva, "Servicemen Say: He Who Has Not Been in the Army Has Lost," *Zerkalo Nedeli*, 15–21 June 1996.

20. For a discussion of the origins and implications of the former KGB's role in business, see James Sherr, "Russia: Geopolitics and Crime," *The World Today* 51, no. 2 (1995): 32–36.

6

Civil–Military Relations in a Sovereign Ukraine: Contributing or Detracting from the Security of a New Nation?

Stacy R. Closson

> It is not within the army that one is likely to find the remedy against the vices of that army, but within the country as a whole.
> Alexis de Tocqueville, *Democracy in America*, vol. 2

In 2001 Ukraine embarks upon an important milestone in its efforts to create a democratic state.[1] Almost a decade into independence, Ukrainian senior leaders understand the value of the transformation of the defense establishment as part of the larger democratization process and espouse the establishment of proper civil–military affairs as crucial to this effort. What this state of civil–military affairs should comprise, however, remains to be defined. Ukraine's primary consideration, of course, is to address the dire straits of the economy and serious social and political challenges. A consolidated national consciousness must be formed to create new democratic and legitimate political institutions that address these challenges. As part of this effort, a strengthened civilian body must have political decision-making supremacy over the military, which in turn must accept this relationship not just in word, but as a core value in its professional ethos.

The military, however, is one of the institutions that is most constrained by a lack of resources, clear mission, positive image, and an as yet undemonstrated ability to rapidly adapt to the new realities of a sovereign, modern Ukraine. In order to address these deficiencies, defense reform must become part of the senior Ukrainian government decision makers' common vernacular. Previously, as both the Ukrainian presidential elections of 1994 and 1999 have shown, the government and public are primarily concerned with establishing a stable democratic society built on an accepted set of legal norms and economic prosperity. "Defense reform"—a term used by the NATO allies and others when referring to the restructuring and transformation of Ukraine's armed forces—is only marginally discussed in the context of the economy, thus viewing the military primarily as a consumer and not a guarantor of security. This is largely due to the fact that Ukraine, to date, has not faced an immediate threat to its security. However, the government cannot continue to take this for granted.

Ukrainian public opinion on defense reform is increasingly voluminous, through unions, nongovernmental organizations, and the media. This has played a part in the heightened sense of urgency in the Ukrainian government's agenda to conduct a comprehensive review of the entire security apparatus, beginning with the creation of an interagency panel to conclude an updated National Security Concept and Military Doctrine. In the interim, the general staff of the armed forces has created the "2005 State Program for the Re-development and Reform of the Armed Forces," which, unfortunately, will require financial resources beyond the current allocated means. On a deeper level, it will require Ukraine to overcome behavioral factors, such as ideology and political culture, party politics, and personalities of leaders, to meet the goals set out in this plan. Paramount to this effort is a new understanding of civil–military relations in order to effect both the internal reform efforts as well as Ukraine's relationships with Euro–Atlantic institutions.

There is an abundance of theoretical and practical literature on civil–military relations, with a concentration on the former Soviet Union and Eastern Europe, and one can also refer to the comparative studies of Latin America, where military dictatorships are common. After a preliminary review, there appear to be several specific case studies by Western scholars of civil–military relations in Ukraine in the early 1990s taken up by a few Ukrainian scholars publishing works in Ukrainian and English from 1996 to the present. This in itself is a sign of progress; independent Ukrainian scholars are addressing civil–military relations and, in the case of Anatoliy Grytsenko of the Ukrainian Center for Economic and Political Studies, are offering prescriptions.[2]

However, the limited number of Ukrainian case studies by non-Ukrainians produces a gap in the literature concerning Ukraine's overall efforts to address this fundamental issue in democracy building. Further, whereas the traditional notion of civilian control is addressed in past literature and comparative studies referencing Ukraine, the role of the various security units is not addressed in any detail.[3] Civilian control of the various security units as well as their intrarelationships can play a key stabilizing or destabilizing role in building newly sovereign democratic states. Therefore, this chapter will attempt to evaluate the relationship, at present, between the armed forces—restricted to the Ministry of Defense—and their relationship with civilians on four levels: (1) the role of the presidential administration and the *Rada* in creating legislation and determining the direction and development of the armed forces, (2) the relationship between the Ministry of Defense and the other security units, (3) the role of civilians within the Ministry of Defense, and (4) the relationship between the armed forces and society.

For Ukrainians (and non-Ukrainians alike) who are confused about what defines civilian–military affairs or civil control of the military, or for those who are not convinced of the necessity and/or parameter of civilian control in a transitioning state, this chapter will address some relevant questions, such as, What is civilian control of the military? and Why is civilian control of Ukraine's armed forces so important, particularly at this time? The word "control" often is construed to mean a restrictive regime. Anatoliy Grystenko explains that the translation in the common Ukrainian usage connotes the access to information about the activity of power structures, and the right of state authorities to audit and inspect military units and supervise the observance of human rights in the army.[4] This chapter argues that proper civil–military affairs, or civilian oversight of the defense apparatus, is a sign of a developing democratic society and an end to the authoritarian regime, and is therefore a strategic and necessary reform effort that Ukraine should continue to work toward.

STATUS OF CIVIL–MILITARY AFFAIRS IN UKRAINE

The evolution of civil–military affairs in Ukraine appears to be hampered by a governmental system that has failed to address sociological, political, and economic factors. Sociologically, the Western model, for Ukrainians, is perhaps reminiscent of the commissariat of the Soviet system, where the Communist Party dominated the Ministry of Defense and decisions of senior officers. At the root of civil–military affairs is the notion of transparency and the role of society in government affairs. This requires an open evaluation of the "redevelopment" of the armed forces through multiple layers of society and its organizations, from the highest levels of government to the mothers of the sons and daughters serving in the military.

Politically, the choice of a strategic orientation for Ukraine, and the ability to openly state that choice, varies among political orientations within the Ukrainian leadership and among political parties, particularly concerning Russia. Growing regional divisiveness and disillusionment with the West are also posing challenges for Ukrainian senior leaders to establish clearly defined national interests and a resultant national security strategy and military doctrine for all security services. A lack of strategy is further exacerbated by hyperinflation and an unrelenting economic crisis hampering the reform of the armed forces. A nation of people that blame a bloated officer corps on competition for scarce resources are likely to pressure the leadership to decrease the size of the armed forces. Ukraine needs a cadre of professional defense and security analysts to take it into the next decade, with the task of clearly defining the mission of the military based on realistic threats and ensuring that a national force is adequately trained, equipped, combat ready, and in place to meet future challenges. The current institutional structure is not configured to do this.

WHAT DOES "CIVILIAN CONTROL" OF THE MILITARY REALLY MEAN?

Since 1996, Ukrainian leaders have been members of the NATO Partnership for Peace Program, have conducted bilateral military engagement with allies, and have participated in the Organization for Security and Cooperation Europe (OSCE). Political–military engagement requires that member nations of these organizations attain a proper level of civilian control of the military. Ukraine is versed in NATO's 1991 Strategic Concept, which espouses civil–military relations as a shared democratic value between East (Central and Eastern Europe) and West. Further, the Partnership for Peace Program's Framework Document lists many aspects of democratic civil–military relations:

- Transparency in national defense planning and budgeting processes.
- Enduring democratic control of armed forces.
- Clear legal and constitutional frameworks.
- Chain of command from the military to government through a civilian minister of defense.
- Qualified civilians working with the military on defense policy, requirements, and budget.
- A clear division of professional responsibility between civilian and military personnel.
- Effective oversight and review by parliament.[5]

What Ukraine may ultimately seek to attain is not civilian control—a term that tends to have a negative connotation for general officers across nations—but democratic control, of which proper civilian oversight is a basic ingredient. NATO allies and PfP partners agree that to enhance democratic control of defense establishments (i.e., armed forces and various security units) is important for three reasons.[6] First, it is widely accepted that democratic control of defense establishments increases the likelihood that a country remains at peace, thus improving its security and the security of its neighbors. Democratic control balances the whole spectrum of national interests against those of the military, which would prevail if the military were allowed to become the key foreign policy-maker vice of one the instruments of foreign policy. Second, democratic control of defense establishment provides oversight, which should result in greater transparency and spawn a more effective and efficient military. Third, it provides the military with the legitimacy it needs to be respected by society.

From recent experience, the Ukrainian government understands that the notion of civil–military affairs is more complex than appointing a civilian to the helm of the Ministry of Defense or creating the position of deputy minister of defense for military policy. Further, over six years of courses at the George C. Marshall Center in Garmisch, Germany, and Monterey's Center for Civil Military Relations, as well as NATO–sponsored and bilateral conferences on this subject, have provided adequate information on the parameters of civil–military affairs.

At the very foundation of a professional armed force is a successful civil–military partnership. This may take the form of a constitutional mandate, a parliament that affects reform laws and appropriates an adequate budget, a civilian head and professional civilian staff leading the defense ministry, or a carefully orchestrated public-affairs campaign on roles and missions that takes into account the public voice. A functioning civil–military relationship contains parts or the sum of all of these ingredients. Along these lines, Samuel Huntington writes that the ordering of its civil–military relations is basic to a nation's military security policy. This is achieved through a complex balancing of power and attitudes between civilian and military groups: "Nations that have achieved this balance have a great advantage in the search for security by increasing their likelihood of reaching right answers to the operating issues of military policy. Nations that fail to develop a balanced pattern of civil–military relations squander their resources and run uncalculated risks."[7]

Relationship between the Armed Forces and the State

In general, Ukrainian government guidance for the military leadership is ambiguous at best and limited and outdated at worst. In addition, the role of various governmental bodies, particularly parliament

(*Verkhovna Rada*), in providing civilian oversight of the military is weak. Ambiguous guidance can be found in the 1996 constitution and subsequent documents, including the National Security Concept (1997), the Main Directions of Ukraine's Foreign Policy (1993), the Military Doctrine of Ukraine (1993), various laws establishing the armed forces and other security forces (1991–1994), and foreign policy speeches given by senior administration officials.

The constitution and National Security Concept both call for civilian oversight of the military, while outlining the main purpose of the Ukrainian armed forces and key aspects of military doctrine. These include the protection of Ukraine's sovereignty and territorial integrity and the affirmation of Ukraine's neutrality and nonnuclear status. The president is named the supreme commander in chief and the National Security and Defense Council is the main coordinating body for the president's actions to uphold the constitution.

The definition of state bodies' roles and missions pertaining to security and defense matters are defined in the "Law of Ukraine on the Defense of Ukraine" and other related laws. Depending on the issue, oversight of the armed forces is administered by (1) the president, including the General Military Inspectorate, Cabinet of Ministers, and the National Security and Defense Council; (2) *Rada*, particularly the Committee on National Security and Defense and the Budget Committee; and (3) Ministries of Finance and Economics and various state committees responsible for the military industrial complex. However, given the lack of civilian experts on military matters in some or all of these organizations, particularly the Cabinet of Ministers and the National Security and Defense Council, deference is given to the military for filling this role.

The *Rada* was an important early actor in the creation of Ukraine's security apparatus, including its instrumental role in creating the armed forces of Ukraine and the first Ukrainian Ministry of Defense, and in establishing a neutral and nuclear-free defense policy. However, after its initial role in 1990–1991, oversight by the *Rada* of the armed forces has been weak, including limited accountability of power structures to it. For example, parliament has no authority over the appointment of ministers and deputy ministers in charge of the defense sector.

Presidential decrees and not legislation adopted by the *Rada* have served as the system of military law. For example, parliament plays no role in the drafting or approving defense and military–technical policy documents. In fact, the *Rada* does not even have a role in the creation of the "2005 State Program for the Re-development and Reform of the Armed Forces," including the force structure and size, something it is charged to determine. Ukraine's legislation also does not provide for oversight of combat readiness and broad functions of control ascribed to specific committees. Once the budget is provided to the Defense Ministry, there is little to no accountability to the *Rada* on the expenditure of funds and whether defense officials met its goals. Heorhly Kriuchkov, a parliamentary deputy, writes, "In contrast to democratic countries of the world, the Parliament of Ukraine is deprived of legal grounds to influence personnel policy in the military sector, which reduces the effectiveness of control. Parliamentary committees are not empowered with any supervisory functions. Although they scrutinize implementation of specific laws, formally, this is not in line with the norms of the Constitution."[8]

Civil–military reform cannot proceed without a firm political foundation and sound economic basis and, as previously mentioned, the major guidance documents are outdated and vague.[9] This is due in part to the continued division among the civilians leading the government as to the strategic orientation of Ukraine. The battle between the Kuchma administration and the leftist *Rada* from his first election in 1994 until 1999 has affected the administration's ability to openly address the strategic orientation of Ukraine. The east–west and north–south variances on ethnic and security orientation have necessitated this "cold truce" between the two factions. More recently, the escalation of challenges in the Ukraine–Russia relationship, related to energy dependency, economic linkage of Ukraine's market with the CIS, Russian Black Sea forces in Ukraine's Sevastopol, and the role of the Russian language in a sovereign Ukraine, have probably put a hold on Ukraine's forthright Euro–Atlantic security orientation.

The Relationship between the Ukrainian Armed Forces and Security Units

A less studied but significant element of the civil–military relationship is cooperation between the armed forces and other security units in Ukraine. This relationship is important for four primary reasons: (1) the ability of the units to work together to address civil disaster and humanitarian crises situations, such as the 1986 Chernobyl disaster; (2) the level of civilian oversight and/or direct command of various security units; (3) the economic burden placed on the Ukrainian economy by maintaining ten different security units that must share limited resources; and (4) the necessity of the state to clearly define modern threats and assign units to meet these threats.[10]

First, a threat to the Ukrainian state remains natural and manmade disasters. Ukraine's armed forces have a mission to assist the Ministry of Emergencies, Ministry of Health, and other units in protecting society from civil disasters and providing humanitarian relief. Cases of flooding in eastern and western Ukraine necessitate that the various units work together effectively and rapidly. Workshops with NATO on civil emergencies as well as the May 1999 *Rough and Ready 2000* exercise sponsored by the U.S. National Air Guard in cooperation with units from Ukraine's Ministries of Emergency and Health proved the need for more joint planning and interoperability between Ukraine's units. By presidential decree, there is one combined joint training exercise per year, but more effort should be placed on detection, monitoring, and planning for relief services.

Second, in the early 1990s a newly formed Ukrainian government made clear and decisive progress in "dismantling and democratizing" all noncombatant militarized elements under the supervision of nonpolitical civil authorities. However, at present the ministries view themselves less as servants of the people and instruments of policy and more as independent reservoirs of power, which are wielded more often for personal advantage than for the benefit of the state. Two things remain to be accomplished in the "civilianizing" of armed security units: They should be led by senior civilian leaders within the organizations themselves (the Ministry of Emergencies is in the lead with almost 80 percent of their executive positions filled by civilians) and should be civilianized by rank and uniform and restricted to light armaments and basic police duties.

Third, these units are often assigned redundant missions and compete for the same dwindling group of aspiring professional military personnel within society and limited resources. Ukraine retains three heavy armies (Ministry of Defense's Ground Forces, Ministry of the Interior, and the Border Guard), and two navies (Ministry of Defense's Navy and Border Guard). Often, the military's missions overlap to a considerable degree, including the protection and transportation of state officials, patrolling city streets, and the protection of the transportation of precious goods, and provision of aid in the event of catastrophes. There has been little visible effort to include these nine forces in the reform of the armed forces. In fact, while the armed forces have been reduced from over 800,000 to just under 320,000, the non–Ministry of Defense forces have grown to 1.4 million people.

After President Kuchma's reelection in 1999, he dissolved the National Guard. This was viewed by some as a money-saving effort; however, the forces were not retired but subsumed under the armed forces and Interior Ministry. Western analysts thought that the dissolution of the guard was a visible sign that the presidential administration felt comfortable in the allegiance of the armed forces to the state, as well as the strength of other units to protect the sovereignty of Ukraine. In some ways, the guard was truly a civil force: Only the most loyal of Ukrainian patriots were sought for its service, and they were trained to face potential separatist forces in Crimea and Donets'k. Other military units, such as those under the Ministry of Interior and the Security Services, could have served this mission, but Ukraine was quick to form five regional divisions of heavily armored units under the guard. Despite its origins, the National Guard played an important role in curtailing separatists in Crimea in the early to mid-1990s. However, it was never used to suppress extremist groups in any region.[11]

Fourth, perpetuating a large number of forces, besides historical legacy, is the lack of an agreed-upon national security concept and updated, comprehensive national military doctrine. The 1997 National Security Concept has two flaws according to Ukrainian experts. The first is that it is vague on delineating missions between the various militaries. This is compounded by a lack of subsequent legislation defining duties. In fact, the existing legislation does not regulate the armed forces' involvement in internal functions. Therefore, limited resources spread across ten militaries, compounded by an ambiguity of roles and missions, leads to an inability to measure whether the militaries are adequately performing their duties.[12]

In order to leverage resources, the Ukrainian effort to reform the armed forces should be undertaken simultaneously with the paramilitary units. Instead of independent organizations, there should be horizontal lines of communications for planning and executing defense, particularly if the major security threat is internal. A transparent reformation process of all nine organizations could help in building trust with the civilian population that lives with these various units and explaining their missions as it applies to the functioning of a lawful and peaceful state.

The Ukraine Ministry of Defense as a Civilian Organization

Ukraine has experience with civilian leadership within the Ministry of Defense. It was the first former Soviet State in 1995 to assign a civilian, Valeriy Shmarov, as minister of defense. However, the early negative experiences have been judged by most as premature and may prevent another civilian from leading the ministry for some time. Neither the system nor the ministry would support a civilian leader then or now. Experts pose several reasons for the first civilian minister of defense's demise, but perhaps the one most pertinent to this study is the fact that civilians have no effectual or influential role in the Ministry of Defense. This is because under the Soviet system there was no civilian expertise on defense and security matters: It was left to the military. Besides former Defense Minister Shmarov, there have been only two civilians in leadership positions in the ministry, both of whom were appointed by Shmarov and have subsequently been relieved.

Anatoliy Dovgopoliy, who was made the deputy minister for armaments (1996–2000), and O. Urban, who was the director of the Foreign
Relations Department in the general staff from 1995 to 1996.

There is an effort underway to increase the role of civilians within
the Ministry of Defense, led by the ministry's Main Staff Directorate.[13]
The *Rada* is in the process of drafting a legal basis for civilian oversight of the armed forces called the "Law of Ukraine on Civilian Control over the Military Organization and Law Enforcement Activities
in Ukraine." The law encapsulates the 1994 "OSCE Code of Conduct
Regarding Political–Military Aspects of Security," to which Ukraine is
a signatory. The primary impetus behind this policy is a financial one;
it is less expensive to pay civilians than the military personnel in
Ukraine. In the early stages of this effort, many of the civilians are
retired military, which is not uncommon in transitioning governments
of Central and Eastern Europe that are selecting from a limited pool of
candidates. In fact, by placing a soon-to-be retired military officer in a
"civilian" billet, the government plans to be spared pensions.

In addition to passing legislation on the range of posts and the authority held by civil servants in the Ministry of Defense, there must be
a concerted effort to create a system of education, recruiting, training,
and retention to acquire a solid professional civilian cadre of defense
experts. General Major Tuituinnyuk of the National Security and Defense Council notes that while many in the government understand
the need for more civilian leadership within the Ministry of Defense,
the country is simply short on civilian defense experts.[14] There are attempts to alleviate this problem through education, through the offering of courses this year at the National Defense Academy for civilians in
defense and security matters. However, Ukraine's civilian educational
system must support the instruction of civilians in national security
and defense topics, a serious recruitment effort must be undertaken,
and competitive salaries are required, which again depends on a
strengthened economy.

The Ukrainian president has instructed the defense minister to place
civilians in the highest possible positions in "central command bodies" in over 20,000 newly civilianized posts, including military units,
logistics, medical and financial facilities, and military schools. It remains the authority of the minister to determine what positions are
civilian and who occupies the leadership positions, as opposed to the
U.S. system in which the president appoints and congress approves
the political civilian appointments down to the deputy assistant secretary level in the Department of Defense. Currently, the number of
civilians in the Ukrainian Ministry of Defense amounts to only 33 percent, occupying primarily low- to mid-level administrative and technical staff in the services, in operational commands, and in the fields

of command, control, communications, and intelligence. There are some heads of directorates and departments, but it is unknown to what degree they have influence. Most of the civilians are technical specialists with little opportunity to move into managerial positions. Many civilians constitute the workforce of the former Soviet military industries across Ukraine, in some cases in nonproducing complexes.[15]

On a very basic level, displacing military officers with civilians provides an avenue for downsizing the military in roles that would not otherwise be occupied by the military. It also provides the military with the valuable time and personnel it needs to focus on the military mission. Some examples include the provision of support to the military, including medical, communications, logistics, administration, mechanical, and clerical, which can be provided by civilian personnel. Research and development responsibilities of the military should fall to civilian laboratories with a dual-use technologies focus. Acquisition program evaluation should be in the hands of civilian professionals. Resource management (financial, acquisition, personnel, installations, etc.) should be out of the hands of the military, and instead be transferred to civilian staff who are separated from the parochial interests of the services. A professional civilian staff that has experience liaising with parliamentarians and committees should complement the budgeters. Even defense policy development and strategic planning, program and budget development and execution, contingency planning, and military operations should be the responsibility of a professional civilian staff within the ministry.[16]

When analyzing Ukraine's experience, it is useful to conduct a comparative study of the relationship between civilians and the military in developed NATO governments such as the United States. Even in the United States, where civilian control of the military is an established system grounded in the Constitution and tested through two major world wars and the restructuring of the armed forces after the Vietnam War, some Americans still cannot fathom the number of civilians in the Department of Defense. Civilian defense experts number 670,780, including four undersecretaries appointed to lead directorates of policy, acquisition, technology, and logistics; personnel and readiness; and the comptroller, as well as four service secretaries and agencies. These numbers do not include civilians working in private defense industries on government contracts. Just a decade ago, at the height of the Cold War, there were over 1.1 million civilians employed by the Department of Defense.

Yet in such an established system, in which education, law, and precedence support a strong civilian corps of defense analysts, tension between the civilians and military exists. Civilian control is particularly tested during and after times of war, when actual and perceived threat scenarios change. The post–Cold War threats of drugs, thugs, and (chemical and biological) bugs often do not fit under the mission of the traditional armed forces and this poses a problem for civilian authorities, who are sometimes more concerned with future threats than traditional territorial defense. And since most of these threats tend to be internal or transnational, authorities must strike a delicate balance as they seek to define the role of the armed forces in resolving civil disputes.

Society and the Armed Forces

A fourth but no less important ingredient of civil–military relations is the relationship between the armed forces and society. The essence of the symbiosis is accountability. Accountability can be accomplished through transparent mediums such as the media, education of civilians in defense matters, and an enhanced role of nongovernmental organizations. Because the military is ultimately from society and of society, it is therefore shaped by it. Chris Donnelly, secretary general of NATO's Special Representative to Central and Eastern Europe, sums up the cyclical patterns of symbiosis between civilians and the military as follows: "The essence of this symbiosis is accountability. The army is accountable to the government, the government is accountable to the army and to parliament, and parliament is accountable to the people."[17]

Since Taras Kuzio's writings on civil–military affairs in the early 1990s on the role of civic groups, media, and democratically controlled councils in forming an independent Ukrainian force, the role of society in building the armed forces has significantly declined.[18] To some extent, civil–military relations have become more sophisticated—put into the hands of the presidential administration's elite—but not necessarily more effective.

It is interesting to note that in the former Soviet Union it was the Committee on Soldier's Mothers, the Union of Ukrainian Officers, and other groups' protest against the abuse their children suffered as conscripts in the Soviet Army that led, in part, to a nationalized Ukrainian force. Ukraine inherited the old Soviet system of conscription and a force that was subordinate to the Party and ultimately in charge of preserving the Party. It is now this same issue—mandatory conscription and the desires of mothers to keep their children from serving—that has raised the level of interaction with society on the future of the armed forces. The Committee of Soldiers Mothers monitors conditions of soldiers, protects their interests, and conducts investigations. This grassroots effort has perhaps played a role in the minister of defense's decision to slowly phase out conscription over the next fifteen years and create a volunteer, professional (and presumably pro-fessionally treated) force. The Ukrainian government plans to limit conscription to twelve months by 2005 and complete transition to an all-volunteer force by 2015.

As described by Richard Spence in his article "The Military in the New Russia," moving to a professional force, while perhaps alleviat-ing the treatment of conscripts, has important implications for civil–military relations.[19] As the armed forces pulls more from the "elite," the members will tend to be less accountable to, or influenced by, the attitudes and values of the majority of civilian society. The military may become less responsive to society, which in turn could be danger-ous in a state struggling to redefine its basic values and institutions. The fact that the Ukrainian military is not 100-percent ethnic Ukrai-nian and instead has a solid base of approximately 25-percent Rus-sians may actually help to desolidify homogenous feelings, thus leading to internal cohesion and tendencies toward elitism.

In general, however, the role of society in influencing the reform of the armed forces remains weak, including grassroots interest groups, the media, nongovernmental organizations, think tanks, and political parties.[20] As with the building of a cadre of defense experts to serve within the Ministry of Defense, it is important to build civilian de-fense and security competence in various sectors, including the media and the public. Chris Donnelly explains, "Western policy is heavily influenced by knowledgeable journalists, who can evaluate and criti-cize policy initiatives in a realistic manner and bring public and ex-pert pressure to bear on policies they scrutinize. Journalists with no understanding of military affairs are likely, in a free press, not only to miss the important points, but to criticize unfairly attitudes adopted and actions taken by the military because they do not understand mili-tary realities."[21] There are a few regular publications that publish thought-provoking pieces on the military, particularly *Nauka i Oborona*, but more are needed.

What does the military mean to Ukrainian society? The answer to this question is ambiguous. While recent opinion polls suggest that the majority of the Ukrainian public supports the armed forces, it is less understood if Ukrainian society understands the roles of the vari-ous forces in protecting them. Transparency is necessary, including an open dialogue on strategic orientation leading to a rational force struc-ture and improved state of readiness. It is necessary that the popula-tion have the pertinent information to understand the need to invest in defense. Questions remain as to whether there is a broad civilian support network for draft evasion and desertion. If so, this strain of antimilitarism in society suggests a rift between civil and military cul-tures. Is the army seen as a foundation to democratic society or a hindrance to its development? As with most post–Cold War militaries, as the mission becomes blurred, the work is demoralizing. This is compounded in Ukraine by the lack of equipment, training, and reward for service.

CONCLUSION

An independent and sovereign Ukraine has been able to prevent the military from dominating the state, with its own political, judicial, and religious systems excluding civilian agencies. Ukraine has also "depoliticized" the armed forces and with the proclaimed neutrality of the state, civilian leaders have not used the military to resolve their disputes, particularly interstate and regional ones. The Ukrainian military generally appears to be less politicized than the Russian military. Ukraine should avoid those periods of history in neighboring states when the internal forces were used to quell, for example, an attempted coup in 1991 and the 1993 storming of the White House in Russia, and the use of interior troops for armed struggles in Chechnya or to protect Russian minority populations in Georgia and Moldova.

The challenge remains to rest accountability for the armed forces restructuring and reform with elected officials, government, and parliamentary sovereignty, and not the military. This can be accomplished on four levels: by the presidential administration, within the Ministry of Defense, and between paramilitaries by and of society. As Chris Donnelly writes,

Effective civil–military relations will lead to a strong Ukrainian army able to defend the sovereignty of Ukraine. The transformation of Ukraine's defense establishment will be a major ingredient in a strong democratic society. This, in turn, creates a national sense of security, which will contribute to good relations with neighboring states. Thus, defense transformation becomes a supportive element in the transformation of the rest of society.[22]

Proper civilian oversight of the military is not only vital for the military security of the nation, but for economic security as well. At a time when Ukraine is struggling to bounce back from the fall 1998 devaluation of the Russian ruble, break free of energy dependency on Russia, and privatize formerly government-owned industries, the security apparatus is a drain on the economy, both in terms of manpower and the military industrial complex. Ukraine is approaching a critical ten-year mark at which civil–military relations must function in support of the development of a rational and ready-armed force to enhance the security of the nation. For society, democratic civilian control is a guarantee of the effective use of budget funds, civil order and peace in everyday life, protection and assistance in case of emergency, and a guarantee of human rights within power structures and society in general.[23]

What senior Ukrainian military leaders perhaps do not yet believe, but will in time, is that civilian oversight, if not control, is actually in their own best interests in the long term if they wish to meet their ambitious reform goals. As Western models demonstrate, positioning civilians in leadership roles in the ministry can provide clear definitions of organizational structures, roles, and missions within which to operate. It can promote the combat readiness of the troops and prestige of military service, as officers and soldiers are left to military missions. Thus, while the military may at first balk at the idea, their subordination to civil authorities within the ministry makes the civilians, and not the military, directly responsible for the effectiveness of the structures and accountable to society for a stable and effective security apparatus.

NOTES

1. Larry Diamond and Marc F. Plattner note in their introduction to *Civil–Military Relations and Democracy* (Baltimore: Johns Hopkins University Press, 1996) that the notion of civil–military relations is missing from modern democracy-building debates.

2. Anatoliy Grytsenko, *Civil–Military Relations in Ukraine: A System Emerging from Chaos*, Harmonie Paper 1 (Kyiv: Centre for European Security Studies, 1997). Also see Anatoliy Grytsenko's work done in 1999 during his fellowship at the Centre for European Security Studies at http://www.uceps.com.

3. See T. Kuzio, "The Non-Military Security Forces of Ukraine," *Journal of Slavic Military Studies* 13, no. 4 (2000): 29–56, which details the structure, roles, and missions of the ten security forces.

4. Anatoliy Grystenko, *National Security and Defense* 11 (2000): 4.

5. Partnership for Peace, Framework Document (NATO Online). Available at: <http://www.nato/int/docu/facts/fpf.htm>.

6. Marco Carnovale, "NATO, Partners and Allies: Civil–Military Relations and Democratic Control of the Armed Forces," *NATO Review*, June 2000, 3–5.

7. Samuel Huntington, *Soldier and a Statesman* (Cambridge: Belknap Press of Harvard University Press, 1957), 1–3.

8. Heorhly Kriuchkov, speech obtained via FBIS 2000.

9. The latest deadline for an updated National Security Doctrine and National Military Doctrine is July 2001. An interagency committee, including military personnel, are in charge of drafting the documents, with the military-dominated general staff taking a leading role in writing the Military Doctrine.

10. In addition to the armed forces, the units in Ukraine include the Ministry of Interior internal troops, security service units, border troops, customs service units, tax policy, Ministry of Emergencies civil defense troops, National Space Agency, and State Communications Department.

11. Kuzio, "The Non-Military Security Forces of Ukraine."

12. In winter 1999, Minister of Defense Oleksandr Kuzmuk gave a speech in which he defined three threats to Ukraine: an unstable relationship between NATO and Russia, internal unrest provoked by an outside force, and regional conflicts, such as Chechnya, spilling over into its borders. Taking these threats into account, the future role of security units, particularly the border guard and the Ministry of Internal Affairs in coordination with the armed forces, would appear essential in ensuring Ukrainian security.

13. *Narodna Armiya*, 31 March 2000 (obtained via FBIS).

14. General Major Tuituinnyuk, National Security and Defense Council, interview, Kyiv, Ukraine, 24 May 2000.

15. In addition to the *Narodna Armiya* article, some of this information was clarified during an interview with CPT Lihotkin, Ministry of Defense Chief of Personnel, Kyiv, Ukraine, 25 May 2000.

16. Stephen D. Olynyk, "Civilians in the U.S. Defense Establishment" (paper). He was citing *Report of the Secretary of Defense to the President and Congress 2000* (Washington, D.C.: U.S. Government Printing Office, 2000).

17. Chris Donnelly, "Defense Transformation in the New Democracies: A Framework for Tackling the Problem," *NATO Review*, January 1997, 17.

18. T. Kuzio, "Ukrainian Civil–Military Relations and the Military Impact of the Ukrainian Economic Crisis," in *State Building and Military Power in Russia and the New States of Eurasia*, ed. Bruce Parrott (Armonk, N.Y.: M. E. Sharpe, 1995), 157–192.

19. Constantine Danopoulos and Daniel Zirker, *Civil–Military Relations in the Soviet and Yugoslav Successor States* (Boulder, Colo.: Westview Press, 1996), 13–34.

20. Tuituinnyuk, interview.

21. Chris Donnelly, "Developing a National Strategy for the Transformation of the Defense Establishment in Post-Communist States," *NATO Review*, 4 December 1996, 13.

22. Ibid., 15.

23. Anatoliy Grystenko, *National Security and Defense* 11 (2000): 12.

Part III

FOREIGN AND SECURITY
POLICY ORIENTATIONS

7

Defining a Ukrainian Foreign Policy Identity: Business Interests and Geopolitics in the Formulation of Ukrainian Foreign Policy 1994–1999

Tor Bukkvoll

> The West has made it its goal to exploit all our reforms and efforts at restructuring, to ruin everything for us, and to turn the mighty Soviet Union, including the present independent Ukrainian state, into an economic appendage providing raw materials and cheap labour. Nobody, neither in the USA, England, France or Germany, has any interest in a strong Russia and a strong Ukraine. We must find our own way out of the crisis, expecting help from nobody.
> Leonid Kuchma, Prime Minister of Ukraine, 1993[1]

> Ukraine's strategy is decided by the country's geopolitical location, historical and cultural traditions. And all these factors clearly identify Ukraine with Europe. Integration into European structures—that is the strategic direction of our foreign policy.
> Leonid Kuchma, President of Ukraine, 1999[2]

In the summer of 1994, Leonid Kuchma was elected president of Ukraine on a program of redirecting the country's strongly pro-Western foreign policy in favor of closer relations with Russia. In this enterprise Kuchma was strongly backed by those sectors of the Ukrainian business elite that saw their future in the restoration of broken ties with Russia. Of particular importance here was the Ukrainian military–industrial complex, in which Kuchma himself had spent most of his professional career. Five years on, a major shift of orientation had taken place. It was now a dominating view in the Ukrainian president's administration that the country's foreign policy identity should be European rather than Eurasian.

In this chapter the shift in foreign policy identification will be investigated, and it will be explained both why it came about and why it came to be seen by substantial parts of the Ukrainian elite as an ultimate choice. In particular, I will highlight the relationship between Ukrainian national interests as interpreted by the ruling elite and the personal, political, and economic interests of this same elite. The chapter thus aims to make a contribution to a growing debate within international relations about how to develop a better theoretical understanding of the state. Here I refer to the body of theory known as state theory.[3]

There are three main schools of thought within state theory: the Weberian school, the pluralist school, and the Marxist school. I will concentrate on the differences between the Weberian school and the pluralist school, since, for the purpose of this chapter, the positions of the pluralist school and the Marxist school largely coincide.

To the extent that state theory has been discussed at all in connection with foreign policy theory, the perspective of the Weberian school has largely been taken for granted. The Weberian school maintains that the state should be seen as "much more than a mere arena in which social groups make demands and engage in political struggles or compromises."[4] Thus, it highlights the state's autonomy from society. In his acclaimed article on state theory "The State as a Conceptual Variable," J. P. Nettle claims, "Whatever the state may or may not be internally, . . . there have . . . been few challenges to its sovereignty and its autonomy in 'foreign affairs.'"[5] Nettle ascertains that whatever is the case in domestic politics, in foreign affairs the Weberian perspective is the appropriate one.

An alternative school of state theory is the pluralist school. In its modern form this school conceives of the state as a place where "separate interests constitute a functioning holistic system where the state forms the combining framework for the endeavors of the parts. The state is regarded as an arena in which different social groups compete. It coordinates competition and regulates arising conflicts. The coordinating and regulating functions are beyond the capability of the individual actors."[6] The pluralist school therefore allows for very little state independence from society.

This chapter does not aim to give a full explanation of the change of foreign policy identity during Kuchma's first five years. The focus is more narrow. Instead, this chapter will investigate how the relationship between the economic self-interests of elite groups and the interests of the Ukrainian state as a political organization independent from these same groups has affected Ukrainian foreign policy. By doing this I also aim to reach some general conclusions about the usefulness of the Weberian versus the pluralist perspectives in foreign policy analysis.

However, before proceeding, two issues have to be clarified: What alternative positions on foreign policy identity were discussed during Kuchma's first five years in power, and what kind of state is Ukraine? My conclusion on the second issue is that Ukraine is what Michael McFaul has termed a "privatized state."[7] McFaul sees the Russian state's privatized nature in that it "functions to defend the interests of a small capitalist class."[8] Ukraine too, is a privatized state, and these kind of states pose a particular challenge to the Weberian perspective in explaining foreign policy. This is because by nature they should be especially prone to letting the state's policy in foreign affairs be dominated by the interests of leading societal groups. If the Weberian perspective explains the foreign policy of these states, this makes it less likely that the pluralist perspective can make substantial contributions to foreign policy analysis.

In the first section of this chapter I give a brief overview of the foreign policy debate in Ukraine from 1994 to 1999. In the second, it is argued why it is justifiable to refer to Ukraine as a privatized state. In the third section, I examine more closely the foreign policy perspectives of the major sectorial interests in the Ukrainian economy. Finally, changes to a European foreign policy identity under Kuchma are discussed, and this identity's persistence, in light of the Weberian and pluralist perspectives of state theory, is explained.

FOREIGN POLICY WITHIN THE KUCHMA ADMINISTRATION

Three alternatives have been repeatedly proposed in the debate on Ukraine's foreign policy identity: European, Eurasian, and transitional. They all include clear proposals for the course of Ukrainian foreign policy: integration with European structures (EU, NATO), integration with Russia, and maintaining a neutral position.

The national democrats, a large portion of the intellectual elite, and substantial sections of the Ukrainian economic elite support the European identity view. The basic historical claim here is that Ukraine is a European country that was forcefully taken away from Europe and now has its historic chance to return. Former chairman of the Ukrainian parliament's foreign policy committee, the nationalist–Communist Dmytro Pavlychko, carried this thinking to extremes. In outlining the direction of Ukrainian foreign policy, he stated, "Our foreign policy has to lead us to Europe, where we were born and where we grew up as a nation, and from where we were torn away and put in Asian imprisonment, redressed in Muscovite clothes, and educated in the Slavic–Russian language of Genghis-Khan's great-grandchildren."[9]

The Eurasian identity view is supported by most of the Communist Party, the Progressive Socialist Party, a number of small non-communist pro-Russian parties, substantial portions of the general population of eastern, southern, and partly also central Ukraine, and in the Crimea. The view is also supported by leading agents of Ukrainian agriculture. They emphasize the common historical and cultural roots of the eastern Slavs, and call attention to the common Orthodox faith.

The transitional identity is supported by the Socialist Party, influential members of the early Kuchma administration, and many intellectuals from eastern Ukraine. They emphasize how much Ukraine was marked by having been a Russian province since the middle of the eighteenth century, and also by the seventy years of Communism. They are in principle positive about Ukraine slowly becoming a European country, but only after it has overcome the legacy of Communism, and most probably in tandem with Russia. Dmytro Tabchnyk, former close presidential adviser, and the intellectuals Vasyl Kremen and Vasyl Tkachenko, wrote in 1996, "The engulfment of Ukraine by the Russian empire, and the centuries as a part of that empire, led not only to the formation of a tight web of economic relations, but also to the formation of certain cultural, spiritual, and traditional commonalties, which made Ukrainians, Russians, and the other peoples of the former Soviet Union very close in many respects."[10] However, they also concluded that "the presence of a Eurasian influence over centuries, after all did not make Ukraine Eurasian."[11]

During Kuchma's first five years in power, the supporters of the transitional and the European foreign policy identities lived in uneasy coexistence. While Kuchma chose the side of the Europeanists in shaping the long-term strategy for Ukrainian foreign policy, he needed the transitionalists for short-term purposes. The transitionalists were especially needed for solving the remaining controversies with Russia. These included the conclusion of the major Cooperation and Friendship Treaty, the division of the Black Sea Fleet, and the restructuring of the oil and gas debt to Russia. Because of this need, the policy toward Russia was largely removed from the responsibility of the Ukrainian foreign ministry. This was especially the case after Boris Tarasyuk was appointed foreign minister in April 1998.

The individual put in charge of relations with Russia was the transitionalist Oleksandr Razumkov, largely due to his diplomatic skills and his extensive personal contacts in the Kremlin. According to former staff member of the powerful National Security and Defense Council and Razumkov ally, Anatoliy Hrytsenko, "There were times when our civil servants who went to Moscow for negotiations did not get further than to Sheremetevo airport. They were met at the airport by a leader of Gazprom or some other company, and asked a single question: did you bring money? If the answer was no, they would get no further. Razumkov was able to overcome all of this."[12]

Razumkov had Prime Minister Pustovoitenko as his channel for consultation with the president, whereas the Europeanist Tarasyuk had the leader of the powerful NSDC, Volodymyr Horbulin, as his channel for consultation. The two groupings at times clashed strongly, and in public. In February 1999 Razumkov told a Kyiv symposium arranged by the Konrad Adenauer Foundation that Ukrainian membership in NATO would not be on the agenda for at least another ten years. Horbulin later rebuked his subordinate by publicly stating that Razumkov had "erred both in form and in substance."[13]

Still, the coexistence of the two opposing views in the administration was not necessarily the result of ambiguity in Kuchma's own foreign policy outlook. He knew very well that good relations with Moscow would ease rather than worsen the prospects of Ukrainian integration with the West. Putting a relatively pro-Russian person in charge of the Russia policy and making a very strong pro-Western person responsible of the rest of the foreign policy were, therefore, not contradictory, but mutually reinforcing measures.

UKRAINE AS A PRIVATIZED STATE

According to a Ukrainian parliamentarian, the Swedish economist Anders Åslund gave a rather sarcastic characterization of the state of Ukrainian politics to a visiting group of Ukrainian parliamentarians in Washington in early 1999. He described Ukraine today as a "closed joint-stock company, led by four clans: the Rabinovich–Volkov clan; the Bakay–Holubchenko clan; the Surkis–Medvedchuk clan; and the successors of Alik the Greek."[14]

Although Åslund's characterization might go too far, it seems fair to claim that Ukraine is no less a privatized state than is Russia. The most blatant example of the privatization of the Ukrainian state is found in the gas-trade sector. Several Ukrainian gas traders, by exploiting the high political positions they achieved in the government and the presidential administration, have secured enormous profits for themselves. However, their activities have had very negative effects for Ukrainian society. The gas traders are middlemen that buy gas from Russia and resell it to Ukrainian consumers. During the five years covered by this chapter, many of these gas traders received huge sums in payment from Ukrainian consumers but paid very little of that money back to the Russian suppliers. Instead, they put the money in their own pockets.

For Ukrainian society this meant recurring halts in gas supplies to both commercial and private consumers, damage to the international economic reputation of Ukraine, and the accumulation of an enormous foreign debt. The Ukrainian authorities stated that the part of the energy dept accumulated by private gas traders was the gas traders' own and not the government's problem. However, this changed after the reelection of Kuchma in 1999. Following substantial pressure from the Russian government, the newly appointed Ukrainian minister for energy, Yuliya Timoshenko, went to Moscow in January 2000 and accepted the Ukrainian government's responsibility for the privately accumulated debts. It thus seems likely that the Ukrainian taxpayers will have to pay for the feast of the gas traders after all. If not, they may no longer be able to heat their apartments.

The most notorious of these gas traders was Pavlo Lazarenko. He took advantage of his position as prime minister from May 1996 to July 1997 to monopolize most of the gas trade for his own firm, United Energy Systems. President Kuchma dismissed Lazarenko in 1997 after severe international pressure, but the use of influential political positions for the promotion of private economic interest did not stop with his dismissal. Oleksandr Volkov and Viktor Pinchuk gradually became public figures in Ukraine during Kuchma's first five years in power. Both were successful businessmen who held influential positions in the presidential administration, and both used their positions to promote personal business interests.

The Ukrainian business elites have two principal strategies for influencing the political leadership. The most efficient one is to get their own people into leading government and administrative positions. Alternatively, they can create an interest organization that engages in public campaigns and the lobbying of state institutions. The latter strategy, however, is, according to Yaroslav Zhalilo, Volodymyr Lupatsiy, and Andriy Smenkovskiy, more a sign of weakness than a sign of strength.[15] In their analysis of the interplay between business and politics in Ukraine they write,

The need for formal organizations and for appointing official representatives, only occurs when a certain branch or business group has been excluded from the informal channels of influence. In other words, the need for public politics arises when a certain group feels a need for replay of what happened in the informal channels. They will engage in public politics only after they have tried and failed in exploiting all the options for replay within the informal framework (an example here is the formation of the political party Hromada).[16]

The Ukrainian Union of Industrialists and Entrepreneurs (UIEU) is a prime example of the relationship between business and politics that Zhalilo, Lupatsiy, and Smenkovskiy describe. The UIEU was established to promote the political interests of the Ukrainian business community. However, the UEIU did not look upon itself as an organization established to lobby government for the adoption of preferable decisions. They instead saw themselves as part of that government. After all, their candidate, Leonid Kuchma, won the election. Although occasionally the UEIU could openly criticize the government, public politics was never high on the UEIU's agenda. Their main strategy for influence is to get their own people represented in decision-making bodies at all levels, and to establish the UEIU as a special body for consultancy within the government. In addition to Kuchma himself, who was president of the UEIU from December 1993 to July 1994, numerous other UEIU members have occupied high positions in the government and in the presidential administration.

A further illustration of the UEIU as a part of government rather than as an actor trying to influence it is the Coordinating Council for Social–Economic Policy. This council consists of the ministers in the government who are responsible for social and economic issues and the UEIU. According to the journalist Aleksandr Gurevich, there is good reason to believe that the UEIU has the upper hand in this council.[17] Anatoly Kinakh, president of UEIU and simultaneously first vice prime minister in the government, said at the UEIU Congress in June 1999 that the regional divisions of the UEIU should be included in the bodies of regional administration. UEIU leaders at regional levels were instructed to make sure that their members were included in local organs of power at all levels. Prime Minister Varly Pustovoitenko told the leadership of the UEIU in 1997 that in the process of selecting people to fill ministerial posts the UEIU proposals for candidates would of course be taken into account.[18]

The UEIU's "part of government" identity can also be illustrated by its organizational design. Under the UEIU president there are a number of vice presidents. Their number and thematical specializations correspond more or less exactly to the number and thematical responsibilities of the socioeconomic ministries of the government.

The examples given here illustrate a trend. It therefore seems fair in the case of Ukraine to claim that the state functions to defend the interests of a small capitalist class. The question in this chapter, however, is whether that also applies to Ukrainian foreign policy, or whether foreign policy is kept as an area of fairly autonomous state action in a privatized state.

Before answering that question, however, Ukrainian big business will be analyzed in some more detail. I find it necessary to describe which main branches it consists of, what foreign policy strategies the different branches think would best suit their own interests, and how much influence the different branches have on the executive.

UKRAINIAN BIG BUSINESS:
FOREIGN POLICY PERSPECTIVES

There are many ways of classifying Ukrainian big business according to sectors. The following classification is helpful:

- The energy sector.
- The metallurgical and chemical sectors.
- The civilian machine building and the military–industrial sectors.
- The agricultural sector.

The agricultural sector is the one most clearly in favor of closer relations with Russia. Ukrainian agricultural products have few chances on the protected Western markets, but have traditionally been crucial to satisfy the Russian need for farm produce. Since Ukraine became independent in 1991, however, they have met with ever-higher Russian customs barriers. The agricultural sector hopes that political integration with Russia will remove these barriers. One of the main spokesmen for this sector was the former speaker of parliament and 1999 presidential candidate Oleksandr Tkachenko.

Within the metallurgical sector, we may distinguish roughly between those enterprises that are profitable and able to export to the West, and those enterprises that run at a loss and sell their produce to Russia for less than production costs.[19] According to the scholar Aleksandr Potekhin, the loss makers account for about 70 percent of the enterprises within this sector. However, they are still in business for two reasons. First, some of leaders of these enterprises are able to pocket some personal profit despite the sorry state of affairs of their enterprises. Second, the Ukrainian government is afraid of the social and political consequences that a substantial increase in unemployment could have in eastern Ukraine. The profitable parts of the metallurgical sector and the chemical sector are mostly oriented toward export to the West, and are, therefore, in favor of a pro-Western foreign policy. For this reason, they were some of the strongest supporters of Leonid Kravchuk in the 1994 presidential elections.

The energy sector as a whole is mildly pro-Russian in its foreign policy outlook. Zhalilo, Lupatsiy, and Smankovskiy write that "these groups [the energy sector] are, all things taken into account, an impediment to a pro-Western foreign policy. For them, a 'soft' Ukrainian dependence on Russia and intimate relations with the representatives of the Russian oil and gas sector is most convenient."[20]

The point about personal contacts is especially important here. In Russia the privatization of big industrial enterprises is more or less finished. In Ukraine it is just about to start. Russian big capital is eager to take part in this process. Therefore, in the last year of Kuchma's first term as president, Russian business interests started to build ever-closer connections with Ukrainian oligarchs. They did this to establish channels of influence to the Ukrainian decision makers, hoping to be able to use them when the privatization of major companies gets started. According to *Kyiv Post* staff writer Katya Gorchinskaya, "All of Russia's movers and shakers regularly pay low-key visits to Ukraine, and all of them are working to build close business—if not personal—relations with the Ukrainian elite."[21] One of the most prominent examples of such close connections is the association between Ukrainian presidential confidant Oleksandr Volkov and Russian oligarch Boris Berezovsky. According to *Nezavisimaya Gazeta*, "The media magnate himself made all possible and impossible efforts to support Kuchma, displaying a level of activity that was out of all proportions even for him."[22]

The civilian machine building and the military–industrial sectors were in 1994 pro-Russian, but changed during the period from 1994 to 1999 to a largely pro-Western orientation. It seems that the rocket-cosmic branch was leading in facilitating this shift in foreign policy outlook for the civilian machine building and the military–industrial sectors. The decision of the Ukrainian rocket and cosmic industry to try to enter Western markets was largely initiated in 1994 by Volodymyr Horbulin, and it was an important factor contributing to Horbulin's rise in Ukrainian politics. According to Zhalilo, Lupatsiy, and Smenkovski, "It is no coincidence that the rocket builders and in general the military–industrial complex have become the leading lobbyists for cooperation between Ukraine and NATO and the countries of Central Europe, and for admission of Ukraine to the WTO."[23] There are at least three important reasons why this sector turned from a pro-Russian to a pro-Western foreign policy outlook.

First, the directors of this sector vehemently disliked what they considered to be the superior (imperialist) attitudes of its Russian counterparts. Oleksandr Potekhin, leader of the Foreign Ministry's U.S. and Europe department in the early Kuchma period, stated,

The business interests of the major Ukrainian companies were of course in Russia at that time. However, nobody wanted to be removed from his or her top position. Nobody wanted to become simple servants for Russian masters. Vyakhirev and Gazprom and in general the leaders of most Russian major enterprises, therefore, made a great mistake by behaving in this way. They always made clear that they were not ready to consider these Ukrainian industry barons as equals, and they were never ready to conduct negotiations on equal terms.[24]

Second, representatives of the Russian arms industry have on numerous occasions maintained that the patent rights are Russian for a large number of items that the Ukrainian arms industry is now marketing. Ukraine should therefore not sell them without acceptance from

Russian patent holders, and Ukraine has no right to make any changes to them.

Third, Russia and Ukraine to a large extent manufacture similar products for export, and are thus commercial competitors. This is especially the case with tank production. It was a major blow to any possible remains of cooperative spirit on the Ukrainian side when Russia refused to deliver the turrets to 320 T-80 tanks for which Ukraine had signed a delivery contract with Pakistan. The Ukrainians then developed their own turrets in cooperation with a Swiss company. This Russian decision was seen as a very clear token of the attitudes of the Russian arms industry toward the Ukrainian arms industry. The fact that Russia is a major exporter of arms to India, and that concern for Russia's relations with India probably was a major reason for the refusal to supply Ukraine with turrets, did not particularly soften Ukrainian reactions.

This does not at all mean that Ukrainian industrialists do not want to do business with Russia, but it means that the hopes and expectations connected to an economic and political reintegration of the two countries are no longer dominant. One of the leading experts on the Ukrainian arms industry, Valentin Badrak, says that even if one can point to single episodes of successful cooperation between Russian and Ukrainian arms exporters, the very clear trend is toward ever-deteriorating relations.[25]

THE KUCHMA ADMINISTRATION:
FOREIGN POLICY IDENTITY

It might be useful to combine the Weberian and the pluralist perspectives of state theory with what James G. March and Johan P. Olsen have described as two bases of social action.[26] These are "the logic of anticipated consequences" and "the logic of appropriateness." The first means that individuals are "driven by a logic of anticipated consequences and prior preferences"; the second means that individuals are "driven by a logic of appropriateness and senses of identity."[27]

The logic of anticipated consequences seems to coincide with the pluralist perspective. According to March and Olsen, "Within the consequentialist perspective, politics is seen as aggregating individual preferences into collective actions by some procedures of bargaining, negotiation, coalition formation, and exchange."[28] On the level of the nation-state, this means that "the coherence and significance of the nation-state in international relations is explained as the result of efforts of political actors to find structures favorable to their individual objectives. The major elements of the nation-state are assumed to thrive because they serve the interests of key actors. The interests of the political actors come first; the interests of the nation-states are derived from them."[29]

Similarly, the logic of appropriateness seems to coincide with the Weberian perspective. March and Olson describe the logic of appropriateness in the following way:

Human actors are imagined to follow rules that associate particular identities to particular situations, approaching individual opportunities for action by assessing similarities between current identities and choice dilemmas and more general concepts of self and situations. Action involves evoking an identity or role and matching the obligations of that identity or role to a specific situation. The pursuit of purpose is associated with identities more than with interests, and with the selection or rules more than with individual expectations.[30]

Individuals display both types of behavior, and according to March and Olson there are four broad interpretations of the relationship between the two types of behavior:

1. Whatever is most clear to the actor in any particular situation—preferences and consequences or identities and rules—will dominate his choice.
2. One of the logics is used to make fundamental decisions, and the other is used to make day-to-day refinements.
3. Actors start a relationship using the logic of anticipated consequences, but gradually by developing identities and rules, the logic of appropriateness becomes dominant.
4. Both types of logic are nothing but "a special case of the other."[31]

In the rest of the chapter, when I talk about the Weberian and pluralist perspectives, that should be understood as the Weberian perspective, including the logic of appropriateness, and the pluralist perspective, including the logic of anticipated consequences.

The Choice of a European Foreign Policy Identity

Taras Kuzio, in his book *Ukraine under Kuchma*, argues that the election of Kuchma in 1994 can be seen as the successful conclusion of the efforts of the Ukrainian military–industrial complex to place their own man at the top in Kyiv.[32] Furthermore, Kuzio argues, he came from this industry with an explicit mandate to redirect the foreign policy to a pro-Russian path. This industry largely paid for his campaign, and Kuchma spent more money on his campaign than any of the other candidates.

The industrialists got their reward when a large number of their representatives were placed in influential positions in the presidential administration after the election. The military–industrial complex was so well represented that some Ukrainian observers jokingly talked about a special Ukrainian form of "conversion." Instead of converting military industry to civilian industry, Ukraine converted military industrialists to civilian powerholders.[33] The most prominent of these were Volodymyr Horbulin and Valeriy Shmarov. Horbulin, who had been a colleague of Kuchma's at the missile plant Pivdenmash, became secretary of the NSDC. Horbulin was one of the main architects behind Ukrainian foreign and security policy during the period from 1994 to 1999. Shmarov, from the defense industry in Kyiv, became defense minister, with a special responsibility for developing close relations between the Ukrainian and Russian defense industries.

These parts of Ukrainian big business, however, soon felt let down by the reception of their integration initiatives in Russia. At the same time, in particular the military–industrial complex discovered new opportunities in the West. These included both a limited potential for export to the West, and more important, possibilities for technical and scientific cooperation. The changes in business outlook made these parts of Ukrainian big business change from a pro-Russian to a pro-Western foreign policy perspective. The civilian machine building and military–industrial sectors therefore, together with the profitable parts of the metallurgical sector and the chemical sector, became a powerful lobby for a pro-Western foreign policy. That shift is a major part of the explanation for why Ukrainian official foreign policy also became increasingly pro-Western.

So far, the story corresponds well with the pluralist framework. The change in foreign policy outlook during Kuchma's first five years in office can to a large extent be explained, with the changed interests of Ukrainian big business as the point of departure. However, the change can also be explained by using the Weberian perspective. Once in place as president of Ukraine, Kuchma's object of reference for his self-identity changed from enterprise director to state leader. That meant he was suddenly entangled in a web of norms for how a state leader is supposed to act, how other state leaders were supposed to act upon him, and how his state was supposed to act and be acted toward. That is, the logic of appropriate behavior for a state leader became important. To achieve the integration he was elected to carry out, he would have to play by the rules presented to him by the Russian establishment. These rules were not in agreement with what he and his staff saw as the standard international norms for state-to-state relations. Most important, they constituted a denial of Kuchma's identity as a state leader. According to Alexander Wendt, "Two kinds of ideas can enter into identity. Those held by the Self and those held by the Other."[34] It was not just a question of personal insult; without a functioning identity as a state leader, Kuchma would lack the basis for knowing what would be appropriate action or what would not.

This can be explained by using the distinction between regulative and constitutive rules. The scholar John Gerard Ruggie describes this distinction in the following manner: "Regulative rules are intended to have causal effects—getting people to approximate the speed limit, for example. Constitutive rules define the set of practices that make up any particular consciously organized social activity—that is to say, they specify what counts as that activity."[35] In the eyes of the Ukrainian elite, Russia did not treat Kuchma as the president of an independent country. A February 2000 survey of 100 representatives of the Russian foreign policy elite had as one of its main conclusions that Russians do not see Ukrainians as a separate nation.[36] The situation was similar to the one in which a chess player moves the pieces around on the board in unauthorized ways. By doing this, he not only offends the other player, but he makes the whole game impossible to play.

The Persistence of the European Foreign Policy Identity

What then happened in the latter part of Kuchma's first period was that the energy sector gradually outmaneuvered much of the civilian machine building and military–industrial sectors from the higher power circles in Kyiv. The Ukrainian daily *Kievskie Vedomosti* wrote in July 1997, "The main battle within the shadow economy and power circles today is taking place between the energy clan and the military–industrial and machine building clan."[37] The energy sector could win this battle, first of all because it commanded considerably larger financial resources than the civilian machine building and military–industrial sectors. The companies within the energy sector make up close to 80 percent of the major companies in Ukraine. The largest, Ukrhazprom, would, if it was a Russian company, have occupied third place after PAO EES Rossii and Gazprom.[38] The rise of "oligarchs" in Ukraine started within the energy sector. It was quite clear to Kuchma, who was aiming for reelection in 1999, that either he had to get the energy sector to support his candidacy or this sector would put their money in another basket.

If we look at the situation in 1998–1999, some of the most influential actors in Ukrainian politics were the following: Oleksandr Volkov, Ihor Bakay, Hryhory Surkis, Viktor Medvedchuk, Oleksandr Derkach, Viktor Pinchuk, and Yuliya Timoshenko. Ihor Bakay was former head of the Respublika and Interhaz private gas-trading companies, and later became director of the major state gas company Naftohaz. Viktor Pinchuk controlled the gas and a metallurgical investment group Interpipe. Hryhory Surkis and Viktor Medvedchuk were through several companies heavily involved in the oil and gas sector. Oleksandr Volkov was not himself influential in the energy sector, but took on the role as a coordinator of the political interests of this sector. In February 1999 Volkov gathered the majority of gas-trading MPs into the parliamentary faction For Regional Revival. Volkov was allied with Bakay, and Rabinovych with Pinchuk and Derkach.

The following are the major Ukrainian oligarchs and institutions under their control:

	Oleksandr Volkov	Surkis/ Medvedchuk	Ihor Bakay	Pinchuk/ Derkach	Vadym Rabinovych
Business interests	Naftohaz, Ukrenergo-Sbyte Finansy i Kredit F&C Realty Gas and finances	Slavutich, Ometa 20th Century, Ukrainian Credit Bank, Oil, gas, electricity, ports, and others	Naftohaz (resigned, but still considered influential) Oil and gas	Interpipe, Turbotrast, Belinterpipe, Binako Pipeline building, gas, iron and steel smelting	Nordex (until 1997) Oil and gas
Political parties	Democratic Union of Ukraine	Ukrainian Social Democratic Party (United)	Democratic Union of Ukraine	Working Ukraine	
Parliamentary factions	The Revival of the Regions	The faction of the Ukrainian Social Democratic Party (United)	The Revival of the Regions	Working Ukraine	Parts of the factions of the Green Party of Ukraine
Other public organizations	The charity fund Sotsialny zakhyst (Social Protection)	The footbal club Dynamo Kyiv			The All-Ukrainian Jewish Congress
Media	The TV channel UT-1 (state TV), Hravis The newspapers *Segodnya* and *Noviy Vek*	The journal *Biznes* (Business), the daily *Kievskie Vedomosti*, and the TV channels Inter, Yutar,	The daily *Segodnya* (Today) and the TV channel ICTV	The dailies *Fakty* (Facts) and *Kievski Telegraf*, and the regional TV channel "1+1" and 11th Channel in Dnipropetrovsk	The weeklies *Stolichnye Novosty* (The Capital News), and *Delovaya Nedelya* (Business Weekly), the TV channels ERA, NTU, and UNIAR, and the radio channels Super-Nova and ERA

At the end of Kuchma's first term Ukraine was in a position where Russia both as a political and economic actor was increasing its influence on Ukrainian domestic politics. The political scientist Volodymyr Polokhalo very approximately estimated that Russia stood for 60 percent of the foreign influence on Ukrainian domestic politics, and the West for 40 percent.[39]

In spite of the shift in the balance of power among the sectors of Ukrainian big business in influencing the Ukrainian executive, there was no return to a pro-Russian foreign policy. In fact, a July 2000 survey of the foreign policy attitudes of 100 representatives of the Ukrainian political elite, including high representatives from the presidential administration, the Security and Defense Council apparatus, the government, the Foreign Ministry, and other organs, confirmed how entrenched the pro-European foreign policy discourse had become. In this survey the respondents were asked to state which countries they thought should be the main priority for Ukraine in foreign policy. Russia and the CIS countries were the choice of only 26 percent (17 percent and 11 percent, respectively) of the respondents, whereas the EU and the United States were the choice of 59 percent of the respondents (48 percent and 11 percent, respectively).[40] This does not necessarily mean that all these elite representatives had adopted some kind of a deep personal conviction of Ukraine as a genuinely European country. However, the survey results do suggest that the pro-European discourse had achieved something of a hegemony position in the elite foreign policy debate.

Using the pluralist perspective, one would have anticipated a return to a more pro-Russian foreign policy after the change in the balance of power among economic interest groups. So why then were there few indications of this happening?

One reason is because an identity, once adopted, also becomes a constraint on behavior. Each time the Ukrainian leadership asserted the country's Europeanness, a retreat to a non-European identity became more difficult. This happens, according to international relations scholar Ted Hopf, because "actors reproduce daily their own constraints through ordinary practice."[41] If the Kuchma administration had teetered back and forth between a Eurasian and a European identity, it would have become unable to act as "we," to know where the borders of the Ukrainian self were, and to provide predictability. This is an important part of the explanation of why the changing balance of power among economic interest groups in the presidential administration did not change Ukraine's pro-Western foreign policy. The focus on the explanatory power of identities in state behavior is largely a contribution from constructivist theory, as discussed in Chapter 3.

The analysis, so far, corresponds well with the pluralist perspective. Initial choices are made within the pluralist–consequentialist perspective, but because the actor tends to develop both an identity and a set of rules that build on the initial choice, the Weberian–appropriateness perspective slowly becomes dominant. It can be questioned, however, if that is what has taken place in Ukraine. It could be argued that the pro-European statements of many Ukrainian politicians do not reflect any deep convictions, but are mainly motivated by the wish to attract Western aid and support. That is very possible, but even if this is the case it does not necessarily weaken the standing of the European foreign policy identity, at least not in the short or medium term. If we conceive of the Ukrainian European foreign policy identity in the same way that the scholar Joseph Schull conceives of the term "ideology," individual beliefs become less important as a source of explanation. Schull defines ideology as "a form of discourse or a political language— a body of linguistic propositions expressed as speech-acts and united by the conventions governing them. Its adherents will have varied beliefs about its conventions, yet all will be constrained by them in order to be recognized as competent speakers of the discourse."[42] In this interpretation the European foreign policy orientation takes the form of a framework for acceptable linguistic utterances, where serious deviation from the framework can have serious negative consequences for the perpetrator personally. If that is the case, the pluralist–consequentialist perspective is still dominant. But whereas the European orientation initially was chosen because of the fear that integration with Russia would make the representatives of the economic elite lose their positions and power to Russians, now these same representatives have to stick to that orientation because they might otherwise lose their power and positions to other Ukrainians who stick to that orientation. Most likely, different representatives of the Ukrainian political elite under Kuchma profess the European foreign policy orientations for different reasons. Some follow the pluralist–consequentialist perspective because they think it is expected of them if they want to remain influential, whereas others who advocate the Weberian–appropriateness perspective are personally convinced that Ukraine is naturally a European country.

The second interpretation indicates that one of the perspectives is used to make fundamental decisions and the other is used to make refinements. By the terminology of this chapter, this means that the pluralist perspective can be used to explain fundamental decisions and the Weberian perspective to explain the refinements. This can mean refinements of fundamental decisions, but one can also imagine that smaller day-to-day decisions might not be in accordance with fundamental decisions at all. That is, smaller deviations from the fundamental decision for the purpose of promoting individual interests might be acceptable to the actor as long as he does not think it will substantially damage the fundamental decision.

One example of this is the case of the construction of the Odesa–Brody pipeline. The almost total dependency on Russian oil and gas has been recognized as probably the main security concern of the Ukrainian state since 1991. One way to lessen this dependency is the construction of an oil pipeline from Odesa to Brody, with a connection to the Polish oil pipeline network. The main role of Ukraine in this project is as a transit area for Caspian oil to Europe. This will bring money to Ukraine in the form of transit fees, but the main advantage is that Ukraine will become less dependent on Russian oil deliveries.

The realization of this project came more or less to a halt in 1998. In a joint appeal from the People's Democratic Party and Rukh, First Deputy Prime Minister Anatoly Holubchenko was accused of acting independently to halt the construction of the pipeline. Holubchenko was at that time high in the power hierarchy in Kyiv. The suspicion was that Holubchenko had stopped the construction because he was making substantial personal gains from the resale of Russian oil in Ukraine and feared that the Odesa–Brody pipeline would diminish the scale of that trade. Ukrainian government officials never admitted any truth in the accusations, but Kuchma removed Holubchenko from his position the day before he went to Warsaw for further consultations on the pipeline issue. Kuchma's foreign policy adviser, Yuriy Scherbak, later confirmed that the pipeline project had been almost terminated because certain "civil servants had had private interests in this situation."[43]

The removal of Holubchenko, however, did not lead to the realization of the pipeline project. As of March 2000, 30 percent of the project was still not completed. This was the case despite several explicit presidential orders to complete the project and funds made available for the completion by the Ukrainian parliament. This time Ihor Bakay became suspect for acting in a manner similar to Holubchenko. One Ukrainian journalist, Aleksandr Yurchuk, referred to the Odesa–Brody pipeline as Bakay's personal "sour point."[44] Bakay was considered to have substantial influence on the president, both in his own right and through his political and business ally, Kuchma confidant Aleksandr Volkov. The problem is, of course, that if the number of smaller deviations from the fundamental decision for the purpose of promoting individual interests reaches a critical level, the fundamental decision may be damaged. It can then end up not being taken seriously by domestic actors or by the outside world.

The political game behind the import of Russian gas is a very murky business and something on which it is difficult to find reliable information. What does seem clear, though, is that for this business to continue the oligarchs were interested in stopping plans for a diversification of Ukrainian energy supplies. However, because diversification of the sources of energy supply had been elevated to security question number one in Ukraine, to be seen as fighting against it would be tanta-mount to high treason. Thus, there was great secrecy around these efforts. In addition, it became imperative for the oligarchs to give the impression of being Ukrainian patriots. For this very reason, Ihor Bakay managed to become relatively popular in Ukrainian nationalist circles.

The first serious challenge to the business interests of these oligarchs came after the reelection of Kuchma in 1999. Under influence from the West, Kuchma chose the unscrupulously noncorrupt chairman of the National Bank, Victor Yushenko, as the new prime minister. The choice of Yushenko was a slap in the face of the oligarchs, but worse was to come from the viewpoint of the oligarchs. To tidy up in the energy business, Yushenko chose as his deputy prime minister in charge of energy issues the former oligarch Yulia Timoshenko. Timoshenko had been in the same business as Surkis and Bakay, but the activities of her United Energy Systems of Ukraine had been stopped by a court deci-sion in 1997 on the basis of accusations of massive irregularities. Many Ukrainian observers saw this appointment as a blatant example of sending the fox to mind the geese. Timoshenko herself, however, claimed that she would "use her own experience from 'the shadowy sphere'" to bring order to the branch.[45] Though Timoshenko's ability to act only in the best interests of the Ukrainian state and not in the interest of particular business groups were still questioned, indepen-dent experts characterized Timoshenko's legislative efforts as initia-tives that could truly bring order and transparency to the energy sector.[46] In addition to the legislative efforts, Timoshenko also tried to secure alternative sources of energy supply, thus further challenging the business interests of the oligarchs. In particular, she tried to enlist Turkmenistan as an alternative source to Russia for gas supplies.

Because of Timoshenko's initiatives in the energy sector, she was at constant war with the oligarchs after becoming deputy prime minis-ter. In the mid-1990s, she is still victorious in this struggle.[47] Ihor Bakay, for example, resigned from his position as head of the main state gas and oil company, Naftohaz Ukrayiny, in protest against Timoshenko's policy. Though President Kuchma tried to be on good terms with both sides in this struggle, he was probably well aware of the need for an orderly and transparent energy sector and for alternative sources of energy supplies. These alternative sources probably only increased in importance after the change of president in Russia. There were clear indications that the new leadership in the Kremlin had more difficulty in coming to terms with the energy situation than the previous one. According to one of the most respected observers of Ukrainian poli-tics, journalist Yulia Mostovaya, the new Russian leadership started to make a very strong connection between energy supplies and politi-cal concessions. She gave the following illustration of the conduct of

Russian–Ukrainian negotiations on energy issues under the new Russian leadership: "Schematically it looks like this 'We give you 5 billion cubic meters of gas, and you enter the Customs Union, and we give you an additional 5 billion cubic meters of gas, and you support our position on the missile defense issue.'"[48]

There is also evidence that the first interpretation is useful in explaining Ukrainian foreign policy under Kuchma. According to this interpretation, whatever is most clear to the actor in any particular situation—preferences and consequences or identities and rules—will dominate his choice. What seemed to take place during the final year and a half of Kuchma's first term was a division into separate spheres of economics and politics. Economically, Ukraine, for the reasons mentioned here, again came closer to Russia, but this did not result in any adjustment of Ukraine's foreign policy identity. The interests and preferences of individuals and societal subgroups are probably clearer in economic affairs than in political affairs. The major markets are still in Russia, and old-time business contacts are still strong. In political life, however, the geopolitical picture is particularly clear and makes the Weberian perspective more applicable. It is a dominating idea in the Ukrainian establishment that Ukraine's only alternative to a European identity in the long run is the position of a small obedient brother to Russia. This scenario became particularly clear in the context of the Belarus–Russia union.

The Ukrainian elite seems able to separate economics and politics and act according to the pluralist perspective in economics and the Weberian perspective in politics. A good example of this is the Ukrainian rocket industry. This branch of the military–industrial complex has been one of the major advocates for the European foreign policy identity supported by Horbulin, and at the same time it is this branch that has some of the best personal contacts and functioning commercial cooperation with Russian counterparts. The economic realm, therefore, seems to have a natural bias toward the pluralist perspective, whereas the political realm seems to have a similar bias toward the Weberian perspective.

CONCLUSION

Ukrainian industrial barons from east and central Ukraine paid for Kuchma's campaign in 1994, and were rewarded with numerous influential positions in the government and presidential administration after the election victory. They set out to achieve reintegration with Russia, but on terms that gave them a considerably stronger and more equal position than had been the case during Soviet times. When they learned that this was not how the Russian elite envisioned the reintegration, they became proponents of a pro-Western foreign policy course as an alternative.

Therefore, in order to explain the shift from a Eurasian to a European foreign policy identity in Ukraine during Kuchma's first five years as president, one must take into account the changes of attitude toward Russia among leading economic elites. This finding indicates the necessity of using insights from the pluralist perspective of state theory in foreign policy analysis. It is especially the case when the object of analysis is what may be described as a privatized state.

What the pluralist perspective cannot account for, however, is why the advent of the mildly pro-Russian energy barons in the government and presidential administration, and the ever closer personal relations between these barons and Russian oligarchs, did not result in a return to a more pro-Russian foreign policy.

This, however, can be explained by using the Weberian perspective of state theory combined with insights from constructivist theory. For a number of psychological and sociological reasons, foreign policy identities are not easy to change once established. The Ukrainian case seems to suggest that the relationship between the pluralist perspective and the Weberian perspective is that the first is good at explaining initial major choices, and the second better at explaining what happens after these initial choices have been made.

The Ukrainian choice of a European foreign policy identity seems to persist. However, one cannot exclude that Ukraine in the future might be confronted with the need for a major rethinking of its foreign policy identity. This could happen, for example, if Russia together with Ukraine reached a clear understanding that the expansion of European political and economic institutions will stop at these countries' western borders. Such a message might be perceived by the Ukrainians as signifying a return to square one, putting the country in a situation where it again has to make a major "initial" choice. Here the pluralist perspective could again become dominant. If Ukraine is left with little hope for significant integration with the major European political and economic institutions, the dominant economic elites of the Ukrainian privatized state would be forced to take stock of where the country is going. They would have to decide what would best suit their interests, the identity of a rejected son of Europe or the identity of a smaller brother in Eurasia. If the Russian political and economic elites in this situation would be ready to treat the Ukrainian political and economic elites with more respect and sense of equality than in 1994, and promise the Ukrainian elites that they will not lose their positions of power in politics and economics, then the "smaller brother in Eurasia identity" could well become the most tempting.

NOTES

1. Prime Minister Kuchma, interview, *Ukrayinska Hazeta* 2 (1993), quoted in Yuri Lukanov, *Trety Prezydent—Politychny Portret Leonida Kuchmy* (Kyiv: Taki Sparvy, 1996), 110.

2. Yanina Sokolovskaya, "Ukraina ne otvorachyvayetsya ot Rossii" (Ukraine is not turning away from Russia), *Segodnya*, 10 October 1999.

3. For a focus on how both international relations and foreign policy analysis could be improved by connecting to state theory, see Fred Halliday, *Rethinking International Relations* (London: Macmillan Press, 1994), 74–93; Bruce E. Moon, "The State in Foreign and Domestic Policy," in *Foreign Policy Analysis: Continuity and Change in Its Second Generation*, ed. Laura Neack, Jeanne A. K. Hey, and Patrick J. Haney (Englewood Cliffs, N.J.: Prentice Hall, 1995), 187–200; Brian White, "The European Challenge to Foreign Policy Analysis," *European Journal of International Relations* 5, no. 1 (1999): 54–55; Alexander Wendt, *Social Theory of International Politics* (New York: Cambridge University Press, 1999), 193–245.

4. Theda Skocpol, "Bringing the State Back In: Strategies of Analysis in Current Research," in *Bringing the State Back In*, ed. Peter B. Evans, Dietrich Rueshchmeyer, and Theda Skocpol (Cambridge: Cambridge University Press, 1985), 8.

5. J. P. Nettle, "The State as a Conceptual Variable," *World Politics* 20 (1968): 563–564.

6. Bo Stråth and Rolf Thorstendahl, "State Theory and State Development: States as Network Structures in Change in Modern European History," in *State Theory and State History*, ed. Rolf Thorstendahl (London: Sage, 1992), 13.

7. Michael McFaul, "Russia's 'Privatized' State as an Impediment to Democratic Consolidation," *Security Dialogue* 29, no. 2 (1998): 191–199.

8. Ibid., 195.

9. Dmytro Pavlychko, "Yevropa vidchula shcho vona bilsha nizh zdavalos" (Europe started to feel that she is larger than she would like to be), *Viche* 8 (1992): 141.

10. Vasyl Kremen, Dmytro Tabachnyk, and Vasyl Tkachenko, *Ukrayina: Alternatyvy Postupu* (Ukraine: Alternative roads) (Kyiv: Lybid, 1999), 711.

11. Ibid., 119.

12. Anatoliy Hrytsenko, interview by author, Kyiv, 2 March 2000.

13. *Jamestown Monitor*, 17 February 1999.

14. Mykhailo Pozhivanov, interview, *Den*, 3 March 1999.

15. Zhalilo worked from 1994 to 1996 as an assistant to the president of UEIU, and therefore knows the thinking of these groups from the inside.

16. Yaroslav Zhalilo, Volodymyr Lupatsiy, and Andriy Smenkovkiy, *Korporatyvni interesy i vybir stratehichnykh priorytetiv ekonomichnoyi polityky* (Corporative interests and the choice of strategic priorities in the economic policy) (Kyiv: National Institute of Strategic Studies, 1999). Available at: <http://www.niss.gov.ua/book>.

17. Aleksandr Gurevich, "Znakomtyes: Kabmin v promyshlennom ispolnenii" (Get familiar: The government in the service of the industry), *Zerkalo Nedely*, 10–16 July 1999.

18. Mikhailo Romantsov, "Valeriy Pustovoitenko vpershe vyishov 'u narod'" (Valery Pustovoitenko "went to the people" for the first time), *Den*, 1997.

19. Oleksandr Potekhin, interview by author, Kyiv, 29 February 2000. Potekhin at the time of the interview was head of the Centre for Peace, Conversion and Foreign Policy of Ukraine.

20. Zhalilo, Lupatsiy, and Smenkovkiy, *Korporatyvni interesy*.

21. Katya Gorchinskaya, "Western Criticism Pushes Oligarchs toward Russia," *Kyiv Post*, 3 February 2000.

22. Ivan Galperin, "Pustovoitenko ili Derkach?" (Pustovoitenko or Derkach), *Nezavisimaya Gazeta*, 12 November 1999.

23. Ibid.

24. Potekhin, interview.

25. Valentin Badrak, interview by author, Kyiv, 29 February 2000.

26. James G. March and Johan P. Olsen, "The Institutional Dynamics of International Political Orders," in *Exploration and Contestation in the Study of World Politics*, ed. Peter J. Katzenstein, Robert O. Keohane, and Stephen D. Krasner (Cambridge: MIT Press, 1999), 309.

27. Ibid.

28. Ibid., 311.

29. Ibid.

30. Ibid.

31. Ibid., 313.

32. Taras Kuzio, *Ukraine under Kuchma: Political Reform, Economic Transformation, and Security Policy in Independent Ukraine* (New York: St. Martin's Press, 1997), 60–64.

33. Vyacheslav Pikhovshek, Oleksandr Chekmyshev, Olga Lehn, Tetyana Koltsova, and Inna Pidluska, *Dnipropetrovsk V Security Service* (Report by the Ukrainian Centre for Independent Political Research, 1996), 55.

34. Wendt, *Social Theory*, 224.

35. John Gerard Ruggie, *Constructing the World Polity* (London: Routledge, 1998), 22.

36. Valeriy Chaly and Mykhail Pashkov, "Ukraine's International Image: The View from Russia," *National Security and Defense* 3 (2000): 65.

37. Vladimir Lartsev,"Pobeda kakogo klana vygodney strane" (What clan's victory is best for the country), *Kievskie Vedomosti*, 15 July 1997.

38. Petr Vlasov, "Bednye lyudi" (Poor people), *Ekspert*, 1999.

39. Tatyana Ivzhenko, "Kabminu trudno" (Difficult times for the government), *Kompanion*, 2000.

40. Mikhail Pashkov and Valery Chalyi, "Cherez ternii—k yevrozvesdam" (Through thorns to the European stars), *Zerkalo Nedely*, 9–15 September 2000.

41. Ted Hopf, "The Promise of Constructivism in International Relations Theory," *International Security* 23, no. 1 (1998): 180.

42. Joseph Schull, "What Is Ideology? Theoretical Problems and Lessons from Soviet-Type Societies," *Political Studies* 40, no. 4 (1992): 729.

43. Yuriy Scherbak, "Vybor tseli" (To choose the goal), *Stolichnye Novosti*, 22–28 February 2000.

44. Aleksandr Yurchuk, "Volkov i dualizm" (Volkov and dualism), *Zerkalo Nedely*, 16–22 September 2000.

45. Yulia Timoshenko, interview, *Zerkalo Nedely*, 2–8 September 2000.

46. Yulia Mostovaya, "Snimu vitse-premyera" (I remove the deputy prime minister), *Zerkalo Nedely*, 9–15 September 2000.

47. Editor's note: In February 2001 Yulia Tymoshenko was dismissed from her post, arrested, and jailed to face multiple charges of corruption, bribery, tax evasion, and money laundering. The group of energy-controlling oligarchs, which had been undoubtedly harmed by her policies, apparently took its revenge.

48. Yulia Mostovaya, "Politichesky rezus-konflikt" (A political resus-conflict), *Zerkalo Nedely*, 19 August–1 September 2000.

8

The Polish–Ukrainian Interstate Model for Cooperation and Integration: Regional Relations in a Theoretical Context

Joshua B. Spero

> Poland has mastered the role of major articulator of Ukraine's interests in Europe.[1]

Rarely do post–Cold War studies on state alignment and international relations theory explore why medium-size states cooperatively align with larger, traditionally stronger hegemonic states, especially post-Communist states.[2] The important nexus between the state and international system underscores the complex relationship between bureaucratic change and institutional transformation at the domestic level for foreign policy outcomes. By focusing on the underpinnings of comparative foreign policy, this chapter examines if post–Communist Poland promoted a nonthreatening, pragmatic security policy and offered a post-Communist model for the relations built with Germany during the early 1990s and those attempted with Ukraine today.

The main question focuses on whether post–Communist Poland designed predominantly conciliatory policies during the post–Cold War era to increase stability in turbulent Central East Europe, particularly toward Ukraine, and if such policies demonstrated how a post–

Communist European state tried to overcome a security dilemma. Such a state model of behavior contributes to future research regarding other post–Communist European foreign policy comparisons, especially states desiring integration into or developing close ties toward NATO and the EU.

Few works explore the important post–Cold War Polish–German relationship and how it presents a starting point for assessing post-Communist and Western interstate relationships and alignment strategies.[3] This chapter contributes to international relations and comparative politics by studying the design and formulation of Polish foreign policy toward Ukraine to reveal if Warsaw–Kyiv ties showed an important conciliatory model of state behavior.

In order to profit by forming what neorealists Randall Schweller and Charles Glaser, among others, characterized as nonthreatening and cooperative state behavior, the chapter attempts to exhibit that post–Communist Poland bandwagoned with its neighboring states more than it balanced in an attempt to create new, nonpredatory alignments. The chapter uses neorealist theories of bandwagoning, balancing, and aggressive alignment to examine nonthreatening and cooperative behavior among traditional adversaries. Specifically, cooperative rather than competitive bandwagoning exists when a weaker state aligns itself to a stronger state or coalition to gain a reward. The state responds to an opportunity, not necessarily by trying to achieve greater security because of a direct threat or to reduce the security of other states. Balancing results when a state attempts to ally with another state or coalition against a perceived threat. Aggression underscores threatening behavior, often leading to war, and opposes bandwagoning and balancing.[4]

Given this theoretical context, more of which generally follows, the chapter defines independent and dependent variables. The chapter applies the rapidly changing security system in Central Europe as the independent variable and employs the foreign policy Poland developed, crafted, and promulgated toward Ukraine and how Ukraine responded as the dependent variable. Initially created and implemented by Poland's first post-Communist foreign minster, Krzysztof Skubiszewski, from 1989 to 1993, successive foreign ministers built on his foreign policy template and early successes.[5] Thus, neorealism underpins the chapter's objective to increase understanding about whether post–Communist Poland sought to aid post–Communist Ukraine's security and stability without threatening Russia.

Analysis of Polish–Ukrainian post–Cold War politico-military relations provides the foundation for examination of cooperative behavior to demonstrate whether Poland and Ukraine peacefully bandwagon

with, rather than balance against, each other to achieve national security objectives. This chapter argues that Polish–Ukrainian ties do not
threaten Russia. Rather, Warsaw aims to foster a similar path with Kyiv
as it did with Bonn–Berlin during the immediate post–Cold War period, to increase regional stability in Central East Europe and offer a
bridge to Russia based on democratization.[6] The reasoning stems from
the premises that Poland

1. crafted new interstate relations with Bonn in the early 1990s and considerably increased Warsaw's chances for European reintegration.
2. tried to solidify relations developed in the early mid-1990s and expanded
   significantly by the end of the decade with Kyiv to strengthen Ukraine's
   independence and peacefully reduce Russian regional imperialist aims.

Hence, according to the Polish argument, if Poland and Ukraine
could overcome their historically conflictual tendencies toward one
another, both Warsaw and Kyiv could greatly increase regional stability
in the post–Cold War era, particularly with their respective ties to NATO.[7]
Moreover, this analysis presents implications for other post-Communist
states and might be applied beyond this chapter's conclusions.

Within this context, the chapter views Polish–Ukrainian relationship in terms of the impact post–Cold War transnational security dilemmas have on institutional change and foreign policy priorities.
These dilemmas not only often lead to international conflict, such as
the Yugoslav wars during the 1990s, but also provide a basis of investigating potential solutions for models of crisis management and conflict resolution, even for conflict prevention, as it will be argued
Polish–Ukrainian ties demonstrate. By analyzing if change via such
multilateral institutions as NATO creates a new type of contemporary
realism in post–Cold War state relationships, the chapter contends that
Polish–Ukrainian politico-military cooperation underscores significant
and concrete successes during the past several years.

Such successes stem from the series of nonthreatening military training exercises to promote capabilities in peace support operations (peace
enforcement and peacekeeping), search and rescue, and humanitarian
relief. Polish and Ukrainian civilian and military leaders and staffs conducted these events, which consisted of hundreds of activities within complex exercises on both Polish and Ukrainian territory and under the
auspices of NATO's Partnership for Peace process.[8] From this politico-
military cooperation came the creation of the Polish–Ukrainian peace
support battalion, operational fully in 1998 and deployed as part of
the NATO–led Kosovo implementation force (KFOR) in June 2000.[9]

THE NEOREALIST FRAMEWORK
FOR STATE ALIGNMENT

To have a better understanding of Polish–Ukrainian relations and their importance to European security regionally, the following theoretical section elaborates distinctions within neorealism. The arguments here distinguish bandwagoning and balancing alignment, taking some of the key arguments to illustrate why states ally and realign.[10]

Neorealism signifies that the anarchical international system, its unequal distribution of power, and its structural pressures shape how states exercise their political, economic, and military capabilities, rather than just actions stemming primarily from key decision makers. According to neorealism, states try to maximize security and self-preservation, not simply to expand power, as realists argue. Both security and distribution of power represent key neorealist variables, but unlike security, power remains a means not an end in itself for changing political relationships between and among states. Distribution of power does, however, define the international system's structure.[11] Some neorealists assert that particular interdependent categories of inquiry for states define certain historical periods in relation to the independent variable, the international system, and the dependent variables, such as interest, security, and power; perception and reality; and cooperation and conflict.[12]

COMPETITIVE ALIGNMENT IN NEOREALIST
BALANCING AND BANDWAGONING

Waltz first defined neorealism as a theory where states compete to increase security and strengthen or maintain their places in the international system. He argued that balancing and bandwagoning, and the distribution or redistribution of power within the system's balance of power, lead to a weaker state's alignment with the strongest state. In the system, Waltz felt states needed to preserve or restore the system's balance via power plays. He viewed balancing and bandwagoning as opposite alignment with periodic "balancing of would-be leaders" among states, and asserted that "as soon as someone looks like the winner, nearly all jump on the bandwagon rather than continuing to build coalitions intended to prevent anyone from winning the prize of power." Therefore, he maintained that "power is a means and not an end, [and] the goal the system encourages them [states] to seek is security; the first concern of states is not to maximize power but to maintain their positions in the system."[13]

A variation from Waltz's "security-based" neorealism, however, stems from the arguments regarding threat more than power made by neorealists such as Walt. For Walt, states not only measure the merits of bandwagoning with or balancing against other states by determining which state or states appear the strongest, but also, more important, which state or states seem the most threatening. He contends that states attempt to align with or against the most threatening state, a state not necessarily the strongest one in the system. On the one hand, Walt believed that "bandwagoning refers to alignment with the dominant power, either to appease it or to profit from its victory." Such behavior, Walt explained, "involves unequal exchange [when] the vulnerable state makes asymmetrical concessions to the dominant power and accepts a subordinate role." The state bows to bandwagoning pressure, whether latent or manifest, when it displays a willingness to support or tolerate illegitimate actions by the dominant ally. Moreover, "bandwagoning requires trust; one assists a dominant power in the hope that it will remain benevolent."[14] In other words, Walt's threat-based system identified a proclivity to bandwagon when no allies or potential allies existed, a threatening power looked appeasing, or an endangered state remained vulnerable to domination, notwithstanding allied help. On the other hand, Walt explained that balancing signified state "alignment against the threatening power, to deter it from attacking or to defeat it if it does." Many states, then, consistently discern threats by either one or several states. Furthermore, even if threats appear unfounded, Walt contended that a state's leaders need seriously to consider such potential risks, decide how to respond, and calculate whether to balance against a threatening state. Therefore, the widespread anarchy anticipated by neorealism among competitive states, Walt argued, makes states wary about others' readiness to aid during emergencies or confrontations.[15]

Based on the Waltz and Walt models, the upheaval resulting from the Cold War's end presumably would have states allying to protect themselves from either the strongest or the most threatening state in the emerging post–Cold War system. Both Waltz and Walt argued that most states would resort to balancing for power against other states or balancing against threats, rather than either bandwagoning with the winning side toward the end of a conflict or allowing themselves to become an easy victim of a larger power's expansion.[16] Despite the conventional wisdom held by many neorealists that certain balancing alignments develop when the international system changes, others, such as Glaser and Schweller, believe that the end of bipolar Cold War Europe witnessed more than most states simply balancing. Hitherto, Waltz argued that, throughout the Cold War, the superpowers continually balanced against one another to preserve the bipolar European regional and conventional military balance of power. In such a system, Waltz believed that states, "at a minimum, seek their own preservation and, at a maximum, drive for universal domination."[17] Even if some weaker states bandwagoned with the perceived stronger and threatening states, according to Walt, this occurred in bipolar Europe. The Cold War's demise, however, resulted in heated debates by realists and neorealists about why bipolar and multipolar systemic structures generate different types of alignment, what problems concerning the maintenance of the system arise, and how states preserve themselves within the new system.[18]

COOPERATIVE ALIGNMENT IN NEOREALIST BALANCING AND BANDWAGONING

This section explains cooperation theoretically to discern insights in the next section on the basis for the Polish–German model and then to impart why bandwagoning and balancing do not necessarily denote opposite geopolitical behaviors when viewing Ukraine.[19] Rather, the chapter uses bandwagoning to portray actions states conduct to gain a reward, while balancing characterizes effort states take to achieve security. The results from balancing, however, frequently entail costs to states because such alignment involves balancing with a state or coalition vigorously against a strong predatory state or states. This balancing, whether offensively or defensively, by a state or states against a seriously perceived external threat aims to preserve and protect the state.[20] Unlike the more conventionally held realist notion of the defense of the state's economic and military capabilities and the pessimistic neorealist view that adversarial states rarely cooperate, the chapter employs the neorealist definition of cooperative alignment by Schweller and Glaser, alternatively, to analyze post–Communist Poland's self-preservation and security.[21]

By comparing the Waltz and Walt competitive neorealist arguments with the cooperative ones by Glaser and Schweller, the chapter demarcates a state's willingness to incur a cost, often by balancing with a weaker state or states, but distinguishes it from a state that bandwagons with a stronger state or states to profit. According to Schweller, the objective of bandwagoning centers on the opportunity by a state, especially an unthreatened state, to gain by seeking to join the security system it values. The security system comprises a stronger state or coalition of stronger states and the bandwagoning state attempts to align, usually during a time of geopolitical change. Furthermore, Schweller maintains that bandwagoning by one state or states need not occur by threatening another state's security or the security system to which the bandwagoning state desires to belong. Bandwagoning emphasizes a state strategy to gain a reward for alignment, but not necessarily through appeasement of a threat. Nonthreatening bandwagoning states seem to ally with others, not solely because of the external security and stability sought, but in the expectation of distributive gains to many of the states involved.[22]

Bandwagoning states try to attain such gains, not through war but from extending the bandwagoning state's value system, such as promoting peacefully the values of democracy, free markets, and cooperative military programs. Alignments or even alliances become positive-sum experiences for bandwagoning states, not behavior motivated mainly by power and threat leading to aggression or war, as neorealists Waltz and Walt contend. Moreover bandwagoning frequently occurs voluntarily, particularly after geopolitical changes.[23] The chapter uses this theoretical context to examine the motivations behind Poland's strategy and how Warsaw defined what it meant to achieve security to disclose if Poland demonstrated a new post–Communist European alignment paradigm. Therefore, the chapter attempts to test why Poland displayed bandwagoning alignment as a "nonthreatened" state more than balancing as a "threatening" state toward Germany and Ukraine. Given the new geopolitical chances in Poland's view to reintegrate into Europe, the result of Central East Europe's democratic revolutions, the bipolar European security system's collapse, and the USSR's disintegration, this chapter's examination sets a foundation for future research to explore post-Communist state alignment.[24]

This chapter also raises the question of whether balancing frequently revolves around the costs of security, even of survival. By taking Schweller's assertion that "profit rather than security drives alliance choices" and applying it to post–Cold War Europe, the chapter contends that states often willingly "climb aboard the bandwagon through the promise of rewards, not the threat of punishment."[25] States often cooperate because of the "values of the security system they covet," particularly post–Communist Poland's desire to reach new accords with all neighbors and to join NATO's pluralistic security community.[26]

NATO, POST–COLD WAR EUROPE, AND POLISH ALIGNMENT

According to the neorealist framework of competitive states within either Waltz's power-based or Walt's threat-based system, states presumably compete against each other as a result of a collapse like the Cold War's bipolar system and the increased anarchy in Europe. Given this competition and Central Europe's war-ravaged history, the premise underlying examination of post–Communist Polish foreign policy might assume antagonism or submission toward neighboring states. The reduction of superpower tensions in crumbling bipolar Europe at the end of the 1980s, however, actually began to invigorate many of the states comprising NATO to adapt its Cold War institution for post–Cold War missions. Although this chapter remains focused on Poland and its potential cooperative state model without presuming an exhaustive rationale for alliance theory and NATO's post–Cold War evolution, it does base its rationale on NATO providing states a more stable security system. The rationale results from the number of crises NATO decreased from escalating into regional or European war. The chapter takes into account how Polish and Ukrainian foreign policy makers considered options toward NATO at the end of the 1990s, given their geostrategically important location between larger Germany and resurgent Russia. More important, the restrictive norms and behavior standards NATO members needed to uphold during the Cold War reduced uncertainty, miscalculation, and war. Within the context of Poland's 1999 NATO accession, this chapter accounts briefly for how NATO institutionally adapted and defined post–Cold War missions as threats substantially declined and different types of challenges emerged.[27]

As the Cold War ended, NATO members started to change NATO's structures, and "enemies" such as Poland and Ukraine began to reevaluate whether to remain a member of the opposing Warsaw Pact or to move closer toward the Western alliance. The emerging democracies desired either to join or begin linkages to NATO's stability-enhancing and democratic institution. The demise of the Warsaw Pact and then the USSR initially gave rise to the notion in alliance theory that NATO's institutional raison d'être no longer applied to post–Cold War Europe and, hence, NATO's existence appeared in doubt.[28] Yet NATO launched confidence-building measures toward its former enemies and, more important, toward neutral Eurasian states by defining new post–Cold War missions focused partially on membership for former adversaries by the end of the 1990s.[29] Though this chapter concentrates on neorealism to assess Poland's behavior toward Germany and Ukraine within anarchical post–Cold War Europe, institutional theory offers an important perspective to view the growing importance of NATO to both Polish and Ukrainian foreign policy makers.

NATO's cooperative institutional norms and lowered costs of security for its members allowed for institutionalization of politico-military links among its members to develop over fifty years. Some realist arguments favoring NATO's lasting value focus on how NATO reduced tensions between former enemies such as France and Germany while providing the United States with the leading role to arbitrate European security within NATO's intricate politico-military structures. Unlike realist interpretations of institutionalist structures in an anarchical world, however, institutionalist theorists depict NATO's role differently within the system comprised of cooperative and antagonistic states. Institutionalists argue that NATO's framework plays the key role in influencing state expectations and behavior in Europe's security system, resulting more often in enhanced state security. This chapter considers theoretical debates about Europe's evolving security system, Polish decision making toward Ukraine, and Polish–Ukrainian relations vis-à-vis NATO, an institution in which its members states behaved primarily according to politico-military principles, rules, and procedures.[30]

Why Poland Bandwagoned toward Germany from 1989 to 1993

At the outset of the post–Communist Polish period, Foreign Minister Skubiszewski crafted a dynamic German policy that remained relatively consistent until he left government four years later, having achieved the majority of his goals and setting the long-lasting foundation for important Polish–German relations.[31] The relationship with Germany, particularly during German unification, focused on obtaining four objectives to begin Poland's European reintegration. First, Poland required that Bonn unambiguously agree to Poland's western border in a treaty to conclude peacefully the outstanding uncertainty from the post–World War II territorial settlements. Second, to achieve this critical objective, Skubiszewski believed Poland needed to gain Bonn's support for Poland as an independent actor in Central European security, primarily in the unification process. Furthermore, he recognized that Germany's rapid unification necessitated four-power control. Last, the Polish foreign minister believed strongly in trying to coordinate with a unified Germany regarding the orderly withdrawal of Soviet troops from both Poland and Germany.

Skubiszewski wanted Poland to play not only a useful and independent role regionally, but also recognized the need to promote a practical set of policies to influence Central Europe's rapidly changing security architecture. Within the limitations of Warsaw's politico-military capabilities between Bonn and Moscow, Skubiszewski navigated cautiously and peacefully between larger, stronger, and transforming states. During the fall of 1989, before the Berlin Wall fell, Skubiszewski recognized the need for four-power control of the likely political and legal German unification process. The Polish foreign minister reiterated the concern that all parties involved in German unification consider Poland's legitimate security dilemma over the Oder–Neisse western border's integrity. Though the Germans focused on the four powers rather than Poland regarding unification, Skubiszewski's early caveats proved accurate when the four-power process started at the Open Skies Discussions and then the 2 Plus 4 talks.

Even as the first European foreign policy maker to raise the importance of four-power control over unification, Skubiszewski tried several policy maneuvers to break the Oder–Neisse impasse with Bonn,
but ended bowing to FRG domestic reelection politics. On the one hand,
Skubiszewski's bold move to bandwagon with Bonn by supporting
unified Germany in NATO surprised Moscow, and, Warsaw calculated,
stood Poland in good stead with Bonn as a means to mitigate tensions
over the Polish–German border. Certainly, Skubiszewski and the Polish
leadership feared a potential neutral Germany and advocated unified
German NATO membership. Yet Poland's support for Bonn failed to
persuade the Germans on the border. On the other hand, Skubiszewski
tried to balance Moscow against Bonn temporarily, when he threatened not to request Soviet troops withdraw from Poland to hedge
against German obstinacy on the Oder–Neisse. Bonn ignored Poland's
ploy and Skubiszewski dropped it quickly. Soon it became more important for Poland to participate as the seventh member in the emerging 2 Plus 4 talks. Moreover, Skubiszewski understood the diplomatic
ramifications for Poland's exclusion from the talks and needed Bonn's
support to participate with the six powers. Paradoxically, Poland's
maneuvering on Soviet forces in Poland gave Moscow not only reason to back Poland's 2 Plus 4 participation, but also played into the
Soviet hard-liner strategy when Poland faced major obstacles on troop
withdrawal negotiations. Eventually, Germany agreed to Poland's 2
Plus 4 participation and Skubiszewski claimed foreign policy successes
regarding the unification process on four-power terms and the resolution of the Oder–Neisse border with the signing of the 2 Plus 4 Treaty.

Although Polish–German tensions existed on Soviet force withdrawals from both states, Skubiszewski continued entreaties toward Bonn
to coordinate on troop transit issues. By the time of the failed Soviet
coup d'état, Bonn finally responded more favorably to Warsaw's re-
quests and began a dialogue on troop withdrawal coordination. Warsaw finally convinced Bonn that Germany's policy of supporting
Gorbachev's USSR without considering options such as Yeltsin's rise
proved detrimental when the USSR disintegrated. After the failed Soviet coup d'état, Bonn upheld stability-enhancing policies more actively with Poland, both to bring Poland closer to NATO and the
European Community (now EU) and to attempt to evict Russian troops
from Germany by 1994. Even if Poland and Germany coordinated regularly on Russian troop withdrawals from late 1991 through to the end of
Skubiszewski's leadership, Bonn still considered Russian troop withdrawals from Poland a Warsaw–Moscow matter separate from Bonn–Moscow
negotiations. In that respect, Skubiszewski's strategy toward Germany
proved only partially successful. Poland stood up for its sovereignty

and provided Germany with many options to weigh, but Bonn preferred to work directly with Moscow. In fact, Bonn agreed almost to any terms Soviet hard-liners defined for force withdrawals to ensure swift Soviet force withdrawals from eastern Germany. Still, though Bonn negotiated most aspects of unification and troop withdrawals with Moscow without consulting Warsaw, the FRG worked with Poland as an independent actor and overcame the Oder–Neisse border controversy.

The great geopolitical shift caused by the USSR's demise also strengthened Poland's ability to coordinate more closely with Germany because Warsaw became a bridge of stability for Bonn to post–Soviet Russia. By signing the June 1991 Polish–German State Treaty just before the failed Soviet coup and then fortifying support from Bonn for Poland's membership in both NATO and the EC, Skubiszewski sought to bandwagon with Poland's larger, stronger, and more stable Western neighbor. Such support for Poland's European reintegration into the emerging post–Cold War security structures signified Skubiszewski's successful pragmatic, nonpredatory, and nonthreatening bandwagoning strategy. Except when Skubiszewski tactically pressured Bonn by mistakenly using Soviet forces as a bargaining chip to secure the Oder–Neisse border, he projected an image for Poland that neorealist Schweller termed primarily that of "security-maximizer," not "power-maximizer." When it came to strategic decisions to help Germany with unification and integration into NATO, Skubiszewski chose to assist, not hinder Bonn, even when most of Europe opposed unification. He also demonstrated stability-enhancing policies between Bonn and Moscow by redefining post–World War II Polish–German relations into true partnership that both stable Poland and secure Germany might engage an emerging Russia more effectively. As Schweller argued, such alignment underlined the decision to create opportunities and gain rewards rather than play states against one another or threaten them.[32]

Poland bandwagoned with Germany to reintegrate into the Western pluralistic value system it coveted, according to Schweller's bandwagoning theory. Skubiszewski's foreign policy personified primarily cooperative bandwagoning more than balancing or aggressive behavior vis-à-vis Poland's larger and stronger Western neighbor. Poland's strategy toward Germany showed cooperative state alignment that, as neorealist Glaser argued, "Under a wide range of conditions, adversaries can best achieve their security goals through cooperative policies, not competitive ones, and should, therefore, choose cooperation when these conditions prevail."[33] Thus, Poland's bandwagoning policies toward Germany strengthened democratic principles, solidified Poland's sovereignty, and began Warsaw's real road toward European reintegration.

THE POLISH–UKRAINIAN INTERSTATE MODEL FOR REGIONAL COOPERATION AND INTEGRATION

Post–Cold War assessments of Polish–Ukrainian ties comprise a myriad of depictions, most often complimentary of the great strides both post-Communist states made since they consolidated their sovereign foreign policies and began to integrate into Europe in various ways during the late 1990s. Specifically, these assessments provide important chronologies of the events describing the high and low points between the two states politically, economically, militarily, and socioculturally.[34] They illustrate comprehensive insights into the benefits of strong bilateral and regional security relations between Warsaw and Kyiv, but they don't present a theoretical context for analyzing the development of those linkages for larger European security questions. Therefore, this chapter's final section views Polish–Ukrainian relations somewhat differently. The following analysis accounts for both the regional politico-military decisions that Poland and Ukraine employed to promote cooperative relations to integrate Kyiv more effectively into Europe and the theoretical arguments to demonstrate a security model for other post-Communist states beyond this chapter's analysis.

The previous section argued that Polish–German cooperative bandwagoning aided Central European security by decreasing regional tensions, allowing both states to overcome historic tensions and building relations to eliminate their traditional security dilemma, particularly with Poland's NATO accession in March 1999. The critical linkages established by Poland and Germany gave Warsaw a policy baseline to pursue with Ukraine that significantly developed once Poland realized its regional Central European security role increased with its NATO membership after late 1995. Analyses portray the dimensions of this major turning point for Poland and for Polish–Ukrainian ties. Yet they don't take into account how bandwagoning, balancing, or aggressive state alignment may have played a role in the success of Polish–Ukrainian politico-military ties, and how those ties theoretically might be seen in Kyiv's future long-term, even permanent linkages to NATO via Warsaw.

The historic success in European security of German and Polish integration attest to the benefits of first solidifying politico-military ties and then progressively broadening economic linkages. West Germany's membership in NATO in the mid-1950s set the stage for its economic integration after the European Community's creation in the late 1950s. The evolution of Poland's ties to NATO during the early and mid-1990s and its accession from 1997 to 1999 established the foundation, albeit a challenging one, for Warsaw's EU integration over the next several years. Ukrainian independence in 1991 and formulation of a sovereign foreign policy separate from Russia by the late 1990s gave Kyiv the ability to seek closer bonds to NATO and the EU, particularly via Warsaw.[35] Yet Ukraine's membership in both of the two key European security institutions remains distant, if realistic, given continuing security concerns from Moscow and greatly limiting reform requirements from Brussels. For the immediate term, then, the Polish–Ukrainian regional security relationship demonstrates an enduring cooperative model for Kyiv's long-term European integration through consistent effort bringing both states ever closer bilaterally and regionally.[36]

The May 1997 Joint Presidential Declaration on "Understanding and Unity," like the interstate treaty of May 1992, marked a major turning point in bilateral and regional relations. Not only did both states articulate the need to overcome their harsh histories of ethnic conflict against each another, but also their mutual role "in strengthening security and stability in East–Central Europe."[37] This declaration completed yet another stage in their bilateral ties as part of Poland's regional and stability-enhancing role toward Ukraine. More important, the interstate ties during ten years of consistent cooperation between Warsaw and Kyiv, although faltering in the early 1990s, never descended into historic tensions and attendant confrontation. Indeed, Polish and Ukrainian leaders displayed cooperative bandwagoning state behavior when Warsaw could easily have abandoned Kyiv in Poland's quest for both NATO and EU membership. Instead, Poland continued to assist Ukraine, even when confronted by stringent, constraining EU membership stipulations that threatened to decouple Warsaw–Kyiv ties because of the onerous EU visa regime. Warsaw still rejects this detrimental economic restraint, arguing against its probably damaging impact bilaterally and regionally.[38] Moreover, Warsaw upholds Kyiv's fledgling economic reforms by raising concerns over the Russia–Belarus–Poland–Germany gas pipeline that Moscow intends to construct to bypass Ukraine. According to Polish and Ukrainian analyses, such Polish decisions underscore the objective not to "support anything that would be aimed against Ukraine and that would have an overtly anti-Ukrainian character."[39] Given that the progressive market-based Polish economy stands to lose significantly by supporting Ukraine over EU and Russian economic and geostrategic strains, Warsaw and Kyiv continuously project cooperative rather than competitive bandwagoning toward each other. Finally, these two post-Communist states refuse to balance against the EU as well as to threaten Russia, arguing constantly for the necessity to build bridges economically, politically, and militarily. Poland simply seeks to maintain open markets and borders with Ukraine as a means both to increase regional stability and to encourage Moscow to overcome its historic imperialism.[40]

Perhaps, though, the magnitude of change in European security since the Cold War ended also highlights the critical politico-military role that Polish–Ukrainian relations play for other post-Communist states. When one thinks back to the September 1994 NATO–PfP military exercise, Cooperative Bridge, the first of thousands of politico-military training and exercising events that have occurred up to the present day, we can see how important cooperative state linkages among historic adversaries have become in post–Cold War Europe. Notably, Cooperative Bridge occurred on Polish territory at a former Soviet military training base and witnessed not only German troops on Polish territory for the first time since World War II, but also included Ukrainian forces, who took part in the event with ten other NATO and former Warsaw Pact states, including American troops, who organized a great deal of the exercise.[41]

The development on a large scale of the NATO–Partnership for Peace bilateral and multilateral civil emergency planning and military exercising strategy, demonstrated by numerous events on both Polish and Ukrainian territory, in North America, and throughout Europe and Eurasia, provide a long-lasting if not permanent framework for Poland and Ukraine to cooperate. Such cooperation may broaden for years to come, and Exercise Trans-Carpathia 2000 entailed the most recent in a long line of important events. This illustrative set of events occurred from September 20 to 28, 2000, when Ukraine hosted a NATO–PfP disaster relief exercise in the Trans-Carpathian region of western Ukraine and participating states included Belarus, Croatia, Hungary, Moldova, Poland, Romania, Slovakia, Slovenia, Sweden, and Switzerland, as well as the U.N. Office for the Coordination of Humanitarian Affairs. The flood-simulation exercise, one of the major activities in the NATO–Ukraine work plan, brought together more than 350 personnel from disaster-response elements of eleven of NATO's Euro–Atlantic Partnership Council (EAPC) states. First, the exercise tested the capabilities of the NATO Euro–Atlantic Disaster Response Coordination Center (EADRCC) in response to a scenario-based request for international assistance from Ukraine. It involved national disaster-response coordination centers in EAPC capitals as well as the EADRCC. Second, a field exercise took place in Uzhgorod, Trans-Carpathia, and encompassed a simulated flood-response exercise by disaster-response teams from assisting EAPC states operating for the first time as a Euro–Atlantic Disaster Response Unit. Both the scenario for the command-post exercise and the field exercise built upon actual experience and lessons learned by Ukraine and the EADRCC to deal with major floods in the Trans-Carpathian region two years before. Finally, Trans-Carpathia

2000 exercised abilities in search and rescue activities, the provision of life support and medical care, water purification and cleaning of contaminated rivers, and, most important, a train accident involving a damaged railcar containing toxic materials.[42]

The creation of the Polish–Ukrainian peacekeeping battalion, deployed as part of the NATO–KFOR mission, also allows both states to expand politico-military and operational–technical ties to NATO for long-term linkages. Secure in its NATO membership, Poland now accelerates Ukraine's national security objectives and encourages Kyiv's leaders to remain steadfast, as Ukraine did during the Kosovo bombing campaign in the spring and summer of 1999 by not severing its NATO ties. The peace support operations battalion, operating in KFOR Multinational Brigade East sector, comprises the Polish Eighteenth Air Assault Battalion and the Ukrainian Thirty-Seventh Support Company. Its soldiers patrol through both multiethnic cities and small towns scattered across nearly 1,500 square miles of mountainous territory and open plains. The majority of the complex missions comprise civil affairs requirements—a crucial factor in most real world post–Cold War operations—but also peace enforcement monitoring and verification of the provisions of the Military Technical Agreement in order to create a safe and secure environment, provide humanitarian assistance in support of the U.N. High Commission for Refugees efforts, enforce basic law and order until this function is fully transferred to the appropriately designated agency, and establish and support resumption of core civil functions.[43] These commanders, officers, and soldiers, like thousands of other Polish and Ukrainian military who participate in PfP events, especially enhanced PfP rotating operational and exercise planning slots at NATO commands, and other real-world operations such as Bosnia, forge integral politico-military links. The serious cooperative capabilities attained also reduce regional tensions and strengthen ties economically and socioculturally. Poland's pivotal role in assisting Ukraine allows Ukraine to become secure enough in its ties through NATO's Partnership for Peace process and via the 1997 Charter on a Distinctive Partnership between NATO and Ukraine. Like the Polish–German model, the Polish–Ukrainian politico-military relationship may decrease concerns about Ukraine's need to consider NATO membership and may result in long-term, even permanent links that undergird Ukraine's connection to NATO.[44]

CONCLUSION

This chapter has sought to analyze how Poland sought and seeks to help Ukraine increase its security and stability without threatening Russia. Furthermore, the analysis of Polish policy toward Ukraine provides the foundation for further examination of cooperative behavior that shows the merits of states peacefully bandwagoning with rather than balancing against each other for profitable linkages, not territorial aggrandizement. Post–Communist Poland remains an example in its post–Cold War relations with both Germany and Ukraine for comparing foreign policies of other post–Communist European states, states that desire integration into or close bonds with such institutions as NATO. It follows that for states such as Ukraine concerns about NATO membership possibly become less pressing with such developed ties to NATO member Poland. Therefore, this chapter attempted to offer a paradigm for how post–Communist European states tried to overcome their historic security dilemmas without promoting predatory alignment against each other and strengthening sovereignty to contribute to European security regionally.

NOTES

1. "The Polish Factor in Gas Transit Issue: Responsive Rationale of Ukraine's Western Neighbor" (Monitoring Foreign and Security Policy of Ukraine Occasional Report no. 28, August 2000). Available at: <http:// www.cpcfpu. org.ua>.

2. Realist Joseph Grieco raised questions about "key interests" that lie behind cooperative policies by medium-size states toward larger, stronger, and domineering "partners" within NATO's institutional alliance. He referred to cooperative behavior by France and Italy, which tried to "avoid German domination" by maneuvering toward one another, separately from and significantly within NATO. See Joseph M. Grieco, "Understanding the Problem of International Cooperation: The Limits of Neoliberal Institutionalism and the Future of Realist Theory," in *Neorealism and Neoliberalism: The Contemporary Debate*, ed. David A. Baldwin (New York: St. Martin's Press, 1995), 335. Yet few studies analyze interstate behavior for Central East Europe within post–Cold War international relations theory. For notable exceptions, see Mark Kramer, "Neorealism, Nuclear Proliferation, and East–Central European Strategies," in *Unipolar Politics: Realism and State Strategies after the Cold War*, ed. Ethan B. Kapstein and Michael Mastanduno (New York: Columbia University Press, 1999), 385–463; Richard Weitz, "Pursuing Military Security in Eastern Europe," in *After the Cold War: International Institutions and State Strategies in Europe, 1989–1991*, ed. Robert O. Keohane, Joseph S. Nye, and Stanley Hoffmann (Cambridge: Harvard University Press, 1993), 342–380; and Margarita M. Balmaceda, ed., *On the Edge: Ukrainian–Central European–Russian Security Triangle* (Budapest: Central European University Press, 2000).

3. Important exceptions that contribute to comparative understanding of the Polish–German interstate pragmatic model include Andrew A. Michta and Ilya Prizel, eds., *Post–Communist Eastern Europe: Crisis and Reform* (New York: St. Martin's Press, 1993); Ilya Prizel and Andrew A. Michta, eds., *Polish Foreign Policy Reconsidered: Challenges of Independence* (London: Macmillan, 1995); Karen

Dawisha and Bruce Parrott, eds., *The Consolidation of Democracy in East-Central Europe: Authoritarianism and Democratization in Postcommunist Societies* (Cambridge: Cambridge University Press, 1997); Ilya Prizel, *National Identity and Foreign Policy: Nationalism and Leadership in Poland, Russia, and Ukraine* (Cambridge: Cambridge University Press, 1998), 112–124; and Elizabeth Pond, *The Rebirth of Europe* (Washington: Brookings Institution Press, 1999).

4. This chapter's rationale comes mainly from Randall L. Schweller, "Bandwagoning for Profit: Bringing the Revisionist State Back In," *International Security* 19, no. 1 (1994): 72–107, and "New Realist Research on Alliances: Refining, Not Refuting, Waltz's Balancing Proposition," *American Political Science Review* 91, no. 4 (1997): 927–930. For explanations about cooperative and competitive realist actions, see Arthur A. Stein, *Why Nations Cooperate: Circumstance and Choice in International Relations* (Ithaca, N.Y.: Cornell University Press, 1990); Charles L. Glaser, "Realists as Optimists: Cooperation as Self-Help," *Security Studies* 5, no. 3 (1996): 122–163; and Michael W. Doyle and G. John Ikenberry, eds., *New Thinking in International Relations Theory* (Boulder, Colo.: Westview Press, 1997).

5. For a thorough analysis of Polish bandwagoning, balancing, and aggressive alingment in the early post-Communist era, see Joshua B. Spero, "Poland's Security Dilemma between Germany and Russia Again: Bandwagoning and Balancing in Foreign Policy from 1989 to 1993" (Ph.D. diss., Johns Hopkins University, 2000).

6. See Jan Barcz and Mieczyslaw Tomal, *Polska–Niemcy: dobre sasiedztwo i przyjazna wspolpraca* (Poland–Germany: Good neighborly and friendly cooperation) (Warszawa: Polski Instytut Spraw Miedzynarodowych, 1992), for November 14, 1990, border treaty and June 17, 1991, state treaty; "Deklaracja o zasadach i podstawowych kierunkach rozwoju stosunkow Polsko–Ukrainskich" (Declaration on principles and directions of development of Polish–Ukrainian relations), *Zbior Dokumentow* 4 (1991): 25–30; "Treaty between the Polish Republic and Ukraine on Good Neighborliness, Friendly Relations, and Cooperation," in *Ukraine in the World*, ed. Lubomyr A. Hajda (Cambridge: Harvard University Press, 1998), 304–312; and "Joint Declaration of the Presidents of the Polish Republic and Ukraine on Understanding and Unity," in ibid., 317–318.

7. For important analyses on Polish–Ukrainian relations in the post–Cold War era, including some important Cold War–era literature as a foundation for crucial post–Cold War foreign policy tenets, see Juliusz Mieroszewski, *Materialy do Refleksji i Zadumy* (Materials for reflection and musing) (Paris: Instytut Literacki, 1976); T. Kuzio, "The Polish Opposition and the Ukrainian Question," *Journal of Ukrainian Studies* 12, no. 2 (1987): 26–58; Zdzislaw Najder, ed., *Polskie Porozumienie Niepodleglosciowe: Wybor Tekstow* (Alliance for Polish independence: Electoral text) (London: Polonia, 1989); Ian Brzezinski, "Polish–Ukrainian Relations: Europe's Neglected Strategic Axis," *Survival* 35, no. 3 (1993): 26–37; Stephen R. Burant, "International Relations in a Regional Context: Poland and Its Eastern Neighbors—Lithuania, Belarus, Ukraine," *Europe–Asia Studies* 45, no. 3 (1993): 395–418; T. Kuzio, *Ukrainian Security Policy* (Westport, Conn.: Praeger/The Washington Papers, 1995); Ilya Prizel and Andrew A. Michta, eds., *Polish Foreign Policy Reconsidered: Challenges of Inde-*

pendence (London: Macmillan, 1995); Margarita Mercedes Balmaceda, "Two's Company, Three's a Crowd: The Role of Central Europe in Ukrainian Security," *East European Quarterly* 32, no. 3 (1998): 335–351; Sherman W. Garnett, *Keystone in the Arch: Ukraine in the Emerging Security Environment of Central and Eastern Europe* (Washington, D.C.: Carnegie Endowment, 1997), 85–91; Prizel, *National Identity and Foreign Policy*; Zbigniew Brzezinski, "Ukraine's Critical Role in the Post-Soviet Space," in Hajda, *Ukraine in the World*, 3–8; Stephen R. Burant, "Ukraine and East Central Europe," in Hajda, *Ukraine in the World*, 45–78; and Stephen R. Burant, "Poland, Ukraine, and the Idea of Strategic Partnership," *The Carl Beck Papers in Russian and East European Studies* 1308 (1999).

8. Though Russians almost always received invitations and rarely participated with units in these military exercises, they often sent exercise observers. Notably, the Russians, like the Poles and Ukrainians, frequently received financial support from the United States and other NATO states to participate, but the Russians almost invariably refused assistance as a matter of pride. The Russian rationale then ensued that financial constraints prevented them from participating. See *Report to Congress on Implementation of the Partnership for Peace Initiative* (Washington, D.C.: Department of State, U.S. Government Printing Office, 1998), 18–19, and *United States Security Strategy for Europe and NATO* (Washington, D.C.: Department of Defense, U.S. Government Printing Office, 1995), 10–12. Note that the author directed the U.S. Joint Staff positions on NATO's PfP policies as part of his responsibilities to develop and implement the larger American National Security and Military Strategy of Enlargement and Engagement.

9. See F. Stephen Larrabee, "Ukraine's Place in European and Regional Security," in Hajda, *Ukraine in the World*, 249–270; Martha Brill Olcott, Anders Aslund, and Sherman W. Garnett, eds., *Getting It Wrong: Regional Cooperation and the Commonwealth of Independent States* (Washington, D.C.: Carnegie Endowment, 1999), 204–208; and Roman Wolczuk, "Ukrainian–Polish Relations between 1991–1998: From the Declarative to the Substantive," *European Security* 10, no. 1 (2000): 127–156.

10. For some important theoretical studies that examine linkage between a state's domestic and foreign policies, see Jack Snyder, *Myths of Empire: Domestic Politics and International Ambition* (Ithaca, N.Y.: Cornell University Press, 1991); Richard Rosecrance and Arthur A. Stein, eds., *The Domestic Bases of Grand Strategy* (Ithaca, N.Y.: Cornell University Press, 1991); Fareed Zakaria, "Realism and Domestic Politics: A Review Essay," *International Security* 17, no. 1 (1992): 177–198; Ethan B. Kapstein, "Is Realism Dead? The Domestic Sources of International Politics," *International Organization* 49, no. 4 (1995): 751–774; Colin Elman, "Horses for Courses: Why Not Neorealist Theories of Foreign Policy?" *Security Studies* 6 (1996): 7–53; and Matthew Evangelista, "Domestic Structure and International Change," in *New Thinking in International Relations Theory*, ed. Michael W. Doyle and G. John Ikenberry (Boulder, Colo.: Westview Press, 1997), 202–228.

11. See Kenneth Waltz, *Theory of International Politics* (Reading, Mass.: Addison-Wesley, 1983), and "Realist Thought and Neorealist Theory," *Journal of International Affairs* 44, no. 1 (1990): 21–37.

12. For example, Waltz, *Theory of International Politics*, 125–128, 132, and Steven M. Walt, *The Origins of Alliances* (Ithaca, N.Y.: Cornell University Press,

1987), 29–31. It should be noted that international historians such as Paul Schroeder caution that neorealists who use predictive prescriptions for specific historical eras to depict the order and disorder in the international system need to consider more specifically the relevant historical evidence. However, he accepts some of the generalizations that political scientists, mainly neorealists, conclude in their analyses. See Paul Schroeder, "Historical Reality vs. Neo-Realist Theory," *International Security* 19, no. 1 (1994): 117–119; and Paul W. Schroeder, "History and International Relations Theory: Not Use or Abuse, but Fit or Misfit," *International Security* 22, no. 1 (1997): 64–74.

13. Waltz, *Theory of International Politics*, 126.

14. Stephen M. Walt, "Alliance Formation in Southwest Asia: Balancing and Bandwagoning in Cold War Competition," in *Dominoes and Bandwagons: Strategic Beliefs and Great Power Competition in the Eurasian Rimland*, ed. Robert Jervis and Jack Snyder (Oxford: Oxford University Press, 1991), 52–53; Walt, *Origins of Alliances*, 11, 17, 29–31; and Stephen M. Walt, "Alliances, Threats, and US Grand Strategy: A Reply to Kaufman and Labs," in "Balancing vs. Bandwagoning: A Debate," *Security Studies* 1, no. 3 (1992): 469–471.

15. Though Walt doesn't analyze Poland and focuses mainly on the Middle East and Southwest Asia, this chapter describes his theoretical framework for understanding whether post–Communist Polish foreign policy represented Walt's definition of bandwagoning or balancing. See Walt, "Alliance Formation in Southwest Asia," 52–53; Walt, "Alliances, Threats, and U.S. Grand Strategy," 469–471; and also Waltz, *Theory of International Politics*, 91–93. For good analyses about Central European security, including short assessments of post–Communist Polish foreign policy and international relations theory, see Kramer, "Neorealism, Nuclear Proliferation, and East–Central European Strategies," 388–393; and Weitz, "Pursuing Military Security in Eastern Europe," 355–359.

16. Walt, *Origins of Alliances*, 21–26, 263–266; Walt, "Alliance Formation in Southwest Asia," 50–54; and Walt, "Alliances, Threats, and US Grand Strategy," 450–451.

17. Waltz, *Theory of International Politics*, 118.

18. Post–Cold War analysis beyond this chapter's scope concerns debates over nuclear powers and potential nuclear powers and how the dominant powers, primarily the United States, reconcile the dynamics of the international system toward their own national interests. See Benjamin Frankel, "The Brooding Shadow: Systemic Incentives and Nuclear Weapons Proliferation," *Security Studies* 2, nos. 3–4 (1993): 37–78; Scott D. Sagan and Kenneth N. Waltz, *The Spread of Nuclear Weapons: A Debate* (New York: Norton, 1995); Samuel P. Huntington, *The Clash of Civilizations and the Remaking of World Order* (New York: Simon and Schuster, 1996); Barry R. Posen and Andrew L. Ross, "Competing Visions for U.S. Grand Strategy," *International Security* 21, no. 3 (1996–1997): 5–53; Robert Jervis, "International Primacy: Is the Game Worth the Candle?" in *The Cold War and After: Prospects for Peace* (expanded ed.), ed. Sean M. Lynn-Jones and Steven E. Miller (Cambridge: MIT Press, 1997), 291–306; and Robert J. Art, "Geopolitics Updated: The Strategy of Selective Engagement," *International Security* 23, no. 3 (1998–1999): 79–113.

19. Schweller, "Bandwagoning for Profit," 74–75. As analyzed later, theorists disagree whether bandwagoning and balancing denote opposing behav-

iors. Waltz credits Stephen Van Evera with first recommending that "bandwagoning" defines the opposite "balancing" as a theory of behavior among competing states. Waltz, *Theory of International Politics*, 126.

20. Schweller, "Bandwagoning for Profit," 104–107. For some important arguments regarding the offensive–defensive debate, see, among others, Jack Snyder, *The Ideology of the Offensive* (Ithaca, N.Y.: Cornell University Press, 1984); and Robert Jervis, "Offense, Defense, and the Security Dilemma," in *International Politics*, ed. Robert C. Art and Robert Jervis (New York: HarperCollins, 1996), 183–203.

21. See Glaser, "Realists as Optimists: Cooperation as Self-Help," 122–124. The main arguments explaining this chapter's rationale for balancing and bandwagoning stem from Schweller, "Bandwagoning for Profit," 74–75, 104–107, and Schweller, "New Realist Research on Alliances," 927–930. Among the myriad pieces written on "balancing" behavior as part of neorealism, the passage here comes from the prominent works of Waltz, *Theory of International Politics*, 125–132; Waltz, "Reflections on Theory of International Politics: A Response to My Critics," *International Politics*, 342–345; and Walt, "Alliances, Threats, and US Grand Strategy," 471–473. See also Sean Kay, *NATO and the Future of European Security* (Lanham, Md.: Rowman and Littlefield, 1998), 6–7; and Stephen R. Rock, *Why Peace Breaks Out: Great Power Rapprochement in Historical Perspective* (Chapel Hill: University of North Carolina Press, 1989).

22. For an understanding of how the North Atlantic democratic "security community" emerged in the post–World War II and post–Cold War periods, and the attraction of its member value system, see, among others, Karl W. Deutsch, ed., *Political Community and the North Atlantic Area: International Organization in the Light of Historical Experience* (New York: Greenwood Press, 1969); Ole R. Holsti, P. Terrence Hopmann, and John D. Sullivan, *Unity and Disintegration in International Alliances* (New York: John Wiley, 1973); Richard H. Ullman, *Securing Europe* (Princeton, N.J.: Princeton University Press, 1991); Bruce Russett, *Grasping the Democratic Peace: Principles for a Post–Cold War World* (Princeton, N.J.: Princeton University Press, 1993); Keohane, Nye, and Hoffmann, *After the Cold War*; Catherine M. Kelleher, *The Future of European Security* (Washington, D.C.: Brookings Institution, 1995).

23. Schweller, "Bandwagoning for Profit," 74–75, 83, 93, 99, 101, 105–107; and Schweller, "New Realist Research on Alliances," 928–929. Certainly, there remains great debate within international relations about bandwagoning, with some important works depicting bandwagoning differently. Several important arguments originate from Stephen Van Evera, "Primed for Peace: Europe after the Cold War," in *The Cold War and After: Prospects for Peace*, ed. Sean M. Lynn-Jones and Steven E. Miller (Cambridge: MIT Press, 1993), 193–243; Waltz, *Theory of International Politics*, 125–132; Waltz, "Reflections on Theory of International Politics: A Response to My Critics," 342–345; Walt, "Alliances, Threats, and US Grand Strategy," 471–473; Walt, "Alliance Formation in Southwest Asia," 51–56; Robert G. Kaufman, "'To Balance or to Bandwagon?' Alignment Decisions in 1930s Europe," *Security Studies* 1, no. 3 (1992): 423, 436, 438; Eric J. Labs, "Do Weak States Bandwagon?" *Security Studies* vol. 1, no. 3 (1992): 406–408; and John A. Vasquez, "The Realist Paradigm and Degenerative versus Progressive Research Programs: An Appraisal of Neotraditional Research on

Waltz's Balancing Proposition," *American Political Science Review* 91, no. 4 (1997): 904–906.

24. Research and analysis of post-Communist states besides Poland is beyond this chapter's scope.

25. Schweller, "Bandwagoning for Profit," 79.

26. Ibid., 92–93.

27. See, among many others, Charles W. Kegley, Jr. and Gregory A. Raymond, *When Trust Breaks Down: Alliance Norms and World Politics* (Columbia: University of South Carolina Press, 1990); Thomas J. Christensen and Jack Snyder, "Chain Gangs and Passed Bucks: Predicting Alliance Patterns in Multipolarity," *International Organization* 44, no. 2 (1990): 137–168; Charles L. Glaser, "Why NATO Is Still Best: Future Security Arrangements for Europe," *International Security* 18, no. 1 (1993): 5–50; Gunther Hellmann and Reinhard Wolf, "Neorealism, Neoliberal Institutionalism, and the Future of NATO," *Security Studies* 3 (1993): 3–43; Charles L. Barry, ed., *The Search for Peace in Europe: Perspectives from NATO and Eastern Europe* (Washington, D.C.: National Defense University Press, 1993); Jeffrey Simon, "Does Eastern Europe Belong in NATO?" *Orbis*, Winter 1993, 21–35; Joshua B. Spero and Frank Umbach, *NATO's Security Challenge to the East and the American–German Geo-Strategic Partnership in Europe* (Cologne: Bundesinstitut fur ostwissenschaftliche und internationale Studien, 1994); "Special Issue on the Future of NATO," *Journal of Strategic Studies* (1994); Steven L. Burg, *War or Peace? Nationalism, Democracy, and American Foreign Policy in Post-Communist Europe* (New York: New York University Press, 1996); Robert McCalla, "NATO's Persistence after the Cold War," *International Organization* 50, no. 3 (1996): 445–475; Robert J. Art, "Why Western Europe Needs the United States and NATO," *Political Science Quarterly* 111, no. 1 (1996): 1–39.

28. John J. Mearsheimer, "The False Promise of International Institutions," in *The Perils of Anarchy: Contemporary Realism and International Security*, ed. Michael E. Brown, Sean M. Lynn-Jones, and Steven E. Miller (Cambridge: MIT Press, 1995), 332–376; and Kenneth N. Waltz, "The Emerging Structure of International Politics," in ibid., 257–258. For insightful realist alliance analyses concerning how NATO grappled with emerging post–Cold War missions and how members determined to survive as a different institution, see Kay, *NATO and the Future of European Security*, 1–11, 147–156; and Stephen M. Walt, "The Ties That Fray: Why Europe and America Are Drifting Apart," *National Interest* 54 (1998–1999): 3–11.

29. Among the significant NATO declarations and communiqués, three particularly stand out: NATO Press Service, *London Declaration on a Transformed North Atlantic Alliance*, 5–6 July 1990; NATO Press Service, *The Rome Declaration on Peace and Cooperation*, North Atlantic Council, Brussels, 7–8 November 1991; and NATO Press Service, *Declaration of the Heads of State and Government Participating in the Meeting of the North Atlantic Council*, Press Communique M-1 (94) 3, NATO Headquarters, Brussels, 10–11 January 1994.

30. See Hellmann and Wolf, "Neorealism, Neoliberal Institutionalism, and the Future of NATO"; Robert Axelrod and Robert O. Keohane, "Achieving Cooperation under Anarchy: Strategies and Institutions," in *Neorealism and Neoliberalism: The Contemporary Debate*, ed. David A. Baldwin (New York: Columbia University Press, 1995), 85–115; and Robert O. Keohane and Lisa L.

Martin, "The Promise of Institutionalist Theory," *International Security* 20, no. 1 (1995): 39–51.

31. This section provides a summary of the arguments contained in Chapter 2 of Spero, *Poland's Security Dilemma between Germany and Russia Again*, 114–168.

32. Schweller, "Bandwagoning for Profit," 78–79, 88–89, 104–107.

33. Glaser, "Realists as Optimists," 123.

34. Balmaceda, "Two's Company, Three's a Crowd," 345–348; Garnett, *Keystone in the Arch*, 85–91; Prizel, *National Identity and Foreign Policy*, 137–145, 388–396; Brzezinski, "Ukraine's Critical Role in the Post-Soviet Space," 7; Burant, "Ukraine and East Central Europe," 50–59; Larrabee, "Ukraine's Place in European and Regional Security," 257–263; Olcott, Aslund, and Garnett, *Getting It Wrong*, 204–208; Wolczuk, "Ukrainian–Polish Relations between 1991–1998," 148–153; and Burant, "Poland, Ukraine, and the Idea of Strategic Partnership," 22–25.

35. "Treaty on Friendship, Cooperation, and Partnership between Ukraine and the Russian Federation," in *Ukraine in the World*, ed. Lubomyr A. Hajda (Cambridge: Harvard University Press, 1998), 319–329.

36. See especially Balmaceda, "Two's Company, Three's a Crowd"; Garnett, *Keystone in the Arch*; Prizel, *National Identity and Foreign Policy*; Brzezinski, "Ukraine's Critical Role in the Post-Soviet Space"; Burant, "Ukraine and East Central Europe"; Larrabee, "Ukraine's Place in European and Regional Security"; Olcott, Aslund, and Garnett, *Getting It Wrong*; Wolczuk, "Ukrainian–Polish Relations between 1991–1998"; and Burant, "Poland, Ukraine, and the Idea of Strategic Partnership." For extensive elaboration on Ukraine's major economic constraints, see the other chapters in this volume.

37. "Joint Declaration of the Presidents of the Polish Republic and Ukraine on Understanding and Unity," 317.

38. "Polish, Ukrainian Premiers Meet," *Foreign and Security Policy of Ukraine* (Center for Peace, Conversion and Foreign Policy of Ukraine newsletter, 7/15/00–7/21/00). Available at: <http://www.cpcfpu.org.ua/>; and *Joint Statement by the President of the European Council, J. Chirac, assisted by the Secretary General of the Council/High Representative for Foreign and Security Policy of the EU, J. Solana, the President of the Commission of the European Communities, R. Prodi, and the President of Ukraine, L. D. Kuchma*, Paris, 15 September 2000.

39. "Politicians Express Concern over Gas Pipeline Project By-Passing Ukraine," *Radio Free Europe/Radio Liberty Poland, Belarus, and Ukraine Report* 2, no. 26 (2000); "The Balancing Act in Stereo," *Kyiv Post*, 1 September 2000; and "Newspaper Analyses Prospects for Caspian Oil Transit via Ukraine," *Ukrayina Moloda* FBIS, 6 September 2000.

40. "Ukraine–Europe–Russia: Developing New Geopolitical Paradigms" (Monitoring Foreign and Security Policy of Ukraine Occasional Report no. 36, September 2000). Available at: <http://cpcfpu.org.ua/>.

41. *Report to Congress on Implementation of the Partnership for Peace Initiative*, 7–8; and *United States Security Strategy for Europe and NATO*, 10–12.

42. "Exercise Trans-Carpathia 2000" (NATO Press Release [2000]087, 22 September 2000). Available at: <NATODOC@HQ.NATO.INT, NATODATA@LISTSERV.CC.KULEUVEN.AC.BE>.

43. Major Steven R. Shappell, KFOR Spokesman, "KFOR Soldiers Shot At" and "Kosovo Serb Convoy Stoned," KFOR Daily Press Release, SHAPE Announcement no. 10–12 Pristina, Kosovo, 11 October 2000. See also KFOR Web site at: <http://www.kforonline.com/kfor/mnb_east.htm>.

44. See the parameters from the "Charter on a Distinctive Partnership between the North Atlantic Treaty Organization and Ukraine," in Lubomyr A. Hajda, *Ukraine in the World* (Cambridge: Harvard University Press, 1998), 340–346; and also "Foreign and Security Policy of Ukraine Expert Poll" (Monitoring Foreign and Security Policy of Ukraine, Quarterly Report no. 3/2000, September 2000). Available at: <http://www.cpcfpu.org.ua/>.

9

Ukraine, GUUAM, and Western Support for Subregional Cooperation in Europe's Security Gray Zone

Jennifer D. P. Moroney and Sergei Konoplyov

A most interesting test case in the proliferation of new subregional organizations within the Commonwealth of Independent States has emerged in recent years. This organization, loosely defined at present, is known as GUUAM. GUUAM is interesting and important for one specific reason: These five member states are not considered as potential members in Euro–Atlantic institutions, but they have pursued a pro-West foreign and security policy stance in any case. For the last several years they have also simultaneously pursued an anti-CIS foreign policy stance in order to promote their sovereignty and independence separate to Russia.

GUUAM was set to institutionalize its structures at a summit in March 2001. Due mostly to pressures from Moscow, GUUAM's formalization was postponed, and GUUAM was finally institutionalized in June 2001. Now that GUUAM is formalized the West and particularly the United States has been obliged to seriously consider the potential role of GUUAM in European security.

GUUAM as a fully fledged institution should have had the following attributes: clearly defined empirical objectives, a legal charter, a secretariat, a standing committee comprised of representatives for all of the member states, and an economic coordination council charged with drafting a plan of action for 2001. The establishment of GUUAM and other subregional organizations reflects a desire on the part of its members to bring about some kind of institutionalized security or "political normalcy" to the rather underorganized frontier region between Russia and Europe. The crucial question now is if the West will support this movement toward geopolitical pluralism in the region. There is no easy answer to this question. Because of the largely pro-West foreign policy of GUUAM members, recognition by the United States, NATO, and the European Union is of utmost importance to GUUAM in its ability to transform itself into a viable regional organization with international links. Yet Russian opposition to GUUAM has been a key factor in determining the West's attitude toward GUUAM, and, for that matter, any other regional organization of which Russia is wary, reflecting the West's desire not to endorse any regional organization that might provoke or antagonize Russia. Therefore, GUUAM, at best, has been greeted with "cautious optimism" from the United States, NATO, and the EU.

Beginning with a brief history of the organization, this chapter will consider GUUAM's potential role in European security and the "Russia factor" from a theoretical perspective. The motivations or factors that have brought the five members of GUUAM together will then be outlined. Next, GUUAM relations with the West—namely the United States, NATO, and the EU—will be discussed, followed by an analysis of GUUAM's prospects as a viable economic, political, and security institution. It will be argued that without Western and particularly U.S. support for the proliferation of subregional cooperation within the FSU, these "organizations" have no hope of moving beyond the stage characterized as loose-knit political talk shops. Further, the West cannot afford to take the "wait and see" approach to this crucial region, particularly in light of recent Russia moves to bring Ukraine, Moldova, Georgia, and the whole of Central Asia back under its direct sphere of influence.

Further, the GUUAM Summit's postponement for three months clearly illustrates two very important points. First, the extent to which the fate of uninstitutionalized organizations within Europe's security gray zone highly depends on subjective factors, such as the personalities of state leaders, political ideas, and personal agendas. Second, the postponement highlights the extent to which Russia is still able to effectively control the fate of its "near abroad."

HISTORY AND EVOLUTION OF GUUAM

GUUAM was formally founded as a political, economic, and strategic alliance designed to strengthen the independence and sovereignty of these former Soviet Union republics. Some of the key ideas behind the formation of GUUAM was to search for alternative energy routes enabling the members to bypass Russia, to establish closer ties to NATO and the EU, and to lessen the effect of the creation of new dividing lines in Europe following NATO and EU enlargement. During the five years of cooperation, GUUAM was looking to enhance regional economic cooperation through development of a Europe–Caucasus–Asia transport corridor. But it has also evolved into a forum for discussing existing security problems and promoting conflict resolution and the elimination of other risks and threats.

Cooperation among delegations of Azerbaijan, Georgian, Moldovan, and Ukrainian officials started in 1996 in Vienna, Austria, at the CFE Treaty Conference, where four states issued joint statements and proposed common initiatives. In October 1997 the presidents of Azerbaijan, Georgia, Moldova, and Ukraine met in Strasbourg during the Council of Europe Summit and stated their mutual interest in developing bilateral and regional cooperation, European and regional security, and political and economic contacts.

In their joint communiqué, the presidents stressed the importance of the four nations' cooperation in supporting the EU's project for a Eurasian, trans-Caucasus transportation corridor (TRACECA), and underscored the importance of strengthening the quadrilateral cooperation "for the sake of a stable and secure Europe guided by the principles of respect for the sovereignty, territorial integrity, inviolability of state frontiers, mutual respect, cooperation, democracy, supremacy of law and respect for human rights."[1]

In 1998 the U.S. position toward GUUAM changed as a result of President Clinton's trip to Russia. For example, as explained to the author through diplomatic circles, Uzbekistan's accession to GUUAM was largely the result of U.S. encouragement, which was in line with a tougher stance against Russia's expansion into the region. Therefore, in April 1999, GUUAM was enlarged by one with the addition of Uzbekistan, which joined the group at the GUUAM Summit held during the NATO–EAPC Summit in Washington, D.C., on April 23–25, 1999. Following on the heels of the NATO Summit, GUUAM representatives were invited to participate in a conference in the U.S. Congress to discuss the Silk Road energy transportation corridor.

Later that same year, an Institute for GUUAM Coordinators was established, which included Andrii Vesselovskiy from the Policy and Planning Directorate in the Ukrainian MFA; Stephan Gorda, the head of the Department for Political Analysis in the Moldovan MFA; and Araz Azimov, the deputy minister for foreign affairs of Azerbaijan.

In July 1999 during the Florence Summit, Secretary of State Madeleine Albright officially met with GUUAM representatives for the first time.

In September 1999 at the Vienna–OSCE Summit, the GUUAM foreign ministers met again. From approximately May to September 2000, the activities of GUUAM countries' embassies were heightened in the United States. As a result of the GUUAM countries' lobbying efforts, GUUAM representatives met again in the fall of 2000 in Congress to discus energy issues.

In September 2000, at the U.N. Millennium Summit in New York, the presidents of GUUAM countries pledged to intensify multilateral cooperation within the framework of GUUAM by giving it a multi-level character, including an institutionalized status, and to hold a summit in Kyiv to officially lay down the structure and objectives. To this end, it was deemed appropriate and necessary to convene regular summits at the level of heads of state at least once a year, and meetings at the level of ministers for foreign affairs at least twice a year. In the joint communiqué of their meeting, the GUUAM leaders articulated that among other tasks of cooperation, the establishing of favorable conditions for boosting economic growth and raising living standards of their peoples were among the priorities. Moreover, it was intended that "GUUAM departments" of the respective agencies of the member states (e.g., commerce, energy, economics, science and technology, culture, transport, etc) would be established. In addition, GUUAM countries agreed to strengthen and improve the mechanisms of consultations and coordination of actions within the framework of international organizations, and to actively promote the practice of joint statements at various levels (e.g., executive and legislative branches, business circles, NGOs, etc.).

In November 2000 the first high-level diplomatic conference on GUUAM, which included U.S. representation, was held at Stanford University. The point of this conference (as well as the timing) was to discuss the formal institutionalization of GUUAM and the individual positions of its members in the run-up to the planned March 2000 event.

The postponement of the GUUAM Summit scheduled for March 2001, was officially due to the request of Presidents Haidar Aliev of Azerbaijan and Petru Lucinschi of Moldova. Aliev cited a scheduling conflict and Lucinschi was concerned about leaving Moldova so close to the parliamentary election.

Unofficially, there was talk of President Kuchma himself postponing the summit due to political pressure from Moscow, which Putin was able to leverage given the fact that Kuchma is forced to look East for political friends at this time due to the unstable domestic situation, in which Kuchma was accused of ordering the murder of a leading independent journalist in Ukraine, Hryhoriy Honhadze. Kuchma's decision to host the summit and cast Ukraine as GUUAM's locomotive predates the internal political crisis currently facing the president. In December 2000, Kuchma still had enough political clout to pull off the full original agenda of the summit, including a "soft-security" element, but the political situation had deteriorated to the extent that Moscow was apparently able to force Kyiv's hand (as well as the other GUUAM members) in concessions. Kuchma's popularity has since deteriorated significantly. A recent public opinion poll reveals that only 6.1 percent of Ukrainians still support Kuchma.[2] It would seem to make more sense for another member state, perhaps Azerbaijan, to take over this role to try to give GUUAM some additional momentum. It is quite clear that the political climate is such that Ukraine is in no position to do so at this time.[3]

Staff-level preparations were rather far advanced when the summit was postponed. First, establishing the secretariat was a top priority, most likely located in Kyiv. Second, enhancing the role of the five national coordinating staffs was important, which are very underorganized at present. Third, adding an interparliamentary dimension to GUUAM was also on the agenda. Fourth, instituting the rotating chairmanship or its emerging interstate bodies was being discussed. Fifth, approving a consular convention and provisions for simplifying travel across the GUUAM territories was on the table. Sixth, laying the foundation for a GUUAM free-trade zone in lieu of the inability of the CIS to create such a zone was to be a priority.[4] When GUUAM was eventually formalized in June 2001, the provision to establish a military element of GUUAM in the form of a peacekeeping battalion was included on the agenda due to the opposition of several member states (i.e., Moldova). Perhaps most important, the summit was also to include a discussion of conflict resolution issued in Azerbaijan, Moldova, and Georgia as well as the potential role of GUUAM in advancing the EU's pipeline projects and the Europe–Caucasus–Central Asia transit corridor.

THEORETICAL CONSIDERATIONS OF SUBREGIONAL COOPERATION IN THE FSU

Russia's response to GUUAM

In order to try to make some sense of Russia's response to GUUAM, it would perhaps be useful to examine the realist–neorealist model of state behavior and the pluralist model of state theory for some clarification. According to the realist and neorealist theories, the state is the primary actor in international relations. What is seen as "rational" versus "irrational" behavior depends on how closely the state actors are following a foreign policy course, which is in the interests of the state (maintaining and expanding power and influence).

It is clear that Russia has been concerned with regard to the strengthening of GUUAM since the organization's inception. Further, because Russia continues to regard the external world as a "hostile environment," any regional organization in which it does not play the dominant role will be met with disapproval, to say the very least. One might argue that Russia's negative attitude toward GUUAM follows the lines of realist–neorealist theory, and is even testimony to Moscow's neoimperialist tendencies. If a Russia led by Putin seeks to restore its control and influence over the CIS countries, then GUUAM would objectively pose a threat to the realization of such intentions. If Russia follows such a policy, the instinct would be to try to destroy GUUAM, or at least to try to reduce the organization's impact to purely ceremonial functions, and to simultaneously seek to enhance Russia's military presence in the Caucasus and the Black Sea region. However, the price Russia would have to pay for such a policy would be the increase of stability on its own territory, as Chechnya serves to demonstrate.

With Russia continuing to regard the external world as a hostile environment, any regional organization in which it does not play the role of a dominating power would be considered hostile. And if the Russian policy continues to be aimed at the "struggle for dominance in the region" and the preservation of the old imperialist or Soviet-style status quo, GUUAM would naturally be an obstacle to achieving such dominance in the Caucasus region and expanding to adjacent areas.[5]

On the other hand, if Russia's own national security policy is indeed based on the interests of the protection of its own territory rather than on seeking to dominate its neighbors, Russia should, in theory, support the proliferation of regional organizations such as GUUAM, which follows the reasoning of the pluralist perspective. If Russia was interested in increasing security at its present borders, which have explicitly been agreed to in recent border delimitations with its neighbors (and not, say, at the ephemeral borders of the former USSR), then Russia should be interested in GUUAM's regional security objectives that could benefit Russia by securing its southern borders and promoting stability in the North Caucasus. Cooperation between Russia and GUUAM would thus potentially reduce potential domination of hostile centers of power in the region. Certainly the GUUAM countries and Russia have common interests in strengthening regional stability and combating terrorism and drug trafficking. However, since Moscow does not support GUUAM on any level, this would lead one to conclude that Russia's intentions follow the lines of the realist–neorealist perspective.[6]

Furthermore, Russia counterattacked GUUAM on several fronts, both officially and through proxy. Moscow sponsored the "anti-GUUAM" group of Transdniester, Abkhazia, South Ossetia, and Karabakh, territories that have seceded from the countries of Moldova, Georgia, and Azerbaijan, respectively. On January 19 and 20, 2001,

Russia's Foreign Affairs Ministry issued perhaps its sharpest attacks to date on GUUAM's proliferation, accusing the member states of aiming to create a military bloc, thus deviating substantially from GUUAM's original agenda.[7] The Russian Foreign Ministry charged that, first of all, GUUAM had moved beyond its "initial character as an informal consultative group within the CIS." Second, it asserted that GUUAM's agenda—focusing on Caspian oil and gas pipelines and the European transport projects—has departed from the group's original goals, which had in principle been comparable with the "integration within the CIS space." Third, the Russian document accused GUUAM of "forcing up the pace of military cooperation in obvious contradiction to the group's initially stated goals" (the proposed peacekeeping battalion, the so-called GUUAMBAT).[8] But the charge that GUUAM has the potential to develop a military component in the short term is grossly exaggerated. Not least due to the lack of economic resources, there is also a lack of political will on the part of the member states. It is a known fact that Moldova has on more than one occasion denounced any interest in GUUAM's potential role in peacekeeping and/or pipeline security.

All this talk generated an unprecedented international interest in GUUAM in the months immediately preceding the planned March 2001 summit. U.S. government agencies also began to take a greater interest in GUUAM, though the United States did not collectively lend official support to the institutionalization process. The EU was less enthusiastic, though the EU Commission was indeed "interested" in the developments. The talk also "intimidated" some GUUAM members themselves. For example, there have been reports that Moldova and Uzbekistan have been unhappy with the "excessive politicization" of the group. In short, clouds have undetectably been gathering over GUUAM for the past year, and it should, perhaps, not come as a surprise that the intensification of these trends may eventually lead to the collapse of the group.[9]

WAS GUUAM MEANT TO REPLACE
OR DESTROY THE CIS?

It is debatable whether it is the intention of the member states for the deepening of integration within GUUAM to be at the expense of the furthering of CIS integration. Indeed, the two organizations were formed for fundamentally different reasons, and pursue very different goals. Whereas the CIS is united by a common past, GUUAM countries are united by the prospect of a common European future. Most important, unlike the CIS, GUUAM has no center. There is instead an arrangement of equal partners, with no one country clearly dominat-ing. This organization has formed because of common interests based on common economic, energy, and foreign policy interests. The CIS, conversely, was formed by Russia primarily in an attempt to maintain some level of economic, political, and military dominance over the former Soviet republics.

Further, GUUAM and the CIS pursue different objectives. As out-lined in greater detail later, GUUAM members favor the strengthening of political, economic, energy, and security ties with the goal of moving individual members closer to Europe and to the West. Specifically, GUUAM ambassadors have pledged to promote an East–West trade and transportation corridor, to develop interaction within the frame-work of the Euro–Atlantic Partnership Council and NATO's Partner-ship for Peace program, to prevent the proliferation of weapons of mass destruction in the region, and to combat the trafficking in narcotics in their countries (as declared at an international conference on U.S.–GUUAM relations at the U.S. Capitol on May 18, 2000). CIS countries, on the other hand, do not have any generally agreed-upon objectives by all member states. Instead, they pursue three different objectives. Some CIS states, such as Russia and Belarus, advocate the restoration of a single state with Moscow at its center. Other members consider the CIS as an appropriate means for a civilized divorce from the USSR. Still others, such as the GUUAM members, favor the shifting of ties in the CIS from a multilateral to a bilateral approach. They do not, for example, support having CIS "ambassadors" represent individual member states in international forums.

IMMEDIATE AND LONG-TERM GOALS OF GUUAM

There are several key integrating factors of GUUAM members, in-cluding the establishment of a Caspian–European oil transportation corridor, the desire to deepen political and economic cooperation and to create institutionalized security in the region, the desire to establish a peacekeeping role for GUUAM, and their common opposition to Russian domination in the CIS. GUUAM has established roughly four areas that serve to characterize the direction of its integration. These areas are institutionalization, economic and trade cooperation, humani-tarian affairs, and cooperation in the sphere of security.

Institutionalization

First of all, as mentioned, GUUAM members have agreed that they must first and foremost institutionalize the organization if they are to expect external international actors to extend credence to their "club." The establishment of a legal charter, a secretariat, and formalized meetings at the presidential and ministerial levels, for example, are certainly ways to capture the attention and thus, perhaps, the support of influential and powerful states and institutions.

Since the last quarter of 2000, there has been an upsurge of activity aimed at building an institutional structure for GUUAM. The following are some initial and longer-term steps that should be taken to achieve this goal:

- Elaborating the conceptual basis of the GUUAM development.
- Implementing GUUAM's program as an international organization.
- Articulating program purposes, tasks, and functions of GUUAM.
- Drafting and ratifying the charter and organizational structure of GUUAM as an international organization with institutional bodies, including the secretariat.
- Establishing a format and strategic direction for GUUAM's cooperation with other international actors and institutions.

Subregional Economic and Trade Cooperation

Since economic and trade relations are one of the cornerstones of GUUAM's rationale for further integration, the following immediate and longer-term goals in this sphere are conceivable:

- Harmonization of economic interests of GUUAM countries and particulars of economic collaboration within the framework of this organization.
- Creation and implementation of the free-trade zone in the GUUAM framework.
- Establishing overall directions of economic cooperation in the GUUAM framework.
- Defining principles and mechanisms of creation of joint financial and economic structures.
- Defining and developing perspective directions of development of a transport–energy and economic infrastructure in the GUUAM framework.
- Reviving the "silk way" as the pan-European economic project.
- Taking concrete steps toward integration of GUUAM countries in the European economic space.
- Developing a strategy of GUUAM's partnership with the EU in terms of what the best route is to get there (e.g., by way of regional cooperation? Bilateral ties with EU member states? Directly with EU institutions [i.e., commission])?

Humanitarian Development

With regard to cooperation in the humanitarian sphere, GUUAM seeks to analyze migratory processes in GUUAM, analyze the demographic situation in GUUAM countries and interethnic and religious contradiction, investigate the situation in the sphere of human rights and freedoms in GUUAM countries, analyze the level of development of democratic processes in GUUAM countries, and address the problems of adaptation of the national and local legislation to EU standards.

Security Cooperation

In the sphere of security cooperation, which will be discussed in greater detail later, the GUUAM countries have agreed in principle to pursue the following objectives: to establish agreed-upon conceptual bases and strategies of cooperative security of GUUAM, to elaborate the new approaches as to definitive settlement of conflicts in the GUUAM region, to outline the basic directions and forms of military–technical cooperation in the GUUAM frameworks (with the United States, the EU, NATO, and others [bilateral]), and to prioritize the deepening of GUUAM's partnership with NATO to reinforce national and regional security issues.

GUUAM'S RELATIONS WITH THE WEST: THE UNITED STATES, NATO, AND THE EU

As mentioned, the U.S. government has approached GUUAM with cautious, unofficial support at best, though in 2000 Congress took limited steps to "recognize" GUUAM by allocating annual Foreign Military Financing (FMF) to "GUUAM + Armenia." The State Department established a "consultative framework" in December 2000 for engaging GUUAM.

Regarding defense relations, perhaps because the Department of Defense (DOD) has extensive bilateral defense and military ties with GUUAM countries already, it has hinted that it may support the informal GUUAM association if it specifies common interests in the defense sector. In such a case, DOD would be ready to provide assistance. The possible creation of a GUUAM peacekeeping battalion (GUUAMBAT) would naturally be of particular interest to U.S. defense structures. Ukraine has training centers and structures in place as well as relevant forces and means to carry out peacekeeping operations. For example, the Ukrainian Ministry of Defense has established a Peacekeeping and Verification Center in Kyiv, and Yavoriv in Western Ukraine has been transformed into a PfP peacekeeping training facility. Ukraine and other GUUAM members are focused on making a contribution to NATO and U.N. peacekeeping operations (Ukraine through the Polish–Ukrainian peacekeeping battalion—UkrPolBat—in KFOR), and all have an acute interest in settling conflicts on their territories (e.g., Nargano-Karbakh, Abkazia, Ajaria, and Transnistria) and enhancing stability in the Black Sea region as a whole.

However, because GUUAM failed to take such steps in terms of formalizing its structures and objectives, the U.S. government's interest in GUUAM for the moment has been pushed to the wayside. It seems that GUUAM is cracking in front of Washington's very eyes. Moldova and Uzbekistan are also close to withdrawing from GUUAM. If the United States does not do anything, than GUUAM will most likely turn out to be a "stillborn child."[10]

NATO and the EU have been even less enthusiastic in supporting and holding consultations with GUUAM. In the case of NATO, GUUAM asked for consultations within the "19 + 5" format in summer 2000, but this proposal was rejected by NATO. Basically, the attitude is that NATO's partners can pursue cooperation with NATO through the Partnership for Peace program and through bilateral mechanisms. The EU, similarly, has extensive political and economic contacts with the FSU and with GUUAM members, specifically through the Partnership and Cooperation Agreements and executive and legislative consultation, and thus does not see the need to open up formal diplomatic and other contacts with GUUAM, particularly since it has not been institutionalized.

GUUAM'S MOST SIGNIFICANT CHALLENGES: DOMESTIC PERSPECTIVES

The most serious challenges to GUUAM clearly lie within the weaknesses and vulnerabilities of its individual member states. For example, Moldova is virtually paralyzed by Russia's continued refusal to comply with the OSCE–Russian agreements on the removal of Russian forces from the Transnistria. Moldovan President Lucinschi has also spoken out against making GUUAM into a new political organization with corresponding structures, thus moving beyond the "consultative body" arrangement. Lucinschi has stated that the political situation in Moldova has changed considerably and that relations should be advanced more on a bilateral basis, and also within other organizations, adding that Moldova intends to use the opportunities that will arise in the near future when the country enters the Stability Pact for Southeast Europe.[11] In addition, Uzbekistan is deeply involved in the struggle against Islamic movements, in which it feels some dependence on Russia. Further, as discussed, Ukraine is becoming increasingly unassertive, having been confronted by the prospects of an oil pipeline bypassing Ukrainian territory. Azerbaijan is seemingly preoccupied with internal difficulties stemming from contested election results, which has led to mass demonstrations and political clashes. Georgia is in the process of trying to persuade a reluctant Russia to carry out its promise and withdraw its forces from Georgian territory. Furthermore, President Shevardnadze's government continues to be held hostage by the Russian-sponsored separatist movements in Abkhazia and Ajaria. Because of Russia's continued military presence, Georgia is not in control of its own borders and territorial integrity, which is an important symbolic affirmation of the country's sovereignty. Georgia is also constrained by Russia's imposition of a visa regime not levied against other CIS countries, but instead being used to leverage Georgian efforts to obtain the removal of Russia's military bases.

In addition to the domestic situations in the GUUAM countries, there are also higher forces at work that have hindered the integration and formalization of GUUAM. It is evident that Ukraine has been focusing its foreign policy toward Russia since the latter part of 2000, just after the sacking of pro-West Foreign Minister Borys Tarasyuk and the appointment of Anatoly Zlenko to the position. At a meeting held in Astana, Kazakhstan, in October 2000, a group of CIS countries (Kazakhstan, Kyrgyzstan, Belarus, and Tajikistan) headed by Russia decided to transform the customs union into the Eurasian European Community (EEC), and thus signed an agreement that established a new organization that supports a process of "real integration in former Soviet States." The first meeting of the EEC took place in Minsk in September 2001. Thus, essentially, the geoeconomic space in the CIS has been transformed into pro-West versus pro-CIS emphasis on trade agreements, or GUUAM versus EEC.

In addition, a conference opened in Kyiv in mid-March 2001 that focused on the "Zubr" union of Russia, Belarus, and Ukraine. The conference, titled "Union between Ukraine, Belarus, and Russia Is Inevitable," included representatives from the Russian Duma, the Belarusian National Assembly, and the local Communist parliamentary factions. According to "Zubr" followers, GUUAM and other international institutions are just weakening Ukraine's position, and Ukraine should be focusing itself on "life-giving (economic) unions with Russia and the CIS."[12]

THE "RISKS" OF WESTERN AMBIVALENCE TOWARD SUBREGIONAL COOPERATION IN THE REGION

It is the author's opinion that GUUAM should first and foremost be viewed as a test case for the proliferation of new security organizations in the frontier region between the West and Russia. The countries of the FSU (with the exception of the Baltics) that lie outside of NATO's and the EU's direct purview or liability are also targets that Russia strives to dominate on any level it can. Such a situation presents the possibility of new threats and challenges for European security. Logically speaking, it will be more difficult for NATO and the EU to influence those countries that are outside of their immediate zone of liability. Thus, the neutralization of new threats for Europe originated from the post-Soviet space and the reinforcement of its stability can be reached through the creation of definite subregional security outposts. The creation of such zones in the post-Soviet space is made possible due to current fragmentation, which encourages countries in the region to unite in subregional organizations such as GUUAM, the Black Sea Economic Cooperation Organization (BSECO), and others.

GUUAM is the only subregional organization in the FSU distinguished by its pro-Western European and Euro–Atlantic orientations. Hence, the support of subregional development from the side of the Western countries and particularly the United States will bring about establishment on the eastern borders of the EU and NATO something that is not a "buffer zone," but rather a stable subregion seeking to promote European security. However, the creation and development of this organization is not imagined to be constructive without deep theoretical, conceptual, and analytical support.

CONCLUSION

In hindsight it is easy to see why some scholars may have given GUUAM too much credit before it was institutionalized. Taras Kuzio, for example, has argued that "Russia is losing its bid to represent, and perhaps also to reintegrate the Former Soviet Union. . . . Instead, successor states are creating their own regional partnerships and striving to join existing European organizations."[13] To be sure, GUUAM member states have indeed sought to deepen their cooperation in political, economic, and military terms both with NATO and the EU. But the bottom line is that both NATO and the EU have been experiencing a certain level of fatigue with GUUAM countries, particularly with Ukraine, and there have been no steps taken in a credible or formal way to bring these countries closer to membership.

GUUAM member have found themselves in a zone of competing polar interests. Will GUUAM be able to overcome this setback? There really is no clear answer, but several options can be discerned from the current situation: (1) gradual collapse of the alliance (i.e., GUUAM to GUA to GA), (2) postcrisis truncation with further expansion (i.e., to perhaps include Poland, Romania, Armenia, or Turkey), or (3) preservation of the alliance's current structure with considerable depoliticization, which would not include a military element. The first and perhaps the third options would suit Moscow's interests. The second and third options would suit U.S. interests. The first two options are the least likely, and only the third option can possibly become the basis for seeking acceptable compromises.[14]

GUUAM still has some growing pains to overcome. GUUAM has not yet developed clear objectives and goals, has bowed to Russia pressure, and has not captured the full support from the West, which they desperately need. The lesson learned in early 2001 is that the West, particularly the United States, has pursued a "Russia first" policy, particularly given the new war on terrorism, and that subregional organizations such as GUUAM must be formalized before the West will lend economic or political support. This was clearly evident in the case of the Black Sea Economic Cooperation Organization, which until its institutionalization in September 1998 did not fully capture the West's attention.

GUUAM could be doomed to fall apart unless a larger, influential country joins it. Although Romania, for example, has not officially declared that it would like to join GUUAM, according to Georgian Foreign Minister Irakly Menagarishvili the cooperation between GUUAM and Romania is possible.[15] Yet perhaps Poland is more important for GUUAM's future. Poland, which is Ukraine's strategic partner (with ardent U.S. backing) and a participant in the trilateral U.S.–Ukraine–Poland defense-oriented grouping, is the most attractive candidate, since it shares a similar background and similar problems with the GUUAM members.

It is important that GUUAM and future regional organizations take into account the lessons learned from other subregional organizations and consultative bodies, namely the Visegrad group, which actually shares many similarities with GUUAM. Like Visegrad, GUUAM is a consultative body with no secretariat or charter, but unlike GUUAM, Visegrad was an effectively functioning body. Moreover, unlike GUUAM, the West has lent its support to the group.

The question now to consider regarding the proliferation of subregional organzations is this: If the United States and the EU are truly concerned about the geopolitical configuration of Eastern Europe and the CIS and Russia's resurgent role in the region, should the West not lend political and economic backing to those states that have declared their desire to "return to Europe"? We should ask ourselves what the cost is of not doing so. Clearly, the fact that the United States, NATO, and the EU have not officially declared their support to GUUAM was a major contributor to its initial decision to postpone formalization and allowed Moscow to have a stronger influence. Since NATO and the EU are not ready to talk membership with these countries, a logical alternative would not be to follow a wait-and-see approach, but rather to engage these countries in a multilateral and bilateral context and to encourage them to take a more proactive role in safeguarding their own security at the regional level. In the end, taking action can only serve to advance Western interests in the region.

NOTES

A shorter version of this chapter was first published in *National Security & Defense* (no. 12) (Kyiv, Ukraine).

1. See GUUAM Web site (http://www.guuam.org), "History and Principles (of GUUAM)," November 2000.

2. "Opinion Poll Shows Only 6 Percent Support for President," *Kiev Ukrayina Moloda*, 16 March 2001. The poll was conducted between February 26 and March 7 of over 2,000 people by the Ukrainian Center for Political and Economic Research.

3. Fatima Mamedova, "GUUAM National Coordinators to Meet in Baku," *Azerbaijani News Agency*, 24 February 2001; "GUUAM's Growing Pains," *Jamestown Monitor* 7, no. 34 (2001).

4. "GUUAM's Growing Pains."

5. "New Political Aspects of GUUAM Development" (Center for Peace, Conversion, and Foreign Policy of Ukraine Report no. 45, December 2000).

6. Ibid.

7. For a more detailed discussion on military cooperation in GUUAM, see Flemming Splidsboel-Hansen, "GUUAM and the Future of CIS Military Cooperation," *European Security* 9, no. 4 (2000).

8. "GUUAM Attacked by Moscow Ahead of the Group's Summit," *Jamestown Monitor's Fortnight in Review* 7, no. 3 (2001).

9. "Azeri Agency Downbeat about GUUAM Alliances Future," *Azerbaijani News Agency*, 2 March 2001.

10. *Zerkalo Nedeli*, 17 February 2001.

11. "Moldovan President Does Not Think GUUAM Should Become a Political Organization," *Interfax Russian News*, 23 February 2001.

12. "Communist MPs from Ukraine, Russia, and Belarus Demand Return of Union State," *Kiev Novyy Kanal Television*, 17 March 2001.

13. T. Kuzio, "Promoting Geopolitical Pluralism in the CIS: GUUAM and Western Foreign Policy," *Problems of Post-Communism* 47, no. 3 (2000): 25–35. Also, see O. Pavliuk, "The Maturing of a Politics Grouping into Economic Cooperation," in *Building Security for the New States of Eurasia: Subregional Cooperation in the Former Soviet Space*, ed. Renata Dwan and O. Pavliuk (Armonk, N.Y.: M. E. Sharpe, 2000).

14. "Azeri Agency Downbeat about GUUAM Alliances Future."

15. "U.S. Ambassador Kenneth Yalowitz on Caucasus Relations," *Tbilisi News Agency*, 2 March 2001.

PART IV

NATIONAL IDENTITY, IDEOLOGY, AND UKRAINIAN SECURITY POLICY

10

European, Eastern Slavic, and Eurasian: National Identity, Transformation, and Ukrainian Foreign Policy

Taras Kuzio

Placing undue emphasis upon language in contemporary Ukrainian politics misreads the dynamics of post-Soviet transformation and foreign policy in Ukraine.[1] It places too great an emphasis upon language criteria while neglecting other factors, such as political culture and national identity. Throughout Ukraine's post-Soviet transition under both Presidents Leonid Kravchuk (1991–1994) and Leonid Kuchma (1994–) it has backed a foreign policy course defined as "returning to Europe." In reality there has been little to differentiate the strategic guidelines of Kravchuk's and Kuchma's foreign policies. This is more a question of different tactics to be used in attaining the same strategic goals. Volodymyr Horbulin, secretary of the National Security and Defense Council, defined Ukraine as a country lying geographically in Eastern, Central, and Southeastern Europe (not in Eurasia).[2] Ukrainian security policy elites believe that Ukraine, unlike Russia, has historically belonged to Europe, from which it was temporarily isolated.[3]

Kuchma's pragmatic nationalism has elite consensus, which has translated into a strategic objective of affirming Ukraine as both a European and eastern Slavic country. Ukraine's pro-Russian orientation has declined as the revival of the USSR becomes increasingly unlikely. While accepting independent statehood as a de facto reality,

Ukrainians do not rule out economic integration and cooperation with Russia and the CIS to improve their socioeconomic plight.[4] Ukraine has pursued good relations with Russia and sought to "return to Europe," two foreign policy objectives not defined as contradictory. While Ukraine is a purely European state, Russia is both European and Asian (i.e., Eurasian).[5] Russia does see Ukraine's twin-track foreign policy agenda as contradictory; in other words, if Ukraine desires to "return to Europe" its back will be to Russia.

Ukraine and Russia have been unable to normalize their relations because they differ over how the east Slavic space should be organized. Russia sees the eastern Slavic space as a region where it will be the cultural, political, and ideological hegemon. Such a view stems from its political culture of pan Slavism that defines itself as the leading Slavic nation. Ukraine, in contrast, has a Central European view of the Slavic region that recognizes no hegemon (i.e., "elder brother") and insists upon equality among nations. Russia sees Ukraine as always having been part of "Russia," and therefore sees its presence outside the east Slavic space as contradictory. Ukraine's identity is derived from a far longer period under non-Russian rule and influence until the late eighteenth century, and a shorter Russian–Eurasian period of rule during the nineteenth and twentieth centuries.

This chapter discusses this foreign policy strategic course in four sections. First, it surveys the theoretical literature on political culture and argues in favor of using it as a framework for understanding the relationship between national identity and foreign policy. Second, it surveys Ukrainian identity, political culture, and post-Soviet transition. Third, it reviews foreign and defenses policies under Presidents Leonids Kravchuk and Kuchma and discusses Russian–Ukrainian relations and the reasons for the failure of a Russian–Ukrainian strategic partnership. The final section outlines ten factors that shape Ukrainian foreign policy from the perspective of national identity and political culture.

NATIONAL IDENTITY, POLITICAL CULTURE, AND FOREIGN POLICY

National identity and political culture are difficult concepts to define, but, nonetheless, they play an important role as building blocks in the formulation of a country's foreign policy. Wilson and Bilous believe that Ukraine lacks any political culture because "Post-communist Ukraine is in effect attempting to create a political culture from scratch." Unlike the Baltic and Central European states, therefore, "Ukraine cannot draw on a rich historical political tradition."[6] This pessimistic conclusion fails to recognize what Holmes points out as the fact that no post-Communist state began with a "clean slate." State and nation building is therefore being undertaken "with citizens who are carrying a considerable amount of baggage from the past."[7] Tismaneanu and Turner also add, "Like individuals, societies do carry with them certain memories, thought patterns (formae mentis), expectations, nostalgia, fantasies, and even culture of democratic procedures, norms, institutions, and values."[8]

This baggage can be both negative and positive in the creation of new civic nations and states upon the ruins of the Soviet empire. But it cannot be ignored, and these historical memories, embedded habits, and behavioral patterns interact through politics and culture. These values and the perspectives they bring, their personality and psychological traits together with the cognitive knowledge and beliefs of one's political culture and the way it operates, are internalized in modern polities. Within those societies that are in democratic transition, where societies exhibit both parochial and participatory elements, political culture will be in a state of flux. In parochial societies the citizen does not feel that his or her action can have an impact upon the political process, or that it is "worthwhile to perform one's civic duties."[9]

Political culture in Western societies is composed of a trinity of a modern "European" system of values (market economy, democracy, and welfare system), often based on a common language, shared religion, a sense of place, and otherness (which defines the "we" from the foreign). This community of choice is at the heart of civic nationalism and the territorially bounded political nation. A country's political (or societal) culture is not required to be uniformly homogenous, and "there is no requirement that everyone share a given belief."[10] Subpolitical cultures can coexist within an overall political culture that goes to make up the societal culture, but it does require that the political culture act in the form of internalized, unconscious assumptions that represent taken-for-granted "control mechanisms" that plan, rule, and govern behavior as well as the course of action. It entails assumptions about who belongs to one's political community, who are the "others," and how they should be related to.[11] This distinct set of norms, rules, habits, traditions, and beliefs, which are still largely absent in societies undergoing transition except among elites and elements of the population, "sit at the heart of each political system, shaping the behavior of the main participants in the political process."[12]

It is not surprising, therefore, that during periods of elite-led transition from old to new regimes there are discrepancies between the political culture of the elites and the masses on the one hand and between generations on the other. These manifest themselves in differing views about foreign policy and the overall domestic transition process.

In societies in transition, such as Ukraine, not all of the elements of the political culture are fully internalized, and its shared values provide the normative culture that defines the situation and underwrites the political goals of its members. In societies in transition, elites, intellectuals, historians, writers, and political activists search for and debate the values, orientations, ideas, and morals newly located in previously banned and/or revived studies and works. These will go toward the construction of a new post-totalitarian and post-imperial Ukrainian political culture and identity to integrate the emerging civic nation and state.

Political culture is composed, in Kavanagh's view, of orientations to political objects and action that "are determined by such factors as traditions, historical memories, motives, norms, emotions and symbols."[13] These national values, elements of Soviet political culture that the newly emerging elites may not wish to discard, as well as the influence of Western values important to underpin the emerging democratic society and capitalist economy, will go into the creation of a political culture and national idea.

NATIONAL IDENTITY AND
FOREIGN POLICY IN UKRAINE

Ukrainian Identity and Political Culture

The study of Ukrainian political culture is still in its infancy. Nevertheless, some elements can already be identified that, at the very least, show important distinctions between Ukrainian and Russian political culture. In a detailed analysis of Ukrainian political culture Zimmerman found that the Ukrainian worldview throughout its regions differed from that held by Russian citizens.[14] The Ukrainian and Russian foreign policy dialogues among elites and the public were therefore fundamentally different and drew upon contrasting myths, culture, beliefs, and values.

Without such differences in Ukrainian and Russian political culture it would be difficult to explain the domestic strength of support for Ukrainian sovereignty, particularly among its economic, political, and cultural elites. Traditionally, Russocentric Western histories of "Russia" ignore the multicultural influences upon Ukraine that have influenced its identity and political culture and focus only upon Russian influences. Yet influences upon Ukraine's formative political culture were multidirectional and multicultural (the Byzantine south, the West, and, from the nineteenth century, from the Russian northeast). Therefore, Ukrainian authors are fond of stating, "Our attitude towards European values does not need any additional argumentation. Ukraine completely belonged to this civilization type at least until the eighteenth century, when, in particular, the total pauperization of the population began. The education system, religious life and the economy were typically European."[15]

Throughout the nineteenth and twentieth centuries Ukrainian thinkers rejected both Russian centralizers and Polish aristocratic democracy. Influential Ukrainian political thinkers and historians ranging from social democrats, such as Mykhailo Drahomaniv, Mykhailo Hrushevs'kyi, and Ivan Franko, to nationalists, such as Dmytro Dontsov, to monarchists, such as V'iacheslav Lypyns'kyi, always emphasized Ukraine's formative links to "Europe." Ukrainian political thinkers usually linked the idea of democracy to social and economic justice because foreign overlords ruled Ukrainian peasants and workers. The social democratic Central Rada of 1917 supported Ukraine's national, socioeconomic, and democratic emancipation. Former Prime Minister Pavlo Lazarenko therefore believed that "social democracy conforms to the mentality of the Ukrainian people."[16] Ukraine's past experience of rule by, and dealings with, Russia have therefore largely discredited the idea that the Ukrainian question can be addressed in union with Russia.[17]

Ukraine's cultural traditions, pre-eighteenth-century history, political culture, and national identity are "European," and Ukraine's return to Europe signifies the "overcoming of long-standing artificial alienation from other nations of the continent."[18] Horbulin wrote, "The values enshrined within the development of Ukrainian education, religion and art are inseparable from the development of the European cultural tradition."[19] On the four-hundredth anniversary of Hetman Bohdan Khmel'nyts'kyi's birth, President Kuchma lauded the fact that Khmel'nyts'kyi had led a national, democratic, and socioeconomic revolution that placed Ukraine firmly within the processes of Europe's awakening. Comparing Khmel'nyts'kyi to the "other great European Oliver Cromwell," Kuchma pointed with pride to how Ukraine had attempted to build a society with free farmers and equal citizens over a hundred years before the United States.[20] Hetman Pylyp Orlyk's constitution of 1710 is likewise seen as Ukraine's democratic contribution to European democratic thought, which appeared before its analogous Polish, French, or American variants.

An analyst and the then director of Ukraine's influential National Institute of Strategic Studies (the former think tank of the National Security and Defense Council) believed that Ukraine's pre-Soviet and preimperial identity still influences its contemporary political culture: "Ukraine, unlike Russia, is an exclusively European country. The Ukrainian people are a European people. Even the fact that for more than three centuries Ukraine was part of a huge Eurasian empire, has evidently not changed the fundamental European nature of the Ukrainian people, culture and identity. After finally achieving its independence,

Ukraine desires to link its destiny more and more with Europe and the West."[21]

Consequently, Ukraine's "return to Europe" signifies a rejection of two calamities that are perceived to have befallen Ukraine during the last two centuries: imperial rule and Soviet totalitarianism. The establishment of an independent state and democracy were, and remain, closely bound together as goals in their own right that can only be attained within "Europe," not in Eurasia, the source of empire and totalitarianism. When Ukrainians voted in the December 1991 referendum for independence they therefore "elected the European way of life," Rukh believe.[22] Vasyl' Kremen', minister of education and a leading Social Democrat, agreed with Rukh that Ukraine's return to "civilization" could only be undertaken as an independent state.[23] Becoming again a part of "civilization" (i.e., Europe) is therefore by definition impossible if Ukraine integrated fully into the so-called Eurasia space because it would lose its state independence.[24]

Europe and Ukraine's Post-Soviet Transition

Ukraine's elite consensus on returning to Europe recognizes that Ukraine is European and eastern Slavic. The manner in which the eastern Slavic geopolitical region should be organized continues to divide Ukraine and Russia. Russia continues to see Ukraine (minus Galicia) as in effect "Russian" (i.e., Little Russian). "It is obvious that Moscow has taken too many liberties not only with our country, but its leaders as well," one Ukrainian newspaper lamented.[25] Independence is therefore a temporary aberration instigated by corrupt elites and the West intent on weakening Russia. Ukraine sees itself as an independent country located in Central and Eastern Europe that desires equal relations with other independent Slavic states. It sees no contradiction between being both European and eastern Slavic.

Europe—rather than Eurasia—continues to be the strategic axis of Ukraine's foreign policy. Kuchma argued in no uncertain terms that "our strategy consists in drawing closer to the European structures. Integration in Europe is our conscious and historic choice."[26] "Ukraine is today a European country with its own identity and future. There is no return to the past, no matter whether Ukraine does or does not join NATO," Kuchma said.[27] This would require, Kuchma believed, that Ukraine "intensify efforts towards the strategic goal of integration with the leading European and Transatlantic organizations, irreversibly codifying Ukraine's status as a constituent region of East-Central Europe."[28]

Kuchma lost the presidential elections in Kyiv city. The central ruling elites are the driving force behind Ukrainian foreign policy and its nation-state-building project. Regions, the language factor, or Ukraine's inherited subpolitical cultures do not therefore play the significant role in the formulation of security policy that some scholars believed. Kuchma could not ignore public opinion and policy makers in Kyiv, who are dominated by those with a pro-European orientation, as clearly seen in the following list of influential think tanks in Ukraine:[29]

Organization	Orientation	Rating (1–5)
Ukrainian Perspectives	European	3.57
Center Economic and Political Research	European	2.82
Institute Transformation Society	European	2.37
Politychna Dumka	European	2.31
Center Political and Conflict Studies	European–Eurasian	2.13
Center Independent Political Research	European	1.92
Democratic Initiatives	European	1.92
Demos	European	1.88

An important driving force of Ukrainian national identity within foreign policy rests upon the feeling that its people and elites should have direct access to the centers of "world civilization" rather than through intermediaries as Little Russians. Then Prime Minister Yevhen Marchuk commended himself on the fact that "we now do the Brussels commute as often as we used to do to Moscow."[30]

Improvement of Socioeconomic Situation	65%
Decreasing Economic Dependence on Russia	38%
Inflow of Credits and Investments	36%
Strengthening Ukraine's National Security	35%
Growth of Ukraine's Exports to the EU	31%
Improvement of Ukraine's International Image	30%
Free Entry of Ukrainian Citizens in EU Countries	28%

Europe is defined as the goal of Ukraine's future path of development, whether she joins NATO or the EU, a path that forecloses any return to a negative Eurasian past. President Kuchma defined a key foreign policy goal as "irreversibly codifying Ukraine's status as a constituent region of East-Central Europe."[31] A key element of the December 1994 security assurances provided to Ukraine and the July 1997 NATO–Ukraine Charter were their definition of Ukraine as a "central European state."[32] Foreign Minister Hennadiy Udovenko, president of the U.N. General Assembly in 1997–1998 and a leader of one of two Rukh parliamentary factions, described Ukraine as the largest country in Eastern and Central Europe, presumably in the process excluding Russia from Europe.[33]

The concept of "Europe" is associated with "stability, security, democracy and well-being." Membership of the Council of Europe will allow "the application of other European countries experience in nation building." By integrating into Europe, Ukraine can "promote democratization and Europeanization" at home.[34] In moving toward Europe, Ukraine can learn, Kuchma believes, from those countries where democracy has existed for a long time. Therefore, analysts within the executive structures believe that "the strategic choice of Ukraine lies in the creation of a democratic society of a European standard."[35] Ukraine's strategic foreign policy course will continue to remain "Westward" as, in so doing, it will "adopt all viable norms and values that for decades have successfully gone through trials in the economy, politics and spiritual spheres."[36]

Democratic values and civil society, still in their formative stage in Ukraine, are associated in the eyes of the Ukrainian public with the West; that is, with Europe.[37] This is important for Ukraine in "choosing the European model of development."[38] In other words, political–economic reform and nation and state building, if they are to be pursued, require an orientation toward Europe. It is from Europe that Ukraine can obtain experience of democracy, because there it "has been in existence for a very long time."[39] The alternative would be to prevent Ukraine's integration into the West and "a civilized path of development": "Turning Ukraine into another Belarus is the right way for Russia to establish a long-term political and economic control over our country."[40]

The mixed election law used in the March 1998 parliamentary elections gave Ukraine an image "of a modern European democratic state with a developed legal system," then Prime Minister Pustovoitenko argued.[41] Ukraine's system of party classification should henceforth be based on the "European system."[42] Reform of Ukraine's judiciary system would be undertaken with the help of the Council of Europe and the EU because Ukraine needed to bring its legislation into line with Europe in order to facilitate European integration.[43]

Ukrainian nation and state building and reform would be undertaken "peacefully and civilized, without victims and force."[44] Returning to Europe means a return to the "European model of actions in the state-political and social life," Kuchma believes.[45] Ukraine would not allow itself to go down Russia's road of violence, first against its parliament and then in Chechnya. The lack of ethnic violence boosts Ukraine's national pride. In contrast to most CIS countries, Ukraine "has repeatedly shown the whole world community that it is wholly committed to democratic reform in the country and is able to find a civilized solution in the most complex, seemingly chaotic, and almost hopeless situation."[46]

Europe is the only source of new technology, financial assistance to cover the budget deficit, and technical aid in the transition process.[47] Ukraine, "if we want to have a civilized state," must be a member of the World Trade Organization. "If we do not, we will sit in the CIS club," then Foreign Minister Udovenko argued, clearly seeing this as inferior to being part of Europe and the West.[48] Presidential economic adviser Halchynskiy also links Ukraine's integration with the outside world and the reorientation of its economy away from the CIS to three factors. First, it will provide a greater source of high technology in contrast to becoming merely a raw-material appendage. Second, it will allow Ukraine to "become a part of a civilized world."[49] Third, the level of business and economic freedom reflect "how civilized a state is," President Kuchma believes.[50]

Ukraine's post-Soviet transition is linked with movement toward "European civilization." If Ukrainian economic reform does not progress, Anatoliy Kinakh, head of the Union of Industrialists and Entrepreneurs and a member of the People's Democratic Power, says it "will simply find itself in the backyard of world civilization" (i.e., the CIS).[51] For Ukraine's Westernizers (both romantic and pragmatic nationalists) "civilization" is therefore associated not with Eurasia but with Europe, the "community of civilized countries."[52] Former Foreign Minister Borys Tarasiuk put the choice for Ukraine in simple terms: "to be in a common, rich, and thriving European home or somewhere else."[53] Clearly, "somewhere else" (which probably refers to Eurasia) loses hands down in any competition with Europe.

EUROPE, EASTERN SLAVDOM, AND EURASIA

Political Cleavages and Foreign Policy Orientations

Ukrainian foreign policy orientations are divided not along linguistic lines but by attitudes to Ukraine's post-Soviet transformation (economic and political reform, state and nation building). Those in favor of these four aspects of the transformation process seek to return Ukraine to Europe, while those opposed to this transformation project support the policies adopted in neighboring Belarus of returning to Eurasia. This has been defined as a pro-statehood–anti-statehood cleavage.[54] In the pro- and anti-statehood groups there are Ukrainophones and Russophones.

Mykola Ryabchouk, a Kyiv-based writer, pointed to the close links between Ukraine's national and democratic revolutions and its desire to return to Europe. Ukraine's "national emancipation," Ryabchouk argued, "has a clear pro-European, all-democratic characteristic." This was because in Ukraine "no kind of antipathy between 'Ukraine' and 'Europe' in the Ukrainian liberation movement practically exists today."[55]

Political cleavages and foreign policy among Ukraine's election blocs largely follow the pattern outlined earlier in this chapter, and endorse Ryabchouk's link between the political, socioeconomic, and national planks of emancipation. Those political parties that desire to see a break from the ancien regime's totalitarianism and colonialism support Ukraine's return to Europe as part of the national and democratic agenda. Meanwhile, those that do not (for example, the radical left) are supportive of a pro-Eurasian Slavophile geopolitical orientation. Reintegration with Russia is only popular at the level of elites or at the level of the public at large as a substitute for economic reform to overcome the pain of the reform process (for example, in Belarus, the Trans-Dniester Republic, or Tajikistan). Westernizers in favor of reform therefore look westward toward Europe, while Slavophiles who oppose reform in Ukraine look toward Eurasia. One Ukrainian author therefore divided Ukraine's parties and blocs into two distinct camps (Westernizers and Slavophiles, respectively): "In rough, but realistic terms, so to speak, we have those parties and associations which, despite all their other differences, view Ukraine as an independent entity, its economy as a market economy, and its political structure as a democratic structure, and those who are pursuing the objective of restoration of the Russian empire and the establishment of a Communist–Socialist system."[56]

The following list illustrates the positions of Slavophiles and Westernizers:

Attitudes to Reform	Slavophiles (pro-Russian)	Westernizers (anti-Russian)	Westernizers (neutral to Russia)
Anti	Communists		
	Socialists		
	Peasants		
	Progressive Socialists		
Pro		Rukh	
(a) National Democrats		Christian Democrats	
		Republicans	
		Greens	
		Congress Ukrainian Nationalists	
		Reform and Order	
(b) Centrists			People's Democrats
			Liberals
			Four Social Democratic Parties
			Fatherland Democrats

Slavophiles belong to the radical left camp and are hostile to the reform process. They remain divided over their attitudes toward Russia and the CIS. The Communists and Progressive Socialists are the main supporters of a revived USSR, which is to be achieved as a first step through Ukraine's membership in the Russian–Belarusian union. The soft left may support greater political and economic integration with the CIS but would hold short of full reintegration. They would also continue to support Ukraine's neutrality and oppose Ukraine's membership in CIS military blocs (see Figure 10.1).

Westernizers back reform and Ukraine's strategic agenda of returning to Europe but are divided on the tactics to be used in achieving this goal. The National Democrats, who were influential under Kravchuk, look upon Russia as Ukraine's constituting "other" and believe that it is not a part of Europe. They would support Ukraine's immediate application for membership in NATO and the European Union, regardless of Russian objections.

Pragmatic nationalists, who are influential under Kuchma, also back reform and Ukraine's strategic agenda of returning to Europe, but they do not pursue this strategic agenda in opposition to Russia, believing

Figure 10.1
Foreign Policy Orientations and Domestic Politics

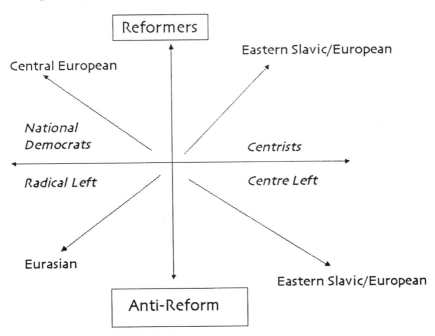

that Russia is also partly a European power. Ukraine's foreign policy elites therefore always state that while Ukraine seeks to integrate into Europe their "natural neighbor and ally" will always remain Russia.[57] Myroslav Popovych, head of the Institute of Philosophy and ideologically close to the Kuchma camp, defines Ukraine's national idea in such a way that it allows for both the continuation of cultural and economic ties with Russia at the same time as a political and even military orientation toward Europe.[58] Kuchma has formulated this policy as "Ukraine has always been a European country. The connection was broken for a long time, but now, we are claiming back our old position. We belong in the EU, NATO, and in addition we will not neglect our historic and humanitarian ties with the east."[59]

Pragmatic nationalists, unlike their romantic counterparts, admit that centuries of Russian influence upon Ukraine have left a "Eurasian" external imprint upon Ukraine that cannot be ignored.[60] The ignoring of these influences was a major criticism of the Kuchma ideologues levelled against Kravchuk in 1994–1995.[61] The three eastern Slavs, Kremen' believes, have close ethnic, cultural, and spiritual ties through sharing a common state for a long period of time. In addition, Russians are the largest national minority in Ukraine and Ukrainians the second largest in Russia.[62]

Pragmatic nationalists therefore attempt to square the circle. While accepting that Ukraine experienced Eurasian external influences they temper this by arguing that these were not internalized, thereby not affecting Ukrainian political culture. In a similar manner to romantic nationalists they therefore also argue that Ukraine has been within the European system of values since it adopted Christianity in 988.[63]

At the same time, pragmatic nationalists have found it practically impossible to support Eurasian integration. Eurasian integration is therefore still commonly associated with a return to an unflattering tsarist or Soviet past, not a democratic, market economic future.[64] Oleh Soskin, leader of the Conservative National Party and a presidential adviser on enterprise development, asked, "Should we move toward the past, to the common abyss, or forward—to a society of developed democracy, Christian morals, private property, and a wealthy middle class that would make up 65 per cent of our society."[65]

While pursuing the vague objective of "integration into European and trans-Atlantic structures" Ukraine has only openly stated its strategic objective of attaining first associate and then full membership of the EU. A government action plan aimed at securing associate membership was published in June 1998.[66] Pragmatic nationalists have ruled out NATO membership for the foreseeable future as too provocative externally to Russia and domestically to large numbers of Ukrainian citizens.[67] At the same time, Ukraine's cooperation with NATO has been developed to the maximum possible as a nonmember. The government program for cooperation with NATO until 2002, presented to NATO in November 1998, has no analogy among other NATO partner countries.[68] Both the EU and NATO action programs were released as presidential decrees and therefore did not require parliamentary approval. In Defense Minister Oleksandr Kuzmuk's view, Ukraine's wide-embracing participation within NATO's Partnership for Peace program is "constantly demonstrating to the world community that Ukraine is a civilized state."[69]

Pragmatic nationalists oppose any integration of the CIS and restrict their activity in it to bilateral economic cooperation. They, like their romantic nationalist colleagues, therefore oppose Ukraine's membership of the Russian–Belarusian union. Even the centrist Social–Liberal SLON bloc, probably the most pro-Russian of the 1998 parliamentary election blocs from the reformist camp, opposes Ukraine's membership in the Russian–Belarusian union.[70] Instead, SLON's founding statement outlines its task of "forming a political force, which is proposing to the Ukrainian people the European path of development."[71]

These cleavages between pro-European–pro-reform and anti-reform–pro-Eurasian attitudes can be seen in the following list. Russia or the former USSR are only regarded as political and economic models of development for Ukrainians who hold Communist views. Those who have reformist views look to the West for political and economic models of development:[72]

Political Model	Reformist Views	Centrist Views	Communist Views
United States	23	18	8
Germany	13	8	4
Russia–USSR	1	3	13
Economic Model			
United States	11	12	8
Germany	19	16	7
Russia–USSR	1	2	16

Foreign Policy under Kravchuk and Kuchma: Different Tactics, Same Strategic Goals

The foreign policies of Kravchuk and Kuchma both looked strategically westward while adopting a more pragmatic approach toward developments in Russia and the CIS. After being elected in July 1994, President Kuchma continued Kravchuk's strategic goal of returning to Europe.[73]

The adoption by Ukraine of social and official nationalism led to good relations with Ukraine's neighbors, denying Turkey, Poland, Hungary, or Russia any pretext to intervene on behalf of their coethnics. But these policies do not rule out problematical relations with neighbors, such as Russia, which may be regarded as the "other" by some sections of Ukraine's population and elites. These feelings of insecurity are further fueled by Russia's unwillingness to accept Ukraine as a permanently independent state or even Ukrainians as a separate ethnic group.[74] The fact that even among democratically minded Russians there is a widespread view that Ukrainians do not command sufficient attributes to constitute a nation creates discomfort among the Kuchma leadership and Ukrainian elites. "Russia's aggressive actions," Yevhen Kushnariov, former head of the presidential administration, believed, "are really pushing Ukraine to a single-vector (foreign) policy."[75] Because Russia does not perceive Ukraine as a "foreign" country, but only as a temporarily lost piece of Russia, Russians do not regard their actions vis-à-vis Ukraine as tantamount to imperialism.

Signs of Ukraine's "obstructiveness" in the CIS are also regarded as evidence by Russia of Ukraine's disinterest in cooperation or integration. Yet this has less to do with obstructiveness per se and more to do with state and nation building and the building of a new national identity, which can only be accomplished within Europe, not Eurasia. It has not been lost upon Ukraine's elites, which are the main driving force in its foreign policy, that to integrate within the CIS and "return to Eurasia" means accepting the status of a quasi-state, something neither Kravchuk nor Kuchma have ever been willing to accept. A Ukrainian identity distinct from Russia, which is the basis for the creation of a new Ukrainian civic "we," can therefore only be constructed by maintaining Russia and the CIS at a distance. Therefore, under both Kravchuk and Kuchma Ukraine continues to remain a participant—not a full, legal member—of the CIS (associate member status does not exist).[76]

Ukraine's successful entry into European institutions would be an indicator of the success of Ukraine's post-Soviet transformation and modernization drive. Under both Kravchuk and Kuchma Ukraine defined herself as a state-nation with a European and, more specifically, a Central European identity. Perhaps ironically, Ukraine has been more successful at trans-Atlantic and European integration under Kuchma than it was under his predecessor. Ukraine's return to Europe always rested upon it maintaining both good relations with Russia and launching a reform program. These twin policies were pursued more energetically by Kuchma than by Kravchuk. A Belarusian-style arrangement for Ukraine was therefore never likely to be considered by Ukraine's non-Communist elites.

Russia as Ukraine's Constituting "Other"

Ukraine's desire to return to Europe had become an all-embracing policy supported by the Ukrainian leadership already one year into Kuchma's presidency. But Kuchma's desire to return to Europe has been undertaken using different tactics to those under his predecessor. In the Kravchuk era Ukrainian foreign policy had adopted three planks. First, it had consciously depicted Russia as Ukraine's main security threat. This is not unusual during the early years of independence of a former colonial dependency. Second, it had attempted, like all former dependencies in their first years of independence, to distance themselves as far as possible from their former imperial metropolis (Russia). This was also undertaken to convince a still skeptical West that Ukraine was indeed different from Russia.

Finally, the National Democratic–National Communist alliance under Kravchuk had portrayed Ukraine as the last Central Eastern European bastion of Europe, with Russia therefore relegated to Asia. Ukraine was promoted as a buffer, a cordon sanitaire protecting Europe from an imperial Russia.[77] This was reflected in Kravchuk's proposal for a Central European Zone of Security and Cooperation, made in Budapest in February 1993 at the OSCE meeting (when Kuchma revived the idea in 1995–1996 it did not exclude Russia, which was invited to regional meetings of its heads of state). Vladimir Lukin, former Russian ambassador to the United States and head of the State Duma Committee on International Relations, complained that Ukraine under Kravchuk had wanted to "draw a new de facto border between the West and Europe— somewhere along the Don river, as the ancient Greeks did—thus remaking Ukraine into some kind of 'front line' of Western civilization."[78]

Not surprising, these three policies under Kravchuk only served to worsen Ukraine's relations with Russia. At the same time, relations remained strained with the West because of three factors: first, the unresolved issue of nuclear weapons; second, the lack of a serious domestic reform program meant the West could not therefore see in Kravchuk someone to whom they could relate to as "their man" (in the manner of then reformist Russian President Borys Yeltsin); and third, the West had yet to come to terms with accepting Ukrainian independence as a permanent factor on the international stage.

An Unviable Strategic Partnership

Neither Kravchuk nor Kuchma would ever have evolved into "Ukrainian Lukashenkas." This was for two related reasons. First, Lukashenka is a specific phenomenon related to Belarus. Nowhere else in the CIS (or among the world's former colonies) have state leaders desired to give away their sovereignty to the former imperial metropolis. Second, both Kravchuk and Kuchma were, and remain, staunch defenders of Ukraine's national interest. Neither would, nor will, accept the status of a Russian vassal.[79] Kravchuk's views about the necessity for equal, good relations with Russia were always close to Kuchma's. Kravchuk therefore believed, "I think that Ukraine must be together with Russia, but not subordinated to Russia—that is all. I have a realistic view on facts. There is no other way for Ukraine but to be together with Russia. We have been together for 300 years and it is in our genes. We have had quarrels, weddings and unification amongst our peoples and these relations cannot be broken."[80]

The following is a comparison of the policies of Kravchuk and Kuchma:

	Kravchuk	Kuchma (1994 Elections)	President Kuchma
Russia as Strategic Partner	ambivalent	yes	yes
Russian temporary lease of Sevastopol	yes	yes	yes
United States, Germany, and the United Kingdom as Strategic Partners in Ukraine	yes	West lacks interest in Ukraine	yes
CIS Economic Union	Associate Member	Full Member	Associate Member
CIS Economic Integration	disinterest or ambivalent	yes	bilateral cooperation, not integration
CIS Charter	Ukraine should not sign it	Not mentioned	Ukraine should not sign it
Tashkent Security Treaty	Ukraine should not join it	Ukraine should not join it	Ukraine should not join it
Inter-Parliament Assembly	Ukraine should not join it	Ukraine should not join it	Ukraine should not join it
Revival of USSR	Opposed	Opposed	Opposed
Russian–Belarusian Union	Ukraine should not join it	Ukraine should not join it	Ukraine should not join it
NATO Enlargement	good	bad	good
NATO Membership	future possibility	no	future possibility

Kravchuk's views are not dissimilar to those found within the Kuchma leadership. "For Ukraine, it is clearly illogical to separate itself from its northern neighbor with an 'iron curtain,'" cautioned Kremen', then deputy head of the presidential administration.[81] But without breaking off relations with Russia, Ukraine still needed to maintain a discreet distance from her. "Under such conditions Ukraine is fated to pursue a policy of balancing within the force fields of geopolitical interests," Horbulin argued.[82]

President Kuchma has always linked good relations with Russia to domestic stability within Ukraine and the decline of separatist feelings. Russia therefore belongs to "Ukraine's top priority."[83] Ethnic or religious animosities against Russia or Russians are not widespread in Ukraine, except perhaps in western Ukraine, where feelings are similar to those found in the Baltic states. But this does not mean that Russian leaders as individual personalities are popular. Former Russian President Yeltsin ranked as the second-most-negative foreign politician in Ukraine, only slightly less popular than Iraq's Saddam Hussein and only slightly higher than former Soviet President Mikhail Gorbachev.[84] Yeltsin's boorish character, together with his responsibility for instigating violence against his own parliament and in Chechnya, all played a role in providing him with a negative image throughout Ukraine.

The absence of widespread anti-Russian feelings among the public at large is seen in the following list:[85]

Country	Very Positive or Positive	Very Negative or Negative	Don't Know
United States	64%	8%	27%
Russia	60%	16%	25%
Germany	65%	7%	28%
Japan	64%	6%	31%
Canada	66%	6%	29%

They also point to the low number of negative views the Ukrainian population has toward Western countries such as the United States. Among non-Communists the United States and Germany are seen as the best political and economic models for Ukraine to emulate. This probably explains the lack of domestic support for creating anything resembling a Ukrainian–Russian military bloc, which in Ukrainian eyes would be both anti-Western–NATO and anti-Turkish. The top politicians with the most positive images in Ukraine are all Western leaders. Only two are Eurasian: Borys Nemtsov and Lukashenka (both with 3 percent each). Yeltsin did not make it onto the list.[86]

Nevertheless, the views of Ukrainian elites are very different. Even after the signing of the Russian–Ukrainian treaty in May 1997,

Ukraine's elites still perceived Russia as its greatest security threat. The following list illustrates the Ukrainian elites' views as to the main allies of and greatest threats to Ukraine:[87]

	Main Ally	Biggest Threat
Russia	27%	48%
United States	13%	11%
Germany	12%	0%
Former Soviet Republics	3%	1%
Eastern Europe	8%	—
Western Europe	5%	—
Turkey	—	3%
China	—	1%
Others	6%	5%
Don't Know	26%	31%

Establishing a working strategic partnership between Ukraine and Russia is near impossible at a time when both countries are suffering from national identity crises and both countries are nations in the making. There has been progress with Russia moving away from "ultimatums and misunderstandings" to "mutual understanding and good neighborly relations."[88] At the same time, Russian–Ukrainian dialogue "was and still is incorrect," believed Anatoly Halchynskiy, Ukrainian presidential economic adviser.[89] The Russian–Ukrainian relationship cannot be a strategic one until they "first develop the guidelines of the equal partnership."[90] Such an equal partnership, as defined by Kuchma, rests upon equality in international law, respect for one another's sovereignty and territorial integrity, equal rights, and taking into account a commonly perceived history.[91] Progress toward this was made by the State Duma's and Federation Council's ratification of the Ukrainian–Russian treaty in December 1998 and February 1999, respectively.

The United States and some other Western European countries now recognize the strategic significance of Ukraine to Russia's post-Soviet and postimperial transformation into a state-nation within the borders of the Russian Federation. In other words, the continued independence of Ukraine will hinder the emergence of a new Russian empire (or great power). Ukraine could therefore "turn out to be the central external force shaping Russia."[92] Horbulin has pointedly linked Ukraine's security to the continued democratic transformation of Russia. By remaining independent, Ukraine would help to "Europeanize" Russia by preventing it from again becoming an empire.[93]

But Russia may not see this in positive terms. Surveying the growing Western and, in particular, U.S. interest in the geopolitical territory of the former USSR, one Russian analyst complained that "the hostility of the Baltic countries and Ukraine are growing before our very eyes (and being very capably nourished from outside)."[94] Support for NATO, GUUAM, and different views on the CIS have all foiled the establishment of a viable Russian–Ukrainian strategic partnership. The overwhelming majority of Russian elites believe that Ukrainian–Russian relations are negative.[95] The following are some factors negatively influencing the attitude of Russians toward Ukraine:[96]

Deepening of Ukraine's Cooperation with NATO	84%
Problems with the Black Sea Fleet and Sevastopol	84%
Control over the Interstate Border	79%
Status of Russophones in Ukraine	77%
Debts for Russian Gas	71%
Limited Participation in CIS	57%
Inconsistency in Foreign Economic Policy of Ukraine	55%
Negative Attitude toward the Union of Russia and Belarus	50%
GUUAM	18%

Russia and Ukraine define their strategic partnership in different ways. Russia perceives such a strategic partnership in geopolitical terms as a political–military alliance that would help her to regain her great-power status. The first Russian visitor dispatched to Kyiv after the signing of the Russo–Ukrainian treaty in May 1997 was none other than its defense minister. The Peace Channel–97 Russian–Ukrainian military exercises held in October 1997 off the Crimean coast were defined by Russia as combat training within an emerging "strategic cooperation" in the Black Sea. Ukraine, on the other hand, defined it purely as a peacekeeping exercise similar to countless others it had undertaken within NATO's Partnership for Peace program. Ivan Bizhan, Ukrainian first deputy defense minister, stressed that Peace Channel–97 "should not be seen as the start of joint Russian–Ukrainian actions in the Black Sea."[97] The Ukrainian elites, unlike their Russian counterparts, do not see the United States, Turkey, and NATO as threats within the Black Sea region that need to be counterposed by a Russian–Ukrainian military alliance.[98] Perhaps it is therefore not surprising that Ukraine cancelled plans for a Peace Channel–98 exercise the following year.

The following is a breakdown of Ukrainian identity and foreign policy:

European	Eastern Slavic	Eurasian
Center Left (Socialists, Peasants)	Center Left (Socialists, Peasants)	Radical Left (Communists, Progressive Socialists, Pan-Slavic groups)
Center (parties of power, Social Democrats, Liberals)	Center (parties of power, Social Democrats, Liberals)	
Center Right (National Democrats)		
Radical Right (Nationalists)		

UKRAINE'S STRATEGIC CHOICE: RETURN TO EUROPE

The strategic goals of Ukrainian foreign policy are fundamentally different to those of Russia. Ukrainian security policy is largely defensive, protective of its territorial integrity and the post-Yalta status quo in Europe.[99] Domestic support for Ukraine's territorial integrity is high throughout the country and separatism was only a serious threat in the Crimea between 1994 and 1995.[100] After the adoption of the Crimean constitution in October 1998 and its ratification by the Ukrainian parliament three months later, this threat receded completely. It is a policy that aims to create a favorable external environment through good relations with the West and Russia, which would provide the breathing space required for political–economic transformation and state and nation building.

Ten factors explain why Ukraine's strategic foreign policy goals have remained consistent:

1. The allegedly "pro-Russian" orientation of Kuchma, propounded by some outside observers, was always highly exaggerated. Even Russian observers of Ukraine accepted by 1996 that there was no longer any alleged division between supporters of Europe and a Eurasian orientation within the Ukrainian elites. This explained the consensus reached within the Ukrainian elites of its even more determined pro-European course under Kuchma.

2. The West largely dropped its Russocentric policies after 1994 when Ukraine ratified the START I and Nuclear Non-Proliferation Treaties. The West's gradual appreciation of Ukraine's strategic importance to European security occurred parallel to its growing disillusionment with Russia from 1993 to 1994.

3. The West was eager to support Ukraine's reform program under Kuchma in gratitude for its agreement to denuclearize.

4. When Kuchma was first elected he believed in the chances of a rapid and full normalization of relations with Russia. Kuchma had therefore proven

to be as "romantic" about Russia as his predecessor had initially been about the West openly welcoming Ukraine into its ranks. Russia remained reluctant to legally recognize Ukraine's frontiers in an interstate treaty and continued to insist on the lease of the entire city of Sevastopol. Only in May 1997 did Russia finally agree to sign the interstate treaty initialed in February 1995 by both governments and concede to the division of Sevastopol's five bays between both countries for their separate navies. It then took until the winter of 1998–1999 for Russia to ratify the treaty.

5. Ukrainian nation and state building together with the development of a national identity different to Russia's could not be constructed in a Russia-dominated Eurasia. After all, between two-thirds and three-quarters of Russians would like to have a unified state with Ukrainians.[101] Between 56 and 75 percent of Russians are of the view that Ukrainians are not a separate ethnic group.[102] There is little room for Ukraine to maneuver in the Eurasian CIS, except as a Belarusian-style dominion. As President Kuchma pointed out, "I do not want Ukraine to be in Russia's shadow or to be sidelined in world history. They are not waiting for us. We must push our way into Europe because that is where our future lies."[103]

6. Successful foreign integration, which primarily refers to European structures, is dependent in Ukrainian eyes upon successful domestic integration into a viable, cohesive political community and civic nation.[104] Ukraine's return to Europe is therefore dependant upon a successful outcome to its state- and nation-building program.

7. Ukraine formulated its foreign policy strategy as "Cooperation with the CIS—Integration with Europe."[105] While rejecting political–military–economic integration within the CIS, Ukraine used its presence in the CIS framework as a vehicle to promote its bilateral economic interests while obstructing the creation of CIS multilateral institutions. Ukraine therefore supported bilateral cooperation—not reintegration—within the CIS.

8. Ironically, Kuchma's greater pragmatic approach to the CIS has not benefited Russia. The CIS has divided into pro-Russian and non-Russian camps, with the latter led and organized by Ukraine. The GUUAM strategic axis has grown in importance, with Ukraine backing this regional organization at the international diplomatic level and in structures such as the OSCE and the Council of Europe.[106] Their interests coincide in a number of areas, including energy and opposition to Russian-backed support for separatism. Ukraine's greater "participation" within the CIS may ironically not be in Russia's interests.[107] Two members of the GUUAM group (Georgia and Azerbaijan) did not renew their membership in the Tashkent Collective Security Treaty in April 1999. Another CIS member, Uzbekistan, which is close to GUUAM, also withdrew from it at the same time and joined GUUAM.

9. Ukraine's foreign policy under Kuchma continued to pursue the same pro-European strategic agenda using different tactics. Russia was therefore no longer portrayed as an "(Asian) other" by elements within Ukraine's elites, and both Ukraine and Russia were defined as belonging to the "European common home." Ukraine was no longer promoted as a "buffer"; instead it was described as a "bridge" linking Europe to Rus-

sia.[108] Ukraine therefore championed Russia's membership in the Council of Europe during the height of the Chechen conflict, as well as arguing in favor of Western recognition of Russian interests during NATO's enlargement process. This policy allows Ukraine to rejoin Europe without antagonizing Russia, a policy that the West, Russia, and the majority of Ukraine's domestic population look favorably upon.

10. Ukraine does not see that there is a contradiction between defining itself as both European and eastern Slavic (only the radical left define Ukraine as Eurasian). Possessing a European and eastern Slavic identity requires Ukraine to seek good relations with both the West and Russia; integrating into Europe is not seen as having a negative impact upon Russia, but a positive one. Defining Ukraine as both eastern Slavic and European has support within the center left (i.e., Socialists) and pro-reform centrist camps. This pragmatic nationalist group dominates the Ukrainian elites, preventing any radical move toward the West or Eurasia.

CONCLUSION

Ukraine's elites hold a strategic consensus on the need to return to Europe. When Tarasiuk was confirmed as Ukraine's new foreign minister in April 1998 he outlined three tasks for Ukrainian foreign policy. The first was to achieve a "more active foreign strategic cooperation" with the United States. The second was to affirm Ukraine's "European choice." The third and final priority was relations with Russia.[109]

The main tactical difference between Kravchuk and Kuchma was that this was undertaken at the expense of Russia under the former. "Europe," as defined by Kuchma, does not necessarily exclude Russia because he recognizes Ukraine as an eastern Slavic (but not Eurasian) country. This has allowed Ukraine to continue to pursue the strategic foreign policy course outlined by Kravchuk immediately after the disintegration of the former USSR, while not arousing strong opposition to this course domestically or within Russia. The continuation of this foreign policy course by Kuchma was possible because the alleged "pro-Russianism" of Kuchma was always highly exaggerated, as was Ukraine's division into two foreign policy camps neatly divided along linguistic lines. It also built upon Ukraine's pre-eighteenth-century history, traditions, and political culture, representing the majority opinion of its intellectuals and cultural literati as well as those who formulate opinion and policy makers in the central ruling elites.

Although Kuchma's tactical approach to returning to Europe is more popular than that pursued by his predecessor, three major problems remain. First, nation building requires foreign "others" against which a common "we" is created as the basis for the emerging political community. Second, it is difficult to see how Russia and Ukraine can jointly return to Europe. Only Ukraine has a strategic agenda of its full integration into European and trans-Atlantic structures. Russia, on the other hand, has not expressed an interest even in the EU, let alone in NATO membership. For both Westernizers and Slavophiles alike, Russian national identity since the eighteenth century, Liah Greenfeld and Iver Neuman have pointed out, has always defined the West as the "other." In contrast, in Ukraine only the Slavophiles (the radical left) define the West as Ukraine's "other."[110] Ukraine and Russia differ fundamentally on their relations with the West.

Ukraine's foreign policy has evolved from romantic to pragmatic nationalism between the Kravchuk and Kuchma eras. Although this is undoubtedly a positive development, Ukraine's strategic agenda of returning to Europe, as defined by its foreign policy elites, still remains elusive. Successful transitions in Ukraine and Russia, defined in terms of not only reform but also state-nation building, will determine the future success of this foreign policy goal.[111]

NOTES

1. Dominique Arel, "Ukraine: The Temptation of the Nationalizing State," in *Political Culture and Civil Society in Russia and the New States of Eurasia*, ed. Vladimir Tismaneanu (Armonk, N.Y.: M. E. Sharpe, 1995), 179. This line of argument is also found in A. Wilson, "The Nationalist Agenda: External Affairs: Untying the Russian Knot," in *Ukrainian Nationalism in the 1990s: A Minority Faith* (Cambridge: Cambridge University Press, 1997), 173–193; Ilya Prizel, "Ukraine between Proto-Democracy and 'Soft' Authoritarianism," in *Democratic Change and Authoritarian Reaction in Russia, Ukraine, Belarus, and Moldova*, ed. Karen Dawisha and Bruce Parrott (Cambridge: Cambridge University Press, 1997), 333; and Andres Wilson, "Redefining Ethnic and Linguistic Boundaries in Ukraine: Indigenes, Settlers and Russophone Ukrainians," in *Nation-Building in the Post-Soviet Borderlands: The Politics of National Identity*, ed. Graham Smith, Vivien Law, A. Wilson, Annette Bohr, and Edward Allworth (Cambridge: Cambridge University Press, 1998), 131–133.

2. V. F. Horbulin, "Natsional'na Bezpeka Ukraiiny ta Mizhnarodna Bezpeka," *Politychna Dumka* 1 (1997): 78.

3. P. Terrence Hopmann, Stephen D. Shenfield, and Dominique Arel, *Integration and Disintegration in the Former Soviet Union: Implications for Regional and Global Security*, Occasional Paper 30 (Providence, R.I.: Thomas J.Watson Jr. Institute for International Relations, Brown University Press, 1997), 15. See also Leonid Kuchma, "Speech in Budapest," *Interfax-Ukraine*, 27 October 1998.

4. Yevhen Holovakha, interview, *Den*, 24 October 2000.

5. On Eurasianism, see Dmitry V. Shlapentokh, "Eurasianism: Past and Present," *Communist and Post-Communist Studies* 30, no. 2 (1997): 129–151.

6. A. Wilson and Artur Bilous, "Political Parties in Ukraine," *Europe–Asia Studies* 45, no. 4 (1993): 696.

7. Leslie Thomas, *Post-Communism: An Introduction* (Durham, N.C.: Duke University Press, 1997), 16.

8. V. Tismaneanu and Michael Turner, "Understanding Post-Sovietism: Between Residual Leninism and Uncertain Pluralism," in Tismaneanu, *Political Culture and Civil Society in Russia and the New States of Eurasia*, 7.

9. See Carole Pateman, "Political Culture, Political Structure and Political Change," *British Journal of Political Science* 1, no. 13 (1971): 291–306.

10. David J. Elkins and Richard E. B. Simeon, "A Cause in Search of Its Effect or What Does Political Culture Explain," *Comparative Politics* 11, no. 2 (1979): 128.

11. See T. Kuzio, "Identity and Nation Building in Ukraine: Defining the 'Other,'" *Ethnicities* 1, no. 3 (2001).

12. Ben Rosamond, "Political Culture," in Barrie Axford, Gary K. Browning, Richard Huggins, Ben Rosamond, and John Turner, eds., *Politics: An Introduction* (London: Routledge, 1997), 78.

13. Roger Eatwell, "Introduction: The Importance of the Political Culture Approach," in *European Political Cultures: Conflict or Convergence*, ed. R. Eatwell (London: Routledge, 1997), 7.

14. William Zimmerman, "Is Ukraine a Political Community?" *Communist and Post-Communist Studies* 31, no. 1 (1998): 52–53.

15. *Heneza* 4 (1996): 13. Leonid Zalizniak also argues that "Ukraine from the moment of the appearance of Kyiv Rus' to the end of the eighteenth century developed within the realm of European civilization" in "Ukraiina na Evraziys'komu Rozdorizzhi," *Vechirnyi Kyiv*, 16 August 1996. See also Ilya Prizel, *National Identity and Foreign Policy: Nationalism and Leadership in Poland, Russia, and Ukraine* (Cambridge: Cambridge University Press, 1998), 365, 379.

16. *Kievskiye Vedomosti*, 11 October 1997.

17. Prizel, "Ukraine between Proto-Democracy and 'Soft' Authoritarianism," 335.

18. See the comments by an analyst and the then director of the National Institute of Strategic Studies, respectively, Leonid Kistersky and Serhii Pirozhkov, "Ukraine: Policy Analysis and Options," in *Perceptions of Security: Public Opinion and Expert Assessments in Europe's New Democracies*, ed. Richard Smoke (Manchester: Manchester University Press), 224. Quoted from Vasyl' Kremen' (then deputy head of the presidential administration), "Ukraine Returns to Europe" (speech given at the Ukrainian Studies Day, School of Slavonic and East European Studies, University of London, 3 October 1997).

19. *Demokratycha Ukraiina*, 3 February 1996. In a lengthy report the Ukrainian nation and its culture were identified as part of the European historical and cultural process. See V. Kremen', *Sotsial'no-Politychna Sytuatsiya v Ukraiini: Postup P'iaty Rokiv* (Kyiv: National Security and Defense Council–National Institute of Strategic Studies, 1996), 32.

20. *Uriadovyi Kurier*, 23 December 1995.

21. L. Kistersky and S. Pirozhkov, "Ukraine: Policy Analysis and Options," in R. Smoke, ed., *Perceptions of Security*, 224.

22. *Holos Ukraiiny*, 26 March 1997. A young Kyivite said, "I voted yes on independence for myself, my children and my people. Today we are returning to our European home and to civilization." *The Times*, 2 December 1991.

23. V. Kremen', "Shist' rokiv poshukiv I spodivan," *Uriadovyi Kurier*, 9 August 1997.

24. V. Horbulin, "Nasha Meta, Nasha Dolia, mistse Ukraiiny v suchasniy Evropi," *Polityka I Chas* 1 (1996): 6.

25. *Zerkalo Nedeli*, 2 December 2000.

26. *Itar-Tass*, 2 April 1996.

27. *Interfax-Ukraine*, 17 March 1997.

28. *Interfax-Ukraine*, 21 March 1997.

29. *Ukraina Segodnia* 13 (1997): 109. The pro-European-oriented National Institute of Strategic Studies is not included here because it is the former think tank of the National Security and Defense Council and currently of the presidential administration. I have added the geopolitical orientation of the think tanks. All the think tanks are proreform and hence are pro-European.

30. *UPI*, 12 January 1996. See also Roman Szporluk, "Ukraine: From Imperial Periphery to Sovereign State," *Daedalus* 126, no. 3 (1997): 107.

31. *Interfax-Ukraine*, 21 March 1997.

32. As defined by Foreign Minister Hennadiy Udovenko in Demokratychna Ukraiina, 23 June 1997 on the assurances, and President Kuchma in *Ukrainian Weekly*, 13 July 1997, on the charter. The then head of the directorate on Foreign Policy of the presidential administration, V. Ohryzhko, said, "Ukraine is a European state, we identify with Europe. This is our perspective and our choice." *Uriadovyi Kurier*, 23 March 1996.

33. *Interfax-Ukraine*, 20 March 1997.

34. Leonid Kuchma, "Comments at the Geneva International Conference Center," *Radio Ukraine World Service*, 23 March 1996.

35. Oleksiy Kalevskyi, ed., "Humanitarna Polityka Dlia Ukrainy: Stratehichnyi Vybir," *Viche* 8 (1996): 23. See also Ihor Kharchenko, "Za p'iat' rokiv nezalezhnosti. Nayholovnishyi pidsumok," *Polityka i Chas* 7 (1996): 8–11, and "Povernennia v Evropu: Pomizh Metoiu I Diysnistiu," *Polityka i Chas* 5–6 (1997): 3–14.

36. V. Kremen', interview, *Imenem Zakonu*, 12 September 1997.

37. Victor Stepanenko, "Natsional'no-derzhavne budivnytsvo i problema sotsiokul'turnoii identychnosti," *Politolohichni Chyttania* 1 (1994): 16.

38. *UNIAR*, 1 January 1996. Ukraine's integration into Europe was into a zone of "stability, security, democracy and welfare," Kuchma said in Geneva (*Uriadovyi Kurier*, 28 March 1996). Foreign Minister Udovenko also linked Ukraine's integration into European and trans-Atlantic civilization with prioritizing human rights, the rule of law, democratic government, and a social–market economy in his interview in *Den*, 22 August 1997.

39. Leonid Kuchma, interview, *Ukrainian State Television—1*, 31 March 1997.

40. *Zerkalo Nedeli*, 2 December 2000.

41. *Interfax*, 25 September 1997.

42. Viktor Medvedchuk, head of the Union of Ukrainian Lawyers and chairman of the United Social Democrats, in *Kievskiye Novosti*, 31 January 1997. Medvedchuk was elected first deputy chairman of the Ukrainian parliament in January 2000.

43. Foreign Minister Tarasiuk, interview, *Holos Ukraiiny*, 3 February 1999.

44. S. Pirozhkov, "Suverenna Ukraiina: Postup u XXI Stolittia," *Narodna Armiya*, 26 July 1996.

45. Leonid Kuchma, "Fifth Anniversary of Independence Speech," *Uriadovyi Kurier*, 29 August 1996.

46. Mykhailo Chechetov, deputy head of the parliamentary committee on Economic Policy and National Economic Management, *Golos Ukrainy*, 10 September 1997.

47. See the comments by then Deputy Foreign Minister Anton Buteiko, *Kievskiye Vedomosti*, 3 April 1997.

48. Udovenko, interview, *Vysokyi Zamok*, 11 February 1997.

49. *Uriadovyi Kurier*, 14 October 1997.

50. Leonid Kuchma, "Speech to Conference on Entrepreneurship," *Ukrainian Television—1*, 10 February 1998.

51. *Ukraiina Moloda*, 14 October 1997. The same argument was used by Kuchma in addressing the Investment Council, referring to tax laws that "fully meet European standards" and the changeover to the "European accounting system." *Uriadovyi Kurier*, 7 October 1997.

52. Valerii Pustovoitenko, "Speech to the Inaugural Congress of the Zlahoda Election Bloc," *Uriadovyi Kurier*, 16 January 1999. Tabachnyk also believed that Ukraine should take the road of "civilized European processes." *Nezavisimost*, 25 December 1998. Oleksandr Zavada, head of the Anti-Monopoly Committee, believes this means the pursuit of a "well-weighed civilized economic policy" that would "transform Ukraine into a flourishing civilized European state." *Uriadovyi Kurier*, 24 January 1998.

53. *Uriadovyi Kurier*, 18 April 1998.

54. See T. Kuzio, "Slavophiles versus Westernizers: Foreign Policy Orientations in Ukraine," in *Between Russia and Europe: Foreign and Security Policy of Independent Ukraine*, ed. Kurt R. Spillmann, Andreas Wenger, and Derek Muller (Bern: Peter Lang, 1999), 53–74; and Sarah Birch, *Elections and Democratization in Ukraine* (London: Macmillan, 2000).

55. Mykola Yu Ryabchouk, "Hromadians'ke suspil'stvo I natsional'na emansipatsiya," *Filosophska I Sotsiolohichna Dumka* 12 (1991): 19.

56. *Nezavisimost*, 7 October 1997.

57. Volodymyr Ohryzhko, then head of the Foreign Policy directorate of the presidential administration, *Itar-Tass*, 1 September 1998.

58. Myroslav Popovych, "Shcho zhe Take 'Ukraiins'ka Natsional'na Ideia?'" *Kul'tura I Zhyttia*, 27 November 1996. Popovych joined the Democratic Platform of the Communist Party of Ukraine and became a founding member of its successor, the Party Democratic Revival of Ukraine (PDVU). The PDVU transformed into the People's Democratic Party in 1996 and is allied to Kuchma.

59. *Algemeen Dagblad*, 29 November 1997.

60. See T. Kuzio, "Nationalism in Ukraine: Towards a New Framework," *Politics* 20, no. 2 (2000): 77–86.

61. V. B. Hryn'iov, *Nova Ukraiina: Iakoi ia ii Bachu* (Kyiv: Abrys, 1995); and Dmytro Tabachnyk and Dmytro Vydryn, *Ukraiina na porozi XXI stolittia: Politychnyi Aspekt* (Kyiv: Lybid, 1995). See my review article of these two volumes in *Journal of Ukrainian Studies* 22, nos. 1–2 (1997): 145–165.

62. Vasily Kremen', "The East Slav Triangle," in *Russia and Europe: The Emerging Security Agenda*, ed. Vladimir Baranovsky (Oxford: SIPRI and Oxford University Press, 1997), 271.

63. V. Kremen', D. Tabachnyk, and Vasyl' Tkachenko, *Ukraiina: Alternatyvy Postupu. Krytyka Istorychnoho Dosvidu* (n.p.: ARC-UKRAINE, 1996), 109, 119.

See my review of this 778-page volume in *Journal of Ukrainian Studies* 23, no. 1 (1998): 137–140.

64. On the negative association for Ukraine of Eurasian integration, see Tabachnyk and Vydryn, *Ukraiina na porozi XXI stolittia*, 136; and Hryn'iov, *Nova Ukraiina*, 4. Heorhiy Manchulenko, a Rukh member of the parliamentary Committee on National Security and Defense, linked Slavic unions to "misery," "poverty," "endless conflict," low living standards, and a poor record on human rights. *Holos Ukraiiny*, 20 October 1998.

65. *Vechirnyi Kyiv*, 9 April 1998. Soskin warned against Ukraine repeating past historical mistakes: "We must prevent Ukraine's colonisation by Russia." *Vechirnyi Kyiv*, 29 October 1998.

66. "Pro satverdzhennia stratehii intehratsii Ukraiiny do Evropeis'koho Soiuzu," *Uriadovyi Kurier*, 18 June 1998.

67. A Ukrainian author explained why this was so: "Not a single influential political force in Ukraine propagates against membership in the EU unlike, for example, in the case of NATO." See Ruslan Osypenko, "Evropeis'kyi vybir Ukraiiny," *Uriadovyi Kurier*, 11 June 1998.

68. A copy of the Ukraine program on NATO is in the possession of the author. See also T. Kuzio, "Ukraine and NATO: The Evolving Strategic Partnership," *Journal of Strategic Studies* 21, no. 2 (1998): 1–30.

69. *Ukrainian Television—1*, 24 August 1998.

70. Mykhailo Bilets'kyi, interview, Ukrainian Center for Political and Conflict Studies, Kyiv, 22 October 1997. This think tank has close links to the Social–Liberal alliance.

71. Quoted from the appeal of the inaugural congress of SLON. Copy in the author's possession.

72. Elehie Natalie Skoczylas, *Ukraine 1996: Public Opinion on Key Issues* (Washington, D.C.: IFES, 1997), 48.

73. On Ukraine's consistent foreign policy, see Paul D'Anieri, *Economic Interdependence in Ukrainian–Russian Relations* (Albany: State University of New York Press, 1999).

74. Igor Kliamkin, "Russian Statehood, the US and the Problem of Security," in *The Emergence of Russian Foreign Policy*, ed. Leon Aron and Kenneth M. Jensen (Washington, D.C.; United States Institute of Peace, 1994), 111–112.

75. *Interfax-Ukraine*, 19 March 1997. A typical Russian view of Ukraine and how its "artificial" independence is being buttressed by the United States is S. M. Samuylov, "O nekotoykh Amerykanskykh Stereotypakh v Otnoshenii Ukrainyi," *ShCha. Ekonomika. Polityka. Ideologiya* 3 (1997): 84–96, and 4 (1997): 81–90. V. Kremen', who was then arguably the main ideologue of the Kuchma administration, replied to this article in "Konstytutsiya provela istorychnu mezhu," *Uriadovyi Kurier*, 21 June 1997.

76. *Rossiyskiye Vesti*, 24 October 1997, complained that "on the very eve of it [the CIS summit] Ukraine undertook something like a demarche by announcing that it had come to the Moldovan capital not even as an associate member of the CIS but as a free listener, as it were. It would attend certain measures in the role of an observer."

77. See Alexander J. Motyl, *Dilemmas of Independence: Ukraine after Totalitarianism* (New York: Council on Foreign Affairs, 1993), 89–90.

78. V. Lukin, "Our Security Predicament," *Foreign Policy* 88 (1992): 63. See also Hryn'iov, *Nova Ukraiina*, 73.

79. Leonid Kuchma, "Ia Ne Budu Nich'ym Vassalom," *Nezavisimaya Gazeta*, 28 October 1994.

80. *Krymskiye Vedomosti*, 26 March 1994; and *Demokratychna Ukraiina*, 19 August 1997.

81. V. Kremen', interview, *Imenem Zakonu*, 12 September 1997.

82. *Vechirnyi Kyiv*, 17 January 1997.

83. Leonid Kuchma, "Speech before the Kyiv Diplomatic Corps," *Uriadovyi Kurier*, 14 January 1997.

84. *Den*, 12 July 1997.

85. *Den*, 24 July 1997.

86. *Den*, 31 July 1997.

87. *Den*, 18 June 1997. The poll was undertaken by the Independent Experts Fund among 420 members of the Ukrainian political, economic, business, civic, and journalistic elites.

88. Leonid Kuchma, *Interfax-Ukraine*, 24 October 1997.

89. *Uriadovyi Kurier*, 14 October 1997.

90. S. Pirozhkov, director of the National Institute on Ukrainian–Russian Relations, Kyiv, as quoted by *Intelnews*, 30 October 1997.

91. *Itar-Tass*, 28 October 1997.

92. Volodymyr Polokhalo, ed., *Politolohiya Postkomunizmu. Politychnyi Analiz Postkomunistychnyi Suspil'stv* (Kyiv: Politychna Dumka, 1995), 324–326.

93. V. Horbulin, "Natsional'na Bezpeka Ukraiiny ta Mizhnarodna Bezpeka," *Politychna Dumka* 1 (1997): 85.

94. *Kuranty*, 15–21 October 1997.

95. "Ukraine's International Image: The View from Russia," *National Security and Defense* 3 (2000): 68.

96. *National Security and Defense* 3 (2000): 61.

97. *Jamestown Monitor*, 3 November 1997. Unnamed news article.

98. See the article arguing this case, Oleg Myasnikov, *Flag Rodiny*, 15 October 1997. Admiral Vladimir Kuroyedov, spokesman of the chief of staff of the Russian navy, argued in favor of the Russian and Ukrainian navies being capable of jointly resolving any tasks, "without any third country" (i.e., NATO or the United States). Quoted in *Itar-Tass*, 30 October 1997. This Russian view is rebuffed in Yuri Shcherbak, *The Strategic Role of Ukraine: Diplomatic Addresses and Lectures (1994–1997)* (Cambridge, Mass.: Ukrainian Research Institute, 1998).

99. Kuchma told the diplomatic corps in Kyiv, "It is understood that unconditional and resolute endorsement of Ukraine's political sovereignty, territorial integrity and the inviolability of its borders will remain the focal point of our foreign policy." *Uriadovyi Kurier*, 14 January 1997.

100. See T. Kuzio, "The Crimea Returns to Ukraine," in *Ukraine under Kuchma: Political Reform, Economic Transformation and Security Policy in Independent Ukraine* (London: Macmillan, 1997), 67–89, and "Federalism, Regionalism and the Myth of Separatism," in *Ukraine: State and Nation Building* (London: Routledge, 1998), 69–99. Sergei Shuvaynykov, head of the Congress of Russian People of the Crimea, admitted, "It is practically impossible to unite

all Russians and pro-Russian organisations of the Crimea." *Holos Ukraiiny*, 1 November 1997.

101. The figure of 64 percent is given by *Argumenty i Fakty* 27 (1997), while that of 75 percent is quoted from Roman Laba, "The Russian–Ukrainian Conflict: State, Nation and Identity," *European Security* 4, no. 3 (1995): 477.

102. The figure of 56 percent is given in *Interfax*, 27 October 1997, while that of 75 percent is quoted from the *Christian Science Monitor*, 21 July 1994. Only 37 percent of Russians believed that Russians and Ukrainians were separate peoples. The poll was conducted by the Center for the Study of Public Opinion, *Interfax*, 27 October 1997.

103. *Reuters*, 21 December 1996.

104. Volodymyr Ihnatov and Luidmilla Kryshtal', "Suchasni Sotsial'no-Politychni Tendentsii Nashoho Rozvytku," *Politolohichni Chyttania* 3 (1995): 8.

105. See Oleksandr Kupchyshyn, "Spivrobitnytsvo z SND, intehratsiya z Evropoiu," *Polityka i Chas* 7 (1996): 13–16.

106. See T. Kuzio, "Geopolitical Pluralism in the CIS: The Emergence of GUUAM," *European Security* 9, no. 2 (2000): 81–114, and "Promoting Geopolitical Pluralism in the CIS: GUUAM and Western Foreign Policy," *Problems of Post-Communism* 47, no. 3 (2000): 25–35.

107. On GUUAM before Uzbekistan joined, see *Holos Ukraiiny*, 5 November 1997.

108. M. A. Kulinich, "Ukraiina v Novomu Heopolitychnomu Prostori: Problemy Rehional'noi iy Subrehional'noii Bezpeky," *Nauka I Oborona* 1, no. 4 (1995): 17–18. See also Shcherbak, *Strategic Role of Ukraine*, 32.

109. *RFE/RL Newsline*, 20 April 1998.

110. See L. Greenfeld, *Nationalism: Five Roads to Modernity* (Cambridge: Harvard University Press, 1993), 254–270; and I. Neuman, *Russia and the Idea of Europe* (London: Routledge, 1996), 210.

111. See T. Kuzio, "The Domestic Sources of Ukrainian Security Policy," *Journal of Strategic Studies* 21, no. 4 (1998): 18–49, and "Ukraine: A Four-Pronged Transition," in *Contemporary Ukraine: Dynamics of Post-Soviet Transformation*, ed. T. Kuzio (Armonk, N.Y.: M. E. Sharpe, 1998), 165–180.

11

National Identity and Foreign Policy Orientation in Ukraine

Mikhail Molchanov

Ukrainian foreign policy is that of oscillation. Sitting uneasily on the porch between East and West, official Kyiv makes no commitment to either side. This may reflect a millennial divide between Christian Orthodoxy and Catholicism, a divide that, as Samuel Huntington noted, cuts contemporary Ukrainian state in two vastly different parts and makes it into a natural arena of the perennial fight of civilizations. It may also speak to the enduring power of the hated legacy of statelessness, which profoundly affected Ukrainian elites, leaving political culture of dependency and accommodation in its wake. It may betray the nation's inability to cope with a very recent trauma of double betrayal: first by Communists and second by nationalists, who both promised material abundance and expanding opportunities for individual self-fulfillment and both reneged on the promise. Finally, the lack of coherence in foreign policy may reflect different understanding of national interest by conflicting political communities in Kyiv and beyond, a confrontation of variously oriented business interests or even the lack of proper concern for the national interest, understood as well-being of the nation, on the part of politicians more concerned with their personal well-being.

An important source of tides and ebbs in Ukraine's pro-Western or, alternatively, pro-Russian orientation must also be found in domestic politics of identity. Ukraine is a nation in the making that embraces several dozen ethnic groups and political communities whose visions of the goals of national development may vary to the point of direct opposition and mutual exclusion. Sometimes political and ethnic cleavages overlap, as in the case of more radical Ukrainian nationalist groups whose membership is practically mono-ethnic. However, more often than not they cut across each other, which makes any attempt to make sense of the Ukrainian politics of identity complicated and by necessity incomplete.

Identity in Ukraine is in turmoil. Not only does this mean that there is no singular, all-encompassing national identity in place; it also means that among several competing identities, each posing as a national representative, not one can be considered uncontroversial. Yet this does not moderate sweeping ambitions of the contestants, nor make the competing discourses any less influential or policy relevant.

In a somewhat dramatic rendering, one may say that Ukrainians do not know who they are or what kind of national state they want to build.[1] This confusion is appropriately reflected in the absence of a generally recognized classification of the identity claims. Researchers tend to agree on only two of them, which constitute a well-defined opposition between the nationalist mobilized, nationally conscious Ukrainians and their opposite Russian numbers. The in-between categories are subject to intense debates thanks to a double obfuscation of the meaning of modern "Ukrainianness" by a billion shades of gray between Ukrainian and Russian, on the one hand, and a lingering shadow of Soviet cosmopolitanism, on the other hand.

We will not attempt a definitive categorization. Nonetheless, since some of the identity profiles figure in academic and popular discourses more often than the others, there is a need to address them, specifically tracing the assumed implications of a given profile for foreign policy. On a more general plane, whether perceptions of identity that are spread among various groups constituting modern Ukrainian society have an impact on foreign policy formulation in Kyiv and what the exact nature and relative weight of such an impact might be are themselves debatable questions. As Taras Kuzio correctly observes, Ukraine's foreign policy is "determined largely by the country's central ruling elites."[2] Available data show that, for example, the pro-NATO course of the government does not enjoy the support of the majority of the population, while a stable plurality that votes for some form of greater accommodation with Russia is routinely ignored by policy makers (see Tables 11.1 and 11.2). This may imply that a large segment of the population has no say in matters of foreign policy, which makes the "dissenting" voice practically inconsequential for the pur-

Table 11.1
Foreign Policy Orientations of the Ukrainian Population (Percentages)

What is your preferred vision of Ukraine's political development?	1994	1995	1996	1997	1998
Closer ties with country members of the Commonwealth of Independent States	40.5	38.8	31.8	23.7	22.8
Cooperate with Russia; strengthen East Slavic Union	17.5	14.8	14.4	28.8	22.7
Develop the Baltic-Black Sea Alliance	1.7	0.8	0.9	0.8	–
First of all, develop relations with Western countries	13.3	13.9	15.9	13.8	15.3
Self-reliance; strengthen independence	13.3	14.4	18.5	16.1	28.7
Different regions of Ukraine should choose their own ways	4.2	4.4	4.5	4.1	–
Don't know, no answer, other	12	12.8	13.9	12.7	10.5

Source: Politychnyi portret Ukrainy 20 (1998): 6; Democratic Initiatives Research Center, Kyiv, Ukraine.

Table 11.2
Attitudes Toward Pro-NATO Course of the Government in Ukraine (Percentages)

Closer collaboration with NATO	1997			1998		
	yes	no	hard to say	yes	no	hard to say
is in Ukraine's national interests	36	17	47	35.4	27.3	37.3
runs contrary to Ukraine's interests, its nonallied status, etc.	22	26	52	32.7	26.6	40.7
makes Ukraine a "buffer" country between NATO and the Tashkent alliance	26	9	65	35.4	15	49.6
undermines stability of relations with Russia	40	10	50	51.1	15.2	33.7
is, by necessity, driven by the goal of further integration with Europe	28	10	62	31.9	18.4	49.7
serves the goal of Ukraine's prospective membership in NATO	40	3	58	51.2	5.8	43

Source: Politychnyi portret Ukrainy 18 (1997); Democratic Initiatives Research Center, 1998.

poses of this study. Marginal and liminal identities can also hide themselves behind a surface of political passivity and withdrawal from participation ("don't knows" and "undecided" in survey returns). Should we ignore them altogether? Alternatively, should we introduce a new label that we believe best characterizes these absentees? What would be the empirical ground for imposition of such a label? These are all difficult questions, and I attempt to answer them in the sections that follow, concentrating specifically on the "Russian dimension" in Ukrainian identity debates and the so-called Eastern orientation in Ukraine's foreign policy.

NATIONAL IDENTITY IN UKRAINE: ONE, TWO, MANY?

The debate on Ukrainian national identity began well before the first modern Ukrainian state came into existence in the wake of the Russian revolution of 1917. Writing in the mid-nineteenth century, the Ukrainian historian Mykola Kostomarov (1817–1885) proposed that we distinguish between what he called two Russian nationalities: the Great Russians and the Little Russians (Ukrainians). While the first were characterized as intrinsically collectivist and supporters of a strong authoritarian state, the second were thought of as spontaneous democrats and individualists.[3] The distinction, though probably far-fetched in its essentialist reading, nevertheless did capture an important element of culture that found empirical manifestation in the patterns of land use by the peasantry.[4] As noted by a historian,

By the last part of the eighteenth century most peasant households were the permanent possessors of their holdings. At this point the Little Russian experience diverged from that of the North. Instead of going back to communal control and equalization . . . individual landholding persisted. Each homestead continued in the possession of its specific holding, and no communal efforts were made to achieve equality in the amount of the land held, or to provide landless peasants with holdings.[5]

References to the famous "peasant individualism" of the Ukrainian people could draw from this reality, which became singularly significant with the advent of collectivization. Be it for reasons of culture and identity or because of exceptionally rich natural endowment, Ukrainians proved powerful opponents to Soviet agricultural policies: "Resistance to collectivization was naturally strongest among those who had the most to lose—the kulaks . . . and the bulk of the peasants in the surplus-producing areas of the Ukraine, southern Russia, and western Siberia, where landlordism and the village commune had been much weaker."[6]

The ensuing Stalinist terror closed most avenues of private initiative, wiping out resisters in a long wave of repression that, in the Ukrainian case, continued into the early 1950s, when the Soviet regime finally managed to crush armed resistance in western Ukraine. By the late

1970s it seemed that the "socialist way of life" indeed had created a type of Ukrainian personality that was hardly distinguishable from its Russian counterpart in its complete allegiance to internationalism and collectivist values.[7]

This illusion was shattered a decade later, when the newly created Rukh (originally named as the Popular Movement of Ukraine in Support of Perestroika) devoted much energy to convince the Ukrainian public of the opposite.[8] Drawing on prerevolutionary and émigré sources, the mouthpiece of the movement, the newspaper *Literaturna Ukraina*, defined Ukrainian identity as exactly opposite to Russian. The term "Little Russian," originally used as a neutral descriptor of nationality, acquired, under this influence, a distinctively pejorative meaning.[9] Modern Ukrainian nationalists use it to designate an identity that is less mature, less "nationally conscious," and, hence, less distinct from the Russian than the standard Ukrainian identity must be. In this view, not infrequently repeated in research literature emanating from Ukraine, a "Little Russian" identity is found in "people, Ukrainian in their ethnic origin, who feel (and try to pretend) that they are Russian rather than Ukrainian."[10]

The view is interesting in its essentialist emphasis on blood ties (presumed genealogy) over subjective ethnic self-identification, which, according to most specialists, must be considered the key element of ethnicity. In both Soviet and post-Soviet contexts, the view of ethnicity as objectively derived from verifiable genealogy has been paramount. The Soviet regime developed this idea into a practice of labeling, which, through the instruments of state censuses, employment records, and internal passports, officially affixed ethnicity (called "nationality") to the individual. Under these circumstances, individual ethnic reidentification was severely restricted and frequently impossible. Thus, a person born to, say, Armenian parents but raised in Lithuania would be considered an Armenian even if he or she had no knowledge of Armenian language and culture, used Lithuanian in day-to-day communication, and would consciously opt for Lithuanian, rather than Armenian, identification.

The idea that the so-called passport nationality (the nationality assigned to ex-Soviet citizens by the state) is somehow more "authentic" than individual perceptions of ethnicity not only flies in the face of modern science but, no less important, reveals a lingering shadow of totalitarian contempt to the sovereign powers of the individual. Recent studies demonstrate that Ukrainian nation-building efforts have led many "passport" Russians to redefine themselves as Ukrainians.[11] Similarly, a not negligible number of those officially designated as "non-Russians" reveal their Russian national identity: In one study, up to 11 percent of "passport" Ukrainians and 2 percent of Jews in

Kyiv, 5 percent of Ukrainians in Simferopol, and 4 percent of Ukrainians and 1 percent of Belarusian respondents in L'viv.[12] A view that there is just one "true" identity that the individual must stick to, though not uncommon among nationalists and fundamentalists, is out of place in modern pluralist society. Its derivative, the notion that there must be one "standard" ethnic identity for a state-bearing ("titular") nation portends not only a division between titular and nontitular groups, but also rifts within the former, between subgroups judged more and less authentic representatives of the standard. The state that takes it upon itself to pass judgment on the ethnic authenticity of its citizenry may only be illiberal, obtrusive, intrinsically arrogant, and contemptuous of its subjects. It is not wholly unexpected to find these features in the post-totalitarian environment of delayed (and therefore goaded by the state) national development.

Unfortunately, certain scholarly analyses, even when pledging a "Western perspective," convey an impression that being Ukrainian "by ethnic origin" somehow requires a person to speak standard literary Ukrainian language, relish Ukrainian "native" culture and be "much more comfortable" with it than with other cultural material, and denounce both Soviet history and larger-than-ethnic "political–ideological identity" that is now deemed incompatible with the ongoing nation-building "struggles" (Ukrainian *zmahannia*) of the elite. The very notion of "interidentity," introduced by an otherwise perceptive analyst, implies that all of its enumerated subtypes (Russophone Ukrainian, internationalist Soviet, and dialectal–localist, *patois* identity) are no more than deviations, hybrids, or semifinished products that fill the space between the clearly defined opposites of Russian and Ukrainian.[13]

The concept of identity is elusive. Identity might be perception of the self, or it might be what "really" separates one self from another. Most researchers prefer subjective definitions of identity, which allow one to capture the process of meaning attribution by the group itself. Thus, national identity is commonly defined as the "comprehension of the character and limits of the nation," rather than the "objectively" established and presumably open to external verification markers of a nation.[14] Since national identity is something more than regional, ethnocultural, or linguistic identity characteristics of the constituent parts of the nation, it is looked upon as "a feeling of solidarity among members of the political community delimited by the state."[15] It can therefore be considered one for the nation, but only in a sense of both posited and actually shared feeling of national loyalty and civic distinctiveness grounded in the collective experience of living in the same state. If such a unity is absent and the meaning of collective experience is contested among several competing groups, it is fair to say that the national identity in question is as yet incomplete and transitional.

The transitional phase in the development of national identity is characterized by a movement in several directions simultaneously. It involves differentiation from the "other," appropriation of the ideal self, and identification of those who belong against those who do not. The process of transition fragments and often completely eliminates identity inherited from the ancien régime and seeks to construct a new identity that would provide a boundary separating the newly constructed polity from the rest. It is especially important to mark off differences with progenitors and neighbors, since allegiance claims those may advance against the young polity tend to be powerful enough to create a not negligible following characterized by a special "in-between" or liminal identity. The state of liminality, writes Anne Norton,

provides for the differentiation of self and other, subject and object, by establishing a triadic relation: the self, an object of likeness, and an object of difference. Liminars serve as mirrors for nations. At once other and like, they provide the occasion for the nation to constitute itself in reflection upon its identity. Their likeness permits contemplation and recognition, their difference the abstraction of those ideal traits that will henceforth define the nation.[16]

It is clear that invectives against the so-called Little Russian identity in Ukraine, as well as frequent lamentations decrying a "complex of inferiority" allegedly inherent in the Ukrainian mentality, are both informed by the desire to find a liminar against whom the nationalist construction of identity could prop its own claims to intellectual and political superiority. Since the process of transition from the Russian–Soviet past toward an as yet undefined Ukrainian future involves both demolition of an internationalist Soviet outlook and relegation of ethnocultural Russian affiliations from previously dominant to a newly subdominant position, there are at least two obvious candidates for this role: individuals and groups that identify themselves primarily with the whole population of the former Soviet Union ("Soviet people") and those with the predominantly pro-Russian orientations variously manifested in language, culture, and political and ideological orientations. Both groups have been well represented in the overall structure of the Ukrainian population, with significant numbers of "Russophiles" hiding behind localist–regional affiliations (see Tables 11.3 and 11.4). Reappropriation of these liminal groups for the nation-building cause in Ukraine may take the form of ethnicization, politicization, resocialization, or redefinition of group boundaries.

Ethnicization of Ukraine's national identity, though a seductive option in view of ingrained ideas of what the "classic" nation-state must look like, leads to a dead end of racialized, ideologically postulated divisions that pitch a de facto majority of the nation (Russianized, cos-

Table 11.3
Self-Identification of the Ukrainian Population

Which of the population groups mentioned below do you primarily identify yourself with? (please choose one)	1994 March	1994 May	1995 June	1998 April
Population of the locality or city of your residence	29	n/a	n/a	30
Population of your region (territory, province)	8	23	14.5	10
Population of Ukraine	34	34	48.3	37
Population of Russia	n/a	3	2	n/a
Population of the former Soviet Union	17	27	20.5	n/a
Population of the Commonwealth of Independent States	n/a	7	6.7	n/a
Population of Europe	3	1	2.3	7
Population of the world	3	n/a	n/a	n/a
Don't know, difficult to answer, other	6	5	5.7	16
N	1,799	1,807	1,808	1,161

Source: Politychnyi portret Ukrainy 9 (1994), 15 (1996); A Political Portrait of Ukraine 4 (1994); Richard Rose and Christian Haerpfer, New Democracies Barometer V: A 12-Nation Survey (Glasgow: University of Strathclyde, 1998), 68, 100.

Note: The 1998 survey employed different methodics, as respondents could pick more than one choice, and the questions on Russian–Soviet identity were not all offered. The table reproduces first choices only.

mopolitan, urban, and less responsive to ethnonationalist appellations) against its "nationally conscious" minority. The bulk of the latter is to be found in the western, least-modernized regions of the country, where ethnonationalism feeds off a rich history of foreign domination, frustrated ambitions of local elites, isolation, and parochialism.[17] When intellectual leaders of this strata attempt to remodel the country in its image, suggesting the westernmost land of Galicia as a springboard for national revival (Ukraine's "Piedmont"), in a sense they continue to fight the struggles of 1848 when the task is to synchronize the country's development with the realities of the twenty-first century.[18]

Politicization of national identity is an equally erroneous avenue for theoretical speculations and practical policy alike. This error is not infrequently committed by those who take fleeting political affiliations and lingering ideological attachments of a group as definitive of its self-image or projected patterns of behavior. Hence, the so-called Soviet identity, a reflection of present deprivation and longing for the "good old times" of guaranteed jobs and a readily available social safety net, becomes, under the pen of a writer, a singularly important characteristic of a good one-quarter to one-third of the nation that votes socialist and communist and is presumed to have no other anchors of identity of equal significance. Whether or not this group will vote the

Table 11.4
Ethnonational Self-Identification in Ukraine, 1997

Which one of these statements better fits your personal perception of the self? I consider myself	N	%
solely Ukrainian	5,712	55.9
both Ukrainian and Russian	754	7.4
as much Ukrainian as Russian	1,466	14.4
both Russian and Ukrainian	496	4.9
solely Russian	1,099	10.8
undecided	102	1.0
don't know	539	5.3
no answer	43	0.4
TOTAL	10,211	100

Source: V. Khmelko, M. Pogrebinskii, A. Tolpygo, E. Golovakha, and N. Panina, *Predvybornye nastroeniia v Ukraine: National survey, November–December 1997* (Kyiv: KTsPIK and KIIS, 1997).

same way should the circumstances change is not at all clear. It is illustrative that pro-Russian sympathies traditionally associated with Ukrainians exhibiting a "Soviet mentality" vary depending on Russia's domestic situation, the war in Chechnya in particular, from full support of Ukraine's reunification with the Russian Federation to a much more cautious economic cooperation.

It is a staple of modern scholarship on nationalism to discern the tension between ethnic and civic national identities in recently democratized polities. While the identity grounded in territorial affiliation, patriotism, and civic values is assumed to be open to all citizens of the state irrespective of their ethnicity, ethnic identity is commonly seen as intrinsically illiberal, since being based in ethnic affiliation, parochial culture, and/or language, it must imply exclusion of all those who do not share the same characteristics of ethnicity. However useful, this generalization tends to simplify a rather complex relationship between ethnic and civic components, which by necessity coexist in varying proportions in any real-world polity. The scheme becomes even more confusing if applied to a multicultural society, which undergoes the process of identity change and redefinition, rearranging ethnic and civic anchors of identity on both national and subnational levels.

Several authors discern tension between ethnic and civic national identities in Ukraine.[19] However, if applied to Ukraine, the view of the two competing identities—one ethnic, other civic—tends to gloss over important cleavages within each of the two or streamline those cleavages into a deceptively clear-cut opposition. Hence, when Kuzio argues that "Ukraine inherited two identities at different stages of development," he feels obliged to introduce a caveat: "Some scholars may want to break these two groups down further."[20] Indeed we must. First, there are not one but several ethnic identities in Ukraine, as expressed in the opposition between Ukrainian and Russian ethnic projects, the problem of the Ukrainian–Russian language competition, or the problem of ethnic self-assertion of other (non-Russian) minorities. Similarly, there are important distinctions characterizing various approaches to the civic understanding of identity. Whatever else may be said of lingering Soviet influences on the construction of Ukrainian national identity, Sovietization succeeded in strengthening territorial affiliations and feelings of local patriotism while downplaying the importance of ethnic affiliations stretching across republican borders. Because of this, the identity project informed by socialization in Soviet values tended to support civic rather than ethnic visions, even if the "compartmentalized" nature of the Soviet federal system worked to reinforce ethnic elites' claim to power and, hence, ethnic nationalism. The Western liberal version of civic identity is also present, supported by both Russophone and Ukrainophone parties of a reformist orientation.

A mature national identity includes both civic and ethnic components. The problem is in the right balance between the two, not in the promotion of just one of them and the elimination of the other. An emphasis on Western "civic" models of national identity as a diametrical opposite to the models that seek to anchor the nation in its "root" ethnicity may create an erroneous impression of a suggested civic identity as being essentially indifferent to ethnicity. In fact, ethnicity remains an important element defining the character of the state everywhere, including stable pluralist democracies whose civic national identity is never in doubt.[21]

It is obvious that Ukrainian national identity, formed in a juxtaposition of a universalist Soviet legacy, Russian and Polish influences, and indigenous nationalist resistance to both, should harbor both ethnic and civic elements. The central role of the latter has been confirmed in the Law on Citizenship of Ukraine (October 8, 1991), which extended the rights of citizenship to

1. all citizens of the former USSR who at the moment of proclamation of independence of Ukraine (August 24, 1991) were permanent residents of Ukraine;
2. persons who at the moment of the enactment of the Law of Ukraine "On Citizenship of Ukraine" (1636-12) (November 13, 1991) permanently re-

sided in Ukraine, regardless of their race, skin color, political, religious and other convictions, sex, ethnic or social origin, property status, place of residence, linguistic or other characteristics, and who are not citizens of other states (Article 2).[22]

In an equally accommodating gesture, the 1992 Law on National Minorities in Ukraine guaranteed national–cultural autonomy of minorities (article 6) and equal political, social, economic, and cultural rights and freedoms to all citizens of Ukraine irrespective of nationality (article 1).[23] The adoption of these documents underscored Ukraine's difference from models of ethnic democracy akin to those promoted in Estonia and Latvia. The 1989 Law on Languages, though proclaiming Ukrainian the sole state language in the country, nevertheless preserved important guarantees for the languages of minorities and kept Russian as "the language of international communication of the peoples of the USSR" (article 4).[24]

At the same time, the newly born state made conscious efforts to embrace ethnicity and culture of the nominally state-bearing nation: Ukrainians. These efforts became pronounced in education and mass media, shaping out as an elaborate set of measures designed to promote the Ukrainian language, particularly at the expense of a de facto still-dominant communication in Russian. Ethnicization of an officially promulgated identity tipped the precarious balance suggested in the legislation, aroused bitter feelings among members of the multicultural Russian community in Ukraine, and worsened interstate relations with Moscow. Instilling of a more distinct ethnocultural component into the national profile presented by the state to its neighbors and citizens alike had arguably less to do with the activity of the nationalist pressure groups inside and outside the country and more with the raison d'etre that dictated necessity of these measures in view of Russia's growing assertiveness vis-à-vis its former sister republic.

UKRAINE'S RUSSIAN CONUNDRUM: POLITICS AND SOCIETY

That the problem of Ukraine's relations with Russia must become a major preoccupation of its political establishment was dictated by several factors. Apart from the obvious historic linkages to the Russian Empire and the USSR, let alone Kyivan Rus, claimed by all eastern Slavs as mother state, Ukraine was in a sense left hostage to its geopolitically squeezed position between Russia and the West. Second, both countries suffered from the breakup of manifold ties that connected their heretofore integrated economies. Third, the 11.3-million-strong Russian diaspora in Ukraine and 4.4-million-strong Ukrainian diaspora in Russia grew accustomed to living in what they believed was their larger common home, the USSR. Many in these groups supported re-integration and were prepared to accept Russia's intervention to that end. Moscow equivocated on the issue of Ukrainian independence, giving rise to the fear that it may attempt to bring Ukraine back to its fold, by force if necessary.

Still more important, Ukrainian national identity remained contested from within, not only by Russian and other minorities, but also by Ukrainians themselves. As late as 1997, 25.5 percent of the Ukrainian population thought of their ethnicity as, to a varying degree, both Ukrainian and Russian.[25] Since, to quote Szporluk, "it is only in the twentieth century that the differentiation of the two nations, realized and accepted by the wide masses of people and not only by the intelligentsia, has been accomplished," an idea that Ukraine properly belongs to the east Slavic family of nations and should forge state alliances accordingly appeared.[26] Historical memories of Ukrainians being part of a larger Russian state became a factor in both countries. In Ukraine, these memories potently manifested themselves in the regions with the longest history of incorporation: southeastern (Donbas), northeastern (Slobids'ka Ukraina, Chernihiv, Kharkiv, and Sumy *oblasti*), southern (Odesa–Kherson–Mykolaiv), and, to a lesser extent, central (Left-Bank *oblasti* to the east of the Dnipro). Crimea, a part of Russia till 1954, remained culturally Russian and resented being controlled from Kyiv. A diametrically opposed view of Russia and Russians as culturally alien and politically hostile dominated the thinking of a hodge-podge group of nationalist politicians in the national capital and in the west of the country, most notably in the historically detached region of Galicia. The Ukrainian parliament, the *Verkhovna Rada*, appeared divided on the Russian issue to no less an extent than were regions and regionally based parties.

In this situation, executive organs of the state, the presidential administration, the Ministry of Foreign Affairs, and the subsequently created National Security Council, had to take the lead in foreign policy formulation toward the east. The overall course of the Ukrainian administration early on coalesced on the idea to move away from Moscow and to preserve as much distance as needed to secure state independence and, hence, fully autonomous power bases secured for the local elite by the December 1991 referendum. Yet Kyiv's actions were more often reactive than proactive, following the scheme of Russian attempts to reassert control, Ukraine's negative reaction, Ukraine looks for international protection and/or mediation of the dispute, Moscow's backtracking, and a compromise solution, not infrequently mediated by the West or reflected through Kyiv's Western policy. Thus, Kyiv is encouraged to continue relying on Western support in its further dealings with Moscow, while Moscow's fears of Kyiv falling into the Western sphere of influence received a new confirmation. The cycle starts anew. Ukrainians show how a principled defense of national interest grows into a self-perpetuating activity, which demonstrates the lack of confidence on the part of the Ukrainian political establishment and its continued dependence on external inputs for policy.

Ukrainian–Russian relations have undergone several stages of development. The first began with the conclusion of the November 1990 treaty, which confirmed both sides' territorial integrity "within their presently existing borders within the USSR" (article 6), extended mutual recognition of sovereignty (article 1), and proclaimed the necessity of a "joint action in foreign affairs" (article 8) and "in the area of defense and security" (article 7). While Russia understood the treaty as essentially tying Ukraine to follow Moscow's lead in foreign policy and security, Ukraine, inspired by its December 1991 referendum on state independence, had early on decided on taking an exception whenever Kyiv believed national interests were at stake. Hence, though Ukraine was a founding member of the Commonwealth of Independent States and affirmed, in the person of its first president, Leonid Kravchuk, its commitment to open borders, a common economic and military–strategic space, and joint "foreign-policy activity" with Russia, it has never signed the CIS Charter or the Tashkent Treaty on collective security and restrained itself to an associate membership in the CIS Economic Union.[27] From 1991 to 1994, Ukrainian authorities sought to put as much distance between Ukraine and Russia as was reasonably possible, which naturally involved revision of the letter and the spirit of both the November 1990 treaty and the Agreement on Creation of the CIS.

The second phase started with the conclusion of the Trilateral Agreement by the United States, Russia, and Ukraine, which addressed Ukraine's nuclear disarmament and external security guarantees (January 1994), or arguably, with the September 1993 Massandra summit, where Moscow linked Ukraine's energy dependency and debt to Russia to its preferred vision of how the Soviet-era Black Sea Fleet must be divided between both countries.[28] Thus, Russia was again seen as an important partner or, at the very least, as a foreign party that could be ignored only at a considerable cost. The election of an ostensibly "pro-Russian" presidential candidate, Leonid Kuchma, in July 1994 confirmed that the pendulum of Ukraine's foreign policy swung back to the East. The inaugural speech of the president called Ukraine a "multinational state" and focused on the Russian–Eurasian direction in Ukraine's foreign policy.[29] Several politicians and presidential advisers published programmatic statements arguing that Ukraine's strategic interests were inseparable from furthering the country's extensive collaboration with Russia.[30] Foreign policy losses in its eastern direction were tied to monoethnic visions of Ukrainian national identity, and the president himself was forced to admit that the "Ukrainian national idea . . . did not bring the desired consolidation, primarily because from the very beginning it was not filled with civic, political, or economic contents, but mostly with ethnopolitical contents."[31]

This phase did not last long, however. Russia's active stance on a number of issues in bilateral relations and officially proclaimed policy of support of compatriots abroad became an annoyance. Speaking during the May 1995 U.S.–Ukrainian summit in Kyiv, Kuchma, in a clear reference to Moscow stated his resolute opposition to the "imperial ambitions, aggressive separatism and desire to rearrange the political map by force."[32] By early 1996 he had fully adopted the image of a national-patriotic *derzhavnyk* (supporter of a strong national state), confirming the choice of a Western nation-state model for Ukraine's political development. Criticism of the "simplified and primitive aggressive understanding of the national idea" made one final appearance in the annual address to the parliament in April 1996.[33] Following that, the president sought to anchor Ukraine firmly in the "European context," which was more often than not done at Russia's expense.[34] Thus, the signing of the bilateral Treaty on Friendship and Cooperation in May 1997 was followed by the adoption of the Ukraine–NATO Charter on Distinctive Partnership (July 1997), while the interstate Program of Economic Cooperation between Ukraine and the Russian Federation for 1998–2007 (February 1998) had its counterpart in the State Program of Cooperation with NATO till 2001 (November 1998) and in Kuchma's Decree no. 615 (June 11, 1998) on Ukraine's integration into the European Union.

Ukraine's "multivectorism" in foreign policy continues to confuse scholars. An authoritative analysis by the National Institute for Strategic Studies even goes so far as to claim that "unfortunately, Ukraine has never had a clearly defined geopolitical strategy."[35] Yet certain regularities in the seemingly chaotic movement of the Ukrainian pendulum can be discerned. Its rhythms are defined by the domestic electoral cycle, the Eastern–Western balance of grants and debt calls, and, perhaps most important, by the necessity to keep Russia at arm's length, using politics of identity to demarcate a political and cultural boundary around the terrain where the local elite's claim to power must remain unopposed. Each of these factors represent a dilemma in its own right, each featuring a certain tension and even opposition between policies and perceptions of the elite and policy preferences of largely disenfranchised and immobilized masses.

Election contenders in Ukraine have to balance between the Russia-averse west and the essentially pro-Russian east of the country, taking into consideration the fact that between 45 and 55 percent of the vote comes from the latter region. Candidates feel obliged to placate Russophile easterners if they want to win the election. However, the western electorate makes a better ally for the incumbent, who must reinforce sovereignty and cannot appear as a Russian client before the world's financial lenders. Pulling in opposite directions, these drives sustain a familiar cycle: drawing closer to Russia before the elections and swinging back when the elections are over. Because of these dynamics, both winning candidates in the presidential elections of 1991 and 1994 had their patriotic credentials questioned at first, moved closer to the critics when in office, and entered the next elections as proponents of a certifiably "patriotic" agenda. Kuchma's second election campaign also started with an assurance—"There is no rupture with my partner and brother Russia and there never will be"—and ended with the pledge of a "continued partnership with the American people" and an expressed desire "to join the Atlantic community."[36]

Ukraine's economic dependence, the balance of grants and debts in particular, represents another problem of standing significance. Between 40 and 50 percent of Ukrainian export–import transactions are generated on the Russian market (see Table 11.5). When Soviet patronage ended, Russia continued financing up to 22 percent of the Ukrainian GDP with subsidized credits. In 1995, support of the Ukrainian economy by Russia and Turkmenistan exceeded disbursements by the IMF and the World Bank combined.[37] The ten-year value of Russian implicit energy subsidies to Ukraine was estimated at $12.6

Table 11.5
Russia's Share in Ukraine's Foreign Trade Turnover, 1994–2000 (Percentages)

	1994	1995	1996	1997	1998	1999	2000
Exports	45.3	43.3	38.7	26.2	23.0	20.7	47.0
Imports	59.1	51.4	50.1	45.8	48.1	47.6	22.8
Total	52.4	47.7	45.0	36.9	36.5	34.3	38.1

Source: S. I. Pirozhkov and A. I. Sukhorukov, eds., *Eksportnyi potentsial Ukrainy na rosiis'komu vektori: stan i prognoz* (Kyiv: Akadempres, 1998), 129; official Web site of the National Institute for Ukrainian–Russian Relations (http://niurr.gov.ua/ru/econom/inprog/tabl_2.htm); O. H. Osaulenko, *Ukraina u tsyfrakh u 1999 rotsi* (Kyiv: Derzhavnyi komitet statystyky Ukraïny, 2000); Derzhavnyi Komitet Statystyky Ukrainy, *Ekspres-dopovid'* 187, 6 June 2000.

Note: Not counting trade in services.

billion.[38] However, debts had also grown. By 1996, Ukraine owed $4.6 billion to CIS countries and $2.11 billion to international financial institutions.[39] Ukraine's energy debts to Russia, restructured in 1995 with Western mediation, had grown again to a staggering $1.4 billion by early 2000 and risen to $2.2 billion by the end of the year.[40] At the same time, Ukraine not only owed $2.02 billion to the World Bank and $2.9 billion to the IMF but had to restructure its $2.6-billion debt to Western bond holders in mid-April 2000.[41] A pattern thus emerged: borrowing more and more in the West and using money principally to pay debts to Russia and other CIS partners in a vicious circle of ever-growing indebtedness.[42]

Ukraine's foreign policy orientations are obviously influenced by expectations of sponsorship, debt relief, and/or new credits forthcoming from either Russia or the West or, preferably, both. The Russian connection is particularly strong in view of Ukraine's energy dependence, since up to 70 to 75 percent of the country's annual consumption of gas and close to 80 percent of its oil demand are covered by imports from Russia.[43] The West remains a major financial supplier. Hence, Ukrainian foreign policy has to walk a thin line between the two, seeking to woo both and not to antagonize either. Just as Russia uses the economy to elicit Ukraine's concessions in foreign policy and security (Massandra, 1993; Trilateral agreement; the 1997 agreements on the Black Sea Fleet), Ukraine applies bilateral and third-party diplomacy to secure Russian lenience over the energy debt and supplies (the Sochi summit, 1995; the Program of Economic Cooperation for 1998–2007; the Sochi summit, 2000). Political rhetoric may help too, as shown by the ex-chairman of the *Verkhovna Rada*, Oleksandr Tkachenko, using "Slavic ties" to help win ratification of the friendship treaty by the State Duma in December 1998.[44]

Ukraine's refusal to enter into the payment, customs, or monetary unions proposed by Russia, or to participate in the CIS Inter-Parliamentary Assembly in more than a limited capacity of an observer, may seem illogical, given the degree of the country's reliance on the Russian market.[45] It flies in the face of liberal theories of international relations, because of the apparent benefits of cooperation and expressed popular preferences of closer ties with Russia in politics, economy, security, and foreign policy on the state-to-state, society-to-society, and person-to-person levels of interaction. It also speaks volumes of the character of the political regime in Ukraine, which masquerades as a democracy while openly ignoring public opinion and patronizing citizens as being somehow unprepared to make informed choices for themselves.[46]

In fact, the choice of the people is clear to everyone but the ruling elite in Kyiv. In public opinion, Ukraine's national interests point toward a profound rapprochement with Russia. Thus, in 1998, 57 percent of those polled voted in favor of Ukraine joining the Russia–Belarus

Union, while up to 66 percent of participants in another survey saw the bilateral Program of Economic Cooperation in unambiguously positive terms, as "facilitating the expansion of a mutually beneficial, good-neighborly cooperation of the two allied states and peoples."[47] In 1998–2000, a stable 28 to 30 percent of the total supported Ukraine's ascent to the CIS military union (the Tashkent Treaty), versus just 15 to 16 percent convinced of the benefits of Ukraine's potential NATO membership and 31 to 37 percent in favor of equidistancing and non-alignment.[48] Through the first five years of independent existence, a majority of Ukrainians supported awarding the Russian language official status in Ukraine, a proportion that only slightly declined (to 44 to 46 percent) in 1997–2000.[49] The levels of interpersonal trust and tolerance of Russians in Ukraine rival those accorded to ethnic Ukrainians and distinguish both as groups of choice for family and business relationships (see Table 11.6).

Table 11.6
Interethnic Tolerance and Social Distancing in Ukraine, 1994–2000 (the Bogardus Social Distance Scale)

Ethnic and ethno-cultural groups	1994	1995	1996	1997	1998	1999	2000
Ukrainian-speaking Ukrainians	1.70	1.72	2.03	2.27	1.83	1.77	2.07
Russian-speaking Ukrainians	1.78	1.84	2.06	2.34	1.97	1.97	2.32
Russians	1.95	2.06	2.45	2.55	2.25	2.21	2.49
Belarusians	2.32	2.49	3.05	3.18	3.04	2.94	3.13
Jews	3.63	3.74	3.89	3.97	3.96	3.86	4.10
Poles	3.85	3.84	4.16	4.23	4.23	4.20	4.45
Germans	4.03	3.92	4.39	4.30	4.47	4.41	4.69
Romanians	4.27	4.40	4.38	4.51	4.59	4.48	5.03
Gypsies	5.15	5.14	5.15	5.35	5.40	5.46	5.60
Average index	3.60	3.67	3.78	3.85	3.82	3.78	4.06
N	2,181	1,530	1,446	1,973	1,566	1,533	1,935

Source: Kyiv International Institute of Sociology online report (http://kiis.com.ua).

Note: The index equals 1 if all respondents would admit representatives of a given group as members of their families, 7 if all respondents would deny anyone from a given group an entry to Ukraine.

In spite of all this, official Kyiv prefers to keep away from Russia in matters of foreign policy and security and does not sign any collective effort at integration within the CIS if it appears or happens to be spearheaded by the Russian Federation.[50] The Ukrainian elite continues to regard Russia with a mixture of awe and hate, which might be considered a rather typical syndrome of postcolonial mentality. However, Ukraine begs exception from any roster of the typically postcolonial states precisely because the majority of the population does not share these feelings with their leaders. When half of the elite (48 percent) viewed Russia as Ukraine's "biggest threat" and most of it confessed to "the absence of long-term euphoria" despite the "signing of a number of important documents in May, 1997," about one-third of the population, including one in every four ethnic Ukrainians, believed that the two countries should unite into one (Table 11.7).[51]

This discrepancy between elite and mass attitudes sheds an important light on the uses of politics of identity, which in the Ukrainian case is called upon to provide symbolic boundary markers and border guards, principally against Russia.[52] Identity markers insulate the nascent and still-fluid space of nation building from neighbors who might still regard this space as falling under their "rightful" hegemony. The sense of a fully separate national identity is therefore supposed to compensate for the de facto transparency of the state border, for a profoundly Sovietized (on the face, Russian) culture of the majority of the population, and for a majority feeling of being "properly" part of another sociopolitical and cultural space than the one constructed by the nation's leaders.[53] The question is, how can elites instill such a sense, implying both loyalty to the newly formed institutions of the state and the shared identity within the new state boundaries, into the people that have grown accustomed to disassociate themselves from the abusive and manipulative power? A foreign policy conspicuously independent from the expected Eastern influences was one obvious choice.

In Szporluk's observation, "New kinds of international relations are especially important in forming and re-forming post-Soviet national identities and states."[54] If novel international relations are not immediately forthcoming, the "right" political rhetoric, indications of intent, and official representations of foreign policy goals and substance may well play a substitute. Foreign policy becomes a principal means of nation building because of "weak political institutions" and a "precarious basis for the political legitimacy of the state."[55] Institutional development takes time and resources, which Ukraine does not have in abundance, hence the need to rely on such mostly symbolic assets as a unique national identity, geostrategic visions of the state's position on the globe, or its avowed closeness to either "Europe and the West" or Russia and the "Slavic world."[56] Thus, a politician can argue, as Kuchma did, that "our line toward strategic partnership and equitable good-neighborly relations with Russia remains unchanged," while simultaneously calling upon Ukrainians to choose "the European model for our development" as something quite different from a model pursued by Moscow.[57] It is not illogical to placate Russians with a vision of "the two great Slavic nations" that "are ready for . . . cooperation, the results of which could be felt by every Ukrainian and Russian family as soon as possible and in the most graphic manner," but dismiss the idea of a union of East Slavic states for being allegedly "too close to ethnic superiority" and "nothing more than a political trick, an abstract theoretical construct which has no real basis or historical prospects."[58] Manipulating a symbolic boundary between Ukraine and its neighbors by making it more or less passable and transparent depending on political circumstances and economic needs of the moment becomes an important mission in its own right, something of a necessary precondition for Ukraine's eventual "return to Europe."

THE ELITE'S EUROPEAN DILEMMA

Available data show that the question "Europe or Russia?" does not exists in Ukrainian mass consciousness, which unequivocally favors closer integration with Russia conditioned on the preservation of Ukraine's state sovereignty (Tables 11.1 and 11.7). In practical political terms, it means an orientation toward some sort of confederation, strengthening of the CIS, joining the Russia–Belarus Union, or even

Table 11.7
Public Opinion on the Preferred State of Ukrainian–Russian Relations, 1998

What kind of relationship between Ukraine and Russia would you prefer ?	Ethnicity									TOTAL		
	Ukrainian			Russian			Other					
	%	N	%	%	N	%	%	N	%	%	N	%
As with any other foreign state	92	286	13	5	14	2	3	9	6	100	309	11
Independent states with open borders	77	1,210	56	18	281	47	5	78	51	100	1,569	54
Unite in one state	62	564	26	32	296	49	6	55	36	100	915	31
Don't know	86	89	4	7	7	1	7	7	5	100	103	3
No answer	77	18	1	9	2	1	14	3	2	100	24	1
TOTAL	74	2,167	100	21	600	100	5	153	100	100	2,920	100

Source: Kyiv International Institute of Sociology, data set POL-14, 1997–1998, courtesy of Dr. Valeri Khmelko.

uniting into a single state as its coequal founders. This is the substance of one of the two dominant political orientations in Ukraine, which local researchers prefer to label, in my view rather unconvincingly, the "Soviet (Donbasite)."[59] Its opposite, the Ukrainian ethnonationalist orientation (dubbed "Ukrainian/Galician" in the same study), is not so much pro-European or pro-capitalist as it is anti-Russian, supportive of the state promotion of Ukrainian language and culture and oppressive toward the continuing use of Russian in the country.[60] Interestingly enough, in a twelve-nation survey of new European democracies, Ukraine scored the lowest on the degree of European self-identification of its citizens (14 percent), even lower than Belarus (18 percent).[61]

However, Ukraine's elite have firmly chosen to pursue the course of European integration, which, in Kyiv's view, promises both security and maybe prosperity for the country. A Russian orientation in Ukraine's foreign policy became fully associated with the parties of opposition, first and foremost, the Communist Party of Ukraine, which also follows an antireform domestic agenda. Interestingly enough, pro-Russian liberal reformists (Social–Liberal Union) and the more outspoken defenders of reintegration (Soyuz) badly lost the March 1998 parliamentary elections, having been unable to clear the 4-percent barrier established as a representation threshold for the party lists. Both the election and the results of several polls demonstrated a diminishing relevance for the politicization of purely ethnocultural slogans to please either Russian or Ukrainian nationalist constituencies. As the popular idea of rapprochement with Russia failed to translate into the electoral support of several smaller groups whose main concern was with the fate of Russian language and culture in Ukraine, it may be fair to conclude that its principal movers were socioeconomic rather than cultural in nature.

Meanwhile, the establishment chose to believe that the principal political and economic questions may be resolved by Ukraine's full integration into European and trans-Atlantic structures. Because of this, it firmly opposes Ukraine's full membership in the CIS economic institutions, which, in the official view, "can only lead to its political and economic estrangement from Central and Western European countries."[62] The pro-Western course of the country becomes coupled to an anti-Russian position in foreign policy that is further supported by a determined "de-Russification" of the predominantly Russophone and Russian-cultured population at home. Enthusiastic embrace of collaboration with NATO and the EU becomes an important sign of the country's Western mentality, which is symbolically "sold" back to the West for a number of material benefits, financial subsidies, aid packages, and loans. On the other hand, the pro-NATO course of Ukraine serves as a dire warning to Russia: Should Moscow fall short of Ukraine's expectations of "mutually beneficial" policy, Kyiv has a well-prepared ground to land on on the opposite side of the border.

Taking into consideration that certain moves and declarations by Russian politicians from 1991 to 1996 could only be read as, at the minimum, interference in Ukraine's internal affairs and, at the maximum, territorial demands and threats of intervention, the pro-Western position of Ukrainian authorities must be seen as dictated first and foremost by understandable security concerns.[63] It was an acute sense of insecurity that prompted Ukraine to call on formal international guarantees of its territorial integrity, which were initially given in the Trilateral Agreement of January 14, 1994, and then reconfirmed in the Budapest Declaration of December 5, 1994. Ukraine's rapprochement with NATO and the attempts to move closer to the EU and WEU can arguably be seen as stemming from the same line of reasoning. Ukraine's numerous vulnerabilities vis-à-vis Russia, only heightened after its nuclear weapons were surrendered to the latter by midsummer 1996, had naturally prompted the country "to use the power of the international community to reduce these vulnerabilities."[64]

However, the decision to turn to the West has also been inspired by considerations of identity, which realist international relations theory is less prepared to take into account or fully explain. An idea that Ukraine properly belongs to Europe, in contrast to the "Eurasian" Russia, has long-standing support from Ukrainian nationalist elites, who, in turn, borrowed it from the nineteenth-century German and Polish proponents of racial exclusivity. One of those, a Pole named Franciszek Duchiski, went to great lengths to underscore the "Asianness" of Russians in contrast to the "Aryanness" of the Ukrainians: "The Muscovites are neither Slavs nor Christians in the spirit of the [true] Slavs and other Indo-European Christians. They are nomads until this day, and will remain nomads forever."[65]

A discursive expulsion of Russia, cast off beyond the realm of European civilization, has found its admirers among Ukrainian intellectuals of nationalist persuasion, who relied upon it to affirm Ukraine's European identity as fully opposite to its Russian counterpart. Recently these ideas staged a not totally unexpected comeback, influencing political and cultural perceptions of certain small right-wing nationalist groups in Ukraine, such as the State Independence of Ukraine (DSU), whose political program and statute are based on the principle of racial exclusivity. Ukrainian nationalist scholars, though not going as far as to deny Slavic roots to Russians, concurred in arguing Ukraine's primordial uniqueness and its early separation from other Eastern Slavic tribes. An idea that ethnic differences between future Russians,

Ukrainians, and Belarusians can be traced back to the times of Scythians and Sarmatians has been recently reintroduced into the Ukrainian academic debate.[66]

Presenting Ukrainian identity as wholly separate from and hardly influenced by the identity of the Russian "other" solves more than purely security tasks of in-group–out-group separation. Ukrainian state- and nation-building traditions, postulated as democratic antipodes to their Russian counterparts, are brought in line with the all-European historical movement toward liberalism and democracy. Russia, on the other hand, remains rhetorically excluded from this movement. From freedom-loving aristocrats and merchant oligarchs of the Galicia–Volhyn' principality to the egalitarian Cossacks fighting social and national oppression to fledgling national democracies of this century, the mythology of Ukraine's uniquely distinct political and cultural tradition never fails to set it apart from an inescapably despotic and imperialist Russia.

Political myths present the state with an identity profile it cannot afford to decline. A newly forged identity feeds back to structure policies that may seem irrational to traditional theories of international politics. However, the focus on political and cultural symbolism helps to understand them better. Thus, economic cooperation with Russia, potentially beneficial for Ukraine, was undermined by the fear that increased cooperation would jeopardize national sovereignty, compromising it with the former metropole. Cooperation on the issue of nuclear nonproliferation was achieved only thanks to U.S. interference, and only after international guarantees of Ukrainian sovereignty were offered. However symbolic, these guarantees were an important substitute for the new state's inability to sit at the negotiating table of nuclear superpowers.[67] From this point of view, "Ukrainian disarmament was more a question of identity than of military security, where the material issue—nuclear weapons—took a back seat to the symbolic one—sovereignty."[68] Ukraine's national pride was further boosted when the country joined NATO's Partnership for Peace Program and the Council of Europe, in both cases ahead of Russia and in symbolic defiance of Russia's futile efforts at reintegration.

These moves were lauded by Ukrainian Westernizers as indication of the country's final return to the path of development befitting a "normal" European state. Group interests of the political and cultural elites alike converged on the idea of European orientation as Ukraine's best safety valve against potential Russian incursions. Both groups have "come to support . . . the link between their prosperity as an elite" and the state's capacity to defend them "against Russian culture and capital."[69] In addition, the turn away from Moscow, though based on a debatable juxtaposition of "European" Ukraine and "non-European"

Russia, promised not only symbolic but also quite tangible gains from international developmental assistance. Identity symbolism turned out to be a major foreign policy resource and a key instrument for procuring other resources.

An early answer to the completely erroneous dilemma "Europe or Russia" was to declare Ukraine's neutrality and nonaligned status. As a Ukrainian analyst noted, neutrality and nonbloc status of the country "have been from the very beginning addressed not to NATO, but to Russia, taking into account the fact that, as a legal heir to the USSR, it was not going to give up its military–political advances on Ukraine."[70] Declarations of neutrality helped to stave off the plans to draw Ukraine into the CIS Collective Security Treaty, which the Ukrainian government perceived as circumscribing national sovereignty and tying Ukraine to a potentially anti-European alliance. Next came the stage of Ukraine's more active interest in NATO, and the officially sought nonaligned status was put on a back burner.

Whether Ukraine is interested in NATO as NATO or as a gateway to the European Union, and what the exact mix is of these two desires, remains an open question, however. Ukraine's attitude toward the West has fluctuated between naïve adoration of all things Western (the early years of perestroika) and almost unanimous outcry and denial (NATO's bombing campaign in Yugoslavia). George Bush's remarks on the dangers of "suicidal nationalism," made in Kyiv shortly before the collapse of the Soviet Union, poured a cold shower over the heads of enthusiasts. The relations with NATO were strained over Ukraine's backtracking on its earlier proclaimed commitment to denuclearize, which prompted a Russia–U.S. marriage of convenience in forcing Kyiv's final ascension to the NPT treaty.[71] In 1992–1994, Moscow became a choice of necessity for most Western countries, most notably for the United States and Germany, while Ukraine was pushed into a corner. "The West and, particularly, the United States belatedly recognized the geopolitical significance of . . . a sovereign Ukraine," lamented Zbigniew Brzezinski.[72] The situation changed in the mid-1990s, following Ukraine's denuclearization and the withdrawal of Russian troops from the GDR.

The emergence of the "red–brown" coalition in the State Duma and the war on Chechnya gave substance to the criticism of "premature partnership" with Russia. Western policy makers started paying significantly more attention to Ukraine, now perceived as Western *antemurale* and hence, a "linchpin" of European stability.[73] Underlying this change of mood has been "the desire of some . . . to turn Ukraine into a buffer state against a feared (or presumed) resurgence of Russian imperialism," the desire, often coupled with encouragement of anti-Russian nationalism, as a motor of Ukraine's speedier transformation into a desired *cordon sanitaire*.[74] The country, heretofore perceived as a consumer of international security, appeared in a position of security peddler. Since international finance could cover economic mismanagement, corrupt officials and businesspeople found themselves united with reform opponents in the government to jointly support Ukraine's geopolitical position. "If the Congress convinces Mr. Clinton of the futility to stake all bets on Yeltsin's dying regime and pushes through with redistribution of financial aid in Ukraine's favor, our prospects will be even better," went one of the typical accounts. "Ukraine has all the chances to transform itself from the world's Cinderella into a quite respectable lady."[75]

There is no doubt that, as an identity model and benchmark of development, Europe leaves Russia behind. The politics of transition must be oriented by visions of the future, which in Ukraine's case is being part of a united Europe. Both identity and security considerations moved Ukraine to join the NATO's Partnership for Peace Program before Russia or other CIS states. The country applied and was accepted into the Council of Europe while Russia was still struggling to be admitted. Following Leonid Kuchma's meeting with NATO's secretary general on June 1, 1995, Ukraine became a decisive supporter of NATO's Eastern enlargement. A member of the Ukrainian delegation to the Council of Europe linked the idea of Ukraine as Western *antemurale* to NATO's enlargement policy, insisting that, "NATO must not let Russia determine [its] policy. Membership in the Organization must be decided by NATO members, not by Russia . . . Ukraine's status . . . is strategically important for Europe and the whole West from the viewpoint of Ukraine's opposition to the growing expansionism of Russia."[76]

Soon, Foreign Minister Udovenko participated in the first "16 + 1" meeting with the North Atlantic Council. The following year, Ukraine signed an implementation paper spelling out relations with NATO in PfP and other areas, and held the first "16 + 1" consultation at the Political Committee level. By 1997, Ukraine had established its permanent mission to NATO, and by 1998 a NATO liaison officer had been posted to Kyiv to facilitate military cooperation. In March 2000, *Verkhovna Rada* approved the Partnership for Peace Status of Forces Agreement (SOFA), which regularized issues related to the presence of NATO forces on Ukrainian soil. During the same month, Ukraine hosted the first meeting of the NATO–Ukraine Commission in Kyiv, an event that NATO's secretary general Lord Robertson described as "a significant step for bringing Ukraine closer to the Euro–Atlantic community of nations."[77]

By participating in the PfP, the Council of Europe, and the Euro–Atlantic Partnership Council, Ukraine reclaims itself as a sovereign

European power, a would-be candidate for NATO membership. An early indication of such a desire was Kuchma's enigmatic remark that "we do not strive to join NATO because as of today we are not yet expected to be there."[78] A number of prominent politicians insisted that Ukraine's nonaligned status must not be seen as its eternal destiny. Borys Tarasyuk, then minister of foreign affairs, pledged to "do everything possible to help integrate Ukraine into European and European–Atlantic structures and strengthen the country's independence by means of foreign policy."[79] Then secretary of the National Security and Defense Council Volodymyr Horbulin contended that Ukraine had all rights to pursue NATO membership in the future.[80] Kyiv has sought to "institutionalize" its relationships with the Western European Union, and looked for an associate membership with the alliance. A powerful symbolism of membership in European structures, in addition to political and economic reasoning, has made Ukraine's Western choice into an official policy, not to be debated by those who carry it out. Even with an understanding that the success story of Central European entrants can hardly be repeated, the fast-track prospects of the EU (and possibly NATO) membership for Estonia still captivate the elite's political imagination.

Recently Ukraine stepped up its participation in PfP programs, in particular joint military exercises. The State Program for Cooperation with NATO envisions "development of interoperability of the command structure, detachments and units of the Armed Forces of Ukraine and NATO's Integrated Military Forces in order to ensure their preparedness for collaborative efforts at realization of common goals" (article 4.2). Proven interoperability between Ukrainian and NATO troops, apart from solving military and technical problems, sends an important signal to Moscow and reaffirms Ukraine's Western orientation. Domestic analysts believe that cooperation with NATO goes beyond conventionally understood security to further political–economic transition of the country "toward a western model of development, regardless of Ukraine's joining the Alliance." If the European choice is to be taken seriously, it helps to show, they argue, that Ukraine "is not an observer of European events, but an active participant in the construction of a European security structure."[81] Hence, the SOFA agreement has designated a major military base in Yavoriv to host military maneuvers of NATO member states, with or without Ukraine's participation. Kyiv invites NATO to use the Ukrainian sector of the Black Sea for joint naval exercises, some of which, as Sea Breeze–97 demonstrated, suggest in no uncertain terms that Ukraine is prepared to ask for Western assistance in fighting ethnic separatism and civil unrest in the heavily Russian-populated southern areas of the country. Other collaborative efforts include joint training of the Polish–Ukrainian battalion formed under NATO auspices in 1997, and participation in the KFOR forces in Kosovo.

The prospect of Ukraine joining NATO is horrifying for Moscow. Russian policy makers believe that such a move would be counterproductive for all sides: Ukraine, Russia, and NATO. Ukraine especially runs the risk of internal destabilization and nurturing that very enemy that must have been neutralized in the first place. In Richard Solomon's commentary,

Ukraine's acceptance of a Western policy of actively pulling Ukraine into NATO would surely sharpen the appearance of an anti-Russian ideology on the part of the Ukrainian government, thereby severely threatening relations not only between Russia and Ukraine, but also between Russians and Ukrainians in Ukraine. . . . If Ukraine's value to transatlantic security lies in the country's continued internal stability, such an assertive policy of NATO enlargement in this direction would lead to exactly the kind of result the West wishes most to avoid.[82]

Moscow would regard Ukraine's joining NATO without Russia as a hostile action by the alliance. Ukraine's admittance to NATO would automatically spell the end of Russian military presence in the Crimea and western part of the Black Sea, thus crushing Russian naval potential in the area. The Black Sea Fleet would have to be relocated to a less than adequate base in Novorossiisk, where, after losing its capacity for blue-water operations, it would be confined to local patrol duties. A nontransparent state boundary would effectively terminate cross-border cooperation between the adjacent Russian and Ukrainian *oblasti*. Moscow is also afraid that Russians in Ukraine would be subjected to a forceful acculturation into the model Ukrainian identity, while Russia itself would fall prey to a demonization campaign in the media.

Any Russian politician would attempt to block these developments. Vladimir Putin is keen at making connections between Ukraine's European policy and Russian energy supply, the connections that may become painful for Ukraine. Ukraine's Western orientation and assertive policies of distancing from Russia are seen as something opposite to the proclaimed "strategic partnership." Moscow may be tempted to retaliate by calling in Ukraine's debts, erecting protective walls in trade, or obstructing the delimitation of the state border. Since NATO's bombing of Yugoslavia, which Kyiv failed to protest, Russia no longer perceives Ukraine as an ally. As head of the Security Council Sergei Ivanov recently opined, "One can't enjoy Russian freebies, pinching our oil and natural gas, and simultaneously head for a Greater Romania, for NATO or elsewhere."[83] Russian plans to build a gas pipeline to Europe circumventing Ukrainian territory must be read as not only economic, but also a political warning to Kyiv.[84] If Ukraine ever applies for NATO membership, it may expect a much harsher reaction from the Kremlin.

The fear of Russian retaliation narrows the space of foreign policy maneuver available to Ukraine and creates a dilemma: moving closer to the West and risk losing Russian patronage in the strategic area of energy supplies, or accepting Russia's lead in foreign policy at the cost of alienating Ukraine's hardly won Western friends, the United States first and foremost. It is a hard choice for the foreign policy community, almost evenly split between those who advocate Ukraine's speedier integration into NATO and those who back the nonaligned, neutral status of the country, with the remaining 7 to 10 percent supporting some type of Eastern orientation.[85] Though the Ukrainian public at large prefers cooperating with Russia (Table 11.1), no less than one-third of it also believes that collaboration with NATO serves Ukraine's national interest, and still more are ready to consent to the Western course out of "necessity" (Table 11.2). Because of these conflicting orientations, Ukraine lacks a strategic vision of foreign policy and remains stuck between its Western drives and Eastern pressures.

WHAT NEXT?

Ukrainian national identity is as yet undefined, and the political elite must accept a large share of responsibility for that. If leaders could develop and implement a consistent set of policies both domestically and internationally, the nation might obtain a chance to come to terms with its new identity; that is, that vision of identity that is sustained by policy. The preceding analysis has shown that the Ukrainian elite remains divided on the most crucial issue of foreign orientations. While officially supporting the country's Westerly move, Ukraine did little to overcome its multifaceted dependence on Russia, particularly in energy and trade. As actions speak louder that words, one may be forced to conclude that (1) either Ukraine's Western orientation is insincere or (2) Ukraine's Russian ties are more significant than the government has been willing to admit. The analysis of public opinion apparently confirms the second proposition. The glaring discrepancy between the elite's Western choice and mass Russian sympathies may suggest, to a democratic state anyway, the necessity to bring the two conflicting orientations in harmony. The future of Ukrainian foreign policy will be to a major extent determined by the way this task is solved.

One way to eliminate the contradiction would be to make Ukraine's Russia supporters radically change their opinion of Ukrainian–Russian cooperation and Russia in particular by redefining it as alien and a potentially hostile "other." The government must obviously take the lead in the process through some form of a sustained public relations campaign, combined with a policy of a further squeezing out of Russian culture, shrinking the sphere of the effective functioning of the Russian language, and encouraging ethnocultural assimilation of Russia-leaning minorities. There are indications that this option has not been ruled out. As Ukrainian security analysts argue, "A clear definition and consolidation in the public consciousness of basic geopolitical priorities and national interests is one of the most important preconditions for the development of an effective external and internal political strategy for the future."[86] An idea that the government may lay claim to a superior knowledge and understanding of the national interest and, therefore, is obliged to instill the right view of "geopolitical priorities" in people's minds reveals a certain disdain of the masses and does not fit well with the concept of democratic governance.

An alternative, making Ukraine's Eastern orientation compatible with a European choice of development, is a task of cyclopean magnitude that Kyiv may not be able to solve on its own. First, the key to this solution lies in Russia moving sufficiently close to Europe to preserve the momentum that has been already achieved in Ukraine. Until Moscow stops human rights abuse at home, brings a lasting peace to Chechnya, achieves a certain level of accountability in the government, transforms the CIS into a genuine community of equals, and, last but not least, starts working toward "rejoining Europe" the way Ukraine does, Kyiv will remain wary of its eastern neighbor, and has all rights to be. Second, the Russian orientation in Ukraine has been all but monopolized by demonstrably anti-Western parties. Because of a disparity between elite and mass preferences in foreign policy and the predominant association of the eastern "vector" with antireform forces represented by the Communist Party, there are fears that drawing closer to Russia can undermine the elite's precarious support of transition to market democracy. Critics of reintegration with Russia argue that it will lead to the establishment of a Lukashenka-style regime and abandonment of the country's European choice. Electoral weakness of the pro-Russian parties of reformist orientation (Constitutional–Democratic, Interregional Bloc of Reforms, Civic Congress, Social–Liberal Union) does not help in bringing more optimism to counter this dire prediction, and neither does Lukashenka's record of governance.

However, those who attribute Belarusian problems fully to its chosen course of reintegration with Russia give the latter too much credit. Economic feasibility of the merger involving essentially an unreformed Belarus and oligarchic–capitalist Russia gives Moscow as much if not more headache as it does to those who question the project from afar. The effects of the proposed integration on economic structures and policies of the participant states are as yet unclear. It is as plausible to argue that drawing closer to Russia will push Belarus along the path of reforms as it is to deny such a possibility. In post-Soviet contexts, institutions matter less than policies, and there is no direct cause-and-effect relationship between the two. Hence, it is possible to be a CIS member and work toward its demise (Ukraine) or to join a union principally to sustain a regime's isolationist policies (Belarus). Ukraine's coming aboard the Russia–Belarus Union will probably not happen anytime soon. Nevertheless, were it to happen, it would be naïve to decry reintegration as such: What counts are solely policy changes that it might (or might not) bring about. Whether strategic partnership with Russia will be used to promote reforms at home or to avoid them for as long as possible is determined by domestically made choices; the logic and the structural constraints of the alliance itself are very much neutral in this regard.

Ukraine's Russian choice is vital for its prospects of rejoining Europe. First, ethnic nationalism that ostracizes the Russian presence in Ukraine leads the country away from the ideal of a modern multicultural and ethnically tolerant society; that is, away from Europe, not closer to it. Finding a stable modus vivendi for Ukrainian–Russian relations both domestically and internationally is therefore crucially important for Ukraine's admittance to the European community. Second, the EU will expect Ukraine to come politically and economically prepared. Unless a sudden and not currently expected inflow of Western investments arrives in the country, which has been an investment outcast in comparison to its East Central European neighbors, Ukraine's only hope of economic recovery lies in a dramatic expansion of cash-paid exports to Russia and the restoration of the production chains that used to run eastward. Finally, the West cannot afford to alienate Russia by admitting Ukraine as a member to NATO or the EU while keeping Russia out. Ukraine's best hope in this regard is to operate as a mediator between NATO and Russia in anticipation of those times, not utterly improbable, when the two countries will grow ready to join European institutions together. Russia's own interest in such an outcome has been registered in Vladimir Putin's comments on the desirability of eventual NATO membership for the country and in suggestions of strategic partnership with the EU ranging from the "pan-European, non-strategic antimissile defense system" to energy supplies.[87]

Ukraine's understanding of Russia's importance influences its regional see-saw strategy of drawing closer–backing away from Russia still deemed too imposing and potentially menacing for Ukrainians to engage it productively. This understanding has not yet been brought to bear in a constructive way on the Ukrainian idea of returning to Europe, which is erroneously presented as something of necessity opposite to a Ukrainian–Russian rapprochement. Meanwhile, Ukraine's very national identity is tied with that of Russia's in a complex relationship of complimentarity, liminality, mutual reflection, and constitutive counterposition. Mutual economic dependence, ethnocultural intermingling, structurally similar problems and levels of development, and the generally positive historical perceptions of each other all make Ukraine, as influential domestic observers choose to put it, "simply doomed to a strategic partnership with Russia," while remaining no more than "'small change' in a big east–west geopolitical game."[88]

Why, then, is the Russian orientation presumed to be tangential, if not directly opposite, to the European course of the country? Can the two be combined in a harmonious way? It is my contention that they can and they should. Objective determinants of foreign policy are conducive to such a development, as are positional and structural factors enumerated by the realist school of international relations. What lacks are those, in Alexander Wendt's words, "intersubjective systemic structures" that would be built around shared understanding of the underlying unity of interests between Ukraine, Russia, and the West, their shared desire to develop a collective identity where divisive lines of the past would no longer dictate politics or perceptions.[89] Creation of a national identity that would not seek to constitute itself in opposition to an alien "other" is the first and absolutely necessary step in that direction, and it is for the Ukrainian elites to make such a step.

NOTES

1. The point frequently made by members of Ukraine's educated classes, personal interviews, 1992 and 1993–1994.
2. T. Kuzio, "The Domestic Sources of Ukrainian Security Policy," *Journal of Strategic Studies* 21, no. 4 (1998): 34.
3. Mykola Kostomarov, *Dve russkie narodnosti* (Kyiv: Maidan, 1991).
4. I discuss behavioral patterns of Ukraine's distinct political culture in M. A. Molchanov, "Political Culture and Nationality in Russian–Ukrainian Relations" (Ph.D. diss., University of Alberta, 1998), ch. 5.
5. Jerome Blum, *Lord and Peasant in Russia from the Ninth to the Nineteenth Century* (New York: Atheneum, 1968), 522–523.
6. Robert V. Daniels, *Russia: The Roots of Confrontation* (Cambridge: Harvard University Press, 1985), 169.
7. V. I. Shinkaruk, et al., *Sotsialisticheskii obraz zhizni i vsestoronnee razvitie lichnosti* (Kyiv: Naukova dumka, 1979); V. V. Kosolapov, et al., *Sotsialisticheskii obraz zhizni i problemy vospitaniia lichnosti* (Kyiv: Vyshcha shkola, 1979).
8. See more on Rukh in T. Kuzio, *Ukraine: Perestroika to Independence* (2d ed.) (London: Macmilan, 2000); and Andrew Wilson, *Ukrainian Nationalism in the 1990s: A Minority Faith* (Cambridge: Cambridge University Press, 1997).
9. Cf. Ievhen Malaniuk, *Malorosiistvo* (New York: Visnyk OOChSU, 1959).
10. Victor Stepanenko and Sergei Sorokopud, "The Construction of National Identity: A Case Study of the Ukraine," in *Ethnicity and Nationalism in Russia,*

the CIS and the Baltic States, ed. Christopher Williams and Thanasis D. Sfikas (Aldershot: Ashgate, 1999), 194.

11. Stephen Rapawy, *Ethnic Reidentification in Ukraine* (Washington, D.C.: International Programs Center, U.S. Bureau of the Census, 1997).

12. Ian Bremmer and Aleksandr Grushevskii, *Russkie v ukrainskom gosudarstve: konflikt ili integratsiia* (Moscow: Fond "Obshchestvennoe mnenie," 1993), 8.

13. Yuri I. Shevchuk, "Citizenship in Ukraine: A Western Perspective," in *State and Nation Building in East Central Europe: Contemporary Perspectives,* ed. John S. Micgiel (New York: Institute on East Central Europe, Columbia University Press, 1996), 354–357.

14. Anne Norton, *Reflections on Political Identity* (Baltimore: Johns Hopkins University Press, 1988), 48.

15. Stephen Shulman, "The Cultural Foundations of Ukrainian National Identity," *Ethnic and Racial Studies* 22, no. 6 (1999): 1013.

16. Norton, *Reflections on Political Identity,* 54.

17. See more on the Ukrainian regional divide in Wilson, *Ukrainian Nationalism in the 1990s;* Valeri Khmel'ko and Andrew Wilson, "The Political Orientations of Different Regions and Ethno–Linguistic Groups in Ukraine since Independence," in *Contemporary Ukraine: Dynamics of Post-Soviet Transformation,* ed. T. Kuzio (Armonk, N.Y.: M. E. Sharpe, 1998), 60–80; William Zimmerman, "Is Ukraine a Political Community?" *Communist and Post-Communist Studies* 31, no. 1 (1998): 43–55; and Sarah Birch, "Interpreting the Regional Effect in Ukrainian Politics," *Europe–Asia Studies* 52, no. 6 (2000): 1017–1041.

18. A recent study showed this part of the country to be less liberal in popular orientations than the "red belt" of eastern Ukraine. Contrary to a widespread illusion, spatial closeness to Europe of the formerly Hapsburg and Polish western Ukrainian lands has not been translated into a cultural affinity. See William L. Miller, Stephen White, and Paul Heywood, *Values and Political Change in Postcommunist Europe* (New York: St. Martin's Press, 1998), 155.

19. Dominique Arel, "Ukraine: The Temptation of the Nationalizing State," in *Political Culture and Civil Society in Russia and the New States of Eurasia,* ed. Vladimir Tismaneanu (Armonk, N.Y.: M. E. Sharpe, 1995), 157–186; David D. Laitin, *Identity in Formation: The Russian-Speaking Populations in the Near Abroad* (Ithaca, N.Y.: Cornell University Press, 1998), 99–102, 179–180.

20. T. Kuzio, "National Identity in Independent Ukraine: An Identity in Transition," *Nationalism and Ethnic Politics* 2, no. 4 (1996): 604.

21. Cf. T. Kuzio, *Ukraine: State and Nation Building* (London: Routledge, 1998).

22. See *Holos Ukraiiny,* 13 November 1991, and the updated version in *Vidomosti Verkhovnoii Rady* 23 (1997): art. 169.

23. *Vidomosti Verkhovnoii Rady* 36 (1992): art. 529.

24. *Vidomosti Verkhovnoii Rady* 45 (1989): art. 631.

25. V. Khmelko, et al., *Predvybornye nastroeniia v Ukraine,* sociological survey, November–December 1997 (Kyiv: KTsPIK and KIIS, 1997).

26. Roman Szporluk, "Russians in Ukraine and Problems of Ukrainian Identity in the USSR," in *Ukraine in the Seventies,* ed. Peter J. Potichnyj (Oakville, Ont.: Mosaic Press, 1975), 196.

27. Agreement on the Creation of the Commonwealth of Independent States, Minsk, 8 December 1991, arts. 4–7. In Lubomyr A. Hajda, ed., *Ukraine in the*

World: Studies in the International Relations and Security Structure of a Newly Independent State (Cambridge: Harvard University Press, 1998), 298–299.

28. See more on this in Sherman W. Garnett, *Keystone in the Arch: Ukraine in the Emerging Security Environment of Central and Eastern Europe* (Washington, D.C.: Carnegie Endowment, 1997); and Paul J. D'Anieri, *Economic Interdependence in Ukrainian–Russian Relations* (Albany: State University of New York Press, 1999), 69–96.

29. *Holos Ukraiiny*, 21 July 1994.

30. Dmytro Vydrin and Dmytro Tabachnyk, *Ukraina na porozi XXI stolittia: politychnyi aspekt* (Kyiv: Lybid', 1995); Volodymyr Hryniov, *Nova Ukraina: Iakoiu Ia Iï Bachu* (Kyiv: Abrys, 1995); Vladimir Malinkovich, "Soiuz chetyryokh plius . . . Rossiia, Ukraina, Belorussiia, Kazakhstan v summe mogut dat' nechto novoe," *Literaturnaia gazeta*, 20 March 1996.

31. *Novyi shliakh*, 14 October 1995.

32. *Kyivskie novosti*, 19 May 1995.

33. *Uriadovyi kurier*, 4 April 1996.

34. *Uriadovyi kurier*, 25 April 1996.

35. Oleksandr Belov, ed., *Ukraine 2000 and Beyond: Geopolitical Priorities and Scenarios of Development* (Kyiv: NIIS, 1999), 22.

36. *Reuters*, 8 May 1999; *Washington Post*, 8 December 1999.

37. Cf. Anders Åslund, "Eurasia e Turnaround," *Foreign Policy* 100 (1995): 127, 139.

38. Gregory V. Krasnov and Josef C. Brada, "Implicit Subsidies in Russian–Ukrainian Energy Trade," *Europe–Asia Studies* 49, no. 5 (1997): 837.

39. Sergei Fomin, *Ekonomicheskie otnosheniia Ukrainy so stranami SNG i stranami Evropy*, Occasional Papers on Changes in the Slavic–Eurasian World, no. 38 (Sapporo: Hokkaido University, Slavic Research Center, 1997), 62.

40. *Den*, 20 July 2000; *Kyiv Post*, 28 July 2000. According to Ukraine's Deputy Prime Minister Yulia Tymoshenko, the debt could be as high as $2.8 billion. *Reuters*, 12 January 2000.

41. *The Economist*, 6 May 2000; World Bank Country Data, *Ukraine at a Glance*, 12 September 2000, at http://www.worldbank.org/data/countrydata/aag/ukr_aag.pdf.

42. Fomin, *Ekonomicheskie otnosheniia Ukrainy so stranami SNG i stranami Evropy*.

43. *RFE/RL Weekday Digest*, 24 July 2000; *Problemy neftegazovogo kompleksa Ukrainy (neft')* (Kyiv: SIAZ, 2000); Energy Information Administration, *Country Analysis Briefs* (http://www.eia.doe.gov/cabs/ukraine.html); Bohdan Klid, "Caspian Sea Oil and Ukraine's Quest for Energy Autonomy," *Geopolitics of Energy* 20, no. 10 (1998): 6–12.

44. *Holos Ukraiiny*, 22 December 1998.

45. Ukraine became a full-fledged member of the Inter-Parliamentary Assembly of the Commonwealth of Independent States on March 3, 1999. The Rukh faction in parliament interpreted the accession, supported by 230 votes out of 450 total deputies (with 226 needed), as "a farce of selling out of Ukraine," and tried to contest the resolution in the Constitutional Court. *The Day*, 6 March 1999; *Vechirnii Kyiv*, 4 March 1999. I discuss Ukrainian–Russian interdependence in more detail in Mikhail A. Molchanov, "Russia's Policy Towards

Ukraine," in *Towards a New Ukraine III: Geopolitical Imperatives of Ukraine: Regional Contexts*, ed. Theofil Kis (Ottawa: University of Ottawa, Chair of Ukrainian Studies, forthcoming).

46. Cf. a typical elite lamentation of the state of Ukraine's public consciousness, which, it is alleged, begs "a clear definition and consolidation . . . of basic geopolitical priorities and national interests." Belov, *Ukraine 2000 and Beyond*, 16.

47. *Politychnyi portret Ukrainy* 21 (1998); the Institute of Social and Political Psychology of the Academy of Pedagogical Sciences of Ukraine, representative national survey (N = 2013), February 1998.

48. Kyiv International Institute of Sociology, national surveys, October 1998, March 2000. The data files were kindly shared by Dr. Valeri Khmelko, Kyiv International Institute of Sociology.

49. *Politychnyi portret Ukrainy* 20 (1998): 39; E. I. Golovakha and N. V. Panina, "Dvuiazychie v Ukraine: real'noe sostoianie i perspektivy (rezul'taty sotsiologicheskih issledovanii)," *Rossiisko–ukrainskii biulleten'* 6–7 (2000): 142–147. A poll, reported by the closely affiliated with the government *Vlast i politika* on April 25, 2000, gave 39 percent of support to the official status of Russian language in Ukraine, plus 38 percent in favor of its official recognition on the regional–local basis in mostly Russophone regions. *Ukrains'ka pravda*, 30 May 2000.

50. For further discussion of Ukraine's security concerns regarding Russia and its dominant position within the CIS, see Mikhail A. Molchanov, "Ukraine between Russia and NATO: Politics and Security," *Ukrainian Review* 45, no. 3 (1998): 3–16, *Bilateralism and Security in Russian–Ukrainian Relations*, UNU/IAS Working Paper, no. 37 (Tokyo: United Nations University, Institute of Advanced Studies, 1998).

51. Kuzio, *Ukraine: State and Nation Building*, 118; Belov, *Ukraine 2000 and Beyond*, 162. At the same time, 27 percent of the elite respondents saw Russia as Ukraine's "main ally." Ukraine's Russian question aside, the split is illustrative of the level of internal cohesion of the Ukrainian body politic.

52. Excluding Russia, only Romania had territorial claims advanced against the Ukrainian state. The question was solved with the conclusion of the bilateral cooperation treaty on June 2, 1997. A rather weak Rusyn separatism in Transcarpathia serves as another, much less compelling or stable target for politics of identity. State policies of dispersal and cultural assimilation of Ukrainian Poles after World War II go a long way to explain the absence of a mobilized local Polish movement with a potentially state-threatening agenda. Poland was the first country to recognize Ukraine's independence. Though the question of "eastern territories" sporadically reappears in the nationalist press, Warsaw had early on renounced all territorial claims on Ukraine and, in contradiction to Russia, has never allowed any exploitation of the issue in policy debates. All these factors, plus the extent of social and cultural distance between Ukrainians and Poles accumulated over centuries (for western Ukraine, decades) of separate existence, have worked together to alleviate Ukrainian fears of a potential Polish encroachment on the newly created identity terrain.

53. See more on cultural and historical reality behind that feeling in Mikhail A. Molchanov, "Borders of Identity: Ukraine's Political and Cultural Significance to Russia," *Canadian Slavonic Papers* 38, nos. 1–2 (1996): 177–193.

54. Roman Szporluk, ed., *National Identity and Ethnicity in Russia and the New States of Eurasia* (Armonk, N.Y.: M. E. Sharpe), 7.

55. Ilya Prizel, *National Identity and Foreign Policy: Nationalism and Leadership in Poland, Russia and Ukraine* (Cambridge: Cambridge University Press, 1998), 27.

56. For further exposition of a political resource theory of national mobilizations in Eastern Europe, see Mikhail A. Molchanov, "Postcommunist Nationalism as a Power Resource: A Russia–Ukraine Comparison," *Nationalities Papers* 28, no. 2 (2000): 263–288.

57. *Uriadovyi kurier*, 4 April 1996.

58. *Itar-Tass*, 10 November 1999.

59. The share of the population of Donbas (Donets'ka and Luhans'ka oblasti) in the Ukrainian population does not exceed 16 percent, while explicitly pro-Soviet orientations, as measured by self-identification of the people, are retained by no more than one-fifth of Ukrainians (Table 11.3). However, reintegrationist sentiment, in both its Soviet and Russian–Eastern Slavic forms, is harbored, according to the same authors, by almost three-quarters of Ukrainians. Clearly, it is something more general in nature that the local Donbasite Soviet nostalgia or even cross-regional pro-Soviet sentiment, best retained and represented in the Donbas. Characteristically, up to 60 percent of those polled have also been ready to support parties that promote "strengthening of independence of the Ukrainian state" and "revival of the Ukrainian nation." I read these results as witnessing a popular belief in the possibility and desirability of such a rapprochement with Russia that would not erode Ukraine's sovereignty or harm the ongoing process of national consolidation. See M. I. Beletskii and A. K. Tolpygo, "Natsional'no-kul'turnye i ideologicheskie orientatsii naseleniia Ukrainy," *Polis* (Moscow) 4 (1998): 85, 87–89.

60. Ibid., 77–89.

61. Only 7 percent of respondents in Ukraine saw themselves as, first of all, Europeans. Another 7 percent named Europe as a second identity. Belarusians were equally reluctant in their first choices, but chose Europe more often for their secondary identification. Richard Rose and Christian Haerpfer, *New Democracies Barometer V: A 12-Nation Survey* (Glasgow: University of Strathclyde, 1998), 23, 69.

62. Belov, *Ukraine 2000 and Beyond*, 61.

63. Cf. Roman Solchanyk, "Ukraine, Russia, and the CIS," in Hajda, *Ukraine in the World*, 19–43.

64. Jack Snyder, "Nationalism and the Crisis of the Post-Soviet State," in *Ethnic Conflict and International Security*, ed. Michael E. Brown (Princeton, N.J.: Princeton University Press, 1993), 95. Several realist scholars of international relations have made the case for Ukraine to keep its nuclear deterrence option. In Barry Posen's view, "If Ukraine eliminates its nuclear arsenal, as it has pledged to do, it will increasingly come to rely on nationalism to strengthen an army that will only be able to stand against Russia through superior motivation. Eliminating Ukraine's nuclear arsenal will therefore make Russia stronger and Ukraine more nationalistic. This could prove dangerous." Cf. Barry R. Posen, "The Security Dilemma and Ethnic Conflict," in ibid., 118.

65. Cited in Ivan L. Rudnytsky, *Essays in Modern Ukrainian History* (Cambridge: Harvard University Press, 1987), 189.

66. Iaroslav Isaievych, *Ukraina davnia i nova: narod, relihiia, kul'tura* (L'viv: In-t ukrainoznavstva, 1996).

67. Judging by the sheer quantity of nuclear arms inherited by Ukraine after the collapse of the Soviet Union, it could have been considered a nuclear superpower by itself. However, operational control of these weapons continued to reside with Moscow, thus making them largely useless for the purposes of national defense.

68. Paul J. D'Anieri, "Nationalism and International Politics: Identity and Sovereignty in the Russian–Ukrainian Conflict," *Nationalism and Ethnic Politics* 3 no. 2 (1997): 21.

69. Kuzio, *Ukraine: State and Nation Building*, 25–26.

70. G. M. Perepelytsia, *Bez'iadernyi status i natsional'na bezpeka Ukrainy* (Kyiv: NISD, 1998), 7.

71. Cf. Garnett, *Keystone in the Arch*.

72. FBIS-SOV-98-023.

73. Zbigniew Brzezinski, "The Premature Partnership," *Foreign Affairs* 73, no. 2 (1994): 67–82; and John Edwin Mroz and Oleksandr Pavliuk, "Ukraine: Europe's Linchpin," *Foreign Affairs* 75, no. 3 (1996): 55–62.

74. Anatol Lieven, *Ukraine and Russia: A Fraternal Rivalry* (Washington, D.C.: U.S. Institute of Peace Press, 1999), 158.

75. *Rada*, 18 May 1995.

76. Serhii Holovaty, "Kryterii dlia vstupu do ES maie buty iedynyi," *Holos Ukraiiny*, 18 May 1995.

77. NATO Fact Sheets, NATO—Ukraine, http://www.nato.int/docu/facts/2000/nato-ukr.htm.

78. *Prospekt*, 17 August 1995.

79. *RFE/RL Newsline*, 20 April 1998.

80. *Xinhua*, 18 March 1999.

81. Belov, *Ukraine 2000 and Beyond*, 84.

82. See Lieven, *Ukraine and Russia*, x.

83. *Interfax*, 25 April 2000.

84. A publicly stated reason for securing alternative routes for the Russian gas transit to Europe has been its large-scale theft in Ukraine. The European Union has endorsed the project and the prospect of long-term energy collaboration with Russia, grasping at an opportunity "to change the commercial relationship into a long-term strategic partnership." *Interfax*, 17 October 2000; *Washington Post*, 20 October 2000.

85. Belov, *Ukraine 2000 and Beyond*, 147–173.

86. Ibid., 16.

87. Cf. Putin's early remark that Russia would like to seek "more profound integration" with NATO and might even join it if "regarded as an equal partner." *New York Times*, 6 March 2000. On Russia's alternative to the American NMD, see *Itar-Tass*, 2 June 2000 and *Rossiiskaia gazeta*, 12 July 2000.

88. V. K. Vrublevs'kyi and V. I. Khoroshkovs'kyi, *Ukrains'kyi shliakh; Nacherky: geopolitychne stanovyshche Ukrainy ta ii natsional'ni interesy* (Kyiv: Demokratychna Ukraïna, 1997), 363, 397.

89. Alexander Wendt, "Collective Identity Formation and the International State," *American Political Science Review* 88, no. 2 (1994): 389.

12

Conclusion

Mikhail Molchanov

Writing on the eve of the new millennium, Russian Foreign Minister Igor Ivanov went to great lengths to emphasize a "qualitatively new form of close, trusting relations" between Russia and Ukraine.[1] Little more than a month later, the statement of the Russian Foreign Ministry lamented "squeezing out of the Russian language from Ukrainian mass media," and accused Kiev of deliberate "de-Russification of all sides of Ukraine's social life."[2] This sort of development is nothing unusual in relations between the two countries, both faced with structurally similar problems of post-Communist transition and adaptation to the fast-paced international reality against the backdrop of profound change at home.

Ukrainian foreign policy is an attempt to walk a tightrope between the country's Western aspirations and its Eastern Slavic roots and anchors that go much deeper than seventy-something years of Soviet experience. It is also an attempt to reconcile diametrically opposed leanings of the country's historical regions: the anti-Russian, ethnonationally mobilized and Europe-oriented West and the profoundly Russianized, Sovietized, predominantly leftist and often antireform East. In other words, Ukraine's foreign policy is nothing less than an attempt to bridge a civilizational divide and forge a new national identity where many would say there has been none—or more than one. The task may no doubt seem impossible to the skeptics and challenging to even the most optimistic supporters. Small wonder, then, that foreign policy of this newly independent state, hailed as a linchpin of stability in Europe, is also not infrequently criticized for inconsistency and accused of unpredictability.[3]

However, the lack of consistency in the realm of foreign policy is not unique to Ukraine. Apart from Russia's well-known turns and backslides, the American attitude toward Ukraine has had its own swings of mood, ranging from outright ostracism of the first postindependence years to less than fully warranted enthusiasm of the second Clinton administration. The European Union has sent conflicting signals regarding Ukraine's prospective membership, at one point denigrating the idea as an example of wishful thinking similar to an argument for Mexico to join the United States, later backtracking with by now familiar rhetoric of Ukraine as "strategically an important part of Europe," which the EU "can't afford" to leave behind.[4] Should we be surprised, then, that Ukrainian foreign-policy makers often try to adapt by mirroring swings and turns in the world's centers of power? Or that the policy in question frequently appears reactive, rather than proactive, and may trail events rather than shaping them according to the nationally defined agenda?

Though the size of France in territory and population, Ukraine remains a small European country in terms of actual power it can bring to bear upon international politics. Its GDP per capita adjusted for purchasing power parity stood at $2,200 in 1999, below that of Zimbabwe, Mongolia, or Guyana and about one-third of the world's average.[5] With $12.5 billion in external debts, Ukraine has to spend about $2 billion in total debt service annually.[6] It has been estimated that close to 60 percent of Ukraine's gross domestic product is generated in the shadow economy, which exists beyond any fiscal control of the government.[7] This fact accounts for chronic budgetary deficit, wage arrears, and unimpeded capital flight abroad. With its economy less than 40 percent of its former Soviet self, Ukraine at present is hardly capable of entering the unified market of the European Union without sustaining a mortal wound to its still largely unreformed and often obsolete industries.

Ukraine's military capabilities are also limited. After the last of more than 1,600 nuclear warheads left Ukrainian soil in mid-1996, the country's denuclearization was complete—a major victory for advocates of nuclear nonproliferation, but also, ostensibly, a not negligible loss of international status measured in terms of military power. Put under severe strain of reform, underfinanced, disorganized, and understaffed, conventional forces were drastically cut back. If by the end of the Soviet Union Ukraine's armed forces totaled 780,000 military personnel, 6,500 tanks, over 7,000 armored combat vehicles, and nearly 1,500 combat aircraft, they were reduced more than twofold in less than six years.[8] Budgetary constraints and relatively weak political clout of the military dictated the policy. As noted by John Jaworsky, per capita military spending in Ukraine in 1996 stood at $15, compared to $113 in Russia and $674 in France.[9] Ukraine's army, now consisting of approximately 400,000 men (310,000 military and 90,000 civilians), is a pale shadow of itself ten years ago. Its 542 tanks, 2,396 armored vehicles, 429 artillery pieces, 533 combat aircraft, and 249 attack helicopters are within 60 to 75 percent of the CFE-allowed ceilings, and by all indications poised to decline even further.[10]

It would be naïve to expect that Ukraine's foreign policy can be fully independent under the circumstances. Much effort exerted by policy makers to shed the country's traditional dependence on Russia became, in effect, hijacked by a newly found dependence on Western financial regulators, security guarantees, developmental aid, and policy advice. Nevertheless, Ukraine's predicament is not as gloomy as it may seem. The country's strategic geopolitical position between Russia and the West; the sheer size of its population and territory, skilled labor force, and not negligible material resources; retained and newly developed communication infrastructure; unusually high—judging by the GDP benchmark—levels of education and scientific potential all warrant attention of major world players and instill hopes that Ukraine may yet see better times. Where will its sympathies lie then? Will it turn East or West? With the European Union, which has repeatedly snubbed it, with the frequently condescending and potentially neoisolationist United States, with the two-headed Janus of the Russia–Belarus Union, or with some other group of countries? It is this book's contention that, to find the answer, we should rely on a combination of methods provided by international relations theory, instead of just using the insights of area studies, which often fall short of linking domestic and international politics because of excessive preoccupation with the former.

As one of the first attempts to link area studies and international relations theory in a study of Ukraine's foreign policy orientation, this book could not fail to produce a rather wide array of approaches that are not easily reduced to a common denominator. While benefits of a theory-informed deductive strategy of analysis have been reasonably well established, no single school of thought in international relations theory emerged as predominant or particularly well suited for the Ukrainian context. Most authors tend to agree, however, that a billiard-ball presentation of Ukrainian foreign and security policy found in some of the more rigorous variants of structural realism leaves many questions unanswered, as it tends to gloss over important factors of a domestic nature. Domestic politics must be allowed to find a way into any explanatory model of Ukrainian foreign policy. The same is undoubtedly true of the larger international environment, which may not be exhaustively theorized solely on the basis of traditional geopolitical considerations. To gain a better understanding of conflicting factors that shape foreign policy of a newly independent state, we must approach the familiar agent–structure problem through the "unpacking" of its both constituents: the "agent" thus must be presented as a multilayered social and political entity, a juxtaposition of social forces struggling behind the deceitfully monochromous façade of the "state," while the "structure" must be fleshed out through the addition of contextual elements and historical and institutional makeup that can change more than a bit in what "structurally" may appear as an essentially similar positioning of international actors.

This volume's authors accordingly differ in the strategies each of them choose to look at Ukraine's foreign and security policy. While some of them prefer to "unpack" the environment, other take a deeper look at domestic determinants. Thus, Jennifer Moroney seeks to explicate Ukraine's predicament through a prism of globalization theory and frontier studies, which allow her to concentrate on such new features of the international environment in Europe as the changed significance of the boundaries, now defined on the basis of international institutional affiliation (NATO, the EU) or nonaffiliation to the extent that undermines traditional state-centered identities and renders them increasingly subordinate to the idea of an "all-European" project. In contradistinction to that, James Sherr and Stacy Closson in their respective chapters concentrate on such purely "domestic" issue as civil–military relations in Ukraine, arguing that the present state and the ongoing changes in the nature of these relations must be seen as a major internal determinant of Ukraine's security and foreign policy.

Tor Bukkvol is concerned with periodic shifts in foreign policy identification of the Ukrainian elite. He believes that the changes can be best explained by applying state theory insights to the process of foreign policy articulation and development. Two main approaches that he calls upon in this study—the Weberian and the pluralist schools of thought within state theory—broadly coincide with, respectively, realist and liberal traditions of international relations theory. While the first in each pair looks at the state as, in Kantian lexicon, the "thing in itself," a major, if not the only, international relations player, and the sole repository of the "national interest," the second model accords prime attention to political and social groups competing within the state and, consequently, relegates the state to a position of only one motor of foreign policy development among many. It is Bukkvol's finding that both paradigms have certain explanatory value for the theory of foreign policy. In accordance with the pluralist perspective, recent reorientation of a number of key sectors of Ukrainian industry from Russian to Western markets and the firsthand experience of global competition with erstwhile Russian partners in arms trade, civilian machine building, and the space industry goes a long way to explaining the concomitant shift in foreign policy from a pro-Russian to a pro-Western orientation. It is less clear from the pluralist viewpoint why the rising clout of a "mildly pro-Russian" energy–industrial lobby failed to produce foreign policy more receptive to Russian overtures. To account for this discrepancy, the Weberian perspective is invoked, strengthened by neoinstitutionalist insights into the logic of appropriateness as a driving force behind regularized functioning of the state. In the latter model, inculcated rules of behavior in the international arena, based on normalized perceptions of identity, are fed back into the foreign policy, acting as a break on sudden changes of course and perpetuating identity stances that had been earlier presented to the international community.

Russia's failure to recognize Ukraine wholeheartedly as an independent state in its own right threatened both Ukrainian "oligarchs" and the Ukrainian state. Because of that, the pro-Russian ("Eurasian") perspective in foreign policy, though seductive for a number of reasons, came to be associated with submissiveness, translated as the loss of profit for business elites and diminution of power for the state stewards. Ukraine's power brokers turned to Europe, since the choice of European identity seemed the only reasonable alternative to what looked like unconditional surrender to the Russian hegemonist designs. Were it not for Moscow's haughtiness, Ukraine's foreign policy might have been guided by considerations of identity more compatible with Russia. As Moscow was slow in treating Ukrainians as equals, the latter had little choice but to rally around the flag, agreeing to separate economic interest in collaboration with Russia from geopolitical ("national") interest in keeping Russia at arm's length. Prompted by geopolitical reasoning, international politics of the newly independent state acquired the Weberian logic of development even when societal interests now and then pointed toward the opposite direction.

The chapter by Taras Kuzio tackles the problem of Ukrainian national identity and foreign policy by concentrating primarily on divisions that exist within the ranks of political elite. Kuzio argues that the linguistic–regional divide is of lesser importance to formulation of foreign policy goals than policy makers' demonstrated unanimity in choosing Europe as a model of development. Few in the dominant core of Ukraine's politicians and opinion makers dispute the need to move as close to the West as possible, either via membership in such

Western "clubs" as NATO and the EU or independently. Ukraine's traditions, political culture, and national identity perceptions, Kuzio argues, are clearly European, albeit in "East and Central European" incarnation, while their opposite Russian numbers do not really belong to a politically and culturally defined Europe. Ukraine's domestic foreign policy debate divides political parties into two groups: While antireform forces (neo-Communists, radical socialists, and romantic Slavophiles) tend to exhibit a "pro-Eurasian Slavophile geopolitical orientation," reformists of all shades choose the West in juxtaposition to the Russia-led Commonwealth of Independent States. While most parties on the right tend to believe that Russia does not and will not belong to Europe, or at the very least must still prove its European credentials by returning into the embrace of Western civilization, the group identified as pragmatic nationalists try to reconcile an Eastern Slavic identity with a pro-European orientation by arguing that Russia must not be ostracized as the "other." Kuchma's foreign policy has so far corresponded to this pragmatic line of thinking as he sought to avoid antagonizing Russia even while moving closer to the West.

Ukraine's foreign policy under the successive administrations of Leonid Kravchuk and Leonid Kuchma did not significantly deviate from the pro-Western course charted in the first post-independence years. Overall, the political elite in Kyiv believes that cooperation with Russia must be subordinated to the higher aim of integration with the West. Only political parties on the left disagree with that, and despite their influence on between one-third to one-half of the population, they do not hold keys to positions of power in Kyiv. As events of the last five years showed, Kuchma has largely followed in the footsteps of his predecessor as far as the Western vector of foreign policy is concerned. Kuzio is right, therefore, in observing that major changes in Ukraine's foreign policy line have never been in the cards.

While the Western choice is hardly disputed by Ukraine's establishment insiders, the Eastern (Russia–CIS) orientation remains a rallying point for the leftist opposition and regionally entrenched forces in much of Left-Bank (eastern) Ukraine. Mikhail Molchanov argues that the pro-Russian orientation is also largely supported by the masses of the Ukrainian public. Available data show that a significant portion of the Ukrainian population supports some form of greater accommodation with Russia than is currently maintained by policy makers, while up to one-third would back reunification in a single state or federation. One of the reasons for this unprecedented expression of sympathy, Molchanov argues, is to be found in the realm of ethnonational identity, which in Ukraine is by and large compatible with that of its Russian counterpart. Thus, Russians and Russian-speaking Ukrainians are judged by the majority of the population to be significantly closer, in terms of social distance and cultural proximity, than Poles, Jews, diaspora Ukrainians, or any other ethnocultural group, for that matter. Up to 40 percent of the Ukrainian public identifies as at least partially Russian ("both Ukrainian and Russian," etc.), which is far more than the actual percentage of ethnic Russians living in Ukraine.

These perceptions, strengthened by deep economic interdependence, structurally similar to the Russian (and other CIS) position on the world markets, certain shared problems that require interstate coordination of efforts in the international arena (e.g., Chernobyl), not to mention geographical proximity and demographic ties, all account for the fact that on such principled questions as European versus Soviet identity or the attitudes toward eastern NATO expansion Ukrainians more than occasionally tend to side with the Russians. On Ukraine's closer collaboration with NATO, public opinion is divided almost in half, which must be primarily explained by the familiar Russian reservations echoed on the Ukrainian side of the border.

Molchanov argues that the dilemma "Europe or Russia" is a hardly appropriate formulation of Ukraine's nation-building and foreign policy choices. Both "vectors" must be pursued simultaneously in a proactive, rather than reactive, manner. In other words, Ukraine's role is to nudge Russia closer to Europe while serving Europe's better understanding of Russia. Both Kuzio and Molchanov see Ukraine as a bridge, not a buffer, between the two parts of the continent. The country is well endowed to carry out this role, building on its existing strengths. To be able to adequately perform it in the future, it must be prepared to compromise on the issues of tactical importance without compromising its hard-won sovereignty. There are signs that it can. Ukraine's participation in the CIS has been sufficiently independent to preclude its subordination to Russia or otherwise incapacitate sovereign decision making. If so, perhaps Russian attempts at a limited reintegration may also be accorded a more sympathetic reading and need not be perceived as unconditionally hegemonist. Ukraine's recent entry into the CIS Inter-Parliamentary Assembly may show that some part of the country's elite supports this benign view of the merits of cooperation. However, an explanation focused on Ukraine's material dependency and opportunism on the part of the Ukrainian elites is at least as much if not more plausible in this context than the one that focuses on identity.

Material constraints on Ukraine's foreign policy are complemented with constraints of a less tangible nature, which zero in on contested sovereignty and what Paul D'Anieri calls contingent state identity. Because traditional theories of international relations tend to underestimate the importance of the latter, their explanatory potential with respect to Ukrainian politics and foreign policy remains limited. Thus,

Ukraine's voluntary relinquishing of its nuclear weapons is hardly explicable from a conventional realist viewpoint. Similarly, liberal theorists of international relations would probably argue that cooperation with the European Union must surely take precedence over cooperation with Russia, and would find it difficult to explain the persistence of Ukraine–Russia ties.

Neither realist nor ethnic determinist theories, argues Victor Chudowsky, can satisfactorily accommodate such policy inconsistencies as Ukraine's participation in the CIS joint air-defense system against the backdrop of regular military exercises with NATO, or avoidance of the CIS Customs Union paralleled by the acceptance of an expanded program of military cooperation with Russia. Because of that, Chudowsky advocates theoretical flexibility and the levels-of-analysis approach that allows distinguishing between the macro-scale geopolitical, nationally relevant domestic and individual factors as different determinants of foreign policy. He also criticizes what in his view is disproportionate attention given to nationalism by those scholars who see it as one of the defining forces behind Ukrainian foreign policy. Chudowsky believes that a rational-choice argument may better explain Ukraine's decision not to join the CIS Customs Union than either traditional security considerations, preferred by the realist school of international relations, or an analysis that takes nationalism as a key explanatory variable.

However, a rational-choice explanation must be based on the researcher's ability to define preferences in a clear and unambiguous way, and on the achievement of a minimal level of certainty in the projections of relative payoffs. Arguably, neither is realistically possible in the context of Ukraine's multiple transitions. For one thing, preferences are still contested from within and are not easily reducible to a common denominator. More important, there is no way to estimate relative payoffs in the situation where, for example, Ukraine's membership in such international institutions as the WTO or the EU remains an uncertain prospect, tomorrow's level of foreign investment cannot be reliably predicted, and economic reform at home is still being held hostage (for how long?) by powerful domestic interests. The international environment presents Ukraine with few constants apart from the constants of a geopolitical and geoeconomic nature. Hence, Chudowsky argues that Ukraine's foreign policy will of necessity be conducted in a reactive way, reflecting policies and positions of the world power centers. If so, the process of reflection is as important as the substance of the policy being reflected and acted upon. While Ukraine's foreign policy choices are too uncertain to be weighted and computed in advance in a sufficiently reliable way, we can at least agree on the necessity to choose the most appropriate theoretical instruments based on the nature of the situation at hand. Hence, no singular approach at the disposal of international relations theory today may be privileged by such a study to the complete exclusion of its rivals.

To capture various determinants of the evolving foreign policy of such a newly independent, positionally uncertain state as Ukraine, we need to go beyond realism and liberalism, making more room for intersubjective and interpretivist explanations that have been recently summarized in a research paradigm of constructivism. Materialist theories of international relations need, therefore, to be supplemented, if not corrected, with a perspective that pays special attention to the role of symbolic benefits and losses as independent or semiindependent motors of foreign policy. Another important insight of constructivism, summarizes D'Anieri, concerns its assertion of the reciprocal and intrinsically reflective nature of foreign policy: The identity that the country presents to the world is shaped by the international community to no lesser extent than it is by domestic policy makers. Hence, while shared or complementary identities foster cooperation, unsettled or contested identities must be regarded on a par with other risk factors that contribute to international conflict.

As Jennifer Moroney suggests, one of the key manifestations of the identity politics in post–Cold War Europe is politics of the East–West frontier. Ukraine sits right in the middle of what many consider a gray zone separating the European Union countries from the ostensibly "non-European" post-Soviet states. This frontier location contributes to the ongoing identity crisis, while demanding its speedier resolution. Psychological and social dimensions of the frontier predicament have direct bearing on the security situation in East and Central Europe, since the awareness of being excluded from the zone of prosperity and security associated with the EU and NATO contributes to the feeling of alienation and breeds resentment, which may be exploited to fan prospective politics of emerging alliances.

A security analysis based solely on factors of a geopolitical nature fails to appreciate the full weight of the identity considerations brought to bear on politics of the frontier. In the Ukrainian case, the identity stigma attached by the European Union to the former Russian sister republic precludes the country's moving closer to the West and acquires features of self-fulfilling prophecy, as the country's elites, frustrated by the lack of support in Brussels, are nudged to fall back on the beaten path of regional isolationism and preferential collaboration with Russia. Thus, transnational and globalization forces, which tend to reduce international barriers throughout the world, also work to reconstitute some of the old divisions in a new form, and in the process mold national and state identities of recently democratized countries. Contemporary frontier politics is also not free from familiar geopolitical considerations, which helps to explain why NATO was keen to establish a special relationship with Ukraine while the European Union appears in no hurry to follow the suit.

Chapters by James Sherr, Stacy Closson, Joshua Spero, Jennifer Moroney, and Sergei Konoplyov all deal with security aspects of Ukrainian foreign policy. However, the presented approaches differ. While Spero focuses on international environment in post–Cold War Europe at large and discusses factors making states in structurally similar situation (Poland and Ukraine) cooperate, Moroney and Konoplyov concentrate on Europe's security "gray zone" stretching through ex-Soviet borderlands and emphasize international significance of the incipient subregional organizations active in the area. Sherr and Closson present two case studies of development of civil–military relations in Ukraine, which is arguably one of the key issues affecting both the substance and the style of foreign policy conduct in the country.

Spero looks at Ukraine's military contacts with Poland as a worthy example of cooperative behavior in the post-Communist Central and Eastern Europe. The chapter applies a neorealist perspective on such alliance-building tactics as bandwagoning, which, as demonstrated through the study of Ukrainian–Polish and Polish–German relations, helped to generate promising solutions to the traditional security dilemmas that reemerged in post–Cold War Europe. Spero defines bandwagoning, usually understood as alignment with the dominant power, as a form of cooperative behavior informed by a desire to gain a reward, which need not be limited to the sphere of security. Since cooperative bandwagoning goes further than simple maximization of security, it may involve establishment of profitable linkages between the states, none of which is unambiguously dominant or sufficiently strong on its own to guarantee other's security. This is the case in the Polish–Ukrainian encounter, which must be seen as a security success story. The study demonstrates importance of a wider international context, which proved conducive to nonthreatening and mutually cooperative behavior among all states of East Central Europe. Had it not been for a powerful pull that the EU and NATO exert on the post-Communist European periphery, cooperative behavior of a sort described in the chapter might not have materialized in the first place. Thus, international structure, though a powerful determinant of policy, is not overbearing. No less important is the quality of the international environment, shaped by its dominant institutions and practices.

Moroney and Konoplev approach the agent–structure problem from an angle that perhaps serves best to emphasize interrelatedness and mutual causality of the two: that of a small interstate structure, a subregional grouping where individual states are as much shakers and movers of policy as receivers of structural impulses generated by group dynamics. The group in question, the subregional organization of Georgia, Ukraine, Uzbekistan, Azerbaijan, and Moldova, all members of the Russia-led Commonwealth of Independent States, distinguished itself by taking a path of development independent of Russia's views on the necessity of post-Soviet reintegration. The GUUAM members proclaimed a more or less decidedly pro-Western and Euro–Atlantic orientations and sought international recognition of their efforts. While they have been moderately encouraged by the West, most credit for GUUAM's continued existence despite Russia's pronounced displeasure must go to the organization members themselves. The chapter argues that the organization's problems stem from two sources: institutional underdevelopment and the obstructions raised by Russia, which echo in the lack of enthusiasm and limited support on the part of the West. Just as Russia's negative attitude toward GUUAM invites a realist explanation, the harm caused by underinstitutionalization is probably best seen from the liberal–institutionalist perspective. Further institutional development of GUUAM, argue the authors, answers Western security interests in the region and must be supported.

But can we see the West or Russia, together or individually, as solely or even primarily responsible for security developments in the region? Is the Western lack of enthusiasm with respect to GUUAM propelled by Russian objections or by a number of unresolved issues in the domestic and foreign politics of GUUAM members? If the subregional level of international organization reflects individual idiosyncrasies of member countries to no lesser extent than structural determinants of international relations at large, it is at least equally plausible to argue that GUUAM's poor fortunes are in no small part caused by unresolved issues and flaws of a domestic nature. The Gongadze scandal in Ukraine revealed that the country must still go some way to implement democratic standards of transparency and accountability in the government. While pro-Western sympathies must surely be applauded, a considerable stretch of the imagination will be required of anyone willing to see Azerbaijan or Uzbekistan as democracies. A comparison to the Visegrad countries, legitimate as it is from a structural realist perspective, may be disputed on account of deeply different domestic contexts, which centrally influence foreign policy formulation and development in Eastern Europe, as well as international perceptions of East European states in the West.

The chapters by Sherr and Closson present the problem of civilian control over the military as a key domestic determinant of Ukraine's foreign policy. A well-known hypothesis of "democratic peace" advanced by the liberal school of international politics postulates that democracies do not go to war with each other. But can a state where the military shuns independent civilian control be considered a democracy? What does this independence of the military say about the strength of the country's civil society? James Sherr argues that, despite a number of positive signs, much needs to be improved in this respect in Ukraine. The task goes beyond the realm of defense and security policy narrowly defined. Without a strong civil society there cannot be a civic state, and hence no civilized interaction with the outside world. The countries where civil society has little say over the matters of security and practically no input into the questions of day-to-day functioning of the authoritatively created armed formations do not qualify as democracies. Such states might qualify as dictatorships, oligarchies, collapsing, or contested states, the last two categories to include such cases as fragmentation of authority due to a civil war or revolution or compartmentalization of authority through separatism, elite dealignment, or capture of the state by special interests. Whatever the case, the absence of civilian control over the military translates into the lack of public accountability on the part of the rulers, with far-reaching consequences for both domestic and international politics of the country. The matter is simply too important to be ignored or sideswiped by the international community.

The analysis of civil–military affairs in Ukraine leads to a conclusion that the Ukrainian military has so far kept a relatively low political profile and did not attempt to accept an independent role in domestic and international politics, as has been arguably the case with its Russian counterpart, not to mention a number of post-authoritarian regimes in the Third World. Nevertheless, civilian monitoring of military affairs has not yet developed into true civilian oversight and direction of the country's defense and security policies. Civilian control over the military must be both strengthened and advanced to a qualitatively new level to make democratic reform in the army irreversible, contributing, in this way, to enhanced national security and domestic stability. Successful military reform in Ukraine will bring the country closer to Euro–Atlantic institutions, thus underscoring its Western orientation in defense and security. It is no less important to secure a firm civilian control over the large contingent of security and police forces, other armed formations that often continue to exist and conduct their activities in a way that is less than transparent and open for societal input. As Sherr believes, Western institutions have a much larger role to play here, matching the success of military collaboration through NATO's PfP program with equally intense programs targeting Ukraine's security services and other, less transparent institutions of the state. Ukraine's neighbors in Eastern and Central Europe may well prove yet another less than fully explored foreign and security policy resource. Ultimately, however, the task must be resolved by the Ukrainian effort. The "Kuchmagate" scandal dramatically underscored both the level of the stakes involved and the distance that remains to be negotiated to secure democratic civilian and not just presidential–executive control over the so-called power ministries of the country.

Stacy Closson's chapter analyzes different organizational and societal levels where civilian–military interaction takes place. She starts by assessing the role of the presidential administration and the parliament (*Verkhovna Rada*) in creating a legislative base for proper functioning and development of the armed forces. An important observation she makes here concerns the fact that civil–military reform in Ukraine is constrained by the lack of agreement among different factions of Ukraine's political establishment, which in turn is caused by the East–West, Left–Right split. Then she looks at the relationship between the Ministry of Defense and other armed formations, such as the troops of the Ministry of the Interior or the Ministry of Emergencies. Redundant and overlapping missions of these various organizations often preclude smooth coordination of their activities and obfuscate monitoring by civilian bodies vested with oversight and control tasks. However, proliferation of the armed security services is not without its benefit, as some paramilitary units may actually lead the military in adopting democratic procedures of control and governance faster than the armed forces. They may also show the way and cooperate with lesser restraint than the army with the appropriate Western institutions on missions related to humanitarian relief and civil emergencies.

More civilian involvement in the matters of military and defense policy is necessary to overcome that ambiguity in Ukraine's strategic orientation that has characterized it until now, argues Closson. The problem is not so much the number of civilians working for the Ministry of Defense or other "power ministries"; the problem is to reshape these institutions according to civilian norms of governance, transparency, and accountability. The level of society's involvement could be increased if more broad-based nongovernmental organizations showed persistent interest in the matters of security and defense. Unfortunately, this has not been always the case, and the progress, while undeniable, remains limited. Ukraine still has much to learn in this respect from such East Central European countries as its neighbors Poland or Hungary.

Ukrainian foreign policy is formed in a complex juxtaposition of domestic and international factors, which must both be sufficiently accounted for to provide a sound underpinning for any theoretical and practical analysis. While international relations shape foreign policy by providing models to emulate, institutions to court, and a globalized environment to deal with, domestic forces determine the relative measure of influence of various state and societal agents involved in foreign policy formulation and development. The problem of national identity straddles both fields, as identity is at once the external profile that the nation presents to the world and the reflection of national aspirations in public consciousness and political discourse at home. How should the newly independent state in the throes of multiple transition position itself in international relations of a new kind in the world that is at once more tightly knit (globalized) than ever before and yet exhibiting no lesser degree of inequalities and divisions among nations? If both national and international identities can be deliberately constructed, what model must Ukrainian national builders take as a benchmark? Is it inevitable that Ukraine must find its place in Europe through diligent distancing from Russia and the CIS? If not, how must Russia be engaged in a way that answers the Ukrainian national interest and desire to join with the family of European nations? These questions retain their centrality for foreign policy makers in Ukraine and for the country's general public.

While different strategic and foreign policy orientations persist, they are not solidly stratified by social class or membership in one or another dominant linguistic community, but rather by changing political and economic affiliations, regional preferences, and attitudes to reform. It is therefore natural to believe that Ukraine's continuing oscillations between East and West will not lead the country astray on its way toward eventual full membership in the democratic international community. Whether Ukraine will be able to do it with or without Russia is a question of secondary importance. Whether it will attempt the transition on the basis of profound democratic reforms at home or solely through the by-now-familiar balancing act in the international arena is, on the contrary, what makes all the difference.

The overview of Ukraine's foreign policy presented in this volume attempted to gain new insights into the subject matter by bringing several international relations theories to bear on such problems as Ukraine's geopolitical position and politics of alliances, the role of domestic and international forces in foreign policy formulation and implementation, Ukraine's strategic orientation between East and West, its present and prospective behavior in the international arena, its actual and potential contribution to European cooperation, and international stability at large. We also sought to compare and evaluate the explanatory potential of several international relations theories by testing the familiar propositions anew in empirical settings of a recently independent post-Communist country, not so familiar to international theorists. As several contributions to this book suggest, such mainstream approaches in international relations theory as liberalism or realism, while useful in explaining the geopolitical predicament of the country (realism) or its apparent desire for further cooperation with the West (liberalism), are not always helpful with questions related to the international politics of identity. Here, a recent addition to the international relations toolbox, the constructivist paradigm, seems to work better, helping the researcher to ask the right questions and to avoid prejudging answers.

We do not advocate any single paradigm as a key to all complex questions that have arisen in this study. We can only hypothesize that the relevance of any international relations theory in the situation of post-Communist transformation and multiple transitions that engulf both the country and the region—in fact, a good part of the continent—must be limited by the uncertain and precarious nature of the new international system arising on the remains of the old. The international environment in this part of the world is fluid to the point where none of the competing theoretical approaches can be applied in a holistic way to describe the emerging international system or to study the problem of system–unit interaction on the country level. Domestic factors influencing foreign policy are also in a state of flux, which in many instances precludes seeing them as either independent or dependent variables in a theoretically rigorous sense. For one example, can we test certain liberal propositions when we are not sure whether the country's regime qualifies as a democracy, whether protectionist or open practices are supported in trade, whether the country has a functioning market economy, and so on? Questions like these recur when we switch to the realist platform and almost immediately find that the strategic orientation of the country cannot be ascertained at the moment because perceptions of external threat differ, and even the factual nature of the threat most commonly acknowledged by security scholars (Russia) remains uncertain and cannot be unambiguously presented to either the country's elite or its general public.

It is necessary, therefore, to use a combination of methods in a comprehensive study of foreign policy and international relations of such reforming post-Communist state as Ukraine. Even if this book does not claim to have produced a single overarching approach to cover most of the problems involved, it demonstrated the value of such a combination of methods. We have also learned the necessity of caution in a study of the international behavior of a country that has to deal with an internally and externally unsettled policy environment. It is apparent that in an environment like this the flight of theoretical imagination must be curbed, while research has to be guided by methods most useful to the concrete task at hand. Ukraine's foreign policy eludes straightjacket modeling. The fact that the national identity of the country is still being constructed and contested from both within and without accounts for much of the uncertainty in definition of its national interests and corresponding modes of behavior in the realm of foreign policy. One of the lessons that might be drawn from the studies collected in this book is that the frontier between internal and external domains of policy, increasingly transparent even in more stable countries, becomes particularly elusive in transitional societies. Because of the level of uncertainty that these societies must deal with and their rather weak material capabilities, subjective determinants of foreign policy often take the forefront, distorting the picture that might have been relatively uncontroversial should considerations of security or material benefit be allowed to play out without interference. The system of international relations in which the state undertaking multiple transitions finds itself might be best modeled as an array of overlapping fields of action with continuously reinterpreted and renegotiated game rules for each of these fields. Neither realism nor liberalism nor constructivism alone can represent this system with sufficient clarity, and hence, conscious methodological eclecticism may be the best research choice at the moment.

NOTES

1. *Rossiiskaia gazeta*, 25 November 2000, 7.

2. FBIS-SOV-2001-0103, 3 January 2001.

3. John Edwin Mroz and Oleksandr Pavliuk, "Ukraine: Europe's Linchpin," *Foreign Affairs* 75, no. 3 (1996): 55–62.

4. *Reuters*, 25 November 1999; *Bloomberg*, 29 June 2000.

5. *The World Factbook* (CIA, 2000). Available at: <http://www.odci.gov/cia/publications/factbook/geos/up.html>.

6. *World Development Indicators Database* (Washington, D.C.: World Bank, 2000). Available at: <http://www.worldbank.org>.

7. Adrian Karatnycky, Alexander Motyl, and Charles Graybow, eds., *Nations in Transit 1998: Civil Society, Democracy and Markets in East Central Europe and the Newly Independent States* (New Brunswick, N.J.: Transaction, 1999), 624.

8. Embassy of Ukraine in Canada, 19 January 2001. Available at: <http://www.infoukes.com/ukremb/milit-1.shtml>.

9. John Jaworsky, "Ukraine's Armed Forces and Military Policy," in *Ukraine in the World: Studies in the International Relations and Security Structure of a Newly Independent State*, ed. Lubomyr A. Hajda (Cambridge: Harvard University Press, 1998), 227.

10. SIPRI Country Profile for Ukraine, 2000. Available at: <http://first.sipri.org>.

Bibliography

INTERNATIONAL RELATIONS
THEORIES AND CONCEPTS

Allison, Graham. *Essence of Decision: Conceptual Models and the Cuban Missile Crisis*. Boston: Little, Brown, 1970.

Anderson, Benedict. *Imagined Communities: Reflections on the Origin and Spread of Nationalism*. New York: Verso, 1991.

Anderson, Malcolm. *Frontiers: Territory and State Formation in the Modern World*. Cambridge: Polity Press, 1996.

Barber, Benjamin R. *Jihad vs. McWorld*. New York: Times Books, 1995.

Brown, Michael E., Lynn-Jones, Sean M., and Miller, Steven, eds. *Perils of Anarchy: Contemporary Realism and International Security*. Cambridge: MIT Press, 1995.

Brubaker, Rogers. "National Minorities, Nationalizing States, and External National Homelands in the New Europe." *Daedalus* 124, no. 2 (1995): 107–132.

Brubaker, Rogers. *Nationalism Reframed: Nationhood and the National Question in the New Europe*. Cambridge: Cambridge University Press, 1996.

Bunce, Valerie. *Subversive Institutions: The Design and the Destruction of Socialism and the State*. Cambridge: Cambridge University Press, 1999.

Cox, Robert W., with Sinclair, Timothy J. *Approaches to World Order*. New York: Cambridge University Press, 1996.

Dawisha, Adeed, and Dawisha, Karen, eds. *The Making of Foreign Policy in Russia and the New States of Eurasia*. Armonk, N.Y.: M. E. Sharpe, 1995.

Doyle, Michael W., and Ikenberry, G. John, eds. *New Thinking in International Relations Theory*. Boulder, Colo.: Westview Press, 1997.

Evans, Peter B., Rueshchmeyer, Dietrich, and Skocpol, Theda, eds. *Bringing the State Back In*. Cambridge: Cambridge University Press, 1985.

Falk, Richard, and Szentes, Tamás, eds. *A New Europe in the Changing Global System*. Tokyo: United Nations University Press, 1997.

Finnemore, Martha. *National Interests in International Society*. Ithaca: Cornell University Press, 1996.

Fleron, F. J., and Hoffman, E. P., eds. *Post-Communist Studies and Political Science: Methodology and Empirical theory in Sovietology*. Boulder, Colo.: Westview Press, 1993.

Graham, Gordon. *Ethics and International Relations*. Oxford: Blackwell, 1997.

Halliday, Fred. *Rethinking International Relations*. London: Macmillan, 1994.

Hedley, Bull. *The Anarchical Society: A Study of Order in World Politics*. 2d ed. Basingstoke: Macmillan, 1995.

Hobsbawm, Eric, and Ranger, Terence, eds. *The Invention of Tradition*. Cambridge: Cambridge University Press, 1983.

Holsti, K. J. "Change in the International System: Interdependence, Integration, and Fragmentation." In *Change in the International System*, edited by Ole R. Holsti, Randolph M. Siverson, and Alexander L. George. Boulder, Colo.: Westview Press, 1980.

Hopf, Ted. "The Promise of Constructivism in International Relations Theory." *International Security* 23, no. 1 (1998): 171–200.

Huntington, Samuel P. *The Clash of Civilizations and the Remaking of World Order*. New York: Simon and Schuster, 1996.

Jervis, Robert. *Perception and Misperception in International Politics*. Princeton, N.J.: Princeton University Press, 1976.

Katzenstein, Peter J., ed. *The Culture of National Security*. New York: Columbia University Press, 1996.

Katzenstein, Peter J., Keohane, Robert O., and Krasner, Stephen D., eds. *Exploration and Contestation in the Study of World Politics*. Cambridge: MIT Press, 1999.

Keohane, Robert O. *After Hegemony: Cooperation and Discord in the World Political Economy*. Princeton, N.J.: Princeton University Press, 1984.

Keohane, Robert O., ed. *Neorealism and Its Critics*. New York: Columbia University Press, 1986.

Krasner, Stephen D., ed. *Problematic Sovereignty: Contested Rules and Political Possibilities*. New York: Columbia University Press, 2001.

Lapid, Yosef, and Kratochwil, Friedrich, eds. *The Return of Culture and Identity in IR Theory*. Boulder, Colo.: Lynne Rienner, 1996.

Neack, Laura, Hey, Jeanne A. K., and Haney, Patrick J., eds. *Foreign Policy Analysis: Continuity and Change in Its Second Generation*. Englewood Cliffs, N.J.: Prentice Hall, 1995.

Nettle, J. P. "The State as a Conceptual Variable." *World Politics* 20 (1968).

Nye, Joseph S., Jr., and Donahue, John D., eds. *Governance in a Globalizing World*. Washington, D.C.: Brookings Institution Press, 2000.

Posen, Barry R. "The Security Dilemma and Ethnic Conflict." In *Ethnic Conflict and International Security*, edited by Michael E. Brown. Princeton, N.J.: Princeton University Press.

Prescott, R. V. *Political Frontiers and Boundaries*. London: Allen and Unwin, 1987.

Rengger, Nicholas J. *International Relations, Political Theory, and the Problem of Order: Beyond International Relations Theory?* London: Routledge, 2000.

Rosecrance, Richard, and Stein, Arthur A., eds., *Domestic Bases of Grand Strategy*. Ithaca: Cornell University Press, 1993.

Rosenau, James N. *Along the Domestic–Foreign Frontier: Exploring Global Governance in a Turbulent World*. Cambridge: Cambridge University Press, 1997.

Ruggie, John Gerard. *Constructing the World Polity*. London: Routledge, 1998.

Schmitt, Carl. *The Concept of the Political*. New Brunswick, N.J.: Rutgers University Press, 1976.

Siverson, Randolph M., and George, Alexander, eds. *Change in the International System*. Boulder, Colo.: Westview Press, 1980.

Strassoldo, R. *From Barrier to Junction: Towards a Sociological Theory of Borders*. Gorizia: ISIG, 1970.

Thorstendahl, Rolf, ed. *State Theory and State History*. London: Sage, 1992.

Triandafyllidou, Anna. "National Identity and the 'Other.'" *Ethnic and Racial Studies* 21, no. 4 (1998): 593–612.

Walt, Steven M. *The Origins of Alliances*. Ithaca, N.Y.: Cornell University Press, 1987.

Waltz, Kenneth. *Theory of International Politics*. New York: McGraw-Hill, 1979.

Wendt, Alexander. "Anarchy Is What States Make of It: The Social Construction of Power Politics." *International Organization* 46, no. 2 (1992): 391–426.

Wendt, Alexander. "Identity and Structural Change in International Politics." In *The Return of Culture and Identity in International Relations Theory*, edited by Yosef Lapid and Friedrich Kratochwil (Boulder, Colo.: Lynne Rienner, 1996).

Wendt, Alexander. *Social Theory of International Politics*. New York: Cambridge University Press, 1999.

Wendt, Alexander. "The Structure–Agent Problem in International Politics." *International Organization* 41, no. 3 (1987): 335–370.

Wilson, Thomas M., and Donnan, Hastings, eds. *Border Identities: Nation and State at International Frontiers*. Cambridge: Cambridge University Press, 1998.

GENERAL STUDIES OF CONTEMPORARY UKRAINE

Arel, Dominique. "Ukraine: The Temptation of the Nationalizing State." In *Political Culture and Civil Society in Russia and the New States of Eurasia*, edited by Vladimir Tismaneanu. Armonk, N.Y.: M. E. Sharpe, 1995.

Arel, D. "Ukraine: The Muddle Way." *Current History* 97, no. 620 (1998): 342–346.

Arel, D., and Khmelko, Valeri. "The Russian Factor and Territorial Polarization in Ukraine." *Harriman Review* 9, no. 1–2 (1996): 81–91.

Aslund, Anders. "Eurasia Letter: Ukraine's Turnaround." *Foreign Policy* 100 (1995): 125–143.

Blaney, John W., ed. *The Successor States to the USSR*. Washington, D.C.: Congressional Quarterly, 1995.

D'Anieri, Paul J., Kravchuk, Robert S., and Kuzio, T. *Politics and Society in Ukraine*. Boulder, Colo.: Westview Press, 1999.

Dawisha, Karen, and Parrott, Bruce, eds. *The End of Empire? The Transformation of the USSR in Comparative Perspective*. Armonk, N.Y.: M. E. Sharpe, 1997.

Diuk, Nadia. "Ukraine: A Land in Between." *Journal of Democracy* 9, no. 3 (1998): 97–111.

Drohobycky, Maria, ed. *Crimea—Dynamics, Challenges and Prospects*. Lanham, Md.: Rowan and Littlefield, 1995.

Duncan, Peter J. S. "Ukraine and the Ukrainians." In *The Nationalities Question in the Post-Soviet States*, edited by Graham Smith. London: Longman, 1996.

Dyczok, Marta. *Ukraine. Movement Without Change, Change Without Movement*. Reading: Harwood Academic Press, 2000.

Jaworsky, John. *Ukraine: Stability and Instability*. McNair paper 42. Washington, D.C.: Institute for National Strategic Studies, National Defense University, 1995.

Karatnycky, Adrian, Motyl, Alexander, and Graybow, Charles, eds. *Nations in Transit 2001: Civil Society, Democracy and Markets in East Central Europe and the Newly Independent States*. New Brunswick, N.J.: Transaction, 2001.

Kis, T., Makaryk, I., and Weretelnyk, R., eds. *Towards a New Ukraine*. Vol. 1, *Ukraine and the New World Order, 1991–1996*. Ottawa: Chair of Ukrainian Studies, University of Ottawa, 1997.

Kis, T., Makaryk, I., and Weretelnyk, R., eds. *Towards a New Ukraine*. Vol. 2, *Meeting the Next Century*. Ottawa: Chair of Ukrainian Studies, University of Ottawa, 1999.

Krawchenko, Bohdan. "Ukraine: The Politics of Independence." In *Nations and Politics in the Soviet Successor States*, edited by Ian Bremmer and Ray Taras. Cambridge: Cambridge University Press, 1993.

Kuzio, T., ed. *Contemporary Ukraine: Dynamics of Post-Soviet Transformation*. Armonk, N.Y.: M. E. Sharpe, 1998.

Kuzio, T. "'Nationalising States' or Nation Building: A Review of the Theoretical Literature and Empirical Evidence." *Nations and Nationalism* 7 (2001): 135–154.

Kuzio, T. *Ukraine: Perestroika to Independence*. 2d ed. London: Macmilan, 2000.

Kuzio, T. *Ukraine: State and Nation Building*. London: Routledge, 1998.

Kuzio, T. *Ukraine under Kuchma: Political Reform, Economic Transformation and Security Policy in Independent Ukraine*. New York: St. Martin's Press, 1997.

Kuzio, T., Kravchuk R., and D'Anieri, P., eds. *State and Institution Building in Ukraine*. New York: St. Martin's Press, 1999.

Magocsi, Paul R. *A History of Ukraine*. Toronto: University of Toronto Press, 1996.

Miller, William L., White, Stephen, and Heywood, Paul. *Values and Political Change in Postcommunist Europe*. London: Macmillan, 1998.

Motyl, A. J. *Dilemmas of Independence: Ukraine after Totalitarianism*. New York: Council on Foreign Affairs, 1993.

Motyl, A., and Krawchenko, B. "Ukraine: From Empire to Statehood." In *New States, New Politics: Building the Post-Soviet Nations*, edited by I. Bremmer and R. Taras. Cambridge: Cambridge University Press, 1997.

Mroz, Edwin John, and Pavliuk, Oleksandr. "Ukraine: Europe's Linchpin." *Foreign Affairs* 75, no. 3 (1996): 52–62.

Nahaylo, Bohdan. *The Ukrainian Resurgence*. London: Hurst, 1999.

Smith, Graham, Law, Vivien, Wilson, A., Bohn, Annette, and Allworth, Edward, eds. *Nation-Building in the Post-Soviet Borderlands: The Politics of National Identities*. Cambridge: Cambridge University Press, 1998.

Subtelny, Orest. *Ukraine: A History*. 3d ed. Toronto: University of Toronto Press, 2000.

Szporluk, Roman. *Russia, Ukraine, and the Breakup of the Soviet Union*. Stanford, Calif.: Hoover Institution Press, 2000.

Szporluk, Roman. "Ukraine: From Imperial Periphery to a Sovereign State." *Daedalus* 126, no. 3 (1997): 85–119.

Vydrin, Dmytro, and Tabachnyk, Dmytro. *Ukraine on the Threshold of the XXI Century: Political Aspect*. Kyiv: Lybid', 1995.

Wilson, A. *Ukrainian Nationalism in the 1990s: A Minority Faith*. Cambridge: Cambridge University Press, 1997.

Wilson A. *Ukrainians. The Unexpected Nation*. New Haven, Conn.: Yale University Press, 2000.

Wolchik, Sharon L., and Zviglyanich, Volodymyr, eds. *Ukraine: The Search for a National Identity*. Lanham, Mass.: Rowan and Littlefield, 2000.

Zimmerman, William. "Is Ukraine a Political Community?" *Communist and Post-Communist Studies* 31, no. 1 (1998): 43–55.

UKRAINIAN SECURITY POLICY

Albright, David E., and Appatov, Semyen J., eds. *Ukraine and European Security*. London: Macmillan, 1999.

Allison, Roy, and Bluth, Christoph, eds. *Security Dilemmas in Russia and Eurasia*. London: Royal Institute International Affairs, 1998.

Balmaceda, M. M. "Ukraine, Russia, and European Security. Thinking beyond NATO Expansion." *Problems of Post-Communism* 45, no. 1 (1998): 21–29.

Bilinsky, Y. "Ukraine, Russia, and the West: An Insecure Security Triangle." *Problems of Post-Communism* 44, no. 1 (1997): 27–33.

Blank, Stephen. "Russia, Ukraine and European Security." *European Security* 3, no. 1 (1994): 182–207.

Bukkvoll, Tor. *Ukraine and European Security*. London: Royal Institute of International Affairs, 1997.

Garnett, Sherman W. *Keystone in the Arch: Ukraine in the Emerging Security Environment of Central and Eastern Europe*. Washington, D.C.: Carnegie Endowment, 1997.

Hajda, Lubomyr A., ed. *Ukraine in the World: Studies in the International Relations and Security Structure of a Newly Independent State*. Cambridge: Harvard University Press, 1998.

Ham, Peter van. *Ukraine, Russia and European Security: Implications for Western Policy*. Chaillot Papers no. 13. Paris: Institute for Security Studies, 1994.

Kis, Theofil I. *Nationhood, Statehood and the International Status of the Ukrainian SSR/Ukraine*. University of Ottawa Ukrainian Studies Occasional Papers no. 1. Ottawa: University of Ottawa Press, 1989.

Kulinich, Nikolai A. "Ukraine in the New Geopolitical Environment: Issues of Regional and Subregional Security." In *The Making of Foreign Policy in Russia and the New States of Eurasia*, edited by Adeed Dawisha and K. Dawisha. Armonk, N.Y.: M. E. Sharpe, 1995).

Kuzio, T. "Slavophiles versus Westernisers: Foreign Policy Orientations in Ukraine." In *Between Russia and Europe: Foreign and Security Policy of Independent Ukraine*, edited by Kurt R. Spillmann, Andreas Wenger, and Derek Muller. Bern: Peter Lang, 1999.

Kuzio, T. *Ukrainian Security Policy*. Washington Paper 167. Washington, D.C.: Center for Security and International Studies, 1995.

Kuzio, T., and Moroney, Jennifer D. P. "Defining Western Interests in Ukraine: Moving from Stability to Strategic Engagement." *European Security* 10, no. 2 (2001): 111–126.

Larrabee, F. Stephen. "Ukraine's Balancing Act." *Survival* 38, no. 2 (1996): 143–165.

Motyl, A. J. "Totalitarian Collapse, Imperial Disintegration, and the Rise of the Soviet West: Implications for the West." In *The Rise of Nations in the Soviet Union: American Foreign Policy and the Disintegration of the USSR*, edited by Michael Mandelbaum. New York: Council on Foreign Affairs, 1991.

Pavliuk, O. *Securing Sovereignty: Ukraine's First Five Years of Independence*. New York: East–West Institute, 1997.

Sherr, J. "Ukraine's New Times of Troubles." *Journal of Slavic Military Studies* 12, no. 2 (1999): 48–88.

Sherr, J. "Ukrainian Security Policy: The Relationship between Domestic and External Factors." In *Contemporary Ukraine: Dynamics of Post-Soviet Transformation*, edited by T. Kuzio. Armonk, N.Y.: M. E. Sharpe, 1998.

Smith, Mark. *The Eastern Giants: Russia, Ukraine and European Security*. RUSI Whitehall Paper Series 13. London: Royal United Services Institute, 1992.

Spillmann, K. R., Wenger, A., and Muller, Derek, eds. *Between Russia and Europe: Foreign and Security Policy of Independent Ukraine*. Bern: Peter Lang, 1999.

Wolczuk, Roman. "The Evolution of Ukrainian Foreign and Security Policy, 1990–1994." *Slavic Military Studies* 12, no. 3 (1999): 18–37.

DOMESTIC SOURCES OF SECURITY POLICY IN UKRAINE

Haran, Olexiy. "Between Russia and the West: Domestic Factors of Ukraine's Foreign Policy." *Harriman Review* 9, no. 1–2 (1996): 117–123.

Kuzio, T. "The Domestic Sources of Ukrainian Security Policy." *Journal of Strategic Studies* 21, no. 4 (1998): 18–49.

Nordberg, Marc. "Domestic Factors Influencing Ukrainian Foreign Policy." *European Security* 7, no. 3 (1998): 63–91.

Shulman, Stephen. "Nationalist Sources of International Integration." *International Studies Quarterly* 44, no. 3 (2000): 365–390.

UKRAINE, NATO, AND THE EU

Bilinsky, Yaroslav. *Endgame in NATO's Enlargement: The Baltic States and Ukraine*. Westport, Conn.: Praeger, 1999.

Bukkvoll, Tor. "Ukraine and NATO: The Politics of Soft Cooperation." *Security Dialogue* 28, no. 3 (1997): 363–374.

Cambone, Stephen A. "NATO Enlargement: Implications for the Military Dimension of Ukraine's Security." *Harriman Review* 10, no. 1 (1997): 8–18.

Kharchenko, Ihor. "The New Ukraine–NATO Partnership." *NATO Review* 45, no. 5 (1997).

Kuzio, T. "The EU and Ukraine: A Troubled Relationship." In *Enlarging the EU: The Way Forward*, edited by John Redmond and Jackie Gower. Aldershot: Ashgate, 2000.

Kuzio, T. "Kiev Craves Closer Ties with NATO." *Jane's Intelligence Review* 12, no. 10 (2000).

Kuzio, T. "Ukraine and NATO: The Evolving Strategic Partnership." *Journal of Strategic Studies* 21, no. 2 (1998): 1–30.

Lieven, Anatol. "Restraining NATO: Ukraine, Russia and the West." *Washington Quarterly* 20, no. 4 (1997): 55–77.

Light, Margo, White, Stephen, and Lowenhardt, John. "A Wider Europe: The View from Moscow and Kyiv." *International Affairs* 76, no. 1 (2000): 77–88.

Moroney, Jennifer D. P. "Ukraine's Ties to the West." *Problems of Post-Communism* 48, no. 2 (2001): 15–24.

Pavliuk, O. *The European Union and Ukraine: The Need for a New Vision*. New York: East–West Institute, 1999.

Udovenko, Hennadiy. "European Stability and NATO Enlargement: Ukraine's Perspective." *NATO Review* 43, no. 6 (1995): 15–18.

UKRAINE AND THE CIS

Garnett, S. W., and Lebenson, Rachel. "Ukraine Joins the Fray: Will Peace Come to Trans-Dniestria?" *Problems of Post Communism* 45, no. 6 (1998): 22–32.

Kuzio, T. "Geopolitical Pluralism in the CIS: The Emergence of GUUAM." *European Security* 9, no. 2 (2000): 81–114.

Kuzio, T. "Promoting Geopolitical Pluralism in the CIS: GUUAM and Western Policy." *Problems of Post-Communism* 47, no. 3 (2000): 25–35.

Pavliuk, O. "GUUAM: The Maturing of a Political Grouping into Economic Cooperation." In *Building Security in the New States of Eurasia: Subregional Cooperation in the Former Soviet Space*, edited by Renata Dwan and O. Pavliuk. Armonk, N.Y.: M. E. Sharpe, 2000.

Szporluk, R. "Belarus, Ukraine and the Russian Question: A Comment." *Post-Soviet Affairs* 9, no. 4 (1993): 366–374.

UKRAINE AND RUSSIA

Alexandrova, O. "Ukraine and Russia in the European Security System: Perceptions and Reality." *Harriman Review* 9, no. 1–2 (1996): 124–128.

D'Anieri, Paul J. *Economic Interdependence in Ukrainian–Russian Relations*. Albany: State University of New York Press, 1999.

D'Anieri, Paul J. "Dilemmas of Interdependence: Autonomy, Prosperity, and Sovereignty in Ukraine's Russia Policy." *Problems of Post-Communism* 44, no. 1 (1997): 16–25.

D'Anieri, Paul J. "Interdependence and Sovereignty in the Ukrainian–Russian Relationship." *European Security* 4, no. 4 (1995): 603–621.

Feldhusen, Anka. "The 'Russian Factor' in Ukrainian Foreign Policy." *Fletcher Forum on International Affairs* 23, no. 2 (1999): 119–138.

Goncharenko, Alexander. *Ukrainian–Russian Relations: An Unequal Partnership*. RUSI Whitehall Paper 32. London: Royal United Services Institute, 1995.

Kanet, Roger E., and Birgergson, Susanne M. "The Domestic–Foreign Policy
    Linkage in Russian Politics: Nationalist Influences on Russian Foreign
    Policy." *Communist and Post-Communist Studies* 30, no. 4 (1997): 335–344.
Kincade, William H., and Melnyczuk, Natalie. "Eurasia Letter: Uneighborly
    Neighbors." *Foreign Policy* 94 (1994): 84–104.
Lester, Jeremy. "Russian Political Attitudes to Ukrainian Independence." *Journal
    of Post-Communist Studies and Transition Politics* 10, no. 2 (1994): 193–233.
Liesman, Steve. "Can Ukraine Slip Russia's Grip?" *Central European Economic
    Review* (1995).
Lieven, A. *Ukraine and Russia: A Fraternal Rivalry.* Washington, D.C.: U.S. Insti-
    tute of Peace Press, 1999.
Mandelbaum, Michael, ed. *The New Russian Foreign Policy.* New York: Council
    on Foreign Relations, 1998.
Marples, D. "Ukraine's Relations with Russia in the Contemporary Era."
    Harriman Review 9, no. 1–2 (1996): 103–112.
Molchanov, M. A. "Borders of Identity: Ukraine's Political and Cultural Signifi-
    cance for Russia." *Canadian Slavonic Papers* 38, no. 1–2 (1996): 177–193.
Molchanov, M. A. "Postcommunist Nationalism as a Power Resource: A Rus-
    sia–Ukraine Comparison." *Nationalities Papers* 28, no. 2 (2000): 263–288.
Morrison, J. "Pereyaslav and After: The Russian–Ukrainian Relationship." *In-
    ternational Affairs* 69, no. 4 (1993): 677–704.
Neumann, Iver B. *Russia and the Idea of Europe: A Study in Identity and Interna-
    tional Relations.* London: Routledge, 1996.
"Peoples, Nations, Identities: The Russian–Ukrainian Encounter." *Harriman
    Review* 9, no. 1–2 (1996).
Rumer, Eugene B. "Eurasia Letter: Will Ukraine Return to Russia?" *Foreign
    Policy* 96 (1994): 129–144; 97 (1994–1995): 178–181.
Shenfield, Stephen D. "Alternative Conceptions of Russian State Identity and
    Their Implications for Russian Attitudes towards Ukraine." *Harriman
    Review* 9, no. 1–2 (1996): 142–147.
Shulman, Stephen. "Cultures in Competition: Ukrainian Foreign Policy and
    the 'Cultural Threat' from Abroad." *Europe–Asia Studies* 50, no. 2 (1998):
    287–303.
Solchanyk, R. *Ukraine and Russia: The Post-Soviet Transition.* Lanham, Md.:
    Rowan and Littlefield, 2000.
Solchanyk, R. "Russia, Ukraine and the Imperial Legacy." *Post-Soviet Affairs* 9,
    no. 4 (1993): 337–365.
Solchanyk, R. "Ukraine, the (Former) Center, Russia and 'Russia.'" *Studies in
    Comparative Communism* 25, no. 1 (1992): 31–45.
Torbakov, Igor. "A Rebirth of Ukrainian Geopolitics." *Harriman Review* 9, no.
    1–2 (1996): 138–141.
Travkin, Nikolai. "Russia, Ukraine, and Eastern Europe." In *Rethinking Russia's
    National Interests,* edited by Stephen Sestanovich. Washington, D.C.:
    Center for Strategic and International Studies, 1994.
Vydrin, D. "Ukraine and Russia." In *Damage Limitation or Crisis? Russia and the
    Outside World,* edited by Robert D. Blackwill and S. Karaganov. CSIA
    Studies in International Security no. 5. Cambridge, Mass.: Center for
    Science and International Affairs, John F. Kennedy School of Govern-
    ment, 1994.

Zhovnirenko, Pavlo. "The Problem of Security in Ukrainian–Russian Relations: A Search for Common Interests." *Harriman Review* 9, no. 1–2 (1996): 129–132.

CIVIL–MILITARY RELATIONS IN UKRAINE

Baev, Pavel, and Bukkvol, T. "Ukraine's Army under Civilian Rule." *Jane's Intelligence Review* 8, no. 1 (1996).

Chandler, A. "Statebuilding and Political Priorities in Post-Soviet Ukraine: The Role of the Military." *Armed Forces and Society* 23, no. 2 (1996): 573–597.

Fesiak, Andrew. "Civil–Military Relations in Ukraine: Nation Building and the Military." In *Nation Building, Regionalism and Identity in Ukraine*, edited by T. Kuzio and P. D'Anieri. Westport, Conn.: Praeger, forthcoming.

Grytsenko, Anatoliy S. *Civil–Military Relations in Ukraine: A System Emerging from Chaos*. Harmonie Paper 1. Groningen: Centre for European Security Studies, 1997.

Hagen, Mark von. "The Legacy of the Soviet Army for Ukraine's Armed Forces." In *The Military Tradition in Ukrainian History: Its Role in the Construction of Ukraine's Armed Forces*. Cambridge: Harvard University Press, 1995.

Jaworsky, John. "Civil–Military Relations in Russia and Ukraine." *Harriman Review* 9, no. 1–2 (1996): 113–116.

Kohut, Z. "Making the Ukrainian Armed Forces Ukrainian: The Role of National (Non-Soviet) Military Traditions." In *The Military Tradition in Ukrainian History: Its Role in the Construction of Ukraine's Armed Forces*. Cambridge: Harvard University Press, 1995.

Kuzio, T. "Civil–Military Relations in Ukraine, 1989–1991." *Armed Forces and Society* 22, no. 1 (1995): 25–49.

Kuzio, T. "Ukrainian Civil–Military Relations and the Military Impact of the Ukrainian Economic Crisis." In *State Building and Military Power in Russia and the New States of Eurasia*, edited by Bruce Parrott. Armonk, N.Y.: M. E. Sharpe, 1995.

SECURITY FORCES IN UKRAINE

Duncan, Andrew. "Ukraine's Forces Find That Change Is Good." *Jane's Intelligence Review* 9, no. 4 (1997).

Izmalkov, Valerii. "Ukraine and Her Armed Forces: The Conditions and Process for Their Creation, Character, Structure and Military Doctrine." *European Security* 2, no. 2 (1993): 279–319.

Jaworsky, J. *The Military–Strategic Significance of Recent Developments in Ukraine: Operational Research and Analysis*. Directorate of Strategic Analysis Project Report no. 645, Ottawa: Department of National Defence, 1993.

Kuzio, T. "The Non-Military Security Forces of Ukraine." *Journal of Slavic Military Studies* 13, no. 4 (2000): 29–56.

Kuzio, T. "Nuclear Weapons and Military Policy in Independent Ukraine." *Harriman Institute Forum* 6, no. 9 (1993).

Kuzio T. "The Security Service of Ukraine: A Transformed Ukrainian KGB?" *Jane's Intelligence Review* 5, no. 3 (1993).

Oliynyk, Stephen D. "Emerging Post-Soviet Armies: The Case of the Ukraine."
    Military Review 74, no. 3 (1994): 5–18.
Strekal, O. "The New Secret Service." *Transition* 1, no. 10 (1995).

Index

About the Editors and Contributors

Tor Bukkvoll is a researcher at the Norwegian Defense Research Establishment. He is former Associate Professor of International Relations at the Norwegian Military Academy and researcher at the International Peace Research Institute in Oslo. His research interests are in foreign policy analysis, with a particular focus on Ukraine and Russia. He is the author of *Ukraine and European Security* (1997) as well as articles and book chapters on Ukrainian and Russian foreign policy.

Victor Chudowsky is a Program Officer at Meridian International Center in Washington, D.C., a major contractor to the U.S. Department of State and other federal agencies. Dr. Chudowsky designs courses and programs to educate foreign diplomats, journalists, politicians, and policy-makers on various aspects of U.S. foreign policy, federalism, election law, trade policy, and deregulation. In 1996 he was a visiting scholar at the National Institute of Strategic Studies in Kiev, under a Title VIII grant from the U.S. Department of State. His area of academic specialization has been Ukrainian foreign policy, public opinion, and relations among members of the Commonwealth of Independent States. He has taught courses in comparative politics and has hosted and produced local television programs on international relations.

Stacy R. Closson, Caucasus desk officer for the Office of the Secretary of Defense, entered the United States Department of Defense as a Presidential Management Intern (PMI) in December 1996. As a PMI, she held a series of positions in the Joint Chiefs of Staff, Senate Appropriations Committee, Undersecretary for Acquisition, Technology & Logistics, and the U.S. Embassy in Kyiv. From November 1998 to August 2001, Ms. Closson served as the Ukraine Country Manager in the Office of the Undersecretary for Policy and currently works on the Caucasus Desk. Ms. Closson coauthored (with Jennifer Moroney) a book chapter on Ukraine addressing NATO–Ukraine relations and is currently working on an article on Ukrainian national security reform. In January 2001, Ms. Closson was presented the Secretary of Defense Award for Exceptional Civilian Service.

Paul J. D'Anieri is Associate Professor of Political Science and Associate Dean of International Programs at the University of Kansas. He is the author of *Economic Interdependence in Ukrainian–Russian Relations* (1997), and coauthor (with Robert Kravchuk and Taras Kuzio) of *Politics and Society in Ukraine* (1999), as well as articles and chapters on Ukrainian and Russian politics and foreign policy. He held a Fulbright Fellowship in Ukraine in 1993–1994, and was visiting Professor at the Harvard Ukrainian Research Institute in 1998. He is editor of *European Security*.

Sergei Konoplyov is the Director of the Harvard Black Sea Security Program and Executive Director for Harvard Russian–US General Officers Program. He served as Acting Director of the Eurasia Foundation for Ukraine, Belarus and Moldova in 1995–1996. A former officer of the Soviet Armed Forces, he served in several military missions in Africa and Latin America. Since 1998 he has been a member of IISS. Mr. Konoplyov is one of the contributing authors of *Monitoring of Foreign and Security Policy of Ukraine*. He also is a member of the editorial board of *International Security* (Ukraine). He continues his International Security Fellowship at Belfer Center for Science and International Affairs, Harvard University; and he is also a NATO Fellow. Since 2000 he has also served as Assistant to Head of National Security Committee at Ukrainian Parliament.

Taras Kuzio is a former Senior Research Fellow, Centre for Russian and East European Studies, University of Birmingham; Postdoctoral Fellow, Yale University; and Visiting Fellow at Brown University. He was also head of the NATO Information Office in Kyiv. He has written many articles in scholarly journals on the former USSR, Ukraine, international relations, nation-building and nationalism. He is the author of *Ukrainian Security Policy* (1995), *Ukraine: State and Nation Building*

(1998), *Ukraine: Perestroika to Independence* (2000) and coauthor of *Politics and Society in Ukraine* (1999). He is also the editor of *Contemporary Ukraine. Dynamics of Post-Soviet Transformation* (1998), and coeditor of *State and Institution Building in Ukraine* (1999) and *Nation-Building, Identity and Regionalism* (Praeger, 2002).

Mikhail Molchanov is Analyst at Human Resources Development Canada and Adjunct Professor at Carleton University. He previously worked as Senior Researcher for the National Academy of Sciences of Ukraine; served as Chair of the Department of Public Administration at the Institute of Public Administration and Local Government, Ukraine; and taught at the University of Alberta and the University of Victoria, Canada. He is currently a NATO-EAPC Research Fellow. Dr. Molchanov has written articles and book chapters on national identity and foreign policy, postcommunist nationalism, neocommunism and political culture change in Russia and Ukraine. His latest book is *Political Culture and National Identity in Russian-Ukrainian Relations* (2002).

Jennifer D. P. Moroney, an Associate at DFI International's Government Practice, is a project manager for contracts with the U.S. Office of the Secretary of Defense. She is also an Adjunct Professor and a Research Associate in the Elliott School of International Affairs, The George Washington University. Dr. Moroney was a NATO Research Fellow from 1999 to 2001 and has published numerous articles on Ukraine, European security, and NATO/European Union enlargement for several journals. She is currently coediting a book, *Security Building in the Former Soviet Union*, and is also a contributor (with Stacy Closson) to a forthcoming book on NATO's Strategic Engagement in Eastern Europe. Dr. Moroney is a frequent presenter at academic and policy conferences in the United States and Europe, speaking on NATO and European Union enlargement and regional security in the former Soviet Union.

James Sherr is a Fellow of the Conflict Studies Research Centre, Royal Military Academy Sandhurst. He is also Lecturer in International Relations at Lincoln College, Oxford, a consultant to NATO on Ukraine, and a former Specialist Adviser to the House of Commons Defence Committee. He is the author of approximately 100 articles on Russia, Ukraine, and European security. Within the past seven years, Mr. Sherr has made more than forty visits to Ukraine, both as a participant in defence diplomacy and in connection with exchanges and projects with Ukrainian NGOs. He also travels regularly to the Russian Federation and has delivered papers at the first and second official NATO-Russia workshops in Moscow. Publications include "Enlargement and Exclusion: The Dual Enlargements and the Future of Ukraine," in *The Lands Between*, edited by Anatol Lieven and Dmitri Trenin (forthcoming); "A Fresh Start for Ukrainian Defence Reform?" *Survival* (Spring 2001); "A New Regime? A New Russia?" in *The Second Chechen War*, edited by A. Aldis; and "Civil-Military Control of Ukraine's Armed Forces: To What End? By What Means?" in *Army and State in Postcommunist Europe*, edited by David Betts and John Löwenhardt (2001).

Joshua B. Spero is a Visiting Assistant Professor of Political Science at Merrimack College in North Andover, Mass. (2000–2002). He has also taught and researched in the Government Department at Dartmouth College (2000–2001). Dr. Spero consults for various international affairs organizations and has also worked for a number of organizations: 1994–2000, senior civilian Strategic Planner, Joint Chiefs of Staff; 1990–1994, Visiting Fellow/National Security Analyst, Institute for National Strategic Studies, National Defense University; 1988–1990, Deputy Assistant for Europe and the USSR in the Office of the Secretary of Defense; and 1988–1994, Washington Liaison Officer to Ft. Leavenworth Foreign Military Studies Office. Dr. Spero is a member of: The Council on Foreign Relations; American Political Science Association; International Studies Association; The International Institute for Strategic Studies; and Women In International Security.